**Business
Information
Technology**
....

Two week loan

Longman modular texts in business and economics
....

Series Editors
Geoff Black and Stuart Wall

Other titles in this series:

Business Information Technology

Systems, theory and practice

Geoffrey Elliott and Susan Starkings

LONGMAN
London and New York

Addison Wesley Longman Limited
Edinburgh Gate
Harlow
Essex CM20 2JE
United Kingdom
and Associated Companies throughout the world

Published in the United States of America
by Addison Wesley Longman, New York

First published 1998

ISBN 0 582 29802-4

British Library Cataloguing-in-Publication Data
A catalogue record for this book is available from the British Library

Library of Congress Cataloging-in-Publication Data

Set by 42 in 9/12pt Stone Serif
Printed in Great Britain by Henry Ling Ltd., at the
Dorset Press, Dorchester, Dorset.

To Valerie, Emrys and Norman

Contents

Preface

The subject of Business Information Technology (BIT) is a relatively new and innovative discipline which has its academic roots in business computing and information systems. So what is modern business information technology and how is the subject domain different to traditional business computing?

Firstly, BIT fundamentally involves the engineering of information and software systems using a range of computing, communications and information technologies. How such information systems are integrated within business has been affected by the information technology (IT) revolution. This revolution has been significant for integrating and advancing the bounds of computer hardware and software tools and techniques. Furthermore, the IT revolution has been significant in the proliferation and advances made in transmitting and telecommunications technology, from global terrestrial and extra-terrestrial communications and networks, to local area networks and client–server technology. The various disciplines of BIT are concerned with the building and maintenance of IT-based information systems at all levels of a business organisation. In essence the key areas of study are the design and development of information systems in organisations; the capabilities of information technology, its configuration and management within an organisation; the management of information as an organisational asset; and the use and application of enabling technologies to engineer systems for decision making. This book particularly concentrates on aspects of BIT concerned with the building of IT-based information systems for business decision making. This requires an understanding of the analysis, design, implementation and evaluation of information systems using a range of tools and techniques within what are known as fourth generation development environments, most commonly found within dynamic business organisations.

Secondly, computing within business has witnessed major changes over recent years in the manner in which computing is absorbed into the fabric of the business environment. The increasing sophistication and use of various information technologies has been accompanied by a move away from large specialist computing departments towards what is termed end-user computing. Therefore, the development and application of information systems within business has moved away from the pure computing domain towards the business information technology domain which incorporates both computing tools and techniques along with networking and telecommunications technology. At the same time the teaching and learning of information systems within business has significantly changed. The traditional systems development life cycle is no longer predominating as a framework for IT-based systems development because of the existence of a broad range of alternative information systems development approaches. These recognise the fact that information technology is not just about computing, but is more importantly concerned with a range of telecommunications tools and techniques that represent the term *information technology*.

This book is particularly useful to students in year one or two of an undergraduate course in business who wish to study modules in information systems and information technology (IS/IT) within business. It is also particularly useful as a year one text for students that are specialising in degrees in either business information systems or business information technology at undergraduate level.

A graduate or diplomate with an understanding and knowledge of BIT will often be expected to form a conduit between the discipline of business and the discipline of information technology; translating the needs of a business organisation into holistic and tangible IT-based information systems used for decision making. Systems that support decision making are critical to most organisations. Therefore, a person with an understanding of the use and application of BIT should possess a clear understanding of the information requirements of business together with a discerning knowledge of such areas as information systems and information technology strategy, information systems analysis, design and development, and enabling computer and communications technology. In practice, to get the most out of modern business information technology requires knowing how and where to apply IT-based systems: staff at every level of the organisation need to be comfortable in using information systems; and a coordinating body is required to implement and maintain the information systems which will, inevitably, need to adapt to a constantly changing internal and external business environment.

To achieve these outcomes the book has two main aims. Firstly, to address the evolution of computing and information systems within business, to assist undergraduates in learning and understanding how IT-based information systems are developed and integrated into the business environment and, secondly, to reveal how an understanding of BIT can be used to successfully connect the computing domain with the business domain.

Geoffrey Elliott and Susan Starkings
September 1997

Acknowledgements

Firstly, I would like to thank Dr David Ellis for giving me the chance, once upon a time, to become what is termed an academic; to Dr Hedley Rees, Professor David Ashton and Professor Don Egginton for providing opportunities to learn and develop; and to Professor Terry Baylis for releasing the reins and allowing various opportunities to gallop.

I would particularly like to thank my friend and mentor, Mike Wheeler, for trusting in both of us and showing levels of consideration that are difficult to repay. Mike will always be a firm anchor and guide in difficult and changing times. Mike's calm and dedicated approach to life and work is an inspiration; I thank him for his encouragement and total lack of any resentment towards the vagaries of misfortune or favour.

Finally, special thanks go to Paul Lillington for providing material and ideas, particularly for chapter 2 and chapter 7. Paul's inspirational teaching style will always, and affectionately, live in my memory along with his kindness and support over many years. Each person, in different ways, has contributed a pattern to my life so far.

Geoffrey Elliott

PART 1

The theory of information systems (IS)

CHAPTER **1**

The Information Age

Objectives

By the end of this chapter you will be able to:

▶ define the Information Age and understand the importance of information to advanced industrial economies

▶ evaluate the importance of information work and information-based economies in the Information Age

▶ describe the role of information and information technology within the competitive business environment

▶ outline the nature and characteristics of business information technology within the business environment

▶ describe the evolution and integration of information systems and information technology into business organisations.

1.1 Introduction to the Information Age

National economies are engaged in competition with one another on a global scale. This competition is for global markets and a larger share of economic wealth. One of the earliest studies of national economic wealth and competition was by a Scottish economist called Adam Smith in his book *Wealth of Nations* in 1776. Adam Smith stated that the wealth of a nation is dependent on how well a society organises its production in national businesses and factories. Higher levels of industrial effectiveness, described as productivity, will lead to higher levels of national wealth and consequently higher living standards for the population of a society. In the 1990s, and the approaching twenty-first century, the wealth of nations will be dependent upon how well a society can organise information and knowledge. This is because we now live in an information age rather than an industrial age which relied upon producing tangible goods to sell for a profit. An information-based economy is one where the majority of the businesses within an economy are engaged in information work and employ information workers. The wealth of information economies depends largely on the effectiveness and productivity of information workers.

National economies where the majority of wealth is produced by information work are often referred to as information-based economies. Within such economies national wealth, which is often known as Gross Domestic Product (GDP), is created by creating, processing and transmission of information.

Information-based Economies   A national economy where the majority of national wealth is produced by creating, processing and transmitting information.

Information workers can be divided into two sub-categories known as *data workers* and *knowledge workers*. Data workers are those who use, manipulate, process and disseminate information. Knowledge workers are those involved in the creation of new information or knowledge. Knowledge workers are usually formally educated to a higher level than data workers and include, as examples, the following occupations: architects, authors, engineers, lawyers, lecturers, researchers, teachers and scientists. These workers are distinguished by the fact that they need to have and use creativity, discerning judgement and be able to intepret and apply information. By comparison, data workers have less formal education and are restricted to handling and processing data rather than creating and interpreting information.

Information-based economies rely on effective development and use of information systems and information technology (often referred to as IS/IT). The national wealth of an information-based economy will depend upon the efficiency and effectiveness of IS/IT within all business organisations in the economy.

Increasingly, most graduates from higher education colleges will be using, or even building, information systems using current information technologies. These graduates need to be IS/IT literate to cope with the business environment of the twenty-first century. To this extent, many universities and colleges are teaching the importance of the information asset in information-based economies. For instance, there are now many departments and schools of Information Science that address the teaching and learning of a range of information-based studies. The following pause for thought has been reproduced from the Internet home page of Indiana University, School of Information Science.

PAUSE FOR THOUGHT 1.1   *The World of Information*

(Reproduced by permission of Professor Blaise Cronin, Indiana University, Bloomington, USA. From the home page of the School of Library and Information Studies at Indiana University.)

For decades, scholars and futurists have predicted an information revolution. Those predictions have come to life dramatically in recent years. We live in an information age, an age in which the ability to generate and access new knowledge has become a key driver of social and economic growth. The conviction is powerfully reflected in the development of the information Superhighway and in the feverish rate of takeovers and joint ventures in the telecommunications, cable and computer industries, as the major players position themselves to be in the vanguard of the digital revolution. Such developments are transforming both scholarly and lay perceptions of the value of information.

Historically, information has been treated as a public good, freely available to citizens. That model is coming under pressure, as the full economic and social significance of information becomes apparent. In many developed nations, the information sector is among the fastest growing segments of the economy. The emergence of a dynamic global information industry has created a wealth of opportunities for appropriately educated information professionals, but it has also helped throw into relief a raft of complex public policy issues, such as privatisation of government-held information resources, the management of intellectual property rights, and the possible emergence of an information underclass, all of which call for rigorous and informed policy analysis.

The signs of a new age are everywhere: personal computers in the classroom, interactive media in the home, global communication networks, electronic publishing, digital libraries. The statistics are irresistible; the amount of information produced in the last decade alone is greater than all the information created in the past millennia. Public awareness of the importance of information has never been sharper, from national debate on the emerging Infobahn to issues of censorship in cyberspace. The rhetoric of the Information Age has finally become reality. And that reality translates into unprecedented career opportunities for information professionals who know how to organise, manage, and exploit information assets; who combine analytic and technical skills with a sense of the strategic value of information to organisations of all kinds.

The economic and social well-being of nations depends increasingly on their ability to generate and access new knowledge. Hence, a need exists to create information-literate societies. Being information literate means knowing how information is created, stored, transmitted, and used. The 'Informatisation' of society is creating demand for specialists who will function as information resource managers and act as guides, interpreters, mediators, brokers, and quality controllers for the ultimate user, who might be a corporate executive, a scientist, or a school child. Today's information professionals do not merely store and locate information, but analyse and synthesise raw information and data to produce customised, value-added services and products for diverse clientele. The field offers a kaleidoscope of career tracks from which to choose, as the mass of position announcements in both the professional and generalists press makes abundantly clear: database design and marketing, information brokering, medical informatics, systems, competitor intelligence analysis. In a sense, the opportunities are limited only by the imagination.

ACTIVITY **1.1**

The Information Age

Discuss why in many developed nations the information sector is often among the fastest growing segments of the economy and write down four reasons why the economic and social well-being of nations depends increasingly on their ability to generate and access new knowledge.

DID YOU KNOW?
The modern English word for information comes from the Latin word informare *which means to form or take shape.*

Information is a powerful resource which is often referred to as the *life-blood* of a business organisation. Information is important to all organisations and the right type of information can sometimes provide a competitive advantage over other organisations in the Information Age. Whichever way you address information, it is clear that information is a major asset of all business organisations.

1.2 Business activity in the Information Age

The central aim of most business organisations is to generate a profit for the owners, or shareholders, of the business. Organisations compete with one another nationally and often internationally, on a global scale, for a share of business opportunities and markets. Business organisations comprise a range of human and technological resources which are managed, organised and coordinated by the organisation for the purposes of generating a profit. Information systems and information technology are part of the resources of an organisation which are applied and used to generate income and profit.

The three fundamental resources of any organisation are the employees, the organisation and procedures, and the technology. These are sometimes known as the three pillars of a business organisation:

1 People
2 Organisation
3 Technology.

The success of a business is determined by how well it manages and controls these three fundamental resources. The components of these three pillars of a business organisation are described in Table 1.1.

Each of these business pillars will be covered and studied in greater detail in subsequent chapters. The successful *integration of these pillars into holistic business information systems* is the driving force behind effective use and application of business information technology.

Consideration of these three pillars is sometimes known as a *socio-technical* view of information systems and technology within a business organisation. The socio-technical view of organisations gives paramount importance to people within the information systems and information technology domain. Most business organisations aim to be effective and efficient in maximising the utilisation of all three main resources to generate an income or profit. Within the socio-technical perspective, information systems within organisations need to be designed and developed so that people can integrate, use, control and understand the information asset. The study of business information technology (BIT) is an attempt to successfully understand and integrate these three pillars into the fabric of a business organisation.

table 1.1

The three pillars of a business organisation

People	Organisation	Technology
Career	Bureaucracy	Hardware
Education	Culture	Software
Ergonomics	Competition	Telecommunications
Employee attitudes	Environment	Informatics
Employee participation	Management	
Employee monitoring	Mission	
Statutory regulation	Policy	
Training	Strategy	

1.3 Business information technology (BIT)

Business information technology is concerned with a range of factors that determine the effective and efficient design, development and integration of information systems and information technology to permit a business to meet its full potential in generating an income or profit. The academic discipline of BIT relates to that part of computing studies which intersects with business studies and involves all aspects of the building and maintenance of IT-based information systems at all levels of an organisation. In order to understand the academic discipline of BIT it is essential to understand how the domains of information systems (IS), information technology (IT) and business organisation integrate for an understanding of the design, use and application of business information technology.

A business information technology professional in the Information Age is required to understand the nature of competitive business organisations and be able to work with business specialists to achieve IT-based solutions to an organisation's information problems. The BIT discipline pursues the integration of the three fundamental business resources of *people*, *organisation* and *technology*, to develop and maintain well-engineered business information systems. The use of the term 'engineering' is deliberately used to emphasise the fact that business systems and business information technology is taught as a solid and rigorous academic discipline in well over 70 universities in the United Kingdom alone. The discipline is also particularly prevalent in academic institutions in Australia and the United States.

A business information technology professional should act as a conduit at the middle of a spectrum of skills and knowledge found within the disciplines of business and computing. The central aim of the BIT professional is to translate the requirements of business specialists into holistic and tangible computer-based information systems that can be used for decision making within a competitive business environment. Anyone working within BIT should possess an understanding of the commercial information requirements of business together with a discerning knowledge of how to integrate business practices, procedures and technology into useful information systems for eventual *decision making*.

> *Business Information Technology (BIT)* BIT is concerned with the rigorous engineering of computer-based information systems used for competitive decision making within the business environment.

A central aim of BIT necessitates acquiring skills in the engineering and integration of computing and information technology into holistic information systems within the business environment. The academic discipline of BIT should fill the vacuum of misunderstanding that often exists between the pure business specialist and the computing specialist within the business environment. BIT requires an understanding of how information systems are designed, developed and used at all organisational levels. This should be coupled with the desire to build systems that have the highest possible levels of information certainty to allow accurate decision making to be undertaken.

The importance of BIT to organisations is in the considered application of a range of tools and techniques to speed up the information systems development process. Such rapid information systems development ensures less costly and shortened time-frames for systems development. The need to manage information systems and information technology (IS/IT) has, with the evolution of computing, become subsumed into the whole business function rather than concentrated in a specific IT-based department or section of the business organisation. Computing and IT now pervades the whole workplace of competitive organisations. The prevalence and benefits of IS/IT are often taken for granted by business organisations. This can be a mistake because business organisations require a strategy for optimising IS/IT investment in order to maximise the return on such investment.

BIT is concerned with a number of key business issues which will be referred to throughout the content of this book. However, five key issues are outlined in Table 1.2.

So why study the discipline of BIT? The motivation to study BIT is likely to come from a number of personal sources. However, the motivation will also likely be from a number of micro-economic and macro-economic considerations present in the Information Age, as follows:

1   The macro-economic evolution of computing over the last 40 years has moved away from large-scale electronic data processing (EDP) departments towards 'end-user' computing and business systems development.
2   Advanced information-based societies have witnessed a macro-economic decline in the number of IT-literate and appropriately qualified entrants to the business environment.
3   In the Information Age there is a growing need in business and industry for employees with hybrid skills that include an understanding of information technology and its application to business information systems.
4   The Information Age has witnessed a decline in demand for specialist computer programmers, who merely have a skill in one language, and a collateral increase in demand for business systems developers as witnessed by salary differences commanded in the business environment.

An understanding of the disciplines of BIT will go a long way towards meeting the needs of business and industry in the Information Age, and offers the increased potential for generating economic wealth, both nationally and internationally. The following chapters of this book are intended as a means of integrating the pertinent areas of information systems and information technology to provide a framework for developing knowledge and understanding of business information technology within dynamic and often highly competitive business environments.

table 1.2
The five key issues of BIT

1	The relationship of IS/IT to business.
2	The capabilities of IS/IT, its configuration and management within the organisation.
3	The analysis, design and implementation and evaluation of information systems.
4	The management and analysis of information as an organisational asset.
5	Computing science and information technology.

1.4   Competitive advantage through IS/IT
....

A significant reason why rigorously built computer-based business information systems are so fundamental to an organisation can be gauged by the following quote that forecasts the business environment of the twenty-first century:

In the past the economic winners were those who invented new products. But in the 21st Century sustainable competitive advantage will come more out of new process technologies and much less out of new product technologies.

What used to be primary (inventing new products) becomes secondary, and what used to be secondary (inventing and perfecting new processes) becomes primary.

(Thurow, 1992)

Business organisations are realising, especially those operating in dynamic (continuously changing) business environments, that competitive advantage is established not merely by the product or service, but by the quality of the computer-based information systems and processes that deliver those products and services in uncertain and often unstructured decision-making environments.

It has been stated that business competition often takes place on a global scale. The globalisation of trade means larger markets and often more competition. The reward can also be greater income and profits. However, globalisation has led to greater levels of uncertainty within the information environment, through differing national laws, trading practices and competition policies. Information systems need to be focused to address these challenges and allow organisations to compete in the global trading environment. A significant challenge in information systems and information technology (IS/IT) is the need for *competitive advantage* nationally and internationally. The concept of competitive advantage is one that has become synonymous with Professor Michael Porter of Harvard University. Professor Porter wrote three major books on competitive advantage in the 1980s entitled: *Competitive Strategy* (1980), *Competitive Advantage* (1985), and *Competitive Advantage of Nations* (1989).

DID YOU KNOW?
Professor Michael Porter is reputed to be one of the wealthiest academics in the world through the publication and sale of various works on competitive advantage.

Competitive advantage is the ability of a business organisation to compete with other organisations. The competitive advantage of a business is determined and gauged by a number of competitive forces. There are four main generic competitive forces:

1   substitute products and services
2   bargaining power of customers
3   bargaining power of suppliers
4   threat of new entrants to the competitive market.

These competitive forces affect the relationship and position of competing business organisations within a market. Once these forces are recognised then strategies can be developed to counteract these forces affecting competition. There are four main strategies that can be used to deal with the competitive forces outlined above. These are as follows:

1 cost leadership
2 market niche
3 customer and supplier linkage
4 product differentiation.

Cost leadership is concerned with producing products and services at a lower price than competitors. Market niche means focusing products and services to particular markets or customers so that a business can concentrate on providing better products and services than its competitors. Product differentiation is concerned with creating new or different products and services that distinguish one business organisation from another organisation. Finally, customer and supplier linkage involves locking-in suppliers to the price and delivery structure of the purchasing organisation or locking customers into the organisation's products or services. Both of these can be achieved by linkages between the IS/IT of the customers and suppliers and the IS/IT structure of the competing business organisation.

Competitive advantage The advantage that one business has over another business organisation due to more effective and efficient use of information systems and information technology to deal with competitive forces.

Information systems and information technology can be used to implement these strategies to achieve competitive advantage. For example, marketing information systems can be developed to enhance the information available from sales and marketing systems. This information can be used to target customers or suppliers to identify market niches for products and services. Such information can also be used to determine how products and services can be targeted to customers more efficiently and effectively.

IS/IT can also be used to create more attractive products and services. For example, retail banks are one of the main users and providers of IS/IT for competitive advantage. Banking was one of the first industries to recognise the importance of IS/IT. A lot of the banking services we take for granted, such as credit cards and cash till machines, would be impossible if it were not for information systems and technology. In the United Kingdom, Barclays Bank was the first high street bank to place a cash dispenser outside for customers to use with a cash debit card. The competitive advantage was that customers could have access to banking services 24 hours a day and seven days a week. So successful was this venture that all other banks followed suit until it is now a rare occurence to find a high street without an available cash dispenser. Banking is a very competitive business where competing banks are constantly looking for ways of providing more customer services and increasing internal systems productivity. Another successful strategy employed by banks is the introduction of telephone banking which provides the advantage of reducing the overhead costs needed to open and maintain physical branches in high streets all over the country.

DID YOU KNOW?

Cash dispensers, known technically as Automated Teller Machines (ATMs), were first developed by Citicorp Bank in 1977.

Information systems and technology can be used to link customers and suppliers to a business organisation. By doing so it can make it too costly or inconvenient for customers and/or suppliers to switch allegiance to a competitor organisation. In terms of supplier linkage, IS/IT can be used to incorporate the suppliers' information technology into the purchasing organisation. The supplier then becomes a virtual part of the purchasing organisation. This makes it too inconvenient for the supplier to seek costly initial supplier relationships with other business organisations. Linkage with customers can be achieved by providing unique after sales services which make it necessary or desirable for the customer to maintain a relationship with an organisation's products and services.

ACTIVITY **1.2**

IS/IT and competitive strategy

Discuss and identify three ways in which IS/IT can be used to deal with the main competitive forces present in most business environments. If in difficulty, take the example of the competitive motor car industry. Find a case study or newspaper article on how Daewoo cars are marketed and sold in the United Kingdom, or how Ford Motor Company markets and sells cars in the United States. Discuss how after sales servicing and various warranties lock-in customers to certain car manufacturers. What competitive advantage do these car manufacturers gain over their rivals?

Competitive business organisations recognise that information systems and information technology (IS/IT) can be used to innovatively transform organisational structures and the way in which an organisation practices business in relation to its customers. Competitive advantage can be gained by providing superior efficiency, effectiveness and systems sustainability. BIT can be applied to design, develop or re-engineer IT-based business information systems to maintain an organisation's competitive advantage in an ever dynamic national and international business environment.

ACTIVITY **1.3**

Competitive advantage through IS

Information systems can be used to gain a competitive advantage over other organisations in the business environment. Information systems and technology can be used to develop new markets or products, new ways of dealing with suppliers and customers, and new ways of operating processes and systems practices within the organisation. Provide examples of how information systems can be used to transform the processes and practices of a business of your choice. Explain how information systems and information technology can support each of the four competitive strategies of competitive advantage.

1.5   End-user computing

Computer and IT utilisation within business has evolved and altered dramatically over the last 40 years. Computing within business has witnessed a number of underlying trends which have changed the way computing is integrated into business organisations. One of the major trends seen is a movement away from large-scale data processing departments towards *end-user computing* (EUC). Another trend is systems *downsizing* which has dramatically altered business organisational structures and the perception of computing and IT within business and other organisations. The two trends have influenced one another and the way in which IT has been absorbed into business organisations.

The term end-user computing is used in information technology to describe the final consumer of information. End-user computing can be defined as the *systems* and *tools* given directly to staff which allow them to manipulate their own or extracted data, to decide *when* and *how* to use applications and to own their *own* data

End-user Computing (EUC) The ownership and development of systems by the end-users of the information system as opposed to systems analysts and computer scientists.

(Price 1991). The emphasis is on responsibility and control of computing in the hands of the final user of information.

In the 1950s and 1960s computing within business organisations normally took place within specifically defined, large electronic data processing departments where a small number of specific staff generated mainly operational data using large-scale computer technology. However, over time the roles and responsibilities of such staff have become integrated into all aspects of business. This trend was largely fuelled by the introduction of the personal computer (PC) in an affordable and available state and a rise of investment in technical communications and empowering information tech-

DID YOU KNOW?

The year-on-year increase in the number of business organisations introducing PC-based technology for the first time has averaged over 25% in the United Kingdom since 1985.

nology. This trend has coincided with the downsizing of business organisation structures and the movement away from centralisation towards organisational decentralisation.

This trend in downsizing has had an effect on the computer profession and the roles and responsibilities undertaken by computer professionals. In the 1950s and 1960s task specialisation gave rise to three categories of computer person: the analyst, the programmer, and the final user of information. Originally, an enquiry from a user of information within an organisation would have been passed to a systems analyst, who analysed and designed the system problem, then passed on to a programmer to programme and implement a solution. The information would then have been passed to the final user, whose involvement in the analysis, design and implementation of the business information system would have been, in the worst case, non-existent. Over time these task-specific *computing intermediaries* have been replaced and often merged into one person: the information end-user. Consequently, career opportunities in computing have changed dramatically. Twenty years ago computer literate professionals working in large organisations would have started their career as a junior programmer and worked their way up through the ranks to become a systems analyst, then senior analyst through to project manager. This is not the case today because of the following main evolutionary reasons present in the Information Age:

1 Elimination of demarcation in terms of computing roles and responsibilities within business organisations.
2 The downsizing of systems practices and procedures with technological advances in personal computing and IT.
3 Emergence of service computing for operational business systems functions, such as stock control, payroll and even sales and purchase order processing.
4 The growth of the BIT professional as a *facilitator* of IT within the business environment.

Nolan Norton & Co., the strategic consultancy arm of Peat Marwick's, has been studying the growth and impact of end-user computing in both the United Kingdom and the United States since 1986. Nolan Norton forecast in the early 1980s that the cost of information systems in business would rise by 700% up until the 1990s (Price 1991). The actual rise has been far greater.

> **DID YOU KNOW?**
> It was estimated in a survey by Nolan Norton & Co. in 1991 that between 30% and 40% of the total spent in the United Kingdom by business organisations on information systems in the early 1990s was directed at end-user computing.

If businesses are willing to invest so much in end-user computing, it is done either to eliminate a problem or to achieve a *competitive advantage*. In practice, to get the most out of modern IT-based information systems requires managers who know how and where to apply IT; staff at every level of the organisation being comfortable with using IT; and somebody to implement and maintain the information systems to adapt to a constantly changing external environment. It is this latter consideration that is central to the concept within the business information technology discipline for an IT *facilitator* within organisations.

The evolutionary trends in business information technology have been *horizontally* absorbed into United Kingdom business in general. However, there is also a further *vertical* absorption of computing and IT trends into the organisational levels (or strata) of business enterprises. A generalised hierarchical organisation will have three broad levels of organisational decision making, being from top down: the strategic (or executive) level, the management level and the operational level. Each level exhibits different information requirement characteristics (in terms of the decision time-frame, certainty, risk, responsiveness, information structure and technology). The decision-making levels are highly significant, since the purpose of processing data is to produce information for decision making. Business information *systems* fall into these three broad categories within the organisational hierarchy: operational systems, management systems and strategic systems. Operational systems are responsive and deterministic to the extent that the inputs and outputs are known and certain. Such systems are usually found in manufacturing environments, or the lowest levels of a business organisation. Such systems are mechanical in their processes and algorithmic in their decision-making functions. Examples of such systems in business are stock control, payroll, sales order processing and purchase order processing. By contrast, strategic information systems are often only as accurate (or factual) as the level of certainty or uncertainty of the predicted probabilities and forecasted events of the business environment. Within strategic information systems the information environment is uncertain and the decision-making functions are unstructured. This level of decision making is characterised by executive information systems (EISs), decision support systems (DSSs) and expert systems (ESs). Management information systems (MISs), characterised by medium-term budgeting and forecasting functions, lie somewhere on the spectrum between strategic systems and operational systems. Management information systems are characterised by a semi-structured information environment. In operational systems the whole of the decision picture is known; however, in strategic information systems parts of the decision picture are unknown. The aim of all systems is to get as near to decision-making certainty as possible.

In the light of the above, a business information technology professional in the Information Age needs not only an understanding of computing and IT, but also a substantive understanding of the application and characteristics of information systems at each level of decision making within the contemporary information-conscious business organisation. An understanding of the differences in use and application of IS/IT within the various business levels is a significant theme of this book.

End-user computing has caused competitive business organisations to move away from the electronic data processing era of computer science, when organisations invested in data processing technology to automate their core business systems with no involvement from end-users, to an era of information systems to allow *knowledge workers* to make informed decisions in highly competitive business environments. This can often mean transforming a business organisation's processes and systems to make it more competitive or to counteract the advantages held by other organisations. Business transformation can be undertaken by the intelligent use of IS/IT to innovatively transform organisational structures and the way in which an organisation practices business in relation to its employees, customers and suppliers.

Anyone applying business information technology should recognise the evolution and application of *end-user computing* (EUC) within the business environment, where the final user of an information system is responsible for the construction and development of that business information system. End-user computing concerns the development and use of software applications and IT-based information systems by non-information systems professionals. Information systems end-users are now more likely to be directly involved in the day-to-day decisions of IT-based information systems and also in their specification and design. End-user computing impacts on how information systems are built and used by organisations.

With the evolution of computing the need to manage IS/IT has become subsumed into the whole business function rather than concentrated in a specific computer-based department or section of a business organisation. Computing and information technology now pervades the whole workplace within business organisations. The prevalence and benefits of information technology are often taken for granted by a business organisation. This should not be the case because most organisations require a strategy for optimising IS/IT investment in order to maximise the return on such investment. Organisations require a clear understanding of how IS/IT can make business processes more efficient and effective and also deliver new products and services through the strategic application of IS/IT.

Information and end-user computing

Discuss the desirable characteristics that information should possess and outline considered arguments as to whether there are any trade-offs between these characteristics. For example, is there a trade-off between timeliness and information accuracy? Once this is done, provide three examples of information and information systems that may give a business organisation an advantage over other competing business organisations. It is sometimes stated that information is power. In this context discuss whether you believe information should be available to all employees of a business organisation or whether only a restricted set of information *end-users* should possess (or even own) the information available in a business.

1.6   Computing and information technology

Computing and information technology are not interchangable concepts. Computing is part of information technology, but not the same as information technology. Traditionally, computing applications were concerned with the routine processing of raw data to provide basic information. Such computing activities were concerned with structured and algorithmic data processing. (An algorithm is a defined set of instructions used to solve a problem.) Information technology differs in definition to computing in that it includes not only computing technology but also *data communications*. Therefore, the definition of information technology (IT) includes all aspects of computing, integrated with technological developments in networking and telecommunications technology.

Information technology involves understanding that computer systems are no longer isolated from other computer systems. Computer systems can be linked together into various networks of larger IT-based systems, both internally and externally to an organisation. Consequently, communication technologies are inherently important in allowing information systems to be linked together nationally and internationally within the global business environment.

DID YOU KNOW?

The Department of Trade and Industry in the United Kingdom has defined information technology as: 'The acquisition, processing, storage and dissemination of vocal, pictorial, textual and numeric information by micro-electronics based combination of computing and telecommunications.'

Information technology includes all aspects of computing, including the use and application of *computer software* and *computer hardware*. Computer software is the term used to describe the programs of instructions used by a computer to carry out commands, functions and activities. The software instructions coordinate the processes and operation of the physical components of computer hardware, which includes all the electronics, circuitry, storage media, data input technology and data output technology included in a computer system. Therefore, computer hardware is the physical computing technology used for inputting, storage and outputting of data and information within an information system. Communications technologies undertake the activity of transferring data and information from one computer system to another computer system, at a local or remote location. All of these aspects of computer hardware, computer software and computer telecommunications will be covered in detail in subsequent chapters and can be considered part of the definition of IT.

Information technology can deliver a number of benefits to a business organisation by integrating computing and telecommunications to achieve the following benefits:

1 increased capacity and speed of data and information processing
2 wider dissemination and communication of data between information systems
3 effective access to local and remote data storage facilities
4 effective and efficient information control enabling global business competition.

Information technology impacts on business information systems and widens the nature of business practices and competition to the extent that internal and external barriers to trade, such as technological barriers, political barriers and economic barriers, can often be eliminated. Advanced national economies, as we saw earlier, seek to invest heavily in IT in order to maintain or increase future economic wealth. However, heavy national investment in information technology

IT literacy A thorough knowledge about the use and application of information technology in society.

can only deliver the benefits of increased economic wealth if the population is IT literate and educated to a level where IT is developed and applied constructively in society.

Therefore in order to reap the benefits of IT in all aspects of society there is a requirement for people to be *information technology literate*. IT literacy within the business environment refers to an understanding of how to design, apply and use business information technology. In order to maximise the benefits of IT literacy in society there is also a need for people to be *information systems literate*, which involves a knowledge and understanding of how information is used by individuals and business organisations. This area is often referred to as *information science*, which includes the study of all aspects of the retrieval, storage and dissemination of information. The importance of information science in society was alluded to in Pause for thought 1.1. Information science stresses the importance of information as a valuable and essential part of modern business-based economies.

ACTIVITY 1.5

Information technology

Divide up into groups of four people and discuss the importance of telecommunications technology for modern IT-based systems. Once this has been done, outline five benefits of using information technology effectively within a business organisation and deliver your findings to the other groups. Write down a list of all the different benefits of IT found by the various groups undertaking this activity.

1.7 Information systems and information technology

An *information system* within business results from the structured and successful integration of the three main resources of people, organisation and technology. An information system (IS) is a set of inter-related parts that are integrated to handle, store and process data that is in turn transmitted and disseminated to individuals (or groups) within the business organisation to provide *information* for *decision making*.

There are three component parts to an information system, namely, *inputs*, *outputs* and a *process*. The input component of an information system is concerned with the collection and capture of raw data, the type of which may be alpha, numeric or alphanumeric. The processing component is concerned with the *structuring* of raw input data into useful information. The output component of an information system is concerned with the

Information System (IS) A set of inter-related components and parts that act together to achieve some purpose or goal.

transmission and dissemination of information for decision making which has resulted from the processing of raw data.

Data and information should not be considered as the same in definition. It is a fundamental fact of IS/IT that '*Information is data processed for the purpose of decision making.*' Therefore, information is the result of processed raw data. Figure 1.1 shows the relationship and correlation between inputs and outputs and data and information within the fabric of IS/IT.

The activity of data processing has four generic stages. In order for information to have the appropriate *quality* for decision making it must possess certain desirable characteristics. The ideal characteristics that information should possess to be useful and purposeful are summarised below in Table 1.3.

Information should be *relevant* for its purpose and to the end-user of that information. Information should be *accurate* for the purpose, which means that the information is correct in all ways. Information should also be *complete* with all material available to allow that information to be used by a decision maker. Information should be *timely* in order for it to be useful for decision making. For example, information which is produced after the decision-making event is worthless. Information should be *reliable*, which will allow decision makers to have confidence in the information. Confidence in information and information sources has to be built up over time. If information was reliable in the past, and communicated effectively, the decision maker will feel confident in depending on the reliability of the information.

figure 1.1
IS/IT activity

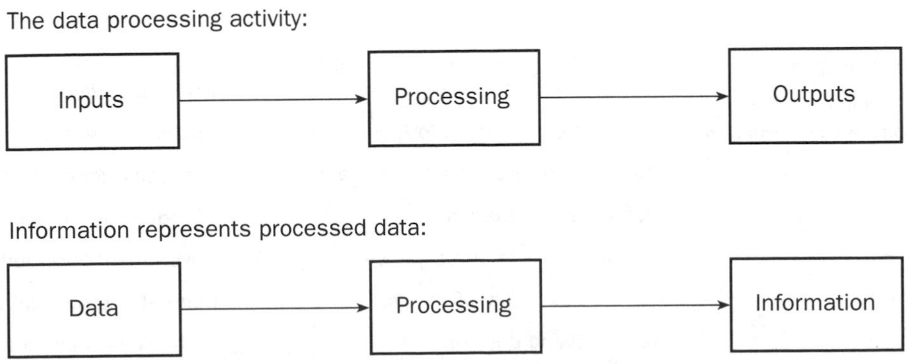

The data processing activity:

Inputs → Processing → Outputs

Information represents processed data:

Data → Processing → Information

table 1.3 **Desirable characteristics of information**	1 *relevant* to the user's needs
	2 *accurate* and factual
	3 *complete* and unabridged
	4 *timely* and delivered to the right person
	5 *reliable* for decision making
	6 *useful* to the end-user's needs
	7 *consistent* and comparable over time
	8 *understandable* to the user
	9 *portable* and easily transmittable

Information should be *useful* to user needs in that the right person has access to the right information. The information needs of different decision makers will vary. It is important that the information is focused to the requirements of the end-user of that information. Information should be *consistent* and homogeneous. The method and approach to preparing information should be consistent from year to year (or period to period) and be consistent between different business organisations. For example, the Annual Financial Accounts produced by all business organisations are produced under consistent rules, guidelines and regulations. This allows the financial information of one organisation to be accurately compared with another business organisation within the same time period or between a number of time periods. Information should be *understandable* to the end-user of the information. The information environment and the language used will influence the degree to which information is understandable to end-users. Information should be *portable* to the extent that it can be effectively communicated between information systems.

Information can be internal to an organisation or external to the business organisation. Table 1.4 lists some of the possible external sources of information and some of the possible internal sources of information affecting a business organisation.

Quality information for decision making is an essential asset for any competitive business. However, the measurement of information value is a difficult

	Internal sources	External sources
table 1.4 **Example sources of business information**	Financial accounting information	Business competition
	Management accounting information	Customer demand and supply
	Marketing information	Economic information
	Production costs and expenses	Government information
	Human resources information	Cultural and political information
	Research and development	Technological information

exercise which is often neglected by organisations. Organisations that are able to measure the value of information are in a better position to assess the value of a business information system. The purchase cost of the hardware and software aspects of information systems is verifiable and quantifiable. Likewise, any business should attempt to apply a quantifiable measure of cost (or economic return) on the value of information.

Quantifiable value is factual, verifiable by documentation, and measured in monetary terms. On the other hand *non-quantifiable value* cannot be measured with such certainty. It may be the case that the information from an information system adds value to the overall business organisation which is not measurable in direct monetary terms. Such value is qualitative rather than quantitative. For example, a marketing information system may store and analyse demographic, social and economic information on customers for transmission to managers for decision making concerning product development in the future. Such information may also be of significance to other sectors of the business both internally and externally. Therefore, the marketing system has added indirect benefit to other sectors of the organisation. The benefits of an information system may have a ripple effect across an organisation and its external environment affecting both customers and suppliers.

ACTIVITY **1.6**
· · · · · · · · · · · · · ·

Information quality

The quality of information affects the quality of decision making within a business organisation. Put yourself into the role of a manager deciding whether to buy new equipment for a factory manufacturing computer components. Discuss and list all the possible information sources the manager would consult to establish a set of criteria for decision making. Explain the qualities that the information set should possess in respect of the manager's decision to buy new equipment. Define whether the information set may include quantifiable and non-quantifiable information and highlight some of the problems associated with measuring intangible (or difficult to quantify) information value.

1.8   Business and technology in the Information Age
· ·

Up to this point in the chapter we have seen how important IS/IT is to business and society and how business information technology is a systems oriented discipline which recognises the importance of business information systems and IT in an information-conscious age. Today the majority of businesses are not just concerned with merely processing data but are intrinsically *information based*. Information is the life-blood of an organisation.

The Information Age has evolved from the industrial age of the nineteenth century, which in turn evolved from the agricultural age preceding that century. The Information Age was a term coined in the 1970s which refers to the fundamental basis of business activity in the late twentieth century. Up until about 1825, the majority of the population of the United Kingdom was engaged in agricultural labour. However, that year heralded a milestone in the industrial revolution. In 1825 the first railway line in England, built between

Stockton and Darlington, heralded the start of a wider-area and faster transportation system, and the beginning of an industrial age based on manufacturing. Railroads in America began effectively with the Baltimore and Ohio railroad in 1830. This development along with the growth of large-scale industrial manufacturing signalled the coming of the industrial age where the majority of the population was employed in heavy industries such as steel, coal, shipbuilding and engineering. Since the 1940s the industrial manufacturing age has declined in importance and has been replaced by the Information Age where the majority of the workforce is involved in some form of information handling, processing and dissemination. This age is often referred to as the *post-industrial society* or by the shorthand description of the *information society*.

Information has even become a saleable commodity in its own right, with organisations engaged in analysing and processing data to be sold on to organisations for profit. For example, mailing lists compiled by market research organisations can be purchased by interested parties. This refers to the concept of the *information industry*. The information society description should not be confused with the information industry. The information industry refers to organisations that earn money from buying, selling and trading information.

DID YOU KNOW?

One of the largest providers of financial and business data and information in the United Kingdom is Dun & Bradstreet, which provides an on-line electronic data service of business information known as 'DataStream'. This service is provided to both competitive business organisations and the academic world of universities and higher education colleges.

Business organisations are often referred to as being information based to the extent that information retrieval, storage and dissemination are the reason for the existence of a business organisation. Information is a particularly important commodity in the financial and banking sectors. The Information Age has led to the study of the science of information, sometimes referred to as *informatics*, which derives from the French word *informatique*, and covers the study of information and its handling especially by means of information technology. The Information Age has necessitated information being considered as a scientific discipline to the extent that there exists in the United Kingdom and the United States professional institutes, such as the Institute of Information Scientists in the United Kingdom, responsible for overseeing the professional application and educational development of information science on a worldwide basis.

The growth of the information society has been fuelled by two factors. Firstly, developments in computing, information technologies and telecommunications which can be termed as *supply side* technology growth. Secondly, market forces and competition among business organisations that has added impetus in acquiring quality information. This can be termed as *demand side* technology growth. Therefore, the demand for information that possesses all the qualities of accuracy, timeliness, relevance, usefulness, understandability and portability by business organisations has encouraged and stimulated advances in information technology to provide more sophisticated information retrieval, storage and communication technologies.

ACTIVITY **1.7**

Business in the Information Age

Discuss and contrast the concept of the *information society* with the *information industry* and outline the main characteristics that distinguish the information society from the information industry. Once this has been achieved, investigate whether your college or university has access to an on-line business information service, such as DataStream, and outline the main categories of information provided to the user of the information service that you have investigated.

1.9   Technology growth in the Information Age

The power and processing capability of information technology grows at an ever increasing rate over time. It is often the case that information technology hardware is advancing far more rapidly than the capability of computing software to support hardware applications. In turn, both hardware and software are advancing faster than the capability of people within business organisations to understand and apply information technology.

It is the case that IT hardware is growing exponentially compared to software and the business organisation's understanding of IT. The relationship between IT hardware, IT software and business understanding of IT is indicated in Figure 1.2. It is estimated that, on average, the capability (or productivity) of IT hardware increases 10 times over a five-year period. The capability (or productivity) of IT software increases by a factor of two every eight years. However, the rate at which business organisations understand and apply IT increases far more slowly. Therefore, there is an awareness that people and business organisations need to increase their knowledge and understanding of IT and the application of IT within the business environment. This can only be achieved by increased

figure 1.2
Business organisation understanding of IT

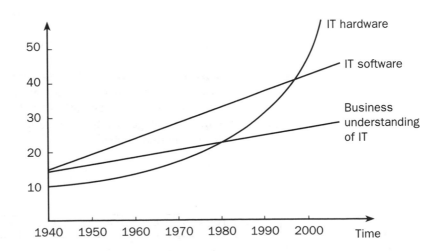

IT Capability Growth
(productivity rate)

education and training in BIT to fill any culture gap that exists in the business environment. For organisations to be competitive they must increase the rate at which people within organisations absorb, understand and apply IT knowledge. The challenge that business faces is to increase the capability (or productivity) of IT understanding within the business organisation.

1.10   Data, information, knowledge and wisdom

Earlier in this chapter it was observed that information is defined as processed data. In the Information Age this relationship can be extended to include consideration of the concept of *information for decision making*. Once information has been obtained, it can be further refined to provide *knowledge* and, with advances in technology, knowledge may even provide eventual *wisdom*. Figure 1.3 shows the progression from data through to wisdom.

Considering Figure 1.3, in order to understand how information technology has impacted on the processing of data; the handling of information; the provision of knowledge for decision making and the possibility of machine independence and responsibility for determining wisdom, a history of the evolution of electronic computer and IT-based technology must be undertaken.

The evolution of computing and information technology is often categorised into generations. The generations are described by the nature and sophistication of the underlying mechanical or electronic technology. For example, the first electronic computers were produced in the 1940s and since then computing and information technology has witnessed a number of advances in the electronics field. Each step up in the power of technology leads to a new generation. The generations of computing can be classified as follows:

First generation computing   This refers to the earliest use of electronic technology in the form of *valves* in the 1940s. The computing systems that categorised this generation of technology were EDSAC, EDVAC, LEO and UNIVAC1. The Lyons Electronic Office (LEO) computer is often referred to as the first business systems computer. It was installed to carry out functional business systems operations, particularly, in a large business organisation of the 1940s called Lyons Tea Houses. However, the LEO system was also later sold to other organisations to automate aspects of their business systems.

Second generation computing   This generation of computing is categorised by the use of more advanced technology in the form of *transistors* that replaced valve technology. This generation evolved around the 1950s. The computing systems that categorised this generation of technology were the LEO mark III, ATLAS and the IBM 7000 series.

figure 1.3
**Progression from
data into wisdom**

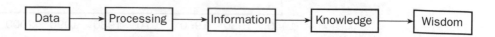

Third generation computing Third generation computers use more advanced technology than first and second generation computers in the form of *integrated circuits*. This generation of computing is also categorised by smaller and more compact technology. The continuing process of miniaturisation of physical technology is known as *downsizing*. Third generation computers are categorised by the ICL 1900 series and the IBM 360 series. Third generation computing can be attributed to the decades of the 1960s and 1970s.

Fourth generation computing This generation of technology uses more complex integrated circuits known as large-scale integration (LSI) or very large-scale integration (VLSI). This generation of technology can be attributed to the 1980s. Fourth generation technology is also categorised by the collateral trends of miniaturisation of computer components, but also massive increases in technology processing power.

Fifth generation computing This is an era that has not yet come to fruition, however, it refers to the development of 'thinking' machines that mimic human reasoning and intelligence with the added advantage of greater information processing ability and power. Fourth and fifth generation technology lies in the realms of artificial intelligence (AI), expert systems (ES) and technologies to support decision making.

1.11 A history of business computing, IT and multi-media

Information can be equated with power to the extent that information provides the knowledge to make informed decisions. Being IT literate is an essential skill in the Information Age. This idea of the importance of information and knowledge can even be found in the early literature of H.G. Wells, who wrote in the 1930s of fictional technological trends, some of which have evolved from fiction to reality in many respects!

DID YOU KNOW?

In his book World Brain, *written in 1938, H.G. Wells wrote:*

"In a few score years there will be thousands of workers at this business of ordering and digesting knowledge where you now have only one."

The earliest *electronic computers* in the 1940s were large and relatively slow with ponderous, unsophisticated processing power. Work on the first digital computer can be attributed to Howard Aitkin, a mathematician at Harvard University in the United States, in the late 1930s. His work, using electro-mechanical switches, began in 1937 and culminated in 1943 with the Mark I computer that contained three-quarters of a million component parts and measured 50 feet long and 8 feet high. The Mark I was designed as an arithmetic machine (that could add, subtract, divide and multiply) and was used by the American Army during the Second World War to calculate ballistic tables for army gunners. The success of this computer led the American government to fund a team (led by J.P. Eckert and J. Mauchly) at the University of Pennsylvania to build a faster computer based on vacuum tubes rather than electro-mechanical switches. The computer was named ENIAC (Electronic Numerical Integrator and Calculator) and its purpose was again to perform arithmetic calculations. Hence, the purpose of computation led the first machines to be named computers. The ENIAC computer was large and a heavy consumer of electrical power.

In 1951 J.P. Eckert and J. Mauchly followed up the ENIAC computer with a more sophisticated computer designed for commercial applications which was known as the UNIVAC (**Univ**ersal **A**utomatic **C**omputer). The UNIVAC, which was based on vacuum tubes, was developed for the American Census Bureau and began work on the American census of 1950. The UNIVAC was significant in using peripheral devices such as magnetic tape and electronic printers. The advances made in computing through the UNIVAC project led to large organisations of the 1950s realising the potential of commercial computing which manifested itself in a movement into the research, design and development of computing technology.

The late 1950s saw the use of vacuum tubes replaced by transistors which were smaller and processed data faster than vacuum tube technology. In 1959 two physicists, named R. Noyce and J. Hoerni, developed the first *integrated circuit* (IC) which entailed the microscopic photo-engraving of transistors on a single chip the size of an average human thumb nail. Integrated circuitry led to the development of smaller but more powerful computers and opened up the possibility of computers becoming available to a wider audience of commercial organisations. In the 1960s International Business Machines (IBM) in the United States realised the potential of computing. The President of IBM in the 1960s, T. Watson, had the vision to appreciate the value of computers to business organisations and actively moved IBM into the development and manufacturing of mainframe computers. IBM eventually moved away from the business of manufacturing and selling business machines, such as cash registers, into computing technology. IBM first of all developed the 7000 series of computers. But in 1964, IBM moved into the third generation of computing technology with the development of the IBM 360 series of computers aimed at satisfying the requirements of large commercial business organisations. IBM was so prevalent in the computing industry that the IBM S/360 computer became a standard business machine in the 1960s. These were supported by a number of peripheral devices, such as tape drives, printers and card readers, but were still very large and required an enormous amount of physical space within an organisation. This in turn led to business organisations establishing departments that were dedicated to the function of electronic computing. These business areas became known as *electronic data processing* (EDP) departments and were supported by numerous computing technicians and various other staff, dedicated solely to supporting the computer technology. The IBM S/360 series of computers were able to process instructions at the rate of around 100,000 instructions per second. These computers were used for carrying out the mechanical and essential functional systems operations of large organisations, such as payroll, stock processing, personnel records and financial accounting. Computers improved the speed, efficiency and effectiveness of data processing within the organisation. These areas were suitable for large-scale *batch processing*, which was the process of putting through the computer a mass of data and information in one computer processing run.

The profit to be made from selling computers to business organisations led to other companies entering the computing industry, such as Burroughs, NCR (National Cash Registers), Honeywell and Hewlett-Packard. If one business organisation acquired a computer it led to other business organisations within the industry acquiring a computer in order to maintain a competitive edge over its rivals. During this period of growth within computing IBM became the front runner within the industry to an extent whereby it dictated the standards to be matched and adhered to by other companies within the industry. In the 1970s attention turned towards the development of more sophisticated peripheral input and output devices to support mainframe computing; input terminals and output devices were consequently improved.

The 1970s saw the start of miniaturisation of computing technology that is perpetually continuing today and is associated with the concept of *downsizing* in the computing and business information technology environment. Downsizing allowed smaller businesses to incorporate computing technology into all of their organisational fabric. Therefore computing was no longer the preserve of the large conglomerate business organisations. The computing industry moved away from mainframes into what were known as minicomputers. Minicomputing introduced the concept of distributed computing within an organisation whereby processing functions were distributed to terminals within various parts of a business organisation. Therefore computing became networked. The dumb (stand alone) terminals used with mainframes were beginning to be replaced with 'smarter' terminals and, by so doing, provided greater participation within an organisation for computing operations and functions. In the 1970s (and more so in the early 1980s) many commercial organisations entered the computing industry to provide cloned IBM technology which greatly challenged the earning potential of IBM. Minicomputers, based on distributed (networked) computing, were cheaper than mainframes and became a standard within the majority of medium size business organisations in the 1970s.

As technology, such as microchips, became cheaper and more freely available, more component manufacturers entered the computing industry which led to the development and supply of 'off-the-shelf' computers and peripheral technology, rather than one-off computer systems for large business clients. The late 1970s saw a dramatic increase in organisations offering off-the-shelf software. Along with hardware technology, software applications for wordprocessing, spreadsheet modelling, graphics and database storage were developed as off-the-shelf applications for commercial business purposes. This eliminated the requirement for business organisations to employ many specialist programmers to write software applications that were specific to one application within a specific organisation. The provision of off-the-shelf generic software is often known as *commodity software*. The early 1970s saw a range of off-the-shelf commercial software applications. Other organisations, such as Lotus 1-2-3, also entered the computing industry during this era to provide readily available software applications for business purposes.

The late 1970s and the early 1980s witnessed computer input terminals proliferating in business organisations. Computing became cheaper and more available to all functional areas within a commercial business organisation to the extent that mainframes were becoming obsolete for the majority of business organisations. The 1980s witnessed computing becoming downsized to the extent that it pervaded all aspects of a business organisation and furthermore proliferated to individuals for personal use and applications. The 1980s is associated with the birth of *personal computing* as the proliferation of technology spread to individuals within society at large.

Personal computing was made possible by the development of microprocessor technology on single silicon chips. The Intel company produced the first available microprocessor, known as the Intel 8008 and the 1080 chip, in the early 1970s and other companies followed suit with the development of other microprocessor-based technology. In the mid-1970s a company known as MITS (Micro Instrumentation and Telemetry Systems) produced a kit-form component computer known as Altair. The availability of such kit-form microprocessor chip technology allowed computer literate individuals to produce their own customised computers which encouraged the development of the microcomputer industry. Indicative of this era were S. Jobs and S. Wozniak who assembled computers in their garage for personal use and to sell to friends. The business took off and the resultant organisation became known as Apple Computers. It was also in the mid 1970s that Bill Gates and Paul Allen formed a company to market software systems that became known as MicroSoft.

By the end of the 1970s it was becoming apparent that personal computers were starting to replace mainframe computing and the peripheral technology that surrounded mainframe computing, such as 'dumb' terminals. PCs could be used not only as terminal emulators for mainframes and minicomputers but also be used to carry out single and stand alone business functions involving word-processing, spreadsheet applications, database applications and graphics. Personal computers were more versatile to an organisation operating in a dynamic and ever changing business environment. IBM was at first slow to appreciate the growing importance of PCs to business, instead preferring to concentrate on the provision of large mainframe computers to business organisations. However, by the early 1980s IBM had moved into the PC market place and had set the IBM standard for personal computers which were cloned by other computer manufacturers. The early IBM personal computers used an 8088 processor produced by Intel in America and a disk operating system (DOS) that was supplied by the MicroSoft corporation. The disk operating system allows the sequencing and processing of computer instructions. The Compaq company and Commodore were examples of computing businesses that grew large on the profits from providing personal computers to business. The increase in companies competing to sell PCs and related business software led to prices being reduced during the 1980s and 1990s to levels at which all business organisations from large to small were able to acquire useful business computing technology. Gradually, computing manufacturers of hardware and software technology moved away from competing on price, when prices fell to levels where it was difficult to generate a profit, to competing on performance and quality. The 1990s is characterised by relatively affordable computing technology with ever increasing performance capabilities. Businesses cannot compete without the effective use and integration of PC-based technology within the organisation.

It is the PC revolution within the business computing world that has led to a cultural change in the way computers are integrated into the business environment, and the way job roles and responsibilities are defined within organisations. Business information technology is a discipline which recognises the nature of business computing and the impact of even newer communications-based information technologies and multi-media. The 1990s were characterised by a large number of computing and IT providers (vendors), with many of the large computer mainframe vendors of the 1970s and 1980s having either gone out of business, merged, or refocused towards selling business and personal computer software. Commercial business software is the largest earner of profit for computing and IT vendors in the 1990s. This trend is forecast to continue into the twenty-first century.

Modern desktop computers have performance criteria that exceeds mainframe computing but which is downsized to fit neatly within the physical area of a common desktop. The language of computing is even starting to refer to such desktop systems as micro-mainframes! Computing and IT vendors, such as Sun MicroSystems, build compact desktop-mountable machines that exceed the capabilities of many of the most powerful mainframe systems. However, the use, management, configuration and integration of such systems into the fabric of an organisation is a prime skill within business information technology.

ACTIVITY **1.8**
. . . .

History of computing and IT

Outline the main distinguishing features of first, second, third, fourth and fifth generation computing. Search your college or university library to find relevant information to construct a chronology of the main decade by decade developments within the computing and IT industry from the 1940s to the 1990s. Discuss the significance of these developments for business. From your discussions, put forward a constructive argument whether the development of personal computers and end-user computing have been the most significant developments over the last 40 years.

1.12   The business systems environment
. . . .

Information systems are shaped by the aims and objectives of the system. However, the shape and development of information systems is often constrained by a number of secondary considerations of the business environment which are internal and external to the typical business organisation. A constraint limits the capacity of a business organisation to achieve its aims and objectives. These constraining factors may be technical, economic, political, statutory, social or cultural. One or all of these factors may constrain or influence the shape and configuration of a business information system. Figure 1.4 shows the various layers of the business systems environment.

figure 1.4
**The business
systems environment**

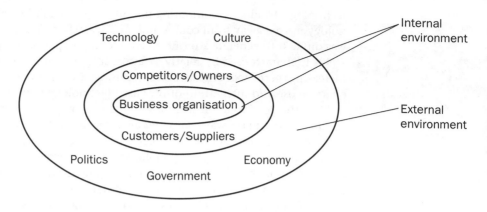

The information systems environment affects the behaviour of a business and influences its technological and business focus. The organisation is affected by both internal and external business environment considerations. Figure 1.4 outlines the internal and external factors that influence and constrain a business organisation. Information systems environments can be either open or closed. Closed information systems are self-contained and isolated from the external constraints. An open information system is influenced by the external business environment.

ACTIVITY **1.9**

The business systems environment

Divide up into pairs and describe the main constraints that might influence the shape and development of a business information system. Outline and try to categorise these constraints influencing the use and configuration of IS/IT into internal and external business factors. Consider and explain what is meant by an *open* system and a *closed* system within the context of the business environment.

1.13 Return on information systems and information technology investment

In any business organisation there are three essential resources that have to be managed and coordinated to allow an organisation to efficiently and effectively maximise its profit potential. These are people, technology and organisation. It is an underlying fact in the business environment of the Information Age that *the profit potential of a business is governed by the competitive nature of the sector in which it operates and how efficiently and effectively the business utilises all its resources.*

The London Stock Exchange of publicly quoted shares separates companies into related areas governed by the nature of the business. For example, the London Stock Exchange separates all listed shares into 40 sectors from alcoholic beverages and banks to transport and water companies. Each sector is expected to provide a return on investment in terms of resources utilised. The situation is the same in the United States where the top 500 business organisations on the American Stock Exchange are known as the Fortune 500.

Some sectors of the stock market have a higher *expected* return on resources than other sectors. The resources of a business are known as its assets. Assets are purchased and managed by a business with the role and intention of producing a profit. The level of profit related to the initial investment in resources can be considered the *return on investment for the business*. The return on investment can be calculated by a ratio of the total value of assets to the profit generated from those assets.

EXAMPLE

SouthWest Enterprises is a small engineering company located in Bristol in the United Kingdom. The company has five staff and assets that can be separated into buildings, vehicles, plant and machinery, and investment in information systems and information technology. For the previous financial year the business made a profit of £60,000. The investment costs of the business were as follows:

SouthWest Enterprises statement of costs

Buildings	£40,000
Vehicles	£12,000
Plant and machinery	£33,000
Information technology	£15,000
Employees costs	£20,000
Total	£120,000

Calculations: The return on investment would be £60,000/£120,000 = 0.5 or 50%. This indicates that 50% of the value of the resources of the business are returned as profit. Therefore, for every £1 spent on resources (assets) there is a return of 50 pence.

The price of a business is governed by its performance, which is a measure of its ability to generate income and create a profit. Computing and IT vendors, particularly of commercial business software, have been significant business performers in the 1990s. For example, the Compaq Corporation of America took only three years to get to a level where it generated over $1 billion of income a year. The computing industry is famous for companies gaining wealth very quickly and in some cases losing wealth very quickly when the tide of technological change eliminates the underlying business and product base. The computing industry is an uncertain and risky sector in all modern national economies. Wealth can be acquired by understanding and correctly predicting computing and IT trends.

DID YOU KNOW?
One of the wealthiest people in the world is Bill Gates, the founder and Chief Executive Officer (CEO) of Microsoft Corporation. The wealth of the corporation is founded upon the development and sale of commercial business software. Bill Gates understood the important trend of personal computing with an avowed aim to put a PC in every business and home in the United States.

Correctly utilising business information technology is imperative to all organisations. The appropriate appreciation and application of BIT principles to developing computer and IT-based solutions to an organisation's information systems problem will result in adding wealth to a business through enhanced business performance.

ACTIVITY 1.10

Return on IS/IT investment (1)

Discuss and explain how appropriately applied IS/IT can improve the return on investment of people, technology and organisation within a business. Once this has been achieved, list and describe the underlying nature of the business base of the top ten performing computing and IT vendors in the United States and the United Kingdom. (Investigate the types of products and the types of markets of such business organisations.)

ACTIVITY 1.11

Return on IS/IT investment (2)

The profit made by Paisley Corporation is £40,000 for the previous trading year. What is the return on the information systems and information technology investment undertaken by the business? The investment costs of the business are as follows:

Paisley Corporation

Buildings	£90,000
Vehicles	£20,000
Plant and machinery	£40,000
IS/IT	£20,000
Employees costs	£30,000
Total	£200,000

1.14 Chapter summary

Computing and information technology is an area of society and business that is growing in performance and influence at an exponential rate. There are thousands of computer vendors selling thousands of different software and hardware products each year. Organisations that compete with each other are affected by technological change in the business environment. In order to be competitive, organisations must understand the nature, role and influence of information technology on business performance. Consequently, technological change must be successfully managed by business in order to compete and earn a profit in increasingly dynamic business environments. The number of business systems functions that utilise IS/IT-literate staff increases each day and pervades the whole hierarchy or fabric of a business. The capability of recognising technological change and developing solutions to meet an organisation's information needs is a discipline that must be acquired and constructively applied in the Information Age.

Systems and IT permeate through all of society, to an extent that national barriers often appear to have disappeared and the world is virtually a smaller place. In the Information Age, information systems and IT are absorbed into everyday life to the extent that their significance is in danger of being overlooked. A key dynamic in this situation is the convergence of the business and consumer markets within people's homes. Individuals and groups have the opportunity in the Information Age to have a mass of information and technological resources at their fingertips to conduct and transact business.

Organisations will increasingly recognise the opportunities that appear with technology and will, consequently, need to address the issues of business information technology that will help them carry out their business activities more effectively and efficiently in an increasingly competitive business environment. Information and information systems are critical for business survival. The imperative of information and knowledge in the Information Age can be gauged from the following quote from the turn of the century at the outset of the age.

This war is a pack of surprises. Both sides are struggling for the margin, the little fraction of advantage, and between evenly matched enemies it's just the extra atom of fore-knowledge that tells.

(Buchan 1919)

The quote indicates the value of information and the need for information systems to deliver knowledge on which to base decision making. The quote describes how a little additional knowledge and information benefits the possessor of that information and ultimately can gain them an advantage over the competition.

Chapter note on the terms *'efficiency'* and *'effectiveness'*.

Throughout this book the terms *'efficiency'* and *'effectiveness'* will frequently be used. The two terms are imperative in the measuring of information systems and IT performance. Evaluating information systems performance requires the use of 'performance standards'. An information systems performance standard is a specific objective or goal of a system.

Efficiency   This is a relative measure of what is produced divided by what is consumed. For example, the efficiency of a mechanical engine could be measured by the ratio of the work done to the work needed to operate the engine.

Effectiveness   This is a measure of the extent to which a system achieves its goals or objectives. A system that achieves all of its goals is totally effective and a system that only achieves some of its goals is, by degree, less effective.

Short self-assessment questions

1.1   Outline and explain the three fundamental resources of a business organisation.

1.2   Define the role and purpose of a BIT professional within a business organisation.

1.3   Explain why such EDP departments are no longer relevant within the current business environment.

1.4 Define the concept of *competitive advantage* and explain the type of strategy that can be employed to deliver an advantage in a competitive business environment.

1.5 Explain the term *end-user computing* as it applies within a business organisation and explain the possible role of end-users in information systems development.

1.6 Outline five key issues for an understanding of business information technology.

1.7 Define and explain the fundamental differences between *information technology* and *computing*.

1.8 Define the term *IT literacy* and explain how such literacy affects the job specifications of *knowledge workers*.

1.9 Explain why it is important to understand the nature and value of information to an organisation.

1.10 State the three component parts of an information system in a business organisation and explain the relationship between these parts.

1.11 Explain the terms supply side technology growth and demand side technology growth and provide examples of *demand* for information and *supply* of technology to meet that demand for information.

1.12 Define and explain what is meant by commercial software and indicate the reasons why commercial software is so important to business in the Information Age.

1.13 Define the terms *efficiency* and *effectiveness* as applied to information systems and information technology in the business environment.

References

Porter, M.E. (1980) *Competitive Strategy*, New York: Free Press.

Porter, M.E. (1985) *Competitive Advantage*, New York: Collier-Macmillan.

Porter, M.E. (1990) *The Competitive Advantage of Nations*, New York: Free Press.

Price, R. (1991) 'What is the payoff from end-user computing: evidence accumulating from the USA and UK', in *IT and Accounting*, B.J. Spaul and B.C. Williams. London: Chapman-Hall, pp. 91–98.

Smith, A. (1776) *Wealth of Nations*, ed. A.S. Skinner. London, Harmondsworth: Penguin 1974.

Further study and reading

Books

Daellenbach, H.G. (1994) *Systems and Decision Making: A Management Science Approach*. New York: Wiley Publishing.

Delamarter, R.T. (1987) *Big Blue: IBM's Use and Abuse of Power*. London: Macmillan.

Koelsch, F. (1995) *The Infomedia Revolution.* Toronto: McGraw-Hill Ryerson.

Laudon, K.C. and Laudon, J.P. (1996) *Information Systems: A Problem Solving Approach.* Orlando, Florida: Dryden Press.

Lavington, S. (1980) *Early British Computers.* Manchester: Manchester University Press.

Manes, S. and Andrews, P. (1994) *"Gates".* New York: Simon & Schuster.

Liebenau, J. and Backhouse, J. (1990) *Understanding Information: An Introduction.* London: Macmillan.

Rowley, J. (1994) *Strategic Management Information Systems and Techniques.* Oxford: NCC Blackwell.

Sculley, J. (1989) *Odyssey: Pepsi to Apple.* London: Collins.

Senn, J.A. (1995) *Information Technology in Business: Principles, Practices, and Opportunities.* London: Prentice-Hall.

Thurow, L. (1992) *Head to Head: The Coming Economic Battle Among Japan, Europe, and America.* Nicholas Brealey.

Journals

Duff, A.S., Craig, D. and McNeill, D.A. (1996) A note on the origins of the information society, *Journal of Information Science*, 22(2), 117–122.

Fairclough, J., *et.al.* (1994) Professionalism in information technology, *Information Technology and Public Sector*, PITCOM. 13(1), 27–35.

Garfield, E. (1979) 2001: an information society? *Journal of Information Science*, 1(4), 209–215.

Grainger-Smith, N. (1994) The role of information systems and technology (IS/IT) in investment banks, *Journal of Information Science*, 20(5), 323–333.

Hoplin, H.P. (1994) Integrating advanced information systems and technology in future organisations, *Industrial Management and Data Systems*, 94(8), 17–20.

Wiio, O.A. (1985) Information economy and the information society, *Journal of Media in Education and Development*, 18(4), 187–191

Other material

West London Training and Enterprise Council (WLTEC) (1993) *IT Skills in the 1990s: overcoming obstacles to growth.* Report, WLTEC.

CHAPTER 2

General systems theory

Objectives
· · · · · · · · · · · · · ·

When you have studied this chapter you will be able to:

▶ describe and outline the development and philosophy of general systems theory

▶ interpret and describe the difference between physical and logical systems thinking

▶ understand the universal principles and characteristics that define a system within the business environment

▶ distinguish the three main organisational levels of a business and be able to describe the information systems characteristics of each level

▶ discuss the nature and characteristics of different types of business information systems found within the business environment.

2.1 Introduction to general systems theory
· ·

The world is made up of systems. Within the world are systems known as human beings. Within the human system exist various sub-systems, like the brain, the blood circulation system, the body temperature system and many other physiological systems. Along with human beings exist various other *natural* and *man-made* systems, such as the climatic system, the four seasons of spring, summer, autumn and winter, and even the planets in our galaxy revolving around the Sun. Other systems exist that are created by human beings, for instance, transportation systems, telephone systems and even the London Underground train network is a system. Therefore, there is a universal understanding that the whole world is comprised of systems! You may even wish to argue philosophically that the universe is a larger system full of smaller sub-systems. The study of systems is known as *systems science*. To be able to appreciate *business systems*, and particularly *business information systems*, we must first of all understand *general systems theory*. Systems theory is a multi-disciplinary study of how things are organised and relate to one another within their environment. Pause for thought 2.1 provides a definition of systems theory prepared for a renowned dictionary of philosophy. When reading the Pause for thought notice that certain words are emboldened; this is to highlight important concepts in systems theory. Study the Pause for thought section carefully and then read on further to discover details of all the concepts highlighted.

PAUSE FOR THOUGHT 2.1   *What is Systems Theory?*

(Reproduced by permission from Systems Thinkers – Principia Cybernetica Web)

Systems theory: The transdisciplinary study of the abstract organisation of phenomena, independent of their substance, type, or spatial or temporal scale of existence. It investigates both the principles common to all complex entities, and the (usually mathematical) models which can be used to describe them.

*Systems theory was proposed in the 1940s by the biologist Ludwig von Bertalanffy (anthology: General Systems Theory, 1968), and furthered by Ross Ashby (Introduction to Cybernetics, 1956). Von Bertalanffy was both reacting against **reductionism** and attempting to revive the **unity of Science**. He emphasised that real systems are open to, and interact with, their environments, and that they can acquire qualitatively new properties through **emergence**, resulting in continual **evolution**. Rather than reducing an entity (e.g. the human body) to the properties of its parts or elements (e.g. organs or cells), systems theory focuses on the arrangement of and **relations** between the parts which connect them into a whole (**holism**). This particular **organisation** determines a **system**, which is independent of the concrete substance of the elements (e.g. particles, cells, transistors, people, etc.). Thus, the same concepts and principles of organisation underlie the different disciplines (physics, biology, technology, sociology, etc.), providing a basis for their unification. Systems concepts include: system-environment **boundary**, **input**, **output**, **process**, **state**, **hierarchy**, **goal directness** and **information**.*

*The developments of systems theory are diverse (G.J. Klir, Facets of Systems Science, 1991), including conceptual foundations and philosophy; mathematical modelling and **information theory**; and practical applications. Mathematical systems theory arose from the development of isomorphies between the models of electrical circuits and other systems. Applications include engineering, computing, ecology, management, and family psychotherapy. Systems analysis, developed independently of systems theory, applies systems principles to aid a decision maker with problems of identifying, reconstructing, optimising, and controlling a system (usually a socio-technical organisation), while taking into account multiple objectives, constraints and resources. It aims to specify possible courses of action, together with their risks, costs and benefits. Systems theory is closely connected to **cybernetics**, and also **system dynamics**, which models changes in a **network** of coupled variables. Related ideas are used in the emerging 'sciences of **complexity**', studying **self-organisation** and heterogeneous networks of interacting actors, and associated domains such as **far-from-equilibrium thermodynamics**, **chaotic dynamics**, **artificial life**, **artificial intelligence**, **neural networks**, and computer **modelling and simulation**.*

Prepared for the Cambridge Dictionary of Philosophy. (Copyright Cambridge University Press)

ACTIVITY 2.1

Systems theory

Briefly discuss why it is important to understand general systems theory in order to appreciate and develop information systems in business. Then after reading Pause for thought 2.1 look in an ordinary or scientific dictionary for the meaning of the following words:

► reductionism
► holistic
► emergence
► organisation
► hierarchy
► cybernetics.

Study these definitions until you are clear about them and provide general systems examples to illustrate the meaning of each conceptual word.

It should now have become clear that certain general concepts and principles underpin systems theory. So what are these principles? Firstly, a *system* is a set of inter-related parts, arranged into an organised whole or orderly structure. This is referred to as *holism*. Such an organised whole is arranged in such a way that it is *systematic*. To be systematic is to be methodical, acting according to a plan, and not casual, sporadic or unintentional. Secondly, all systems can be *decomposed*, or broken down into constituent parts. This is known as *reductionism*. Systems can be broken down into *sub-systems* which can be further reduced down until the most basic constituents of the larger system are reached. For example, a human being can be reduced down to physiological organs, which

A System An organised set of components which interact in a regulated fashion to achieve a goal.

can be further broken down into cells, which can in turn be reduced down to molecules, which can be reduced into atoms, which can be further decomposed into particles (made up of neutrons and electrons). Even these neutrons and electrons can be further reduced down into what are known as quarks.

Organisms often share some common underlying characteristics but are very different in appearance. What emerges from the basic building blocks of a system is determined by the structure, relationship and connectivity of the basic building blocks. In other words, how these building blocks are structured will determine the nature and appearance of the object. This is sometimes referred to as *emergence*. It is important to look at the whole rather than focus on an individual component part that may often be shared by a number of systems.

In the study of *business information systems* it is often not desirable to reduce such systems to their component parts because the reason they exist is only seen in the whole. This is known as taking a *top-down* view of a system. The opposite of studying a system by looking at it holistically is to study the system's component parts without regard to what has emerged from those component parts. This is known as a *bottom-up* approach. The top-down or bottom-up study of systems influences the way business information systems are analysed, designed and evaluated. A further study of systems methodologies in subsequent chapters will reveal that systems design methodologies use various forms of the top-down or bottom-up approach to studying systems.

Systems found within the universe can be categorised into three generic types:

1   natural systems
2   man-made systems
3   social systems.

table 2.1 **Categories of system**	1	Natural systems	Climate, seasons, evolution
	2	Man-made systems	Transportation, telecommunications
	3	Social systems	Economic system, banking system, legal system

Examples of each of the three categories of system can be found in Table 2.1. Business is a *human activity system* which in turn relies on the effective and efficient design, development and maintenance of information systems within the organisation. Business information systems are designed by human beings with reference to human activity and general social systems behaviour. Information systems are concerned with the flows of data and information throughout an organisation which are required for decision making. It is important to note that consideration of the characteristics of an information system should always precede consideration of the technology aspects of the system; technology is merely a tool for making information systems more efficient and effective in their operation.

The sub-systems and component parts of a larger system are normally interdependent. Therefore, a change in one part of the system may often lead to changes in other parts of the system because of sub-system *dependency* within that system. All the parts of a working system should act together in harmony to achieve some purpose or system's goal. It is a fundamental principle that all systems are goal seeking. The reason for a system's existence is directly related to it's *purpose* or *goal*. Goal-seeking behaviour within systems is a major component principle of systems theory.

ACTIVITY **2.2**

General systems theory

Discuss and explain what is meant by the term *holistic* in the context of general systems theory. Then, taking a holistic systems view, define the principle of *emergence* and explain how the composition and nature of systems components often leads to very different emergent systems. Consider whether you think that the same system will, over time, always possess the same goals? If not, what may influence a system's goal-seeking behaviour? This should be considered in the context of explaining why goal seeking is a primary behavioural principle of all systems. Finally, discuss and indicate what *goals* or *purpose* a student might have for being at a university. Are the goals the same for each student? If not, discuss why these goals are different?

2.2   Approaches to systems theory

The doctrine of systems theory states that a *holistic system* provides greater benefit than the component parts of a system all working independently. This provides the fundamental concept that underpins systems theory that: *the whole is greater than the sum of its parts*. The component parts of

DID YOU KNOW?
The systems idea that the 'sum is greater than the parts' is not new. It was stated by Aristotle (384–322 BC) the Greek philosopher and tutor of Alexander the Great.

a system working together within the whole system provides a greater return than the parts working independent of one another and outside of an organised and structured system.

The human being is an interesting example of this doctrine of the system being greater than the sum of the parts. Section 2.1 revealed how the human system can be decomposed down into its constituent parts, even down to atomic particles comprised of neutrons and electrons. However, the reason humans exist can only be seen in the whole and not by looking at the parts in isolation. The idea of contemplating the smallest component parts of a system up to the largest whole is known as a *bottom-up* approach to systems analysis and design. However, this approach misses the idea that the reasons why systems exist can *only* be seen by looking at the system as a whole and in its ultimate *holistic* context. This is normally known as a *top-down* approach to systems analysis and design. The top-down approach views the system in the context of its overall goal or purpose. For example, the physiological organs of the body all work together to achieve the goal of sustaining life in the human body. If the parts of the human body are looked at in isolation then an understanding of the individual purpose and role of these parts will be missed. Therefore, the existence and consciousness of a human being is more than the sum of the parts; a human being has self-identity and a consciousness which is not observed by looking at the individual parts of the body in total isolation. For instance, human consciousness has *emerged* from interlinking together the parts of the human system. The human body is a set of parts that work to a common end, that of sustaining life.

A holistic view observes the whole of a system and not just the parts in isolation, without any recognition of the system's purpose or goal. The additional quality or benefit that emerges from linking the parts together into a system is referred to as *synergy*. A good example of emergence and synergy can be found by looking at the qualities of carbon. The combination of carbon atoms may take on various shapes and forms, which in turn leads to entities that differ greatly in appearance and purpose. For instance, the carbon-based forms of graphite and diamond. Graphite is soft, black and opaque while a diamond is hard and transparent. Nevertheless, both are made up of the same substance: carbon. The difference lies in the way in which the carbon molecules are structured and organised. Therefore, within systems theory, the organisation of the component parts influences the purpose or goal of the holistic system.

ACTIVITY **2.3**

Approaches to systems analysis and design

Explain the fundamental difference between a *bottom-up* approach and a *top-down* approach to systems analysis and design theory. Discuss the idea in systems theory of 'the sum being greater than the parts' and provide two examples of systems in which this is the case. Contemplate and explain what might be 'missing' from the whole if analysis of a human being was modelled using a bottom-up approach.

2.3   Systems principles
•••••••••••••••••••••••••••••

All systems share common underlying characteristics, whether they are natural systems, man-made systems or social systems. The concept and possibility of universal *systems characteristics* was proposed by Ludwig von Bertalanffy in a book entitled *General Systems Theory* published in 1968. This book, which is fully referenced at the end of this chapter, discusses the existence of underlying systems principles to explain systematic behaviour and activity. von Bertalanffy realised that organised processes, from very different backgrounds, seemed to share common principles governing their existence. Therefore, the question that von Bertalanffy asked was whether a system can be defined by its characteristics. For example, a human being can be defined by underlying and common human characteristics, such as, normally, two eyes, two arms, two legs, hair on the top of the head and nails on the ends of the fingers. If only two characteristics such as legs and arms were used to define the human body, this would not be sufficient to clearly define, or distinguish, a human being from an object such as a chair which also may have characteristics called legs! However, if we add more and more characteristics to the distinction list of common characteristics, then a clearer definition of the form of a human being may be gained. Therefore, it is possible to define an object or a system by its distinguishing characteristics. Hence, a system can be defined by its *common characteristics*.

All systems share five common characteristics that allow a system to be defined as a system. A systems framework model can be developed of the five common systems characteristics that allow a system to be more clearly defined. The five defining characteristics of a system are outlined in Table 2.2. In order to be defined as a 'system', all of these characteristics must be present within the framework of the system.

A system is a collection of inter-related parts, some of which may be common to other systems. A system cannot be considered a static object, like a table, chair, pen or other inanimate entity. For a system to be a system it must assume some form of *activity*. In the case of information systems the fundamental activity is processing data and information. For example, the arrangement of inanimate chairs and tables into rows within a room, and the numbering of tables by examination candidate number, may form parts of an examination system's process. However, the component parts of that system, such as the chairs and tables, are not in themselves a system. But the organisation and activity of the component parts will comprise a system.

table 2.2
Common systems characteristics

1	Inputs and outputs
2	Goals or objectives
3	Systems boundary (or environment)
4	Feedback and control — neg/Positive
5	Inter-related parts

From Table 2.2 it can be seen that all systems have *inputs* and *outputs*. In the case of information systems the input to be processed is 'data' and the resultant output of the system is 'information'. The output of one system can often form the input for another system. Therefore, various systems can be connected by their inputs and outputs. It is possible to visualise the whole business environment as being composed of numerous systems and sub-systems. The activities and processes of a system are determined by its *goals*. For example, the main purpose or goal of IT-based business information systems is to make the human activity of information processing more efficient and effective within the organisation. The output from the processes of a system are directly related to the system goal or set of goals.

In order to understand and recognise separate systems and sub-systems within environments it is necessary to be able to define the *boundaries* of the system. This is particularly important when studying the specifics of systems in greater detail. For instance, any analysis of the London Underground train system would be restricted to the environment of the London Underground and not the underground train network operating in Newcastle! A systems boundary (or environment) can be defined as whatever lies within the scope of the system and interacts with that system. The emphasis in establishing boundaries is to determine the specific impact of environmental considerations on a system or sub-system. If something resides outside of the system's boundaries, and does not impact on the system or affect the system in any way, then this would be outside of the system's immediate environment. In any study of system activity it is important to be able to define the boundaries of a system in order to focus attention more effectively on the issues that affect that system. The shape and constituent parts of a particular system are determined by its pre-established boundary.

ACTIVITY **2.4**

Systems characteristics

State and explain the types of inputs and outputs that would usually be found within the general environment of a business information system. Provide an example of a man-made or natural system found in the world at large and define the boundaries of each system.

Another major defining characteristic of systems is the existence of *control* and *feedback*. All systems have regulatory controls that allow a system to maintain or pursue its objectives and goals. The control aspect oversees the processing activities of most systems. In order for a system to meet its goal, or set of goals, some form of control and feedback mechanism is essential to the system's effective operation. The sub-system of control within a larger system may well have its own goals or objectives. For example, the body's blood temperature system is controlled by the central cortex at the back of the brain. The goal of the body's temperature system is to maintain the human body temperature at 96.8 degrees Farenheight (or 36 degrees centigrade). If the temperature of the human body falls or rises from its natural temperature, the body will feed back this information to the body's thermostatic system, so that measures can be effected to bring the temperature back to its natural state. For instance, if the human temperature falls below its natural level the skin starts to get cold, the body will start to shake and pump blood at a faster rate in order to heat the body back up to its natural temperature level. If the body's temperature rises above the normal level, the skin begins to perspire and give up body fluid. This has the effect of cooling the skin down and bringing the body's temperature back to its normal and natural state. The goal of the body is to maintain a determined temperature level. A system that maintains a pre-determined or steady state is known as *homeostatic*. Homeostasis is a movement within a system towards equilibrium. Such homeostatic control systems attempt to maintain a static balance (or equilibrium) within the system. Many other control systems do not try to maintain static balance but are dynamic, ever changing, or *pursuing* target goals. Business is a human activity system which is constantly changing. Therefore, control of change on a broad basis can be a specific objective of business information systems.

Systems *feedback* refers to the information which enables the system processes to modify themselves and in turn meet the system's goals. Feedback can be of two types:

1   negative feedback, or
2   positive feedback.

With *negative feedback* within control systems, the output is fed back as an input to achieve a specified or pre-determined state. Examples of natural systems are the human heart, human kidneys and temperature system; man-made examples are the thermostatic temperature system of a home, a business stock system, or a manufacturing control system. *Positive feedback* occurs when the output of the control system is fed back as an input for growth. For example, a bonfire will burn and cause increasing generation of heat, which in turn will lead to further incineration until the boundaries of the available inflammable material have been totally burnt. The bonfire positively expands and grows as it burns. In the case of business organisations, profits can be reinvested back into the organisation to expand or create increased economic growth within a business. Thus, retaining profits within a business is an example of positive feedback within the business environment.

Normally, all business organisations rely on feedback and control systems. All systems have objectives and, in order to ensure that the systems objectives are met, it is important that control is exercised within the system's processes and activities. Control can only be achieved by accurate and effective information feedback into the system that allows changes to be made to maintain the direction of a system to achieve its goals. Figure 2.1 shows a typical feedback and control system's model.

In Figure 2.1, information flows into a process which is monitored by a *sensor*. The sensor will often use a *comparator* mechanism to compare the inputs being processed with the system's expected *standard*. If the inputs are irregular (or non-standard) the feedback and control mechanisms will activate a change of the inputs. This will cause an action to be taken by the system. If the irregularity is brought back to a standard, then the input will be allowed to be processed and output from the main system. A feedback and control system often forms a closed loop within a system's processing activities.

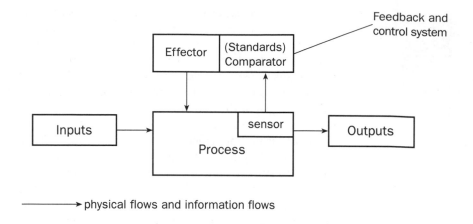

figure 2.1
**Systems feedback
and control model**

The final common characteristic of systems is that they possess *inter-related parts* that work in harmony to achieve the goals of the overall system. Systems can be inter-related to one another by their inputs and outputs. Systems can also comprise component sub-systems which can be decomposed down into a *hierarchical* model, where larger systems are reduced to smaller sub-systems which are in turn reduced to even smaller sub-sub-systems. It should be noted that each sub-system is itself a system with goals or objectives, inputs, outputs and processes, often with its own particular system specific control and feedback characteristics.

When the output of one system can be the input to another system, such systems are said to be *dependent systems*. Systems that are not related to one another are termed *independent systems*. This dependence, or linkage, between systems is often termed *systems coupling*. The measurement of dependence of one system on another system is known as the *degree of coupling*. Systems that are strongly dependent upon one another are said to be highly coupled. The measurement of coupling can be determined by calculating the percentage of output of one system being used as the input for another system. The level of coupling is important in determining the extent to which one system affects another system. This is a particularly important consideration if it is the case that the failure of one system will lead *directly* to the failure of another system. For example, system Y may be highly coupled with system Z. If system Y fails it will also cause a failure in system Z as a consequence of the high level of coupling between the two systems. Coupling has consequences for the development of control mechanisms which control the flow of output from one system to another that are highly coupled. Control mechanisms must be placed between highly coupled systems to prevent one system adversely affecting another dependent system. These basic control mechanisms act as a filter, controlling the flows of physical objects, data or information between systems. In order to ensure that the system's objectives are met it is important that some form of control operates over the system's processing activities. The activity of separating highly coupled systems is known as systems de-coupling. There are three main ways of achieving systems de-coupling:

1 building in marginal capacity into the physical aspects of an information system
2 creating an information buffer between systems
3 establishing an information filter to validate and verify the data or information.

All three of these control mechanisms may be used to assess and validate output information from one system before it is allowed to be used as input information for another system. For example, The NASA (National Aeronautical and Space Administration) Challenger space shuttle is made up of many interconnected systems working in unison to achieve the goal of flight into space with the safe return of its crew to earth, after some pre-defined duration. The failure of one system within the space shuttle, or its dependent systems, may result in life-threatening consequences for a space mission. Therefore, it is important that control systems are put into place to de-couple the dependency of systems. The consequences may not always be life threatening within business systems, but failure to implement adequate and reliable control mechanisms within business systems may certainly threaten the economic well-being of a business.

ACTIVITY **2.5**

Universal systems characteristics

Explain the five main characteristics used to define a system and discuss what is meant by a holistic approach to systems thinking. Do you consider that a personal computer can be classified as a system? Explain your answer in terms of the possible goal or purpose of a computer. If so, outline the possible hierarchical levels into which a computer could be decomposed and consider whether any emergent properties can exist at the lower levels. If all systems are shaped and formed by their respective goals, explain the goals or purpose of the following:

▶ a *student* at university
▶ an aircraft *autopilot*
▶ a *toilet*
▶ a *research and development* department
▶ a *marketing system*.

Systems may incorporate feedback and control mechanisms. In which case, provide a biological, mechanical and business systems example of a negative feedback system and a positive feedback system. Discuss whether the feedback and control mechanisms of the systems you propose are related to the goal or purpose of those systems.

2.4 Deterministic and functional business systems

Systems where the inputs and outputs are defined with certainty are known as *deterministic systems*. Such a system is limited in scope and definition; it is often pre-defined before any systems processing activity has been undertaken. IT hardware and software should be deterministic to the extent that the same inputs will always produce a finite, determined output (as long as no malfunction or error has occurred in the system). Humans and human activity on the other hand are not deterministic. Human activity changes and alters with environmental considerations. Such dynamic activity can be considered to be *adaptive* to the environment in which the system exists. Adaptive systems normally try to be suitable for a purpose, and modify (or alter) with the changing environment and over time. Humans are not static but are dynamic to the extent that human beings and human activity systems are always changing, unlike a passive computer and its technology. Therefore, it can be said that humans are adaptive while computers are deterministic. Likewise, the pursuit of business is a human activity which is adaptive to the circumstances of the internal and external business environment. Information systems can be either deterministic or adaptive depending on the goals or purpose of the information system.

Systems that exist to implement the routine, or day-to-day, activities of business are normally deterministic, while systems that are used for decision making that is not routine are considered to be adaptive. The extent to which a system is either deterministic or adaptive is governed by the level of information certainty of the outputs given a known set of inputs. Deterministic systems within a business are often known as *functional systems* because they carry out a defined function, transaction or routine business activity. For instance, all business organisations utilise common functional systems such as salaries or payroll. However, it is important to understand functional systems in order to be able to understand the use and development of systems that are not deterministic. Typical of functional systems within a *manufacturing organisation* would be the following:

▶ sales order processing
▶ purchase order processing
▶ production control
▶ production planning
▶ input stock controlling (of raw materials)
▶ output stock controlling (of finished goods)
▶ goods distribution
▶ payroll (wages and salaries).

In addition to these functional systems would be further support functions that may or may not be as deterministic, such as:

▶ marketing
▶ research and development
▶ customer service
▶ human resources (personnel)
▶ accounting.

All of these systems will share the five common defining characteristics of systems: goal seeking, possessing defined boundaries, having inputs and outputs, interrelated parts, and some form of feedback and control.

A diagram of how all these functional systems are typically integrated can be found in Figure 2.2. It should be noticed in Figure 2.2 that each system is defined by a box. Each box has an arrow either pointing into or out of the box. These arrows indicate information flows into and out of a system. Each system component of the business is bounded by a box. The linking together of systems by their respective inputs and outputs, but ignoring the internal structure and

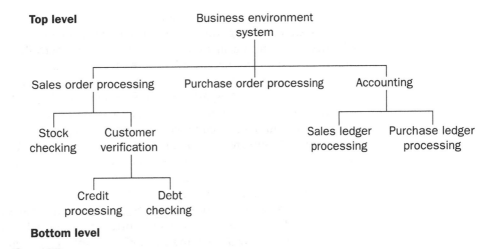

figure 2.2
Systems decomposition

activities, is known as a black box approach to information systems. What is important in this approach are the information flows between the systems. Remember that in *systems decomposition* the outputs of one sub-system may form the inputs of another sub-system of the business organisation.

Since most sub-systems within a business organisation are related to one another by their inputs and outputs, any view of the overall organisation should not consider individual business information systems in isolation. The analysis, design, implementation and evaluation of business information systems requires a view of systems in their *totality*. The total systems approach is central to business information technology in that systems cannot be built without regard to the overall goals of the business organisation. To concentrate on one specific system, to optimise the efficiency and effectiveness of the inputs, processes and outputs, may lead to neglect or sub-optimisation in other related systems to the detriment of the overriding business goals.

ACTIVITY **2.6**

Functional business systems

Discuss and explain the terms *deterministic* and *adaptive* in the context of systems theory and provide an example for each type of systems behaviour. Suggest why functional systems within the business environment are considered deterministic and suggest three possible characteristics such deterministic systems may possess.

2.5 Physical versus logical systems thinking

One of the most important concepts to understand in information systems theory is to be able to separate *logical* systems thinking from *physical* systems thinking. Any manufacturing process requires raw materials to be put together into a finished product; business organisations may also buy and sell services which are more abstract and less prone to physical definition. In systems theory it is imperative to understand the *logical purpose* or goal of a system before thinking about the system in physical and technological terms. For example, the goal of a stock system in a large organisation will be fundamentally the same as the goal of a stock system in a small organisation; they are logically the same. The goal of a stock system irrespective of the size of the organisation and other physical characteristics, will be to monitor and ensure determined levels of stock. However, the physical aspects of a stock system in a large organisation may be very different to the physical aspects of a stock system in a small organisation in terms of the number of employees responsible for the system, the amount of hardware and software needed to maintain the system and the physical location in which the stock system is located. Therefore, the logical basis of the stock system will be the same for all business organisations; however, the physical aspects of each stock system may be very different.

The logical systems process assumes activity, such as sales order processing, purchase order processing and stock controlling. 'Processing' and 'controlling' (and normally any word ending in 'ing') are verbs or action words. However, 'stock', 'employee' and 'order' are nouns, naming physical items. Physical descriptions contain nouns while logical descriptions are verbs or action words. When studying information systems it is the logical processes that are important and not the physical environment and technology in which the system activities take place. A logical representation of physical activities and processes is the fundamental basis for designing and developing business information systems. It is imperative that the logical aspects of a system are separated out from the physical aspects of that system. We now know from earlier study that a system can be classified by its characteristics to determine whether it is a system or not a system. Systems can then be further identified by *type* according to their behaviour. Systems can be any of the following:

▶ goal keeping, aiming or pursuing
▶ deterministic, adaptive, purposeful or homeostatic
▶ possess negative feedback or positive feedback.

Business information systems provide the information needed for managers to make informed and reasoned decisions. When humans interact with a man-made system the whole system can move from deterministic to adaptive. However, some functional systems, such as stock control, are deterministic irrespective of the human element of interaction. Other systems such as marketing do not remain deterministic when the human aspects are added to the system equation. Whether a system is deterministic or adaptive, through the addition of human interaction, depends upon the type and level of the organisational structure in which the business system resides. This means that anyone involved in systems thinking needs to know how systems are absorbed into the fabric of a business organisation. The subsequent sections will describe the typical *organisational hierarchy* and explain the type and role of systems at each level of the organisational hierarchy.

ACTIVITY **2.7**

A

Physical versus logical systems thinking

A system can be classified by its *defining characteristics* to determine whether it is a system or not a system. Systems can be further identified by *type* according to their behaviour. Systems can be either: (a) goal keeping, aiming or pursuing; (b) deterministic, adaptive, purposeful or homeostatic; or (c) possess negative feedback or positive feedback. Identify which of the following are systems and identify which of the above terms within (a), (b) or (c) apply and explain your reasoning:

1 a robot welding machine
2 an aircraft autopilot
3 the British national economy
4 the human body's temperature system
5 achieving a qualification at university
6 selling a business product
7 a computer
8 a software application
9 the weather
10 the human body
11 a stock control system
12 a marketing system
13 the universe.

2.6 Decision levels of the business organisation
· ·

A typical hierarchical business will have three broad levels of organisational decision making; these are, from top to bottom, as follows:

1   strategic (or executive) information systems
2   management information systems
3   operational information systems.

Each organisational level exhibits different information requirement characteristics in terms of the decision time-frame, certainty, risk, responsiveness, information structure and application of technology. These decision-making levels are characterised by information systems that are different in design and composition because of the *level-specific* goals of the information systems at each level of the hierarchy. A diagrammatic representation of the characteristics of information systems and decision-making activity at the three levels of the organisational hierarchy can be seen in Figure 2.3. The decision-making levels are highly significant in terms of systems thinking, since the purpose of processing data is to produce information for decision making.

Within a typical hierarchical business organisation *operational systems* are responsive and deterministic to the extent that the inputs and outputs are known with certainty; such systems are mechanical in their processes and algorithmic in their decision-making functions. Operational systems play a significant part in manufacturing business environments, but are also found to varying extents in normal business environments. Operational systems are sometimes referred to in business systems literature as *transaction processing systems* (TPSs). Examples of such systems within business organisations are stock control, production scheduling and payroll. By contrast *strategic information systems* are often heuristic (random) and only as accurate as the level of certainty (or uncertainty) of the predicted probabilities and expected events of the business information

figure 2.3
**Information systems
decision levels
within a business
organisation**

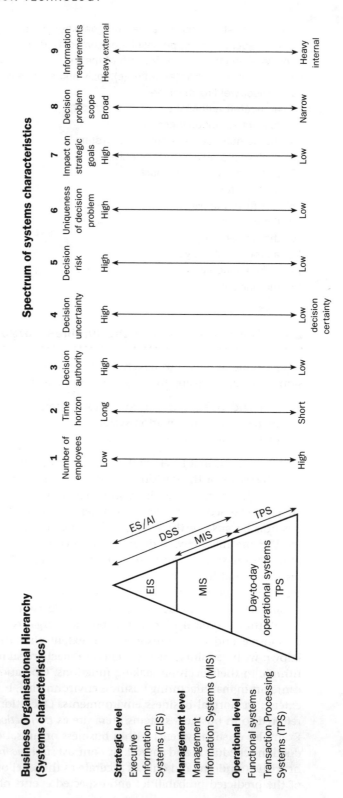

Spectrum of systems characteristics

	1	2	3	4	5	6	7	8	9
	Number of employees	Time horizon	Decision authority	Decision uncertainty	Decision risk	Uniqueness of decision problem	Impact on strategic goals	Decision problem scope	Information requirements
	Low	Long	High	High	High	High	High	Broad	Heavy external
	High	Short	Low	Low decision certainty	Low	Low	Low	Narrow	Heavy internal

**Business Organisational Hierarchy
(Systems characteristics)**

EIS
MIS
Day-to-day
operational systems
TPS

ES/AI
DSS
MIS
TPS

Strategic level
Executive
Information
Systems (EIS)

Management level
Management
Information Systems (MIS)

Operational level
Functional systems
Transaction Processing
Systems (TPS)

environment. Within the strategic information systems environment the information is often unstructured and the decision-making activities are uncertain. This level of decision making is characterised by *executive information systems* (EIS), *decision support systems* (DSS) and *expert systems* (ES). Within the middle level of the business are usually found *management information systems* (MIS). These are characterised by medium-term budgeting and forecasting functions, and lie somewhere on the hierarchical spectrum between strategic systems and operational systems, but normally have characteristics of both the bottom and top levels of business systems.

The *decision-making activities* at the lowest level of the organisation hierarchy are usually routine and repetitive, whereas at the highest level of the organisation hierarchy the decision-making activity is more one-off and user-specific in nature. Figure 2.3 assists in an understanding of the roles of various information systems within the organisation hierarchy. The spectrum of characteristics reveals how information systems requirements are dependent upon the nature of the environment in which the system resides.

The evolutionary trends in computing and IT, described in chapter 1, have been horizontally absorbed into business in general from the top to the bottom of the organisation. The decision-making levels of an organisation are highly significant, since the purpose of processing data is to produce good information for decision making. In the light of what has previously been described in this section, it can be seen that a specialist working within the business information technology environment needs not only an understanding of computing and IT, but also a substantive understanding of the application and characteristics of information systems at each level of decision making within information-sensitive business organisations.

The information which is the life-blood of any organisation may fall into either of two predominent categories of *formal* or *informal* information. Formal information is factual and produced by standard, verifiable procedures and practices, while informal information is subjective and often based on opinion. For information to be formal it must have been acquired and processed within a formalised information systems environment. This does not necessarily mean that formal information is always more accurate than informal information, but only that the procedures used to handle the information were structured and formalised within the organisational hierarchy.

ACTIVITY **2.8**

Decision characteristics within the business organisation hierarchy

This task should be undertaken with reference to Figure 2.3. We have seen how the traditional organisational hierarchy can be segmented into three decision-making levels. Discuss the various characteristics found at each organisational level and describe the type of goals a systems would have at the operational, managerial and strategic levels of an organisation. You should notice from Figure 2.3 that there are arrows indicating the level of absorption of decision support systems (DSS), expert systems (ES) and artificial intelligence (AI) throughout the typical business hierarchy. From the following list of business environment sectors draw an organisational hierarchy indicating the *level* and *extent* of absorption of DSS, ES and AI from the top to the bottom of a typical organisation.

- ▶ stockbroking
- ▶ insurance sector
- ▶ retail banking sector
- ▶ tourist industry.

Discuss why some areas of business activity may show a higher absorption of such systems than other sectors of business.

2.7 Decision making within the organisational hierarchy

The scope of decision-making activity within a typical organisational hierarchy is dependent upon the level and nature of the system being used. As a rule of thumb, the most intensive decision-making activity occurs at the strategic level of an organisation, and the least intensive decision-making activity occurs at the operational level. Operational systems include such activities as payroll, stock control and financial accounting. The activity of preparing payrolls, for example, is a vital but repetitive task which is often done by outside organisations which specialise in providing such mechanical and routine services. Likewise, any manufacturing organisation which maintains levels of stock (known as *inventory* in the United States), in raw materials or finished goods, needs to operate a *stock control system*. Stock must be controlled to maintain the appropriate minimum stock levels across a range of goods. Stock systems should ideally contain up-to-date information on stock quantity levels, prices, minimum stock levels and reorder levels. For instance, a stock system should *automatically* indicate when minimum stock levels have been reached. Stock control systems will also generate useful supplementary reports on sales patterns, stock flow through the manufacturing process and early and late stock orders. In manufacturing environments there are normally two types of stock system working in harmony; one is an input (*raw materials*) stock system and the other is an output (*finished goods*) stock system. The main effect of an IT-based stock control system is that any manager can identify stock levels and the price of any individual item instantly, often at the touch of a button!

All business organisations will have some form of *management accounting* and *financial accounting* system which will generate reports on the transactions and trading performance of the business. Financial accounting reports are produced for *external* information use and are known in the United Kingdom as a Balance Sheet (showing assets and liabilities), a Profit and Loss Account (showing the gross and net profit of the business) and a Source and Application of Funds Statement (showing the movement in liquid or cash assets between two periods). Operational systems are concerned with the recording of day-to-day transactions that occur internally and externally within the business environment. There is very little decision-making activity concerned with operational systems, other than when and how to initiate a transaction processing activity.

ACTIVITY **2.9**

Transaction processing systems

Explain why operational systems are often referred to as *transaction processing systems* and discuss why such systems are usually referred to as *deterministic*.

Once you are happy with the concept of transaction processing, provide two examples of an operational system and determine who (or what) would be responsible for initiating or operating such systems.

Management information systems (MIS) are often characterised by a semi-structured information environment. In operational systems the whole of the decision picture is *known*. However, in a management information system only parts of the decision picture are known; and in strategic information systems, large aspects of the decision picture are *unknown*. The normal aim of all information systems is to get as near to decision-making certainty as possible. Management information systems are concerned with the provision of relevant, timely and useful information for the management *control* of an organisation's resources. Therefore, management information systems are not concerned with day-to-day operational decisions, but with decisions that are in the management sphere; management decisions have a longer decision time-frame than operational decisions.

Management Information System (MIS) A system providing information for decision making usually intended for middle management. The information may be internal to an organisation or external to the business organisation.

Management information systems are designed to select, analyse and produce information that is useful to the activity of management decision making. Therefore, the information systems and technology support the activity of management decision making. The primary role of management information systems is to *plan and coordinate the resources of the business organisation*. Management is a human activity and management information systems must take into account the people aspect of business organisations. Successful management information systems show a due regard to human as well as technical aspects of the business organisation. Management information systems are developed with regard to a range of *knowledge concepts* and techniques that are relevant to the business environment. The knowledge concepts for an understanding of management information systems are as follows:

▶ general systems theory
▶ computing and information technology
▶ the nature of data, information and knowledge
▶ organisational structures and processes
▶ people and human behaviour
▶ planning, decision making and control techniques
▶ organisational levels and functions
▶ interpersonal management techniques.

DID YOU KNOW?
Henri Fayol (1841–1925), a famous French industrialist, is credited with laying the classical academic foundations of the theory of management. Fayol defined the process of management as follows:
'To manage is to forecast and plan, to organise, to command, to coordinate and to control'.

It is the goal of a management information system to provide management with information, based on data from both *internal* and *external* sources; to enable timely and relevant decisions for planning, directing and controlling the resources of the organisation. Management information systems will be tailored to the needs of specific organisations and utilise internal information sources to a greater extent than external information sources.

If an organisation operates in a stable and relatively static and unchanging business environment the management information systems of that organisation will be designed to deal with relatively more structured and mechanistic planning and control of resources. However, in dynamic and volatile business environments such information systems should be adaptive and responsive to deal with change in the internal and external environment. Management information systems are usually characterised by the following factors:

▶ A wider span of organisational coverage and control than operational systems.

▶ Data and information is normally drawn from a wide range of internal and external sources.

▶ Decision making can be complex and uncertain and require reasoned management judgement.

▶ Control is usually assisted by monitoring and feedback provision incorporated into the system.

▶ Use of the system is allied with reasoned and educated management judgement.

▶ Generation of meaningful reports for management decision making and personnel information.

The data used in an MIS will be drawn from internal and external sources within the business environment. Much of the input data for a management information system may originate from output data and information from other, often operational, systems, such as stock, sales order processing, purchase order processing, or even production scheduling. This type of operational information may be processed by a management information system to provide evidence on which to base management decision making.

ACTIVITY 2.10

Management information systems decision making

Discuss the primary role of management information systems within a typical business organisation. You should also discuss the eight basic knowledge concepts that underpin the design and development of management information systems. Indicate who would normally be responsible for using an MIS and explain their possible role and responsibility within a business organisation.

The systems to support such executive or strategic decision making are known as *executive information systems* (EISs). Strategic decision making is concerned with the long-term effects of decisions; and such decisions usually influence the future direction of an organisation. At the strategic level, decisions have a longer time-frame than both management and operational information systems.

> *Executive Information System (EIS)* A system that provides information to senior executive managers on strategic areas of a business organisation's activities to aid strategic decision making. The information may be internal to an organisation or external to the organisation.

Executive information systems are designed to support high-level executives, responsible for an organisation's strategic policies and direction, in the process and practice of decision making. The environment in which strategic decision making is undertaken is normally characterised by high levels of uncertainty within the information environment. An EIS that provides a fraction more certainty than a competitor's EIS, within the decision-making scenario, will gain a competitive advantage within the business environment. Executive information systems are designed to eliminate information overload and provide clear, summarised information that usually highlights opportunities or weaknesses for the organisation. It is critical to a business to be aware of the strategic factors that may influence the direction of the organisation. The strategic direction of an organisation can often be assessed by *SWOT analysis*, which represents a business organisation's

Strengths	(within the internal and external environment).
Weaknesses	(within the internal and external environment).
Opportunities	(for growth and profit within the business environment).
Threats	(from competitors, technology and other trends).

Executive information systems normally comprise powerful data storage capabilities to handle both formal and informal information, which is used and manipulated by a range of sophisticated IT-based applications for simulation and mathematical modelling. Executive information systems are normally characterised by the following factors:

▶ A wider span of organisational coverage and control than operational and management systems.
▶ Concerned with new and unstructured decision-making situations and environments.
▶ Shrewd executive reasoning and judgement in the collection and interpretation of information.
▶ Data and information is largely drawn from sources external to the organisation.
▶ Information sources are usually report based (alphanumeric) and often semi-formal or informal.
▶ Decision making can be uncertain and has long-term significance for an organisation.
▶ Relies on forecasting, prediction and trend analysis of the long-term future.
▶ The information environment is boundary-less and not confined in decision-making scope.
▶ Use of the system requires reasoning, judgement and a broad assessment of multiple variables.
▶ User-specific system that is operated personally by an individual or group of individuals.

Executive information systems must be fast and easy to use by executives who will not necessarily possess a technical background or expertise in information systems and information technology. Therefore, all EIS should be characterised by ease of use through the incorporation of menu-driven windows technology, touch screens, graphics and easy information interchange between systems. Rapid access to data is often permitted through exploration of the data known as *drilling down the data*. Most systems provide easy to use and effective front-end screen applications to permit data simulation and modelling, with the incorporation of presentable report formats. Figure 2.3 shows the link between all of these aspects found within an executive information systems environment.

It is essential that executive information systems, which may be user-specific, are developed with the involvement of the user (or small group of users) in order that the system reflects their requirements. This is essential given the unstructured nature of the decision-making environment in which strategic decision making is undertaken; remember that executive systems are usually built to be specific to one executive or a very small group of top-level executives. Overall, executive information systems attempt to provide a broad and holistic view of the strengths and weaknesses of the business organisation within the competitive business environment.

ACTIVITY **2.11**

Executive information systems

Discuss and then outline the main characteristics that are significant in determining an executive information system. Explain how such strategic information systems may be designed and used to reduce the level of uncertainty found within the executive decision-making environment.

2.8 Decision support systems

Decision support systems (DSSs) are specifically used by organisations as support tools within management or strategic decision making. Decision support systems can be part of the MIS or EIS domains of the business organisation. Such decision support systems are usually characterised by levels of *expert knowledge* built into the system. These expert systems can give advice on areas such as whether a bank should make a loan to a customer, or assess a customer's credit worthiness and make a decision on the loan application. Banking was one of the first industries to use DSSs and general information technology to enable them to increase their profits and gain a competitive advantage. Pause for thought 2.2 describes the use of a 'Lending Adviser' to assist bankers and managers.

PAUSE FOR THOUGHT 2.2 *The use of an IT-based Lending Adviser to assist bank managers*

A major high street bank in the United Kingdom, known as Barclays Bank, installed an IT system in 1996 that was called Lending Adviser. It was used to assist branch bank managers in determining the underlying factors affecting the decision to lend to business customers. The Lending Adviser system is part of the credit risk analysis process and provides a decision support tool to provide interactive and structured analysis for the modelling of likely scenarios. The system presents bank managers with a series of forms (or screen reports) to complete about a business organisation. The information ranges from the finances of the business to the quality of the management and the state of the industry sector in which the business competes.

For example, in assessing a business organisation, a bank manager and the business concerned will work in consultation with the Lending Adviser's accumulated knowledge and the business customer's information. Therefore, in order to assess the industry sector, the bank manager and the business organisation answer questions concerning the degree on competition in the respective industry sector; whether that is changing; how cyclical is demand (sales); the possibility of product substitutes; and the various risks of trading. Once such information is input, the Lending Adviser will produce a score for how good a risk that company is within the relevant sector. The Lending Adviser will also review a range of other information including the organisation's cash flow, balance sheet, size and the quality of debtors and creditors. In addition, there is a subjective assessment of the managerial structure, succession and skills. If the bank manager believes that the financial control is good, but that the financial figures are dubious, the Lending Adviser will ask the bank manager to review the situation again for reassurance. In addition to the information mentioned, the Lending Adviser asks questions related to ethics; for instance, is the organisation 'law abiding', 'law bending', 'law breaking', 'unscrupulous' or 'fraudulent'. These questions rely very much on the bank manager's judgement.

After all the questions have been contemplated and answered, the scores for each screen page are aggregated in a final set that may look something like the following:

Final Report Rating

Overall borrower rating　　　+___-

Key assessments:
1	*Industrial risk*	+___-
2	*Financial management evaluation*	+___-
3	*Management competence*	+___-
4	*Projected financial condition*	+___-

Key strengths and weaknesses:
1	*Stock quality*	+___-
2	*Management expertise*	+___-
3	*Industrial risk*	+___-
4	*Operating performance*	+___-

If at the end of the process the indicators are good (i.e. positive to an acceptable degree) the bank manager will begin negotiating with the business customer about credit security and rates of interest. The main aim of the Lending Adviser system is to improve the process of assessing lending risk. The advantage of such a system is that various variables can be altered in order to carry out 'what-if?' analysis by rerunning the Lending Adviser system until all facets of the lending process have been iteratively analysed.

Decision support systems are useful in situations where there exists only a semi-structured information environment. A DSS is characterised by model building, based on expert knowledge that has been automatically incorporated into the operation of the system. The emphasis of a DSS

Decision Support System (DSS) A system that supports managers and executives by modelling the decision-making process.

is on supporting decision making rather than an automation of the whole decision-making process. Decision support systems are usually designed for individualistic or small group decision making rather than for large monolithic data processing systems found at the operational levels of the business organisation. The main characteristics of a decision support systems environment are as follows:

▶ Best suited to *semi-structured* or *unstructured* problems and within decision-making environments where computer-based analysis can aid a decision maker's judgement.

▶ Decision support systems provide *support for the decision-making process* but do not replace the decision maker's judgement, flair and imagination in the collection and interpretation of information.

▶ Concerned with *predicting and forecasting* the future in terms of trends in the internal and external environment and predicting the effects of business and technology change.

▶ Decision support systems may utilise formal as well as informal information sources as well as qualitative and quantitative information.

▶ The boundaries of the decision-making environment are flexible and changeable in the sense that the DSS is not confined to a specific functional area of activity and must reflect a holistic view of the decision-making environment.

▶ The decision-making activity involves exploring *alternative courses of action* through the analysis and alteration of a range of information variables.

Decision support systems assist unique, non-recurring decision making in environments that are relatively unstructured. Such systems are prevalent in managerial and strategic decision-making environments where *models of reality* are built to describe decision-making environments and provide support for engaging in 'what-if' decision making. Related to the area of decision support systems are applications known as *expert systems* (ESs) and *artificial intelligence* (AI). Normally, an expert system uses heuristic processing techniques, based on an expert's knowledge which can help decision makers investigate alternative courses of action and the likely effects of these different courses of action.

> **DID YOU KNOW?**
> Mortgage lenders often use expert systems to carry out credit evaluation on customers seeking a loan; the system can be interrogated with a range of different variables to come up with the optimum and unique loan analysis for an individual customer's needs.

Expert systems contain the knowledge base of an expert with the ability to mimic the thought processes of that expert. An expert system can be provided with a general set of rules instructing it on how to reason and draw conclusions from the evidence and data submitted to the system. Two areas where expert systems have been operating for some time are medical diagnosis and geological prospecting. In medical diagnosis an

> **Expert System (ES)** A system that acts or behaves like a human expert in a field or area with the facility to replicate the expert's knowledge base.

expert system can be provided with a range of symptoms and taught how to diagnose diseases from the information on the symptoms. In geological prospecting the expert system compares the geological characteristics of an area with its memory of the corresponding characteristics in areas where there is a high probability of finding mineral deposits.

Related to the area of expert systems is *artificial intelligence* (AI), which is concerned with the design of intelligent or thinking machines. AI attempts to mimic the characteristics associated with human intelligence, such as understanding natural language, problem solving, learning and human reasoning. Therefore, what distinguishes an AI system from a decision support system is the ability of the AI system to learn from past experiences and be able to reapply knowledge that has been acquired from past experience and learning.

Artificial intelligence systems attempt to undertake the process of human thought, by reasoning and thinking through the higher and *emergent* aspects of a decision-making problem.

Artificial Intelligence (AI) Systems that replicate the characteristics commonly associated with human intelligence (e.g. problem solving, learning and reasoning).

ACTIVITY **2.12**

Decision support

Outline and discuss the six main characteristics of a decision support system and explain the consequences of using information systems in semi-structured or unstructured decision-making environments. Then consider and highlight the importance of building conceptual models for decision-making activity and indicate the types of models that may be used within a decision support systems environment.

Business information can be categorised into internal and external information, which can be further categorised according to the purpose for which the information is intended, and the organisational level in which the information is used. The underlying purpose of information within the business environment can be broadly categorised into five main areas as follows:

1   *Situation information*   This can be operational, managerial or strategic in nature and its purpose is to keep respectively operators, managers and executives informed of current situations or company policy decisions.
2   *Status information*   This can be managerial or strategic in nature and its purpose is to keep managers and executives informed of continuous progress targets or met objectives.
3   *Feedback and control information*   This can be operational or managerial in nature and its purpose is to provide the more structured and mechanical organisational decision levels with warning or alarm signals concerning occurring or impending problems.
4   *Planning information*   This can be managerial or strategic in nature and its purpose is to describe future events and business policy within the mid-term time-frame for management planning and the long-term time-frame for executive planning.
5   *Environmental information*   This can be used primarily for strategic decision making, but also management decision making, and is concerned with the mass of national, economic and business intelligence and information reports that are generated to provide information on performance (e.g. annual financial accounts, government reports, academic and industrial research).

Information sources are characterised by database applications and technology to store, handle and disseminate information internally and externally within the business environment. Therefore, effective and efficient information retrieval techniques and appropriate technology for *information recall* and retrieval are essential to support the activities of business decision making.

ACTIVITY **2.13**

Information categories

Discuss the nature and type of information required at each level of decision making within a typical organisational hierarchy. Consider and suggest three possible information sources that could be used to provide data and information for decision making.

2.9   Chapter summary

A knowledge of *systems theory* allows an understanding of general systems principles and permits better information systems design through better planning, analysis, implementation and evaluation. An understanding of the principles of systems theory and practice provides a means of building better (more appropriate) systems at all levels within a business organisation, as well as to understand the nature of general systems behaviour. Systems theory or systems science argues that however complex or diverse the world that we experience, we will always find different types of organisation in it, and such organisation can be described by principles which are independent from the specific domain at which we are looking. Hence, if we would uncover those general laws, we would be able to analyse and solve problems in any domain, pertaining to any type of system (*Systems Thinkers* – '*Principia Cybernetica Web*'). The following chapters will look in more detail at the types of systems found within the business environment and how they actually work to the benefit of business organisations.

Short self-assessment questions

2.1   Explain what is meant by modelling a system through a *bottom-up* approach.

2.2   Outline the three main categories of system found within the world at large.

2.3   Define the term *holistic* and explain what is meant by a holistic view of systems.

2.4   Define and explain the concept of emergence within general systems theory.

2.5   Explain the term *homeostasis* and suggest why a system may wish to maintain a static state equilibrium.

2.6   Explain the terms *negative feedback* and *positive feedback* and provide examples of both types of feedback.

2.7   Define the term *systems de-coupling* and explain why coupling is an important concept within systems theory.

2.8 Explain what is meant by a *total systems approach* and indicate why such an approach is an important consideration for business information systems analysis.

2.9 Explain the difference between a *logical system* and a *physical system* and provide an example of a business system to illustrate the difference.

2.10 Define the concept of formal and informal information and provide examples of both sorts of information.

2.11 Highlight the three decision-making levels of a hierarchical business organisation and explain why the characteristics that define these systems are different at each level.

2.12 Explain the relationship between unstructured decision-making environments and uncertainty and explain how and why this relationship affects the strategic and operational levels of a business hierarchy.

2.13 Explain the main characteristics that are significant in defining a management information system.

2.14 Outline and explain the use of SWOT analysis for strategic planning, control and decision making.

2.15 Define the term *decision support system* and indicate the levels of a business organisation in which you would expect to find such systems.

References
• • • • • • • • • • • • • •

Bertalanffy, L. von (1956) *General Systems Theory*. Braziller*

Further study and reading
• •

Books

Edwards, C., Ward, J. and Bytheway, A. (1995) *The Essence of Information Systems*, 2nd edition. Prentice-Hall.

Stair, R. (1996) *Principles of Information Systems: A Managerial Approach*. Danvers, Massachusetts: Boyd and Fraser.

Laudon, K.C. and Laudon, J.P. (1995) *Information Systems: A Problem Solving Approach*. Orlando, Florida: Dryden Press.

Lucey, T. (1994) *Management Information Systems*. London: DP Publications.

Rowley, J. (1994) *Strategic Management Information Systems and Technology*. Oxford: NCC Blackwell.

Thomas, R. and Ballard, M. (1995) *Business Information: Technologies and Strategies*. Cheltenham, England: Stanley Thorne

Journals

Checkland, P.B. (1976) Science and the systems paradigm, *International Journal of General Systems*, 3(2), 127–134.

Klir, G.J. (1988) Systems profile: the emergence of systems science, *Systems Research*, 5(2), 145–156.

Rosen, R. (1986) Some comments on systems theory, *International Journal of General Systems*, 13(1), 1–3.

An asterisk (*) next to a source or reference indicates a '*seminal text*' which means it constituted a major source for later academic development.

Systems thinkers

The following is a list of the most influential theorists in the field of cybernetics and systems theory. (Source: F. Heylighen and Joselyn, *Cybernetics and Systems Thinkers* – Principia Cybernetica Web ©)

W. Ross Ashby   Psychiatrist; one of the founding fathers of cybernetics; developed homeostat, law of requisite variety, principle of self-organization, and law of regulating models.

Stafford Beer   Management cyberneticist; creator of the viable system model (VSM).

Kenneth E. Boulding   Economist; one of the founding fathers of general systems theory.

Peter Checkland   Creator of soft systems methodology.

Jay Forrester   Engineer; creator of system dynamics, applications to the modelling of industry development, cities and the world.

George Klir   Mathematical systems theorist; creator of the general systems problem solver methodology for modelling.

Warren McCulloch   Neurophysiologist; first to develop mathematical models of neural networks.

James Grier Miller   Biologist; creator of living systems theory.

Gordon Pask   Creator of conversation theory: second order cybernetic concepts and applications to education.

Howard Pattee   Theoretical biologist; studied hierarchy and semantic closure in organisms.

Robert Rosen   Theoretical biologist; first studied anticipatory systems, proposed category theoretic, non-mechanistic model of living systems.

Claude Shannon   Founder of information theory.

Ludwig von Bertalanffy   Biologist; founder of general systems theory.

Heinz von Foerster   One of the founding fathers of cybernetics; first to study self-organization, self-reference and other circularities; creator of second-order cybernetics.

John von Neumann   Mathematician; founding father in the domains of ergodic theory, quantum logic, axioms of quantum mechanics, the digital computer, cellular automata and self-reproducing systems.

CHAPTER 3

Information systems development

Objectives
....

By the end of this chapter you will be able to:

► discuss the history of information systems development within the business environment
► outline the role, purpose and effectiveness of the traditional systems development life cycle (SDLC)
► explain the components of the four generic stages of the traditional systems development life cycle
► describe the strengths and weaknesses of the various approaches to information systems development within the business environment
► assess the nature and role of end-user computing (EUC) within information systems development in the business environment
► highlight the development and significance of outsourcing and information centres in the support of end-user systems development
► evaluate the role and development of fourth generation language (4GL) environments in the development of end-user information systems.

3.1 Introduction to information systems development
....

Information systems do not appear randomly in business; their development is a time-consuming and cost-bearing experience that must only be undertaken after careful analysis and consideration of the objectives of an organisation. The *goals* of an information system are paramount in determining the scope, shape and nature of the information system to be developed. The traditional approach to information systems development was known as the systems development life cycle (SDLC). This approach was prevalent in business systems development in the 1960s and 1970s and is sometimes used as a template for systems development in the 1990s. However, the traditional SDLC approach to systems development has been affected by the evolution of technology, end-user computing, outsourcing and growth of information centres to support end-user systems development.

The ultimate objective of all systems development approaches is to build information systems that meet the *requirements of the business end-users* and deliver the optimal benefits of using a structured systems approach to development.

3.2 The traditional systems development life cycle
....

The oldest structured methodology for building information systems is known as the *systems development life cycle* (SDLC) which approaches the development of information systems in a very deliberate and methodical way, requiring each stage of the life cycle, from inception of the idea to delivery of the final system, to be carried out rigidly and sequentially. This is often known as *imperative development*, since it is imperative (or obligatory) to complete one stage before moving on to the next stage of the development cycle. The traditional systems development life cycle originated in the 1950s to develop large-scale *functional* business systems in an age of large industrial business conglomerates. Today this approach is mainly used for very large-scale computer-based information systems development. It still forms the basis of some structured approaches to information systems development, such as the *structured systems analysis and design method* (SSADM), which is used as a framework for building information systems in large government departments in the United Kingdom. Since the 1980s the traditional life cycle approach to systems development has been increasingly replaced with alternative approaches and frameworks that attempt to overcome some of the inherent deficiencies of the SDLC. Particular and alternative approaches to the SDLC will be studied in more detail in chapter 4. However, it is important to understand the traditional SDLC in order to be able to compare, and contrast, the advantages and disadvantages of modern approaches to information systems development within the business environment.

DID YOU KNOW?

The traditional systems development life cycle (SDLC) approach to information systems development originated from the National Computing Centre (NCC) in the United Kingdom in the late 1960s. The SDLC was successfully described and introduced into the academic environment in a book by A. Daniels and D.A. Yeates entitled Basic Training in Systems Analysis, *first published in 1971.*

The traditional SDLC approach to information systems development is an evolutionary life cycle that starts with the inception of the system and ends with the eventual death of the system at the end of the system's useful life. The end of a system's life cycle is indicated by it no longer being relevant or useful for the purpose for which it was initially developed. There are *four generic stages to the systems development life cycle* and these are outlined in Table 3.1.

Each of the four stages of the life cycle can be broken down into *component activities*, which are illustrated in greater detail in Table 3.2. The traditional SDLC approach is known as a *waterfall approach* to systems development. Within this type of systems methodology, the development process is broken down into distinct stages of analysis, design, implementation and evaluation, all of which must be completed in a formalised sequence; one stage must be undertaken and completed before moving on to the next stage of the development life cycle. For example, systems analysis (the first stage) must be completed in isolation and *signed off* as completed before proceeding to the next stage of systems design. Likewise, the systems design stage will be completed in isolation and only after completion is the implementation stage begun. This rigid sequence continues until the evaluation stage has been completed and the finished information system is delivered to the end-users. In this process a higher stage cannot be started before the preceding stage has been formally signed off as

table 3.1
The four generic stages of the systems development life cycle

1	Systems analysis
2	Systems design
3	Systems implementation
4	Systems evaluation

completed. Hence, the allusion to the development process being referred to as a waterfall approach, whereby the development waterfall cascades down each stage of the systems development life cycle in sequential order.

Within the SDLC approach the end-user of the information system under development does not play a major (if any) role in the overall development process. Systems development will normally be carried out by technical specialists in the traditional roles of *systems analyst* and *systems programmer*. The systems analyst would normally interact with the users to establish their requirements and the programmer would convert those requirements to computer language code and undertake the technical integration of the information system into the business environment. The end-user would effectively be redundant in the development process until the eventual system came on-line and was operational. By this stage the end-user is faced with a *fait accompli*, in other words, an action completed and not open to argument. At this point it may be too late in the day for the information systems end-user to rectify any user problems. Therefore, the traditional systems development life cycle relies on the user and *system's requirements* being clearly defined at the beginning of the systems development project. Such levels of certainty are difficult to achieve without the involvement of end-users in the design and development process.

The development of business information systems is a major undertaking that a business organisation cannot afford to initiate lightly. So what reasons are there for seeking to develop new information systems or replace old information systems? The fundamental reason lies in change – business is an *adaptive activity* that must constantly change or modify in order for an organisation to remain competitive. The reasons for initiating the systems development process may be many and various and conditional on the sector of business in which an organisation operates. Some reasons for initiating a systems development project are as follows:

1   The current system may *no longer be suitable for its purpose* or the environment in which it operates. As business requirements change, so do the systems requirements. It is always valuable to continuously assess the effectiveness of information systems to establish whether they align with the current business requirements. Information systems that were established under previous business conditions may no longer be suitable for the prevailing situation. Changes in environmental constraints, such as organisational structure, human resourcing, work practices and statutory obligations, lead to information systems being reassessed.

2   The current system may have become *redundant due to technological developments*. Advances in technology offer systems solutions that are often superior to the existing technology-based or manual systems. Information technology may also offer opportunities that encourage new systems to be established or previous systems to be merged and integrated. Improvements in hardware, software and telecommunications often lead to a rationalisation of systems structures and domains that allow information technology to be exploited for competitive advantage in the business domain.

3   The current systems may have become too expensive or resource intensive which may reduce an organisation's ability to be flexible and competitive. One of the main reasons for building replacement information systems is

to reduce costs or improve the efficiency of current resources, such as human resources, physical assets and technology. New systems can be developed to either cut costs or produce a greater return on existing resources through the focusing of business objectives.

ACTIVITY **3.1**
· · · · · · · · · · · · ·

Information systems development

Discuss and explain what is meant by the term information systems development life cycle (SDLC) and outline three main reasons why the traditional SDLC is considered to be too *inflexible* in the design and development of information systems for business. Discuss and outline some of the consequences of lack of end-user involvement within the systems development process. After discussion of these points highlight some of the reasons for initiating an information systems development project. Provide an example, from your experience or knowledge, of an information system that was developed and explain the reasons behind its development.

PAUSE FOR THOUGHT 3.1 *Farewell to waterfalls!*

The development of alternatives to the traditional systems development life cycle.

Within dynamic business environments very few organisations can afford to use the time-consuming waterfall model for systems development. The rigidity of the waterfall approach requires the systems development team to complete each stage before moving on to the next stage. Consequently, rapid applications development (RAD) has become very popular in the business environment. RAD is often a natural way to do things because the range of tools and techniques available to modern business systems design and implementation allow development teams to work without having to know all the details of an application.

Speed of business systems development is of paramount importance. Often, if a systems development project lasts more than six to nine months there is a higher than normal risk of loss of user's interest or a change in the essential processes of the business organisation. RAD has the advantage of being an iterative approach whereby a systems development team can deliver parts of a system in an incremental manner, all the time incorporating the views and ideas of the end-users themselves. The sooner that end-users can see a tangible product the easier it is for them to accept a changed system. The RAD approach is an excellent way of discovering the concerns and needs of the end-users. The RAD phenomenon is to some extent driven by the availability of visual programming tools and techniques that allow end-users to be a working part of the systems development process. RAD incorporates tools and techniques that allow for the better design and delivery of graphical user interfaces (GUIs). Many business organisations incorporate joint applications development (JAD) into the RAD process with the development and incorporation of employee workshops into the fabric of the organisation.

RAD is a useful approach for developing real-time systems such as bank loan systems and other on-line applications for dealing with financial transactions. Such systems can also evolve over time, with the addition of other applications as and when necessary; a particularly important consideration where user requirements are not well known or easy to define. RAD can be used for developing a decision support system (DSS) that can access data from an on-line transaction processing system (TPS) which might have been developed using the traditional waterfall approach. Therefore, RAD is very flexible and can be used in association with systems developed using the traditional SDLC approach. With RAD, care must be taken with issues of standardisation and systems quality; visual tools and techniques allow users to see what they need through prototypes, rather than reading through textual descriptions of the system. However, because of RAD's lack of a clear methodological framework or process, the end product is not always as inbued with quality as it should be, sometimes because RAD emphasises front-end analysis rather than larger issues of database design and back-end processing.

Therefore, does RAD require a methodology that focuses on the mechanisms of systems development or would such a methodological constraint wipe out the creative aspects of RAD? What is not in doubt is the fact that RAD tools and techniques have had a significant effect on software and systems development in the last decade of the twentieth century, with the majority of business organisations now adopting RAD approaches, rather than the SDLC approaches, to business systems development.

DID YOU KNOW?
The earliest use of computers was for mathematical and scientific applications where the processing of numbers was the primary activity. When computer technology began to be absorbed into the business environment in the 1950s and 1960s the main utilisation of computers was for functional and operational processing system's activities.

The basic business processing activities of the 1960s and 1970s included data and information storage, retrieval, sorting, collating, analysing, calculating and communicating (through the generation of paper-based reports). As computing and IT became increasingly absorbed into the information systems fabric of business organisations, it became apparent that there was a need for a structured method (or methodology) to be applied to the development of information systems. The development of information systems had become an increasingly expensive and time-consuming activity that needed to be carried out with careful thought and planning. This was allied to the fact that information systems end-users were becoming increasingly dissatisfied with the information systems that were being developed on a one-off basis, without any obvious regard to the effect on other related systems within the business organisation.

DID YOU KNOW?
A method is a way of doing something, or a procedure for doing something. A methodology is a branch of human philosophy dealing with the science of method or procedure.

Over time, due to a need for increasingly efficient and effective information systems, business organisations recognised the need for structured development approaches that addressed the issues of information systems analysis, design, implementation and evaluation.

Stage 1	**Systems analysis**	
Activities		
(a)	System definition	Define and state the scope and objectives. Investigate and identify problems and areas of concern.
(b)	Feasibility study	Collect and collate information. Assess project costs. Consider constraints. Assess alternatives.
(c)	Requirements specification	Describe the business requirements. Describe the systems requirements. Integrate and detail the systems requirements.
Stage 2	**Systems design**	
Activities		
(a)	Logical design	Create and document logical design specifications. Model the logical design specifications.
(b)	Physical design	Create and document technical design specifications. Model the technological design specifications. Model the ergonomic design specifications.
Stage 3	**Systems implementation**	
Activities		
(a)	Programming	Construct and write program code. (Applications-based systems development). Integrate hardware and software applications.
(b)	Installation	Business implementation. Technical implementation.
(c)	Conversion	Convert old system to new system.
(d)	Documentation	Systems-user documentation.
(e)	Training	Human training and development.
Stage 4	**Systems evaluation**	
Activities		
(a)	Testing	Technical systems evaluation. Business systems evaluation. Systems and cost audit.
(b)	Organisation	Evaluation of systems integration. Evaluation of human–technical integration.
(d)	Maintenance	Undertake systems maintenance.

3.3 The four generic stages of the systems development life cycle

Systems analysis

This stage of information systems development involves undertaking a *feasibility study* and *systems investigation*. At this stage the scope and objectives of the proposed system must be defined. The aim of the study is to understand the systems *problem* and determine whether it is worth solving. The feasibility study should investigate the current system (if there is one) and ascertain the problems and requirements of the old and proposed new system. The study should determine whether the proposed system is viable and workable on the grounds of legality, organisational structure, technical constraints and cost constraints. This stage will usually result in a set of information systems alternatives within a given set of constraints. This systems investigation and feasibility will normally be delivered in the form of a report (and/or presentation) to the managerial or executive level of the business organisation. Hence, anyone involved in issues relating to business information systems and technology requires good human communication and presentation skills in order to convey ideas and gain approval for the initiation of new projects. At this stage a decision is made to determine whether to progress to the subsequent stages of the development life cycle. Systems investigation involves *fact finding*. The investigation will normally look at the *system requirements* and *business requirements* of the existing system and the proposed new system. The facts are gathered and collated through the use of a number of tools and techniques including interviews, questionnaires, task observation and the analysis of existing systems documentation. The task of systems analysis should determine what the information system must do in order to solve an information-based problem. The result of this investigative stage will normally be delivery of a list of systems requirements and priorities, which will be laid out in what is commonly termed a *feasibility report*. Table 3.3 outlines some of the commonly found issues that are addressed in a feasibility report.

The investigative stage of systems analysis will normally require formal documentation to capture data and information from *people*, *technology* and the *organisation*. Current systems will have to be analysed, assessed and evaluated. The process of systems investigation involves collecting and collating data and information from a range of sources. This can be achieved by various means such as:

table 3.3 **Issues commonly addressed in feasibility reports**	1 Assessment of existing business systems and sub-systems
	2 Purpose and goals of the system
	3 The business environment
	4 Systems integration
	5 Human, technical and legal constraints
	6 Cost and return on investment
	7 Assessment of alternative solutions

- ▶ interviews and questionnaires from employees and other people
- ▶ studying business and other systems documentation
- ▶ data acquisition through human observation
- ▶ data acquisition through technical measurement.

Normally, *interviews* and *questionnaires* are an important method of getting a general feeling for a system. Interviews should be carried out with employees from the specific system and related systems to assess the effects the eventual information system might have on the operation of business. The use of interviewing techniques and questionnaires should not involve open-ended questioning. They should be carefully structured to elicit concise and detailed data or information, which in turn must be clearly documented. An example of a formal questionnaire, by the Institute of Data Processing Management (IDPM), can be found at the end of this chapter. All large and well-controlled business organisations maintain records and documentation that act as a verifiable history of business and systems processes. This documentary evidence can be *numerical* or *alphanumerical* and come from a range of internal and external business sources. Table 3.4 outlines the possible sources of documentation available within the *business environment*. These have been separated into the three pillars of a business organisation; people, organisation and technology.

When studying a business organisation's documentation it is important to consider the nature of that documentation, for instance, whether the information is in date or out of date, and the integrity (or formality) of the procedures that gave rise to the documentation. It is also important to understand that documentation is often an indication of what should be happening and not necessarily what *is* happening in a business organisation.

Data acquisition through human observation is a direct method of analysing systems processes and collecting information. During observation a time and motion study can be carried out of human and systems activity. Observation is a very useful way of gathering information about how human activity interacts with technical systems activity. However, an observer should be aware of the fact that observed people tend to behave differently to their normal unobserved behaviour. This is known as the *Hawthorne effect*, whereby there is an improvement in performance resulting from the interest expressed by researchers and the knowledge that the activity is being measured. Nevertheless, observation is a beneficial source of data and information on the interaction of the human, technical and organisational aspects of a business organisation.

table 3.4
Types of business organisation documentation

People	Organisation	Technology
Personnel records	Mission statement	User instruction manuals
Employment contracts	Policy documents	Systems documentation
Job descriptions	Financial statements	Telecommunications protocols
Time and motion records	Management reports	
Education and training	Statutory regulations	
Monitoring and appraisal	Procedures manual	

Data acquisition through *technical measurement* involves the use of computing and information technology to monitor and measure human and technical systems activity. Such measurement often employs the use of sensors to electronically detect human and systems activity. For example, the number of occasions a system is used can easily be determined by keeping a computerised record of when and how a system was activated throughout a given period of time. Technical measurement is mostly employed to gather *quantitative data* that can be statistically measured and evaluated.

Having collected and collated data and analysed the systems environment, what factors might determine an information systems project going ahead? There are five main *feasibility factors* which might assist in determining the probability of an information systems project being undertaken. These are known by the mnemonic TELOS, which represents:

Technical feasibility
Economic feasibility
Legal feasibility
Operational feasibility
Schedule feasibility.

Technical feasibility is concerned with determining the possibility and practicality of using existing and modern information technology to develop the proposed system. *Economic feasibility* assesses the budgetary and financial constraints of the proposed information system. *Legal feasibility* indicates the existing legal requirements on the business and determines whether any conflict exists between the proposed system and the paramount legal and statutory obligations on the organisation. *Operational feasibility* is concerned with determining whether existing or proposed procedures and practices are adequate for the purposes of the proposed system. Consideration will also be given to the education, training and development required to operate the proposed information system. The last factor, *schedule feasibility*, assists in determining the practicality and acceptability of the time-frame for development of the proposed information system.

ACTIVITY **3.2**
• • • • • • • • • • • • • •

Activities of information systems development

Explain the role and function of information systems analysis within the systems development life cycle and suggest why it is important for the feasibility of a proposed new (or replacement) information system to be investigated. The process of systems investigation involves collecting and collating data and information from various sources within the business environment. Discuss advantages and disadvantages of each of the possible methods, sources and documentation used in the investigation of an information system.

Systems design

This stage involves designing an information system to overcome a particular information-based problem and meet the end-user's requirements. This stage is characterised by the separation of the *logical design* from the *physical design* process. Remember that in chapter 2 it was essential to determine a system's logical purpose before being concerned with the system's physical design. The logical design process describes the functional requirements or *purpose* of the information system. The physical design model follows from the logical design and describes the physical and technological characteristics that the information system should possess. The logical process and physical design models indicate the inputs, outputs, processing technology and human–computer user interfaces necessary for the successful operation of the information system.

The logical design *conceptualises* what the system should do in order to solve the problems identified through the earlier analysis stage. Logical design involves determining the purpose and other aspects of an information system independently of hardware and software considerations. Therefore, the inputs, outputs and processing activities of the system are logically described in terms of their required or desired characteristics. Then the physical design model specifies the hardware, software and human interaction required to convert the logical design into a physical system. The physical aspects of the logical design will normally involve consideration of the following tangible elements:

▶ *Hardware technology*. The input, processing and output devices and their respective performance characteristics.
▶ *Software technology*. Software applications and their integration, specifications and performance within the system.
▶ *Storage media*. The type, structure and function of storage media, such as computer files, databases, CD-ROMs and other data and information storage technology.
▶ *Telecommunications technology*. The specifications, use and characteristics of the technology both internally and externally to the organisation.
▶ *People and organisation*. The description and remit of human interaction, plus the procedures and control aspects of the organisation that impact on the system.

ACTIVITY **3.3**

Systems design

Explain the role and function of information systems design within the systems development life cycle and describe the distinction between *logical* design and *physical* design. Why do you think it is important for an analyst and systems designer to possess logical systems thinking rather than physical systems thinking?

Implementation stage

This stage is concerned with building the components of an information system. This involves the installation and putting into place of a system, inclusive of all its physical aspects. It may also involve the writing of computer programs or the integration of pre-coded applications, which is often referred to as *applications-based development*. This stage is primarily concerned with the acquisition of hardware, software and other telecommunications technology necessary to implement the system. There should also be an element of end-user training incorporated into this stage, assisted by policy and user documentation. The implementation stage should result in the delivery of an installed and operational information system that can be tested and evaluated. The outcome of each stage is sometimes referred to in computing jargon by the term 'deliverable' (e.g. 'what are the deliverables of this stage?'). It is important that any new system should be run in parallel with the old system (if it exists) for a period of time to prevent any changeover or system conversion problems. Once the users are completely confident with the new system then the old system can be removed or taken 'off-line'. The implementation stage will involve acquiring hardware and software technology from computer vendors, who may be an individual or other business organisation. The implementation stage normally includes the following considerations:

- ▶ hardware acquisition
- ▶ software acquisition
- ▶ user familiarisation and training
- ▶ environment preparation
- ▶ information and data preparation.

A number of decisions need to be made, such as whether to acquire externally developed (bespoke) software, or off-the-shelf software, or in-house developed software and other applications. The hardware and software acquired need to be harmoniously integrated into the business organisation.

ACTIVITY **3.4**

Systems implementation

Discuss the role and purpose of *implementation* within the systems development life cycle (SDLC) and highlight five main considerations of this stage of information systems development. Discuss whether you think that these considerations should be undertaken in isolation from the other stages of the SDLC. State three types of computing vendor that might be contacted at the implementation stage of systems development.

Evaluation stage

This stage involves testing and appraisal to determine whether the system is meeting its requirements. An *evaluation report* should be produced to assess whether the system is meeting the requirements set out in the initial feasibility report efficiently and effectively. If the system is not meeting its requirements then the SDLC process may begin again! A number of evaluation techniques can be used to assess the merits of the final system. The following are some commonly used evaluation techniques:

- ▶ user evaluation
- ▶ cost–benefit analysis
- ▶ benchmark testing.

User evaluation involves formal and informal feedback from the end-users of the system to determine whether the system is efficient and effective. With user involvement in the development process this is made easier as the users will be aware of the mutually agreed systems requirements from the start of the systems development project. Cost–benefit analysis attempts to match the aggregate of the costs against the aggregate of the benefits of the system. Hopefully, the benefits will outweigh the costs! The costs will include development and operational costs which can be divided into fixed costs and variable costs*. Table 3.5 lists the possible costs and benefits that may be considered for evaluation.

Benchmark testing involves comparing the actual performance of the system to the ideal standard for that system. The performance of the system is judged by whether it is below or above the standard set.

A detailed study of the tools and techniques often found and used within each generic stage is given in chapter 5.

ACTIVITY **3.5**

Systems evaluation

Discuss in groups the main role and function of information systems evaluation within the systems development life cycle and explain what is meant by user evaluation, cost–benefit analysis and benchmarking within the evaluation process. Once this has been achieved, outline and discuss some of the possible costs and benefits of an information systems project that you have read about or seen on the news. (If you are struggling, find out about the 'Taurus' share dealing system built for the London Stock Exchange, which was terminated because the costs outweighed the benefits.)

table 3.5

Types of systems cost and benefit

System costs	System benefits
Systems development expenses	Reduced salaries and wages
People and resourcing	Reduced environment costs
Information technology purchased	Greater efficiency and effectiveness
Licenses and other fees	New products and services
Equipment rental and leasing fees	Increased customer base
Salaries and wages	Better products and services
Heating, lighting and electricity	Better work procedures and practices
Maintenance and training	
Insurance	

*

Fixed cost = a cost that is fixed and does not vary with systems activity. (e.g. initial equipment purchase costs).
Variable cost = a cost that increases with activity. (e.g. the direct wages of an operator or the electricity consumed).

3.4   Strengths and weaknesses of the traditional systems development life cycle

The traditional systems development life cycle was relevant in meeting the needs of large-scale computer-based systems development in the 1960s and 1970s. At that time computing technology was restricted to only a small section of the business organisation, often known as the *electronic data processing* (EDP) department or function. Therefore, computing technology did not pervade throughout the whole of the business organisation. Today the situation is very different with computing and information technology existing at every level and function of an organisation. Users of information technology are expected to be responsible for using and managing various technologies without regard to a separate EDP function or department; organisations have become more dynamic in dealing with business change and competition. Nevertheless, the traditional SDLC possesses a number of strengths that sometimes make it relevant to the modern information systems environment:

▶ The SDLC is a tried and tested approach that is very suitable for the development of large-scale information systems.
▶ The traditional SDLC relies on the production of systems documentation and standards of development that can be used to guide the development of an information system and can be used as reference and training material for users.
▶ The sequential and phased nature of the SDLC allows a complex systems development problem to be broken down into manageable and understandable tasks.
▶ The SDLC relies on the use of formalised analysis and design tools and techniques that graphically show the nature of data and information flows within the system.
▶ The structured nature of the traditional SDLC allows the incorporation of formal project management techniques and tools to guide the systems development process.

The SDLC was appropriate for the systems environment that existed at the time of its development and use in the 1960s and 1970s. However, the development of information systems in modern day business requires adopting methods of development that are more appropriate to dynamic business environments. The main weaknesses with the traditional systems development life cycle are as follows.

▶ The SDLC ignores or underplays end-user involvement in the systems development process. The end-user is often faced with operating an information system that is user-unfriendly or fails to deliver the user's requirements for the system. The traditional SDLC only permits users to appreciate the system once it has been completed and installed. User dissatisfaction may lead to the user developing their own customised and informal application of the system to the detriment of the overall systems within a business organisation.
▶ Over 90% of computer-based systems development occurs within the business environment. The use of computing and information technology

within business organisations is based on small desktop workstations or personal microcomputers, usually networked locally within the organisation or connected outside to the wider business environment. The traditional SDLC is concerned with large-scale systems development and is not appropriate to microcomputer-based and small-scale development of business information systems.

▶ The traditional SDLC is time consuming and costly in terms of human resourcing and monetary expenditure. The modern day business requirement is for systems to be developed as quickly as is practicable and within certain budgetary constraints. Business information systems are often developed for one-off projects or for functions that are constantly evolving with business changes.

▶ There are many reservations concerning the usefulness of applying a development methodology that is too rigid, sequential and inflexible to change. Time and cost savings can be achieved by developing stages of the life cycle in parallel or out of sequence. The important aim is for an eventual end-user to be able to visualise the final system so that time and energy are not wasted pursuing systems development avenues that are not required by the end-users. Often an inflexible development methodology, which is output driven, does not possess the scope to accommodate changes to the system's output specifications.

▶ The SDLC approach is often a slow and laborious process. This is a problem when there is a need for information systems to be developed as quickly as possible to meet the requirements of dynamic business environments. The use of the SDLC for large-scale systems projects often leads to systems development backlogs where users are forced to wait so long that the system no longer meets its requirements when it is eventually delivered.

▶ The SDLC assumes a sequential, step-by-step approach to development which ignores the possibility of testing the proposed system at an early stage of the life cycle following the discovery of new user requirements. Most human activity systems are fine-tuned through a process of iteration to focus an information system to meet its requirements. Iteration is the process of repeating a series of operations until an ideal solution is achieved.

▶ The traditional SDLC is particularly useful for the development of operational data processing systems where the information processing is structured and routine. However, there is an increasing need within the managerial and executive levels of most business organisations for information systems that process unstructured information and operate within uncertain decision-making environments. The traditional SDLC is not appropriate for the development of such managerial and executive decision-making systems.

These failings of the traditional approach to systems development have led to the evolution of alternative development approaches with the aims of:

▶ reducing development time and cost of systems development
▶ improving the delivery of system and user requirements

▶ recognising advances in computing and information technology
▶ recognising the nature of systems within modern business environments.

The alternatives are development solutions that attempt to overcome the deficiencies of the traditional systems development life cycle approach to building information systems.

ACTIVITY **3.6**

Systems development

Discuss and explain the main characteristics of the SDLC that have led to it no longer being appropriate for many business organisations and environments. Outline some of the possible aims in the search for alternative development methods. For example, should an alternative development methodology try to overcome the weaknesses of the traditional SDLC?

3.5   Overview of alternative approaches to information systems development

The downsizing of information technology within the business environment and the growth of networked desktop computing has seen the traditional SDLC become outdated in many respects. Business organisations that are dealing with desktop microprocessor technology are often making the same mistakes with systems development that the traditional systems analysts and programmers made in the 1960s that led to the formalisation of the SDLC. There are a number of approaches that have evolved as alternatives to the traditional SDLC, some of which utilise the development life cycle approach and some of which are radical departures from the phased approach. Most development approaches and methodologies are underpinned or influenced by aspects of general systems theory, which were detailed in chapter 2. Alternative approaches to systems development acknowledge the fact that most business systems involve human activity which makes systems less predictable. Furthermore, there is a recognition that systems cannot be seen in isolation. Most business organisations, by their very nature of trading with the environment at large, are considered open systems. Business organisations influence, and are influenced by, the wider environment. Five particular alternative approaches to information systems development that utilise the concept of human end-user computing are as follows :

1   rapid applications development (RAD)
2   joint applications development (JAD)
3   prototyping systems development
4   object oriented systems development (OOSD)
5   business process re-engineering.

All of these approaches share a common characteristic of emphasising the importance of human *end-users* in the development process of information systems. It is important to be able to describe the impact of end-user systems development on the traditional systems development life cycle.

ACTIVITY **3.7**
....

Alternative information systems development

Search your college or university library *abstract* and *journal* sources for ten articles related to rapid applications development (RAD) and joint applications development (JAD). Discuss whether the articles you found were from journals in the business area or the computing area or another related academic area and whether each area was addressed from a different perspective.

3.6 End-user information systems development

The evolution of end-user computing was outlined in chapter 1, and described the development of information systems that utilise the knowledge and abilities of the user of the information system to create and build systems that meet the requirements of the business organisation. Unlike the traditional SDLC approach, where the system user is peripheral to the development process, in end-user computing the final user of the system is central to the development process. By including end-users in development it is hoped that the information system that is finally constructed and delivered will better meet the needs of the organisation, and in turn increase the potential for generating wealth for the business. It is the case that the professional roles and responsibilities of the traditional systems analyst and programmer have largely become merged into one single role, that of the *systems end-user*. Within the process of end-user information systems development, IT and other software tools are given directly to the system end-users in order for them to develop specific business systems. Responsibility for the success of an information systems development project is transferred to the end-user rather than held with an intermediary, such as a systems analyst. Therefore, the end-user must be able and competent in deciding how to use and integrate software applications to deliver a working system on time.

End-user information systems development has been encouraged by the distillation of IT into every level of a business organisation and because of the movement away from *centralisation* towards *decentralisation* within business. Decentralisation transfers decision-making powers to departments or individuals to determine their own information systems development projects. Therefore, with people becoming more IT literate there is no longer a need for the centralisation of information system specialisms like programming and systems analysis. Within the business environment, the specialisms that do exist have often evolved into hardware and software maintenance and support roles within what are known as IT support centres or *information centres*. The concept of the information centre is to provide a support mechanism to assist end-user information systems development. In practice to get the most out of end-user information systems development requires an appreciation of the following:

▶ the business knowing how and where to apply IS/IT within the organisation
▶ staff at every level of the organisation needing to be comfortable in using IS/IT
▶ an awareness of the need to build information systems that *adapt* to change in the business environment.

ACTIVITY **3.8**
················

End-user information systems development

Discuss the evolution of end-user information systems development and explain how it may affect the nature and role of systems development within the business environment. Do you think that end-users will require support and assistance in the development of information systems? If so, what type of assistance will they require and how would you suggest that the assistance is implemented within an organisation?

End-user information systems development is often aided by the proliferation of user-friendly fourth generation (computer) language environments which promote the development of business information systems with little formal assistance from technical specialists. The generation of the programming language describes the level of use of *natural language* that is used within the program code; a high-level language has a higher level of natural language used in the program code than a lower level language and should consequently be more user-friendly for the information systems developer. The use of natural language within the program code assists a non-technical specialist to build information systems. Table 3.6 lists examples of programming languages at each generation of language evolution.

Third generation language environments, which are closely tied to programming within the traditional systems development, are imperative, structured, and more suitable for sequential systems development methods such as the SDLC. Third generation development environments do not have the same level of flexibility as fourth generation development environments; consequently, they are less user-friendly for the application of end-user development.

DID YOU KNOW?
Fourth generation programming language environments are often non-procedural and have been developed to be more user-friendly than imperative third generation language development environments.

Fourth generation languages (4GLs) are, by their nature, less structured, non-procedural, and more user-friendly for non-technical business specialists. The main advantage of 4GLs lies in permitting greater end-user involvement in the information systems development process. Fourth generation language development tools provide an opportunity for users to be directly involved in hands-on software development. Furthermore, the less structured program coding domains within 4GLs allow program changes to be constantly made with very little cost, while still maintaining the integrity of the overall information systems development process; programming changes can be made without having to go back to the start of the development life cycle. Fourth generation languages

table 3.6
Generations of programming language

First generation languages	(1GLs)	Asssembler Machine Language Code
Second generation languages	(2GLs)	FORTRAN
Third generation languages	(3GLs)	ADA, C, COBOL, Pascal
Fourth generation languages	(4GLs)	VisualBasic, Visual C++, Smalltalk, Simula

also allow working models (or prototypes) to be developed early in the development life cycle which can be iteratively tested and evaluated by the information system end-users. Iteration is the process of repeated refinement and modification to achieve an optimal solution.

Fourth Generation Languages (4GLs) Non-procedural programming languages developed to replace third generation languages.

In the modern Information Age the business information technology specialist is unlikely to work within information systems development environments, or on computing applications, which deal with highly structured language development tools more associated with third generation language (3GL) environments. Information technology changes over the last 20 years have brought about fundamental changes in working practices within all types of business organisation. Consequently, many business information systems are now built by *integrating* standard software application packages, rather than starting from scratch using Ada, Pascal, C or some other third generation language environment. The practice of using standard software packages, which are often pre-designed and coded, to build information systems is known as *applications-based systems development*. Standard applications packages can be customised, and often integrated, to achieve a technical information systems solution to solve an information problem. Standard software applications packages, for example, within the MicroSoft Office® environment, can be linked and integrated using fourth generation language environments such as VisualBasic®. Therefore, there are a number of underlying advantages in using fourth generation language development tools as follows:

▶ greater end-user involvement in the development process
▶ relatively less program coding with 4GLs compared to 3GLs
▶ user-friendly development tools and environment
▶ less structured and more flexible design and development framework
▶ shorter development time and faster systems delivery
▶ allows end-users with basic computer literacy to be involved in the analysis, design, implementation and evaluation of information systems.

Therefore, within end-user information systems development, fourth generation languages are suitable for customising, tailoring and integrating standard software application packages (e.g. wordprocessors, spreadsheets and databases) that are commonly found and used within integrated electronic office environments. In terms of information systems development, fourth generation language environments involve end-users in all of the four generic stages of the systems development life cycle process of analysis, design, implementation and evaluation. End-user developers play a primary role in defining the information system goals and, through the building of working prototype systems, can evaluate alternative solutions to achieve optimal information system development. The main tools and techniques of fourth generation information systems development include:

▶ applications-based software development (wordprocessors, databases, spreadsheets, etc.)
▶ rapid applications development (RAD)
▶ 4GL environments and other software development tools
▶ information systems prototyping

▶ software tools:
  - software application generators
  - visual programming languages
  - standard query languages
  - graphics languages.

Although 4GLs give end-users a significant role in the systems development process, they do not liberate end-users from developing information systems according to professional programming, documentation and evaluation *standards*. The dominant language generations used in present day business to build software applications for organisations are 3GLs and 4GLs. Increasingly, however, 4GLs are replacing 3GLs as the predominant business systems development language environment. The rigid nature of 3GLs, such as COBOL, ADA, C, and Pascal, and the laborious (often time consuming) coding requirements have persuaded organisations to instigate 4GL development methods. This systems development trend has been fuelled by the rise of *client-server technology* which can make available multivarious software development tools throughout the whole business organisation. Client-server technology is concerned with the networking of software applications throughout an organisation and external bodies, which allows employees freedom of access to software tools and techniques that would otherwise be too specific or customised to be held by individual employee, or departmental, systems.

Client-Server technology A model of computer networking that separates the processing of tasks between the client computer and servers on a network. Each computing device is assigned the functions and tasks that it performs best.

As information systems development tools have evolved, the boundaries between each tool have become increasingly blurred as the tools become more powerful and integrate multiple development characteristics. However, despite having many benefits, 4GLs also have certain weaknesses that must be appreciated in regard to the use and application of 3GLs or 4GLs. Some of these weaknesses of 4GLs are as follows:

▶ The laborious and time-consuming nature of coding in 3GLs is often overcome by using support tools such as CASE (computer-aided software engineering) that reduces development time by automatically generating language code. This makes programming with 3GLs rational and more productive.
▶ The detailed and transparent nature of 3GL program codes may make systems testing and maintenance more apparent, compared to 4GLs that often contain hidden pre-generated language code.
▶ Third generation languages are more appropriate for building large-scale (transactions-based), complex mainframe systems that warrant more sophisticated technical solutions. With large-scale and functional systems, such as national telephone networks and government taxation, these are still better developed and managed using traditional 3GL methods.
▶ By giving up responsibility for development to end-users the business suffers the potential danger of losing control over the design and development process. Furthermore, end-user development using 4GLs may be idiosyncratic and less prone to formal business and computing

standardisation than 3GL systems built by trained technical specialists. Information systems that are operated and managed by multiple end-users require formalised support documentation to confirm the integrity of the data and support the correct use of the system.

Within fourth generation development environments the end-users are normally supported by other technical systems specialists who provide a guiding or supervisory role in the systems development process. It must be remembered that within 4GL development environments there is still a need to be rigorous in the application of verifiable standards to the analysis, design, implementation and evaluation of an information system; irrespective of whether the system being built is large or small scale.

ACTIVITY **3.9**

Fourth generation language development environments

Fourth generation information systems development provides end-users with more control over the definition of system requirements and the overall development process. You are required to give a five minute *presentation* that communicates the following information:

▶ State and describe what tools and techniques are employed by end-user information systems developers within fourth generation development environments.

▶ Outline and describe the use of applications-based systems development and the consequences of using pre-built software.

▶ Summarise the main advantages and disadvantages of fourth generation information systems development to a business organisation.

3.7   The information systems support centre

One of the major ways, adopted by large business organisations, to manage fourth generation development and to maximise the return from end-user development is through *information systems support centres*. These information centres are sometimes referred to as IS/IT support centres. Such support centres provide a facility for guidance, training and support for end-user systems development. The support centre may be operated by one individual or a group of individuals depending on the nature of the organisation within the business environment. The depth of IS/IT support will depend upon the inherent technical abilities of the end-users. The support centre may provide the software, hardware and other applications tools needed for end-user development, or it may only provide training and guidance in fourth generation development tools and techniques. IS/IT support facilities (or information centres) can be used to coordinate and manage the development of end-user systems development within a business organisation. The IS/IT centre could also be responsible for some of the practical systems development in terms of suggesting development approaches, or assisting the building of systems prototypes for evaluation purposes. Some of the services that may be provided by an IS/IT centre are as follows:

▶ Training and advising business specialists on existing hardware and software applications that may be useful to their respective job functions.

▶ Advising on the appropriate use of various development methodologies that can be used to solve particular information systems problems.

▶ Building working prototypes of particular information systems that can be used and iteratively tested by end-users.

▶ Providing reference and other documentation on hardware, software, IT integration and methodologies for the benefit of end-user systems development.

▶ Keeping up to date with current and new IT tools and evaluating hardware and software applications.

▶ Providing a physical resource of hardware and software for end-users to use at will and providing access to communications links to remote information sources.

Figure 3.1 outlines some typical activities undertaken by IS/IT centres. The IS/IT centre can be used to benefit the employees of a business organisation in terms of the spread of IS/IT literacy throughout the whole organisation. Such support activities may also lead to increased job productivity among employees through the more efficient and effective use of IS/IT applications. Some of the advantages of an IS/IT centre are as follows:

▶ It can establish and promote consistent information technology standards throughout the business organisation.

▶ It can improve communications between technical and business specialists and in doing so reduce the culture gap that exists in many business organisations.

▶ It can advise executive management on appropriate hardware and software to be used within the business organisation.

A business organisation must be able to appraise the cost and benefit of providing an IS/IT centre, to assist with end-user information systems development, with the possible alternative policy of employing external technical specialists with a single brief to develop business information systems independently. The alternative policy may lead to an organisation becoming dependent upon the expertise of outside bodies, with the detrimental effect of loss of control over IS/IT strategy within the business organisation.

figure 3.1
IS/IT centre

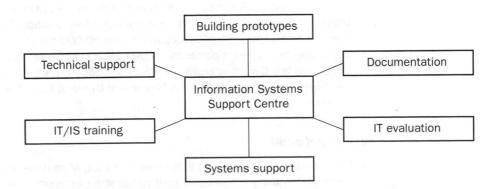

ACTIVITY **3.10**

IS/IT support centres

Discuss the concept of the information centre and outline the main use and purpose of an information centre in a business organisation. Describe the possible costs and benefits to an organisation of an IS/IT support centre. Do you think that the growth of IS/IT support centres has been encouraged by the evolution of end-user information systems development?

ACTIVITY **3.11**

End-users and IS/IT support centres

Information technology support within an organisation can be internal or external to the business organisation. IS/IT centres are a solution to some of the problems of end-user information systems development, such as a lack of consistency and application of common standards in the development process or method. You are required to write a summary *handbook* of rules and regulations that outline the relationship between an information centre and the end-users within a business organisation.

3.8   Chapter summary

This chapter set out to explain the nature and characteristics of the traditional systems development life cycle. This traditional approach to information systems development has been affected by the evolution of end-user computing and the development of user-friendly fourth generation tools and techniques. These trends have encouraged end-user participation in the systems development life cycle. Such participation makes it more likely that the user requirements of an information system will be met when the system is designed and implemented. The next chapter will extend the understanding of systems development acquired in this chapter in a more detailed study of a range of alternative approaches to business information systems development.

CASE STUDY **3.1**

An audit of end-user computing

Corporate overview

Burlington Northern Railroad (BNRR) is one of the largest railroads in North America. Annual gross revenue is approximately US$4.5 billion. Total employees number approximately 32,000. It operates over 60,000 rail cars and 2,500 locomotives on a system composed of over 25,000 miles of track in twenty-five states, and two Canadian provinces. BNRR's headquarters are in Fort Worth, Texas, and it has major offices in St Paul, Minnesota; Overland Park, Kansas; and Denver, Colorado.

Internal audit

The internal audit department is located in St Paul, Minnesota. It is composed of approximately thirty professional staff including an Assistant Vice President and three managers. The department has adopted an 'integrated' approach to information systems (IS) audits and does not contain a specific subset of IS auditors. It does, however, have a number of auditors with IS backgrounds who are used on technical audits. Philosophically, in addition to its role as a reviewer of internal controls, the internal audit department is viewed as a training ground by BNRR management. Auditors are typically promoted to positions in accounting and marketing after spending three to five years in audit.

Information systems

The information systems department (ISD) at BNRR includes over 400 personnel. The hardware used to support the company consists primarily of four IBM compatible mainframes and a number of Wang and DEC minicomputers. A large network of Zerox workstations is also used. The mainframes process about 75% of the production volume, with the other systems processing the remaining 25%.

Role of end-user and departmental computing

A large number of the production applications in use at BNRR have been developed by end users. The use of PCs, however, is relatively light. The emphasis on EUC has been to encourage users to develop applications on the mainframe using fourth-generation languages, such as FOCUS and SAS and TSO. RACF is used to control access to the system and individual datasets.

Departmental computing also plays a large role at BNRR. Historically, individual departments have been free to buy their own hardware and hire specialists to design and program production systems to be used to make the departments more efficient. These departmental systems are typically networked with the ISD mainframe systems to allow the transfer of data between them. ISD technical personnel provide some support for these systems (e.g., systems programming and maintenance), but the systems are considered the property of the department that acquired them. A large number of production applications that were not developed by the central ISD programming staff are now running on these departmental machines.

EUC support organisation

Within ISD, a division called Client Services has been established. It currently contains thirty-five people spread among the corporate locations in St Paul, Fort Worth, Overland Park, and Denver. The primary roles of this group are as follows:
▶ Educating users with regard to how to use and manage the technology available to them
▶ Consulting with the users with regard to the best approach to solving problems using technology
▶ Developing systems in partnership with users, when the users require a good example to follow.

In addition to the thirty-five people performing the above functions, another twenty-five support personnel are used by Client Services to staff user help lines, develop EUC education courses, and test new EUC products that may be recommended to users.

Over the last two years, the Client Services group has been working to develop a list of recommended practices to be followed by end users. They have organised these practices into an end-user computing manual. The manual has been distributed to users after they attend training sessions presented by Client Services personnel on how to adequately control and manage end-user applications. These sessions are typically presented on a departmental basis, and attendance is required by senior management for implementors and managers of EUC. This manual covers a wide variety of topics including the following:

▶ Defining business needs
▶ Evaluating EUC versus ISD development alternatives
▶ Categorising the application by risk and complexity
▶ Developing the EUC application
▶ Following documentation standards and naming conventions.

One of the biggest roles played by Client Services in the past several years has been to establish departmental libraries for EUC applications. This has served to consolidate all EUC applications developed for use within an individual department into a single library. In addition to making it easier to manage EUC production applications from a security and back-up perspective, it has given Client Services the ability to better control and manage the quality of EUC applications.

Client Services controls the migration of applications from the users' individual libraries into the departmental libraries. Before migration the user must show proof of adequate documentation, compliance with dataset naming conventions, consideration of data security, etc. Basically, users must comply with the recommended practices outlined in the EUC manual. The advantages to users who move their production applications to the departmental library include the ability to have the job automatically executed by placing it on the job scheduling system (if it is to be run on a regular basis), automatic back-up on a daily basis, and the ability of others to use it in their absence.

Internal audit role in EUC

Internal audit views EUC as an integral part of production systems. As such, it devotes a portion of the annual audit budget to reviewing EUC data centres and significant application systems.

A variety of approaches is used to identify EUC applications. General EUC controls are reviewed during the course of departmental reviews. Significant applications supporting the department are identified and reviewed if appropriate. Departmental data centres also undergo periodic general controls reviews.

In the past, internal audit has also attempted to perform an annual inventory of major EUC applications at all of the company's major operating locations. A risk analysis is then performed and the most critical or high-risk applications are scheduled for review within the current audit year. The inventory process has been necessary because of the autonomy of each department with regard to equipment acquisition and system development. No one individual or group within the company was aware of all major EUC activity at the various company locations.

The emergence of the Client Services group over the past few years has changed this situation. This group has developed a listing of all production applications that currently reside in the departmental libraries across all company locations.

Internal audit plans to interact closely with Client Services to keep abreast of significant development activity in the future. Client Services, in turn, plans to rely on internal audit to enforce compliance with its recommended practices.

Representative EUC audit

In the course of a departmental audit, internal audit identified a new EUC application that was being used to support the capital projects budgeting and monitoring process. Due to the impact capital projects have on the profitability of the business, internal audit determined that the system should be reviewed more closely. The system has been developed in FOCUS and was executing on the IBM mainframe. It was designed to add functionality by interfacing with the older system master files and adding some additional data and processing options. The entire new system had been created mainly by a single end user and consisted of over 100 FOCUS programs.

As a result of the audit, internal audit noted the following problems:

▶ Redundant data – multiple files contained the same information
▶ Inaccurate data – updates to one file could be made without corresponding updates being made to related files. This situation led to out-of-balance conditions
▶ Inadequate audit trails – audit trails did not exist for all changes to master file data
▶ Inadequate documentation – little or no documentation existed for the EUC system.

The audit served to summarise a number of shortcomings of which many users had been aware for some period of time. Ultimately, the management of the user department responsible for the system and the Client Services group decided that the entire system should be redesigned. As an interim step, management assigned the resources to remedy the most critical weaknesses within the system.

Conclusion

BNRR is a good example of a modern company coming to grips with the issues associated with controlling EUC. Its approach to controlling EUC encompasses the following:

▶ Dedicated personnel in the Client Services department
▶ Internal audit awareness and proactive audit steps (periodic inventory)
▶ Published standards and procedures
▶ User education
▶ Support by upper management of EUC control policies.

BNRR acknowledges that it still has a way to go before it is completely satisfied with controls over the entire EUC environment, but is has laid a solid foundation on which to build the remaining control structure.

Major programmes of The Foundation

Academic Programmes   The Foundation plays a key role in helping internal auditors keep up with the trends in their profession. In today's competitive global marketplace, education is an integral part of becoming and staying marketable to an employer. The Institute of Internal Auditors (IIA), aided by The Foundation, has supported a program to build knowledge and awareness of internal auditing in college and university classrooms. Through supportive professors and university curricula, internal auditing is presented to future practitioners, managers and public accountants.

In 1986, The Foundation began funding IIA-endorsed programs in internal auditing modelled after a pilot programme developed by the Department of Accounting at Louisiana State University. The objective is to add internal auditing curricula and to encourage internal auditing research at colleges and universities. In 1992, The Foundation board of trustees committed $250,000 to support IIA-endorsed programmes in internal auditing over the ensuing five years. The IIA-endorsed school grant programme represented an opportunity to develop and experiment with internal auditing educational programmes and to demonstrate to other schools that such programmes are viable and worth the resource commitment. In 1994, The Foundation completed its 1992 commitment of $250,000 to the IIA's Endorsed Internal Auditing Programme, with the funding of programmes at the University of Texas at Austin and the University of Tennessee at Knoxville.

Internal Auditing Educator's Symposiums   The Foundation sponsors Internal Auditing Educator's Symposiums to discuss the best methods for teaching internal auditing in colleges and universities. Discussions centre on internal auditing topics including analytical auditing procedures, internal controls, operational auditing, evidence, auditing programmes, technology auditing and sampling. Course materials are provided as well as numerous publications and other handouts provided by The IIA.

Foundation Forums   The Foundation sponsors advanced technology forums at two-year intervals. These forums are designed to bring together recognised experts and specialists in specific areas of interest to internal auditors. They provide an intensive and innovative arena of for discussion of technology issues. Forum proceedings are published and distributed to internal auditing professionals who want to stay up-to-date concerning new developments in technology and auditing, control, and security.

Acknowledgement:

© Institute of Internal Auditors Research Foundation.
Systems Auditability and Control.
Module 7: End-User and Departmental Computing, pp. 7–77 and 7–80.

Short self-assessment questions

3.1   Define the four generic stages of the traditional SDLC and outline the nature and purpose of each stage.
3.2   Explain why the traditional SDLC is also called a 'waterfall' approach to information systems development.
3.3   Explain what is involved in a *feasibility study* and outline what would normally be found in a *feasibility report*.
3.4   Highlight and explain the five main feasibility factors (known by the mnemonic TELOS) which assist in determining the probability of an information systems project being undertaken.

3.5   Explain what is meant by the term *computing vendor* and indicate three possible main concerns in dealing with a computing vendor.

3.6   Outline and explain the main strengths and weaknesses of the traditional systems development life cycle.

3.7   Define and explain what is meant by the term fourth generation language (4GL) development environment within business information systems.

3.8   Outline the main software tools and applications used by end-users within fourth generation development environments and explain some of the reasons for using each of the tools and applications.

3.9   Contrast and explain the differences between a fourth generation language and a third generation language in terms of their respective nature and characteristics.

3.10   Explain why fourth generation tools and techniques have assisted the rise of end-user computing and end-user involvement in the information systems development process.

3.11   Define the term *client-server computing* and explain the relationship between client-server computing and end-user information systems development.

References
· · · · · · · · · · · · · ·

Daniels, A. and Yeates D.A. (1971) *Basic Training in Systems Analysis*, 2nd edition. Bath, England: Pitman. (*)

Further study and reading
· ·

Books

Burch, J.G. and Gurdnitski, G. (1989) *Information Systems: Theory and Practice*. John Wiley.

Corr, D. (1995) *Essential Elements of Business Information Systems*. London: DP Publications.

Curtis, G. (1989) *Business Information Systems*. Wokingham: Addison-Wesley.

Gane, C. and Sarson, T. (1979) *Structured Systems Analysis*. Englewood Cliffs, New Jersey: Prentice Hall. (*)

Lucas, H.C. (1992) *The Analysis, Design, Implementation of Information Systems*, 4th edition. New York: McGraw-Hill.

Senn, J.A. (1989) *Analysis and Design of Information Systems*. McGraw-Hill.

Shah, H.U. and Avison, D.E. (1995) *The Information Systems Development Life Cycle: A First Course in Information Systems*. Maidenhead, England: McGraw-Hill.

Yourdon, E. (1992) *The Decline and Fall of the American Programmer*. Englewood Cliffs, New Jersey: Yourdon Press.

Journals

Elliott, G. (1997) 2001 a systems odyssey: is rapid applications development a method or madness of the Information Age?, *Proceedings of the 4th International conference on Financial Information Systems*, Sheffield Hallam University, 2–3 July.

Hoplin, H.P. (1994) Integrating advanced information systems and technology in future organisations, *Industrial Management and Data Systems*, 94(8), 17–20.

Linthicum, D.S. (1995) The end of programming, *BYTE*, August, 69–72.

McCune, J. (1994) Information systems get back to basics, *Management Review*, January, 54–60.

Richardson, M. (1995) 4GL database tools – what's happening?, *CMA Magazine*, December/January, 23–6.

Other journal sources

Journal of Management Information Systems

Journal of Information Technology

An asterisk (*) next to a reference indicates a *seminal text* which means it constituted a source for later developments.

CHAPTER 4

Rapid applications development in dynamic business environments

Objectives
....

When you have read this chapter you will be able to:

▶ evaluate the history, evolution and context of rapid applications development (RAD) within business information systems development

▶ describe the role of user participation in the information systems development process through the use of joint applications development (JAD)

▶ understand the characteristics and explain the function of rapid applications development tools and techniques within information systems development

▶ outline and understand the use of alternative approaches to the traditional systems development life cycle that fall under the RAD development umbrella

▶ understand and describe the strengths, weaknesses and circumstances for adopting various alternative approaches to information systems development.

4.1 Introduction to rapid applications development
....

The previous chapter looked at the traditional systems development life cycle (SDLC) and the role of end-user participation within the process of business information systems development. The traditional waterfall approach to systems development is prone to a number of weaknesses, outlined in the previous chapter, which have led to the use of alternative systems development methods, many of which are more appropriate for information systems development in dynamic business environments. The choice of systems development method, and the approach used, is an important business decision because the process of information systems development can be time consuming and costly to an organisation. Therefore, such decision making should only be undertaken after careful analysis and consideration of the overall business objectives of the organisation and the suitability of the various approaches to systems development available within the business environment. The predominant aim of business systems development is to build information systems that meet the *requirements of the business end-users* and, by doing so, deliver the optimal benefits of well-engineered information systems to the business organisation.

Before progressing further, it is important to be clear about the inherent failings of the traditional approach to systems development within modern business environments. The following business considerations have led to the evolution of alternative development approaches with the aims of:

▶ reducing the time and cost of systems development
▶ improving the delivery of system and user requirements
▶ incorporating advances in computing and information technology
▶ recognising the nature of information systems within dynamic business environments.

The alternative information systems development methods that have evolved are an attempt to overcome the shortcomings of the traditional SDLC approach to building systems within the business environment.

4.2 Alternative approaches to information systems development

There are a number of approaches that have evolved as alternatives to the traditional SDLC, some of which utilise the development life cycle approach and some which are radical departures from the sequential 'waterfall' approach. Most development approaches and methodologies are influenced by aspects of general systems theory. Most alternative approaches to information systems development acknowledge the fact that business systems involve human activity which makes the systems development process less predictable. Furthermore, there is a growing recognition that systems cannot be seen in isolation within an organisation. Most organisations, by their nature of trading with the business environment at large, are considered open systems. Therefore, organisations influence, and are influenced by the wider business environment in which they operate.

Six alternative approaches to information systems development that utilise the concepts of end-user computing within the systems development process are as follows:

1   rapid applications development (RAD)
2   joint applications development (JAD)
3   prototyping systems development
4   object-oriented systems development (OOSD)
5   business process re-engineering (BPR)
6   strategic information systems development.

All of these approaches share a common characteristic of emphasising the importance of *human systems end-users* within the process of information systems development. The last approach to systems development, outlined above, emphasises the strategic nature and effect of information systems to the business organisation.

ACTIVITY **4.1**

Approaches to information systems development
Search your college or university's on-line (or CD-ROM) facilities for journal articles and other academic sources to find one article on each of the following areas:
▶   prototyping systems development
▶   object-oriented development (OOD)
▶   business process re-engineering (BPR)
▶   strategic information systems development.
You are required to use one of your articles as a *case study* to form the basis of an assignment on alternative approaches to systems development.

4.3 Rapid applications development

The term *rapid applications development* (RAD) is an umbrella reference to the use of various fourth generation methods, tools and techniques integrated to achieve fast, rapid information systems development within the business environment. The emphasis within RAD is on the *synergy* created by the effective deployment of these various tools and techniques to achieve delivery of an information system solution in the shortest possible time. Synergy refers to the combined actions of two or more activities or objects which have a greater total effect than the sum of the parts.

> *Rapid Applications Development (RAD)* An umbrella term that uses a number of tools and techniques to speed the information systems development process.

Therefore, RAD applies one of the main principles of systems theory, that the sum is greater than the parts, to the process of developing business information systems. The RAD approach is complimented by the cooperation of technical specialists with business specialists using various participative frameworks such as *joint applications development* (JAD).

The increasing need to develop information systems as rapidly as possible has been driven by the need for organisations to compete effectively in a constantly changing business environment. Organisations have become more customer oriented as they have become more competitive; organisations must now compete with other organisations in other countries and continents on a *global* scale. This type of competition is characterised by continuous *change*. Therefore, it is imperative that information systems within a business organisation are flexible enough to continuously change in line with changes in the overall business environment. Therefore, speed of business information systems development is of the essence to a competitive organisation. The slow, and often laborious, nature of the traditional SDLC approach to building information systems makes it an inefficient development method for most

> **DID YOU KNOW?**
> *Rapid applications development (RAD) is a concept that encompasses a number of methods, tools and techniques that speed up the information systems development process. Although the method is not a proprietary one to a particular individual, it is associated to a certain degree with a systems specialist named James Martin, who wrote a book in 1991 entitled* Rapid Applications Development.
> *There is also further work underway by a consortium of organisations and individuals with the aim of structuring RAD into a methodology which is known as the dynamic systems development method (DSDM).*

organisations competing in dynamic business environments. Consequently, business organisations are turning to the more attractive alternative frameworks within the rapid applications development domain.

The principles of rapid applications development are based on the premise that fast, effective and efficient information systems can only be developed by the careful alignment of specific development methods with suitable software application tools. There are four main principles within the RAD framework:

1 Improving the *speed of systems development* by using tools and techniques appropriate to the business organisation and its competitive environment.
2 RAD does not adhere to the traditional systems development life cycle but instead uses an iterative *prototyping approach to development*.

3   The framework of RAD emphasises concentrated *end-user participation* and involvement in the whole development process via workshops and group meetings to deliberately try to fulfill user requirements.
4   RAD uses a number of known *modelling tools and techniques* which it collates together in the form of a resource toolbox.

The use of RAD techniques encourages efficiency in the systems development process. It is claimed (see Pause for thought 4.1 on The Norwich Union) that RAD can produce information systems applications much faster than conventional methods; this is particularly important for organisations that face customer pressure to provide products and services at ever increasing rates. Information systems must often be developed rapidly to allow the business to support or develop its customer base within the business environment in which it operates. Systems development is usually measured in *function points*, where a function point indicates a specific feature of a software product or application to be delivered. The Pause for thought 4.1 study indicates that by using RAD techniques efficiently and effectively it is possible to increase the delivery of function points by a factor of eight.

> **DID YOU KNOW?**
> The head of RAD development at Norwich Union General Insurance in the United Kingdom asserts that the Norwich Union averaged 64 function points per person month compared with an average of only 8 function points per person month for the insurance industry as a whole in 1995.

The problem with the traditional waterfall approach to the SDLC lies in the fact that what emerges from the development process often is not what end-users need from the information system. In the traditional systems approach development success is measured against how close the finished system is to the original specification, even if the original specification turns out to fall short of the user's requirements. On the other hand, RAD concentrates on measuring the effectiveness of an information system by how well it matches the *business specifications* of the organisation and how well it delivers business benefits of that specification. It should not be inferred that the RAD framework is any less rigorous than the traditional SDLC. The tools, techniques and methods that fall under the umbrella term RAD are increasingly being referred to as the dynamic systems development method (DSDM), which implies that there is a methodological basis to using RAD. To support this idea, and to ensure recognition of alternative methods, tools and techniques for information systems development, a Dynamic Systems Development Method consortium, including many large and reputable business organisations, was set up in the United Kingdom in 1994. The remit of the consortium is to promote RAD methods within the business environment and ensure development framework standards.

Rapid applications development is a group-based, participative activity, relying on business specialists and technical specialists working together in teams and through workshops to analyse, design and formulate information systems solutions. The use and application of RAD methods should never be a solitary activity within an organisation. RAD has had an effect on the structural nature of business organisations in promoting group-based activities. Within this participative environment decision making is devolved to the business specialists, in discussion with the technical specialists, who make decisions in groups, or through workshops, and often by consensus. Therefore, in order for the development process to work, it is important to get the correct and most suitable mix of people involved in the group-based systems development activities. Along with greater involvement comes greater responsibility which should lead to higher levels of commitment and demand on the participant's energies. Such participation is known to be challenging, so it is imperative to employ a group selection criteria that helps to formulate cooperative and effective project groups. For example, the TOBI method can be used for selecting compatible individuals for group-based development activities. The TOBI method allows the profiling of individuals on the basis of whether they show an aptitude for being a *leader, administrator, scheduler* or *maintainer*. Groups can then be more professionally established, which include individuals each with expertise in one of the four areas mentioned.

PAUSE FOR THOUGHT 4.1 *The development of RAD as an alternative for building effective and efficient systems.*

The Norwich Union

Norwich Union is a general insurance business domiciled in the United Kingdom. Between 1994 and 1996 the Norwich Union built and delivered over 20 systems using the RAD appoach to information and software-based systems development. Norwich Union has witnessed high increases in systems development productivity by using RAD. In contrast to traditional waterfall methods, where eventual systems quality is measured by how close the finished product was to the specification (regardless of whether the initial specification was correct in the first place!), in RAD quality is measured against 'business benefits'. By using RAD the Norwich Union has admitted that systems development effectiveness and efficiency has in combination increased eightfold since 1994.

The Co-operative Bank

The Co-operative Bank, located in the United Kingdom, first used RAD tools and techniques when it needed to replace an existing centralised and computer-based application which processed customer application forms. Within the Co-operative Bank existed a range of conventional, mainframe-based, legacy software from the 1960s, 1970s and 1980s. The organisation wished to re-engineer its fundamental processes and procedures and such a significant leap could only be achieved by using a RAD approach. The systems development project was broken into phases because the system that the Co-operative Bank was looking to replace was a fundamental and major system of the business. The phases involved determining user requirements, through the use of workshops and prototyping. The workshops were a critical key to success; it was determined that everyone involved would be allowed to make decisions on the spot as and when necessary. The RAD approach was used to create a sense of trust and empowerment within the workforce and the systems end-users. The application of RAD was a huge success, with the head of technical systems at the Bank declaring in 1995 that because of prototyping and the high level of involvement of business people in the design stage, what emerged was just what was required for the business. This was achieved without providing any formal training and despite the presence of a steep learning curve.

BUPA

BUPA is a private medical insurance business operating in the United Kingdom. When BUPA required a care management system to supervise its new Healthmanager product there appeared to be nothing on the market to match its requirements, so it was recommended that the organisation use a RAD approach because of the time constraints present and the dynamic nature of its changing requirements. BUPA formed a joint development team with another consultancy organisation to deliver the required care management system. The aim of the system was to log all contacts, appointments and hospital stays. Before the new system was developed, BUPA used a range of small systems, including manual paper-based systems, to administrate the Healthmanager product. The old system had become unmanageable because the system was expected to manage over 34,000 incidents of treatment, with each incident report containing an average of 18 separate contacts. By using RAD the first phase of the system was delivered in August 1995 after only an 11-week systems development cycle. A senior project manager at BUPA claimed that had it used traditional systems development methods it would have taken over six months. However, by using RAD tools and techniques the system at BUPA was delivered in the time-scale required with substantial cost savings.

ACTIVITY **4.2**
....

Rapid applications development

Discuss and explain what is meant by the term *rapid applications development* (RAD) and suggest two reasons for its existence as an alternative approach to the SDLC. Then explain why speed of applications and systems development is so important to a competitive business organisation, particularly to organisations competing on a global scale where the sophistication of information technology varies. Outline the remit of the dynamic systems development method (DSDM) consortium and explain why it is important to develop a methodological framework for business systems development.

The rapid applications development approach to systems development has four main phases (not sequential stages) which are laid out in Table 4.1.

table 4.1
The four phases of rapid applications development (RAD)

Phase 1	**Requirements planning**	
	technique:	joint requirements planning (JRP)
	technique:	joint applications development (JAD)
Phase 2	**User design**	
	technique:	joint applications development (JAD)
	tool:	prototyping
	tool:	computer-aided software engineering (CASE)
Phase 3	**Construction**	
	tool:	prototyping
	tool:	computer-aided software engineering (CASE)
Phase 4	**Cutover**	
	tool:	testing and evaluation
	tool:	user training

Requirements planning Emphasis in this phase is placed on the early stages of planning where it is important to establish the correct end-user and business requirements. The two techniques used at this stage for facilitating this process are *joint requirements planning* (JRP) and *joint applications development* (JAD); often these two techniques are used interchangeably. Both techniques attempt to establish an appropriate arena in which all users meet and define the system's requirements. This stage is characterised by structured meetings and intensive workshops where full participation by technical and business specialists is essential. The role of JRP is to establish the requirements of the business at the strategic level of the organisation. Therefore, the executive level of the business organisation is required to participate in the systems development process, which was not necessarily the case with the traditional SDLC. The structured meetings and workshops within the JRP framework are used to identify the goals of the information system under investigation, with a view to achieving a consensus agreement on the priorities and direction of systems development. It is important for the strategic level of an organisation to be included in the systems development process because it is at this level that decisions can rapidly be made without regard to a lower, and longer, chain of command.

User design The main technique used in this phase is joint applications development (JAD). This phase is characterised by full end-user participation in the *analysis* and *design* of the information system. It is essential for the right team of users to be put together, in the most suitable environment, to participate in the JAD process, to achieve the fulfilment of the end-user's requirements. This phase normally uses *diagramming* tools and techniques to rapidly explore the proposed systems processes and user interfaces. The diagrammed prototyping can be used to investigate particular areas of the proposed system, which may be contentious, or the system as a whole. The end-user design is developed by using tools such as functional decomposition, entity modelling and data flow diagrams. (All of these design tools will be looked at in detail in chapter 5.) The results of the end-user design are often represented using computer-aided software engineering (CASE) tools.

Construction This phase involves converting the user design into a more detailed design, then implementing that design by the development of working *prototypes* that can be evaluated by end-users. This phase is mostly given over to technical specialists to build any software-based applications that are required. The process of prototype evaluation by users is brought forward, compared to the SDLC approach, because of the involvement of end-users in the analysis and design aspects of the proposed information system. Then the technical specialists, responsible for physical construction of the system, are required to work rapidly and to utilise any techniques, such as implementing reusable designs and program codes, to build the system. Normally, only a small team of technical specialists are used in the construction process in order to avoid any developmental overlap.

Cutover This phase is concerned with the conversion of the old system to the new system (if an old system is being replaced) and the application of thorough systems testing and evaluation. It is common practice that the old (or in place) system should be run in parallel with the new system until total reliability and confidence is established in the new system. Training is then given to users, although such training will be limited by the fact that users are already familiar with the system from participation in the development process and testing of prototypes, thus reducing training costs for the business organisation.

PAUSE FOR THOUGHT 4.2　　　*Rapid applications development*

Rapid applications development (RAD) comprises a set of tools and techniques for designing and developing information systems in the Information Age. One of the major benefits of the RAD approach is the incorporation of user-friendly programming languages that allow less formalised and detailed computer programming to be carried out within an information systems development project. The RAD approach offers the possibility of a shorter and more flexible systems development life cycle, because of the use of techniques such as prototyping. Another advantage lies in the use of fourth generation programming languages that permit deeper and more effective participation of systems' end-users in the programming process of the systems development project. Therefore, with RAD the amount of time allocated to purer computer programming can be reduced significantly.

Many of the tools and techniques found under the RAD umbrella were used well before the issues of rapid application development became so important. For example, prototyping is a valuable technique in the design stage as it allows the end-users and the development team, in cooperation, to determine the look and nature of an information system more rapidly, which can lead to an early creation of a prototype that looks and acts like the intended system. However, RAD extends the capabilities of prototyping by providing systems developers with everything they need in order to build a prototype as well as turning the prototype into a fully functional set of processes and software applications. In other words, the prototype does not have to be converted to a particular computer language once the development team is happy with the system because the program coding is already implicit in the working prototype. Within the RAD framework developers build systems applications primarily by designing the interfaces of the system. An interface determines how a user interacts with a system. The development team will primarily develop interface components such as menus, windows, buttons and even dialogue boxes that work in a WIMP environment. (WIMP is an acronym for Windows, Icons, Menus and Pointers). The development team should be more concerned with what a systems application does rather than how it does it. Prototyping also allows for a system to be iteratively tested by users in what is often called 'spiral development', which implies a development process of 'getting it wrong' many times before 'getting it right' for the final delivered system. However, care must be taken to ensure that the final system is appropriate and acceptable within the integrated business systems environment. The fixing and refining of a system after it has been delivered wastes money and may lead to user dissatisfaction which is sometimes referred to as the 'prototyping death spiral'! Therefore, a holistic view of a system within the wider system environment is an important and necessary characteristic of RAD.

Another major technique of RAD is the use of object-oriented (OO) development which allow sets of code or parts of various software applications (objects) to be put together along the lines of building something using children's building blocks. Rather than programming from scratch, a system can be developed by building objects to the specification of the users of the system. For example, Borland's 'Delphi' is a RAD tool that allows developers to assemble software applications from pre-built components. Delphi uses an object-oriented variant of the Pascal programming language for development and links to most major database servers. With advances in information technology, particularly the Internet, objects can be located and found across global networks and not just localised business environments. The development team also has wider access to 'good development practice' in other business systems environments. Most RAD tools provide facilities for component re-use. Often simple components are built and re-used throughout the various applications of an information system. This process can be assisted by the re-use capabilities of most RAD tools to build ready-made object code libraries of applications. Furthermore, RAD tools largely incorporate visual programming languages (like 'Visual Basic' and IBM's 'VisualAge') that make the programming aspect of systems development more apparent to the ordinary (or less program-oriented) systems user. Other technological tools and techniques used in RAD include object-oriented analysis and design methods and CASE (computer-assisted software engineering) tools.

RAD does not totally 'eRADicate' the need for programming but it does, by the use of various modern programming tools and techniques (known as the 'programming environment'), allow for a reduction in the programming task that was so time consuming in the traditional systems development life cycle. RAD projects promote development speed but they do not eliminate the requirement for considered analysis and design, nor the need for skilful development through the use of programming tools and techniques. An advantage of RAD is that it encourages systems participation by allowing end-users to become part of the development process and part of a systems development team. However, with speed of development predominating a systems development project there is often a danger of the issues of development consistency, systems standardisation and software maintainability becoming secondary unless they become subsumed into the fabric of the development process. Nonetheless, RAD offers speed of systems development and the possibility of competitive advantage to an organisation that depends upon fast and effective information systems development.

ACTIVITY **4.3**

Rapid applications development within the business environment

Write a brief one-page report outlining the reasons why a business organisation may use rapid applications development (RAD) to develop information systems and, within the report, provide five reasons why RAD tools and techniques may be effective in maximising the productivity of the systems development process. Then, before investigating joint applications development in the next section, discuss the possible *human* and *technical* problems of implementing a RAD approach to information systems development within business organisations.

4.4   Joint applications development

Joint applications development (JAD) is a useful technique for establishing an information system's overall business requirements. JAD can be used in a number of business environments in place of traditional data collection and requirements analysis procedures. JAD involves group meetings between end-users, technical specialists, business specialists and other systems stakeholders all working together to analyse existing systems, propose possible solutions, and define the system's requirements. The concept emphasises the word *joint* to refer to the close working relationship of business specialists and technical specialists. JAD uses *structured meetings* and workshops to bring technical specialists and business specialists together to agree the system's requirements. Therefore, it requires the right people being brought together within the most suitable working environment.

> **DID YOU KNOW?**
>
> *Joint applications development (JAD) is a systems development technique that was originally conceptualised by IBM Canada in the 1970s and was later further developed by James Martin and Associates of the United States, a notable information systems consultancy.*

> **DID YOU KNOW?**
>
> *Joint applications development (JAD) is a group-based approach to end-user participation in overall information systems development; it provides a framework for more concentrated and enhanced user involvement in systems development processes.*

The technical specialist and the business specialist bring two types of mental model to the JAD process. The two mental models are acquired separately by the technical specialist and the business specialist over time and are normally based on the baggage of past experience, expertise and knowledge. The fundamental purpose of JAD is to design a *conceptual model* of the proposed information system that exactly matches the mental design models envisaged by both the technical specialists and the business specialists. The two mental models can only come together into a mutually acceptable *conceptual design model* by a process of continuous iteration, within the modelling process, to break down the differences between the contrasting conceptual models. This can only be facilitated as part of an interactive group-based 'brain-storming' process that airs all preconceived views and overcomes areas of technical and business ignorance. Figure 4.1 shows a typical layout for a JAD meeting or workshop. Within this environment one person acts as *facilitator* to encourage and guide the brain-storming process of the workshop environment.

There are three main principles to the JAD participative framework which are as follows:

1   JAD is characterised by an *intensive brain-storming* meeting of all relevant technical and business users of the information system. These meetings must be structured with an agenda, a set of objectives and a code of conduct between the participants. There should ideally be no more than 15 participants involved in the JAD meetings. The role of the business specialists is usually to decide on end-user requirements, while the role of the technical specialists is to advise on the technical constraints and implications of the ideas being proposed.

2   JAD is characterised by a *structured meeting room* environment. Such a meeting environment is given in Figure 4.1. The layout of the room and

figure 4.1
JAD meeting (or workshop) environment

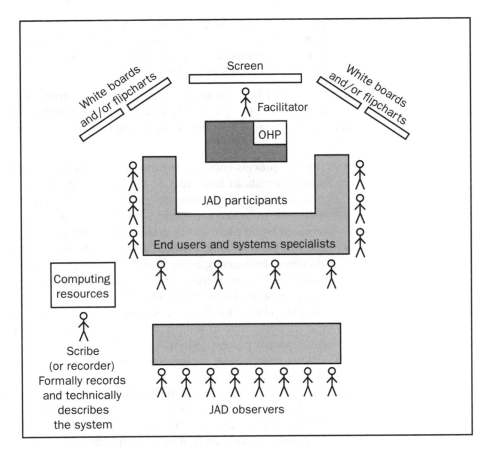

Note: The environment should be isolated from the outside world, apart from possible telecommunications link to or from the 'scribes' computing resources.

The JAD environment does not contain:

Telephones   Pagers/beepers   Mobile phones   Rank/position

The relationship of participants is not based on outside rank or position

the positioning of the participants is vital to the creative process. Many tools, such as white boards and flipcharts, are used to encourage the brainstorming exercise. It is advised that the length of the meeting be determined in advance, with attendance from start to finish of the meeting. Also the meeting should be held away from any possible interruptions usually found within the business environment.

3   The JAD process is managed and guided by a person who acts as *facilitator*. This person performs a task over and above that of the chair of the meeting. The facilitator should be independent of the participants and should be an expert in group dynamics and group behaviour. The facilitator is responsible for controlling the participants and guiding the creative process of the meeting to achieve the stated objectives. The

process is also assisted by a person who acts as *scribe*. This person is responsible for transcribing and documenting the JAD process. This person may also be responsible for guiding the use of various tools and techniques essential for establishing prototypes.

This process of JAD can also be used in environments outside of systems development where there is a need to establish general business organisation requirements. There are a number of advantages of the JAD participative process as follows:

▶ The JAD process encourages *participants to focus on systems problems* and solutions without interruption. This speeds the process of analysis and design. JAD avoids the lengthy process of constructing questionnaires and setting up individual meetings with users. All decisions are agreed and accepted by all participants at the JAD meetings.

▶ The JAD process *brings together all stakeholders* in the system such as the managers, technical specialists and business end-users. Decisions can be made without going through the more usual and formal communications channels of the business organisation.

▶ The JAD meetings *enfranchise participants in the decision-making process* and are better able to achieve a universal commitment to the systems development process. When individuals feel they are part of the decision-making process they are less likely to create resistance to the development of a system.

▶ The JAD meetings involve the employment of an *independent facilitator* who understands group dynamics. This person is neutral within the JAD process and can arbitrate and overcome many of the internal organisational politics that may compromise the development of an ideal information system.

ACTIVITY **4.4**

Joint applications development

Discuss with and advise your colleagues on the use and role of joint applications development (JAD) workshops within a RAD environment. Then proceed to explain the reasons behind including all systems 'stakeholders' in meetings concerned with defining the requirements of the information systems under consideration. Describe the possible strengths and weaknesses of the JAD approach to problem solving and suggest possible effects the approach has on the overall time-frame for delivery of a business information system.

4.5   Prototyping

A prototype is a working and representative model of a system or sub-system, the purpose of which is to permit systems end-users to be involved in the design and development process through the activity of testing and evaluation of the working prototype. Prototyping allows an information system to be tested and evaluated earlier in the overall development process than is the case with traditional SDLC. Prototyping uses a process of *iteration* to refine the system to an ideal; iteration is the process of repeating a series of operations until the desired solution is achieved. The iterative aspect of prototyping provides greater scope for testing alternatives and building an information system more quickly and at less cost. Ideally, when end-users work with a prototype they develop a more focused and discerning idea of the delivery of business system requirements in practice. It also puts a greater emphasis on the development of the human *front-end interface* between the user and the system's technology. Systems users, through working and interacting with the prototype, often demand a higher level of user-friendly IS/IT interface design.

Prototyping places great emphasis on participative end-user involvement at the start of the systems design process in describing the proposed outcome of the information systems development project. However, end-users often have limited training in traditional tools of systems analysis and design so have to rely on transcribing the system requirements in terms of symbols, pictures and narrative illustration. This is a technique known as *story-boarding* which uses rough drawings to describe the requirements of the information system. Such informal analysis, using symbols, icons, and a limited amount of narrative, permits a non-technical end-user to describe and communicate a proposed information system to any technical specialist. The outcome of producing a drawing, with symbols and limited wording, is known as a *rich picture*. The rich picture should act as a graphical representation of the information system's user requirements. Such rich pictures can be developed individually or in group workshops to provide an analytical view of the system's requirements and specifications. Examples of the technique and use of rich pictures within soft system's development methodologies will be discussed at length in chapter 7. However, Figure 4.2 provides a typical example of a rich picture using pictures and icons to represent the marketing systems environment. Furthermore, there are a number of software applications that accommodate the development of user story-boarding for defining an information system.

There are a number of strengths inherent in the prototyping approach as follows:

▶ It overcomes many of the problems of the traditional SDLC, in terms of inadequate requirements definition, by *involving end-users* in the systems development process.

▶ It can be developed using *fourth generation* tools and techniques, which are inherently more user-friendly than third generation computing tools and techniques.

▶ It allows the end-user to work with more *pre-coded software* applications (e.g. spreadsheets, databases, graphics packages) which can be integrated to build business-specific information systems (this is known as applications-based development).

▶ It places a greater emphasis on input and output forms and human–computer *interface design*. It also improves the process of systems investigation and analysis.

figure 4.2

Example of a rich picture to describe a systems environment (marketing function)

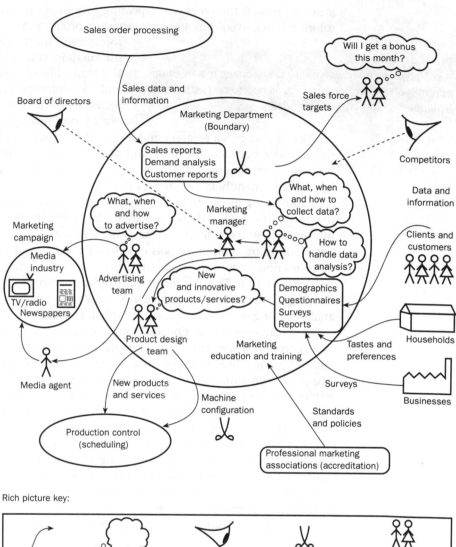

Rich picture key:

Relationship	'Think' bubble (major concerns)	External interested party	Crossed swords (conflict area)	Human aspects (Entities) of system

▶ It involves business specialists in the system problem-solving process to an extent that is not practical with the traditional systems development life cycle. This overcomes the problem of inadequate *communication* between technical specialists and non-technical end-users.

▶ It is a useful tool when the applications area is poorly defined or *fuzzy* or where a business organisation is unfamiliar with the information technology aspect of the proposed information system.

A prototype is normally built by using special tools and techniques to speed up the process of requirements analysis and design of human–computer interfaces.

table 4.2 **The five steps of prototyping**		
	Step 1	Identify and define business and system requirements.
	Step 2	Develop a full working prototype.
	Step 3	Testing and evaluation of the prototype by end-users.
	Step 4	Refine and enhance the prototype through iteration.
	Step 5	Document and deliver the optimum information system.

Examples of PC-based tools and techniques include MicroSoft Access® (for database development) and VisualBasic® (for various applications integration and development). For instance, VisualBasic can be used to enhance the power, capability and integration of software applications by using user-friendly programming to empower pre-built applications software (e.g. spreadsheets), or to integrate software, such as linking a database to a spreadsheet.

A prototype model can also be used as a tool for *organisational learning* as well as supporting the systems development process. In prototyping practice the business specialists will define and illustrate the requirements of the information system, followed by the development of a working prototype built with the cooperation and guidance of technical specialists. Therefore, the business interests predominate in ensuring that the *business* requirements and the *system* requirements are promoted and aligned in harmony. There are five steps to the incorporation of a prototype into the information systems development process, which are illustrated in Table 4.2.

Prototyping is most effective for the development of information systems for decision making in environments that are characterised by uncertainty and subject to dynamic market forces. A prototype can particularly be used where the decision-making requirements are unclear, or where there is a need to clarify the problem-solving process, to deliver a more effective and useful information system's solution. However, this is qualified by the fact that prototyping is most effective for smaller, PC-based, information systems development. Prototyping is often not appropriate for large, mainframe-based, development with incumbent, complex and large-scale data processing requirements. Furthermore, there is a need for any finalised information system to include aspects of *data security* and user *documentation*. However, these aspects often do not fall within the scope of the prototype development framework.

ACTIVITY **4.5**

Systems prototyping

Discuss what is meant by the term *prototyping* as used in information systems development environments and explain the importance of *iteration* to the process of prototyping within systems development. Normally a university or college will operate a system of 'student admissions' to coordinate, control and manage the process of offering places on courses, and the eventual enrolment of students on to those various courses. You are required to investigate the role and nature of university and college admissions and to produce a *rich picture* of the systems environment. Please note that you will first of all have to define the boundaries of the system that is under consideration and then describe the environment with the use of pictures and a minimal amount of wording.

4.6 Object-oriented systems development

The growth of graphical interfaces, Internet browser technology and the increasing use of client-server technology have stimulated an interest in object-oriented systems development. Object-oriented development (OOD) involves the linking together of *objects* to create specific systems applications. These objects may consist of a set of computer codes or an encapsulated collection of data and operations performed on that data. These objects can be interchanged between applications, allowing a systems builder to obtain objects of code and applications from an *object library*. The various objects can be assembled, like building blocks, into a systems application for any business organisation. Therefore, the OOD concept is important in treating data and procedures often within the object.

> **DID YOU KNOW?**
> The concepts and theory of object-oriented development (OOD) originated in the 1970s. However, OOD lay on the margins of information systems and computer programming until the late 1980s and early 1990s when it re-emerged as a systems development framework rejuvenated by advances in information technology.

The advantage of object-oriented systems design lies in the re-usability of computer codes, whereby processing routines and data can be built into objects which can be used in a number of systems software applications. However, it is still a skill to be able to analyse business functions correctly so that they can be encapsulated into an object. Objects possess *classes* and component *members*. For example, a plant may be a class of object with leaves and stem as component members. The importance of OOD is that an organisation can build up a *library of object classes* that deals with all the systems functions of the business organisation. Systems development, involving software applications development, becomes a task of selecting and connecting existing classes of objects into a systems application. This will normally speed along the process of overall systems development.

> **DID YOU KNOW?**
> Object-oriented development (OOD) is a software development method that combines data and the associated instructions for that data into one object or entity that can be used interchangeably and built into other systems' software applications.

ACTIVITY 4.6

Object-oriented development

Discuss and explain the term *object-oriented development* and suggest why there has been a resurgence of interest in a technique that dates back to the 1970s. Describe what is meant by *objects* and explain the possible use, role and function of *object libraries* in applications and systems development within business organisations. Once this has been understood, suggest three possible advantages of using pre-coded or pre-formed objects to build different information systems within one organisation.

4.7 Applications-based systems development

Software applications packages are normally pre-coded and commercially available programs that eliminate the requirement for writing software codes each time a systems application is required by an organisation. Software applications packages perform many tasks and functions and can be divided into the following generic areas within the business environment:

▶ database applications
▶ modelling spreadsheet applications
▶ wordprocessing applications
▶ desktop publishing (DTP) applications
▶ graphics and multi-media applications
▶ operating system (OS) utilities.

Many small-scale information systems can now be built using pre-coded software applications packages. This is a process normally referred to as *applications-based systems development*. This activity reduces the time needed within the traditional systems development life cycle for program coding. In particular, small scale, desktop-based, IS/IT projects lend themselves well to applications-based information systems development. There are a number of advantages of applications-based systems development as follows:

▶ It allows end-users to build systems that meet their individual requirements within the business organisation.
▶ It reduces the need for large numbers of in-house technical specialists and encourages employees to become more information technology literate.
▶ Most commercial software applications come with user support (or help lines) which reduces in-house costs associated with systems development.
▶ Many package environments allow various applications to be integrated so that systems can be built with harmony. (For example the Microsoft Corporation ® encourages user integration of its suite of office applications.)

Applications-based development does not negate the need to thoroughly undertake the stages of systems analysis, design, implementation and evaluation. It is particularly suitable for developing prototypes for information systems used in the managerial and executive levels of a business organisation, where systems applications are specific to individuals and small teams. However, one of the main disadvantages of applications-based development lies in the fact that idiosyncratic systems may be developed without regard to consistent and commonly practiced standards of systems development throughout the whole organisation.

ACTIVITY **4.7**

Applications-based systems development

Explain the term *applications-based systems development* and suggest why it has arisen as a fast method of developing software-based information systems within the business environment. Then proceed to outline and discuss all of the possible advantages and disadvantages of using 'off-the-shelf', pre-coded software for the purposes of applications-based information systems development. What issues of standardisation and development consistency do you think need to be addressed when customising software applications for specific business systems within an organisation?

4.8 Outsourcing of information systems development

The outsourcing of information systems development activities is the practice of employing an external organisation to service a business organisation's in-house IS/IT needs. This concept can also extend to the hiring of outside organisations, or personnel, to develop an organisation's internal information systems. Therefore, in the activity of outsourcing, many of a business organisation's IS/IT responsibilities are given over to outside organisational control. For example, it is common practice for many smaller business organisations to outsource the operational functions of salaries or payroll. Some of the services and facilities offered by outsourcing agents include:

▶ Staffing and managing a business organisation's IT centre.
▶ Advising on, or designing, a business organisation's information systems.
▶ Developing business-specific applications for an organisation.
▶ Total undertaking of a business organisation's functional systems, e.g. stock control, payroll, sales order processing and purchase order processing).

Outsourcing cannot be undertaken lightly by any business organisation and choosing an outsourcing agent requires care and consideration. Important regard must be made to the contractual obligations incumbent upon both parties involved in any business and legal agreement. Nevertheless, there are a number of advantages of outsourcing as follows:

▶ It allows systems and IT applications to be managed and developed by technical specialists who may not be readily available in a business organisation.
▶ It can save a business organisation money by the competitive process of tendering organisations for outsourced business contracts.
▶ It can often turn a variable cost into a fixed cost with the added advantage of the cost being known and clear to an organisation in advance (i.e. there should be no hidden or unexpected costs).
▶ Outsourcing agents have access to a pool of specialist skills and resources that may be beyond the finances of a small-scale business organisation.

These advantages of outsourcing must be weighed against a number of disadvantages of outsourcing as follows:

▶ Outsourcing will often devolve responsibility for business IS/IT to an external body with the possibility of loss of control and over reliance on the outsourcing agent.
▶ It requires a formal contract between two parties, the business organisation and the outsourcing agent, which establishes financial obligations that are enforceable under the law.

ACTIVITY **4.8**

Outsourcing information systems development

Discuss what is meant by the term *outsourcing* as applied to information systems development within the business environment and explain the main advantages and disadvantages of outsourcing. Then, from your knowledge or experience, indicate aspects of outsourcing that may remove information systems control from a business organisation and a pro forma *outline agreement* between a business organisation and an outsourcing agent that covers the outsourcing of any IS/IT activity. How formal do you think this agreement should be?

4.9   Business process re-engineering

So far in this chapter the approaches to business information systems development have deliberately not included account of issues relevant to the strategic level of a business organisation. However, *business process re-engineering* (BPR) addresses the overall nature of IS/IT within a business organisation and looks at business systems issues in the context of the overall strategic direction of the business organisation within its environment. Therefore, BPR does not merely look at the functioning of individual information systems but looks at the purpose, objectives and assumptions of IS/IT to gauge whether the existing business systems are still appropriate to the organisation's strategic objectives. BPR is a concept, rather than a rigid methodology, that attempts to re-engineer business processes that are under-performing, or no longer relevant, in the prevailing business environment. One of the main principles of BPR is that re-engineering of processes is made possible and practicable by advances in information technology.

> **DID YOU KNOW?**
> *Business process re-engineering (BPR) is the process of fundamental and radical redesign of business system's processes and practices to achieve dramatic improvements in critical, contemporary measures of performance, such as cost, quality, service and speed.*
> *(Hammer and Champy, 1993)*

The drive within BPR is in radically changing the way a business organisation perceives the role and purpose of its *business activities*. The emphasis is on what *should* be done to improve business performance, rather than what *was* done in the past (or maintaining the status quo). Therefore, there is a need for business organisations to 're-invent' themselves by determining *what* they should be doing and *how* they should be achieving it. BPR can be a high-risk task which entails the organisation looking at the fundamental nature of its business activities, processes and practices. Ultimately, the task of BPR attempts to find innovative ways to improve overall performance within the business environment. Organisations may attempt to re-engineer themselves for a number of reasons that flow from the belief that an organisation may be under-performing. Some of these reasons for initiating BPR are as follows:

▶ The organisation is facing the prospect of going out of business and has no alternative but to look at the very nature of its business activities and the information systems that support those activities.
▶ Competitive forces and change within the business environment may require a business organisation to rethink the way information systems support the strategic objectives of the organisation.
▶ The business organisation may wish to establish a competitive edge over other organisations within its trading environment.

BPR is not a methodology that requires incremental changes but fundamental organisational changes; which often leads to organisational upheaval, which will necessitate competent management of change measures being employed. BPR is fundamentally linked to improving overall business performance, therefore, a business organisation will need to establish a set of *performance criteria* to judge or evaluate whether improvements in business performance have been achieved through BPR. The use of performance criteria to judge the success of any form of IS/IT engineering may include the following:

▶ end-user or customer satisfaction surveys
▶ reduced systems variable and fixed costs across the whole business
▶ increased systems productivity or efficiency as gauged by income and expenditure
▶ increased human effectiveness and efficiency as gauged by productivity
▶ increased overall business profit as gauged by return on resources employed.

The performance of current information systems can be further assessed by the use of a systems audit grid. Figure 4.3 shows a common systems audit grid, outlined by Michael Earl, to evaluate the usefulness of IS/IT to a business organisation.

The IS/IT 'systems audit grid' evaluates the strengths and weaknesses of IS/IT provision on the basis of *business contribution* and *technical quality*. If a system falls within the upper left-hand quadrant it indicates that the system is of low technical quality and low business contribution. Therefore, the business organisation would divest (or get rid of) its IT-based system. However, if the system falls within the lower right-hand quadrant this indicates that both the technical quality and the business contribution of the system are high. Therefore, the system should be enhanced with resources moved to support the enhancement. This type of evaluation model can also be used to identify IS/IT opportunities which can be aligned within the overall strategy of a business organisation. This is an approach to systems appraisal and construction that attempts to align IS/IT with the organisation's overall business strategy. Nevertheless, there are a number of studies that indicate there is a reluctance among business organisations to undertake such a radical reappraisal of business processes, within BPR, because of a fear of causing unnecessary change and upheaval within the business environment.

figure 4.3
**IT systems audit grid
(Earl 1989)**

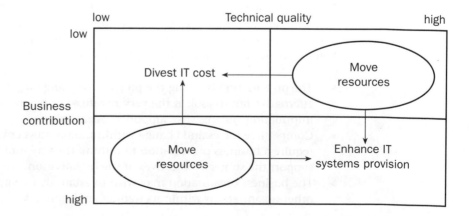

ACTIVITY **4.9**

Business process re-engineering

Discuss with colleagues some of the possible effects on the organisational structure of a business that undertakes BPR. Describe a set of *five* performance indicators that could be used to evaluate whether improvements in business performance have been achieved using BPR and then proceed to explain the relationship between BPR and the alignment of IS/IT with the top-level business strategy of an organisation.

4.10   Strategic information systems development

Strategic information systems development is not a self-contained methodology but an umbrella term for approaches to systems development that take into account the strategic nature of business information systems. The strategic area is particularly concerned with the following four business environment forces:

1   How IS/IT can be used as a means of achieving a *competitive advantage* within the business environment.
2   How IS/IT can be combined to improve overall *business performance* within an organisation.
3   How the appropriate use of IS/IT can develop new *products* or *services*.
4   How the appropriate use of IS/IT can be employed to improve the relationship between the business organisation and its *customers* and *suppliers*.

Strategic information systems development is concerned with finding innovative ways of undertaking business activity and increasing profit. Using IS/IT for competitive advantage is the task when trying to increase income rather than merely trying to reduce costs; reducing business costs is an attempt to improve *efficiency*, while increasing income is an attempt to improve *effectiveness*. Many of the ideas behind the use of IS/IT for competitive advantage evolve out of famous work done by Michael Porter of Harvard University that has been captured in three books on *Competitive Strategy* and *Competitive Advantage*, which are fully referenced at the end of this chapter.

> **DID YOU KNOW?**
> *Professor Michael Porter, who is reputed to be one of the wealthiest academics in the world, has identified five main competitive forces found within the business environment which he detailed in his book* Competitive Strategy *in 1980. These forces are as follows:*
> *1 The threat of new entrants.*
> *2 The threat of substitute services or products.*
> *3 The competition and rivalry between business organisations.*
> *4 The bargaining power of suppliers.*
> *5 The bargaining power of customers.*

The premise of *competitive strategy* is that a business organisation can achieve a competitive advantage within the business environment by dealing with one or all of the strategic forces more successfully than the other business organisations within that environment. For example, by avoiding the threat of new entrants, or even reducing the bargaining power of suppliers and customers within the business environment. The work done by Professor Porter provides a framework for *strategic information systems development* in that it highlights a model for decision making with regard to strategic systems. The work by Porter was taken up by Michael Earl in the late 1980s and early 1990s to highlight and illustrate the strategic role of IS/IT within the business environment. Earl set out a framework which indicated how information technology can be used to deal with Porter's five strategic forces. For example, IS/IT can be used to establish barriers to new entrants to the business environment; IS/IT can be used to reduce the influence of customers and suppliers; IS/IT can be used to add value to existing products and services or to create innovative new products and services.

This leads to the idea that business organisations need to formulate an *IS/IT strategy*. A superior IS/IT strategy can provide a competitive advantage in its own right, but it should include consideration of the following three aspects of the business organisation:

1   strategic aims and objectives of the organisation
2   analysis of current business processes and IS/IT
3   use and application of IS/IT within the organisation.

These three aspects form the tripod on which an IS/IT strategy can be constructed, with each aspect being determined by using various tools and techniques. For example, the aims and objectives of the business organisation can be established by the tools of SWOT analysis, JAD meetings, or ascertaining the critical success factors inherent to the organisation. The analysis of the current IS/IT configuration, which is the second aspect of the strategic model, can be assisted by the use of performance criteria to determine the efficiency and effectiveness of the current information systems. The third aspect of the IS/IT strategy attempts to find possible opportunities provided by IS/IT, which requires a review of current and future systems and technologies. However, care must be taken to avoid merely trying to match the technological configuration of competitor organisations; the investigation should establish how IS/IT can be used to enhance the inherent strengths of an organisation to provide it with an edge in the competitive business environment.

ACTIVITY **4.10**

Strategic information systems thinking

Discuss what is meant by the term *strategic information systems development* and indicate why it is important to consider the strategic level of a business organisation within systems development thinking. Then outline and describe four main forces that impact upon the strategic nature of information systems within a business organisation and compare them to Michael Porter's forces of *competitive strategy*. Do you believe that there are any further forces that can be aded to Professor Porter's list within competitive strategy?

4.11   Chapter summary

You will by this point have reviewed a number of alternative approaches to the traditional systems development life cycle (SDLC). Predominant among these is the umbrella approach known as rapid applications development (RAD) which embraces a number of tools and techniques to hasten the process of information systems development within the business environment. The chapter concluded with a review of approaches which included aspects of *strategic* information systems development. It is important to recognise that information systems development is not a prescriptive exercise, but rather can be a flexible activity that is determined by the dynamics and nature of the business environment in which an organisation operates.

Short self-assessment questions

4.1   Explain why most business organisations are considered to be *open systems* within the business environment.

4.2   Indicate and explain why a knowledge of human activity systems is important to systems development within business organisations.

4.3   Outline and describe the four main principles of rapid applications development (RAD) for information systems development within the business environment.

4.4   Describe why systems development productivity is measured in function points and explain how RAD may increase the productivity of function points in systems development.

4.5   Explain the reasons why group-based activity is important to the philosophy of RAD and indicate why the use of the TOBI method encourages good group composition.

4.6   Outline and explain the four phases of rapid applications development and describe which particular tools and techniques are appropriate in each phase.

4.7   Explain why speed of applications and systems development is so important to a competitive business organisation.

4.8   Define the term *joint applications development* (JAD) and explain the main emphasis within this approach to systems problem solving.

4.9   Outline and explain the three main principles behind JAD and describe the role and function of the independent *facilitator*.

4.10 Describe the function and use of the techniques of *story-boarding* and *rich pictures* to describe a system's overall environment.

4.11 List and explain the main advantages of using *prototyping* and suggest possible disadvantages in relation to end-user information systems development.

4.12 Outline and explain the five main steps of prototyping and suggest how these steps differ from the traditional stages of the traditional systems development life cycle approach.

4.13 Outline and describe six generic areas where software applications are found within the business environment.

4.14 Describe the main advantages and disadvantages of using pre-coded software application packages in the building of business information systems.

4.15 Explain why one of the main weaknesses of applications-based development lies in the fact of idiosyncratic systems being developed without regard to commonly practiced standards.

4.16 Define and explain what is meant by the term *business process re-engineering* (BPR) as used in business systems development.

4.17 Provide three main reasons why competitive organisations may wish to undertake the upheaval of business process re-engineering.

4.18 Explain how the formulation of an information systems and information technology (IS/IT) strategy can provide a competitive advantage to a business organisation.

References

Earl, M.J. (1989) *Management Strategies for Information Technology*. Englewood Cliffs, New Jersey: Prentice-Hall.

Hammer, M. and Champy, J. (1993) *Re-engineering the Corporation: A Manifesto for Business Revolution*. New York: Harper Business.

Porter, M.E. (1985) *Competitive Advantage*. New York: Collier-MacMillan. (*)

Porter, M.E. (1990) *The Competitive Advantage of Nations*, New York: Free Press.

Martin, J. (1991) *Rapid Applications Development*. Englewood Cliffs, New Jersey: MacMillan.

Porter, M.E. (1980) *Competitive Strategy*. New York: Free Press. (*)

Further study and reading

Books

Coad, P. and Yourdon, E. (1991) *Object Oriented Analysis*, 2nd edition. Englewood Cliffs, New Jersey: Prentice-Hall.

Davenport, T.H. (1993) *Process Innovation: Re-engineering Work through Information Technology*. Boston: Harvard Business School.

Rowley, J. (1994) *Strategic Management Information Systems and Technology*. Oxford: NCC Blackwell.

An asterisk (*) next to a book reference indicates a *seminal text* which means it constituted a source for later academic developments.

Journals

Beynon-Davies, P., Mackay, H., Slack, R. and Tudhope, D. (1996) Rapid applications development: the future of business systems development?, *Proceedings of 6th Annual Business Information Technology Conference*, Manchester Metropolitan University, 7 November, pp. 133–43.

Elliott, G. (1997) 2001 a systems odyssey: is rapid applications development a method or a madness of the Information Age?, *Proceedings of 4th Annual Financial Information Systems Conference*, Sheffield Hallam University, 2–3 July.

CHAPTER 5

Information systems tools and techniques

Objectives
....

After you have studied this chapter you will be able to:

▶ contrast and explain the difference between process modelling and data modelling within information systems development

▶ indicate and describe the use and application of tools and techniques for modelling information systems within the business environment

▶ understand and explain the difference between hard and soft tools and techniques for building effective business information systems

▶ evaluate and explain the advantages and disadvantages of the various tools and techniques for process modelling and data modelling

▶ describe the characteristics and usability of the various tools and techniques for analysis, design, implementation and evaluation of information systems.

DID YOU KNOW?
The definition of a 'tool' is anything that is used to assist a person in their activities; and the definition of a 'technique' is the body of procedures and methods of a science, art or activity.
(Websters Encyclopedic Dictionary)

DID YOU KNOW?
A 'model' is defined as a representation of the facts, factors and influences of an object or real world situation.

5.1   Introduction to information systems
....

This chapter will introduce a range of business information technology tools and techniques used to assist delivery of an information systems development project. Many of the tools and techniques covered are employed, to varying degrees, within the traditional SDLC and alternative approaches to information systems development, as described in the previous chapter. However, before listing and explaining the role and nature of each development tool and technique, it is important to understand the difference between *process modelling* and *data modelling*. Each of these modelling techniques requires a range of different tools and techniques.

A central theme of systems development is modelling the information systems environment. A model can be described as an abstract representation of the real world. The analysis and design stages of the information systems development process use modelling techniques to describe aspects of the proposed information system; a model is a useful way of describing and understanding how an information system will operate in reality. Modelling is also flexible, in that it allows various *parameters* (or constant variables) to be altered at will to analyse what influences and effects might impact on the proposed information system.

In the context of information systems development, the modelling activity is concerned with studying the functions and processes of information systems. A process is a progressive series of activities or changes that carry through the stages or phases of the development process. The systems analysis and systems design aspects of information systems development rely on a number of tools and techniques for describing business systems activity. These activities can be separated into three business processes as follows:

1 decision-making processes
2 information-based processes
3 functional processes.

These various processes must be decomposed into their *logical* parts so that a *conceptual model* of the information system (or sub-system components) can be constructed. The development aspects of systems analysis and systems design are concerned with two primary activities:

1 process modelling
2 data modelling.

Process modelling seeks to represent the various processes that are found within information systems, while data modelling is concerned with understanding and documenting data which forms the body and content of information systems. More recently, in the 1990s, there has been a resurgence of interest in object-oriented development (OOD) which attempts to include processes and data within *one* model and this was alluded to in the previous chapter.

5.2 Process modelling

Process modelling is concerned with identifying and analysing the various processes of an information system. This technique attempts to decompose the range of processes and functions of information systems into more manageable and understandable parts. For example, a complex information system can be decomposed down from the highest level into greater levels of detail which we know from chapter 1 is normally known as functional decomposition. A systems process will usually have one (or more) of the following characteristics:

▶ inputs and outputs
▶ control areas of the organisation
▶ involves decision making.

The technique of decomposition will normally continue until the most elementary processes are identified. Figure 5.1 shows an example of a business area known as business area '1' decomposed into three processes, known as A, B and C. Process C is further decomposed into elementary processes known as D, E and F. Figure 5.2 shows the activities of a finished goods *stock control system*, which has been hierarchically decomposed into various sub-processes. Process modelling is normally performed in a structured and disciplined fashion and will continue until the most elementary processes are identified within the overall information system.

It must be remembered that what is being modelled is the *logical* aspects of the information system and not the *physical* aspects of that system. Therefore, for analysis and design purposes, the logical must be separated from the physical within systems development thinking. The first task of *process modelling* is to define the boundaries of the system under analysis, then the main subsequent task is to

figure 5.1
**Process
decomposition**

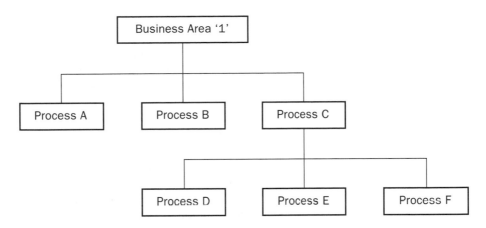

decompose higher-level processes into lower-level constituent processes. Decomposition is a *top-down* approach to the analysis of business systems processes. All systems *processes* should be defined as verbs (or action words), such as 'recording', 'handling' or 'processing', and there will usually be an *object* of the process which should be defined as a noun (or naming word), such as 'stock', 'product' or 'department'. For example, within the process of 'handling stock', handling is the (action) verb and stock is the (object) noun. It should be noticed that the processes often end in 'ing' as in handling and recording, which indicates activity, which is an underlying principle in defining a system from an inanimate object.

DID YOU KNOW?

Conceptual modelling requires an understanding of grammatical language in order to separate the logical thinking from physical thinking in the analysis and design of information systems. A 'verb' is an action or doing word (e.g. talking, computing, processing). An 'adverb' is a word that modifies an adjective or verb that expresses a relation of place, time, manner (e.g. gently, now, where, why). An 'adjective' is an attribute added to the name of something to describe it more fully, and a 'noun' is a word used to name a person, place, thing, state or quality (e.g. Edward, Susan, London, America).

It is during the activity of *process analysis* that the major group interaction often occurs between business specialists and technical specialists. Therefore, it is important that all the identifiable systems processes must be mutually agreed and confirmed by both the parties involved in the systems development project. *Process modelling* assists the activity of analysing and designing an information system by using structured tools and techniques which bring the technical specialist and user views of the system into line; this is particularly useful in the designing of systems that do not stand alone, but are integrated with other systems within the business environment.

figure 5.2
**Stock control
system
decomposition**

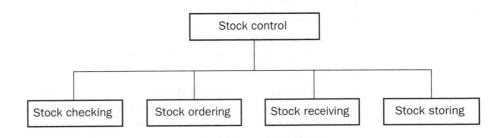

ACTIVITY **5.1**

Process modelling

Discuss and outline the main characteristics of *process modelling* and explain what is meant by functional decomposition. Once this has been understood, explain why *process analysis* should describe business systems processes as 'verbs' (or action words) which implies an activity within the business environment.

5.3   Data modelling

Data modelling is concerned with data structures and the *elements* of data, rather than information systems processes which are the preserve of process modelling. Data modelling is strongly related to aspects of *data storage* and *data structuring*; it is concerned with understanding, analysing and documenting data and information which forms the body of an information system. In a similar vein to process analysis it is important to separate out the physical data model from the logical data model; the idea being for the data model to be implementation independent. In other words it should not matter whether the technology used is IT based (such as a relational database), or even manual (such as a card file), as long as the logical model is correct. Therefore, the logical model will not be dependent upon the prevailing technology and should not be affected by technological change in the business environment; consequently a *logical data model* can be transcribed across a range of different information technologies and business environments.

Data modelling should systematically attempt to identify the data in a business environment and the relationship between data elements within the organisation. This analysis of the relationship between data elements is known as *data structuring* and the objective is to identify the data elements and analyse their structure and meaning within a business organisation. This data analysis activity relies on the gathering of data and information from the employees of a business organisation and other related sources. This can be done through observation of work tasks, interviews, analysing formal output documentation from various processes, and other human and electronic data capturing techniques. Once the data is collected and collated it can be modelled.

The data model is produced by using a number of tools and techniques, one particularly important technique being *entity modelling*. The essence of entity modelling is to establish the relationship between data elements within a business organisation; an entity can be described as a body or object such as customer, supplier, or employee. There are a number of techniques and tools used in the data modelling activity of information systems development as follows:

▶   entity-relationship diagrams (ERDs)
▶   entity life histories
▶   normalisation.

Since data and information is the life-blood of most business organisations, data modelling is an important activity in the analysis and design of information systems. Data modelling has a number of benefits as follows:

▶   Data models describe logical data relationships and not physical data relationships. This makes data modelling a stable activity even in environments of technological change. Therefore, data modelling is technology independent.

▶ A data model can be used by both technical specialists and business specialists. It can also be used to establish and confirm the user's data requirements of an information system.

▶ Data modelling is usually deterministic and rule based which permits it be understood across systems and organisations. Therefore, data modelling is not specific to any one business organisation and it can be readily translated into a computerised database model.

ACTIVITY **5.2**

Data modelling

Explain what is meant by the terms *data structuring* and *entity modelling* and explain the various ways by which data may be captured and recorded within a business organisation. Data capture can be carried out by investigating existing business documentation, or by a range of other means such as observation of employees and work practices, interviews and questionnaires. You are required to list and explain six methods of capturing and recording data, of which three must be electronic (or IT-based) methods and three must be human-based methods (or a mixture of both). For example, lorries that deliver building-site raw materials, for construction purposes, are often electronically weighed on a platform sensor which automatically calculates the weight of raw materials being carried by the lorry. (Clue: think of the retail and banking sector and how data is captured and recorded.)

5.4 Tools and techniques of process modelling

There are a number of tools and techniques used to document the analysis and design activities of information systems development. The most widely used tools within *process modelling* are the following:

▶ flowcharting
▶ data flow diagrams (DFDs)
▶ decision tables
▶ Structured English.

Flowcharting

One of the underlying problems with agreeing a logical (or conceptual) model of processes within a system is the fact that people will generally describe work processes in physical terms. For example, the recording of accounting data may be described as 'I sit at a computer and type in various numbers each morning!', or the handling of stock may be described as 'I move this box from the stock room to the distribution department each Tuesday afternoon'. The latter description may be indicating the *logical* activity of handling stock but this is not apparent from this given *physical* description. Therefore, it is imperative to convert physical activity to logical processes by using a structured framework of systems tools and techniques. The tools mentioned above help to ease the task of converting the physical description of existing activities into a logical process model. Before a logical model can be constructed there is a need to document the processes in some form of descriptive language. System flowcharts show the

figure 5.3
**Basic systems
flowcharting symbols**

Process   File storage   Input/output   Document

Auxiliary
operation   Keying operation   On-line input   Preparation

Direction of flows

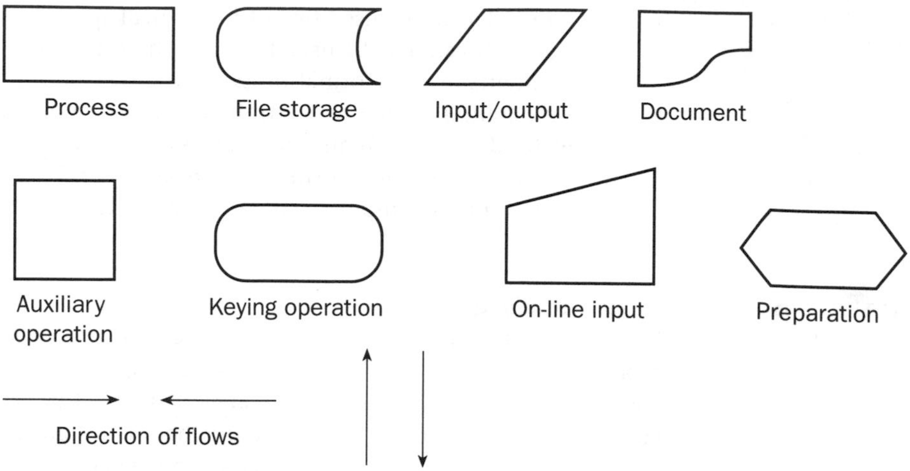

relationship between systems (or applications) within a business organisation; such flowcharts can exist in two main forms as follows:

1   system flowcharting
2   program flowcharting.

Figure 5.3 shows a set of basic systems flowcharting symbols. Notice that the central symbol is the square box which represents the systems process.

Figure 5.4 shows a set of basic program flowcharting symbols. Program flowcharts graphically describe the steps that are followed in a specific computer program as opposed to systems flowcharts that describe an entire information system.

figure 5.4
**Basic program
flowcharting symbols**

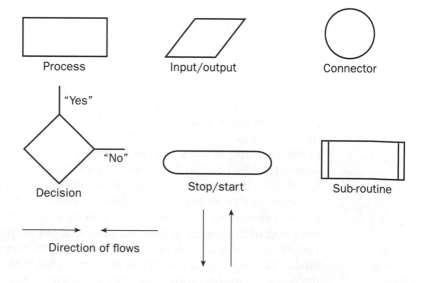

Process   Input/output   Connector

"Yes"

"No"

Decision   Stop/start   Sub-routine

Direction of flows

figure 5.5
**Simplified systems
flowchart**

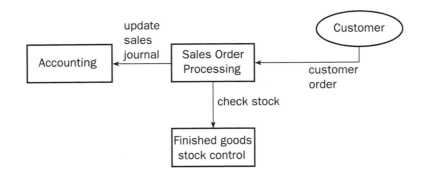

figure 5.5
**Simplified systems
flowchart**

System flowcharting can be further divided into (a) simplified systems flow-charts and (b) detailed systems flowcharts. A simplified systems flowchart merely shows the relationship between various systems processes within a business organisation. For example, Figure 5.5 shows the simplified relationship between three systems processes of *sales order processing, finished stock control* and *accounting*. A detailed systems flowchart shows all the various documents, files and activities that impact on a particular systems process. Figure 5.6 shows a detailed systems flowchart for a typical accounting system process.

Program flowcharting is similar to systems flowcharting. Program flow-charting graphically documents the steps that are followed in a specific software program rather than systems flowcharts which depict an entire information

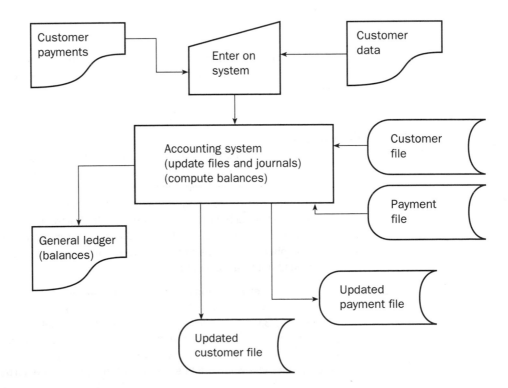

figure 5.6
**Detailed systems
flowchart**

system. Program flowcharts are drawn using three control structures for executing instructions. These are as follows:

1 *Sequence structure.* A series of statements that are executed in the order in which they appear. For example, statement B will follow statement A.
2 *Selection structure.* A series of statements that test a condition, such as, 'true' or 'false', 'yes' or 'no', 'off' or 'on', '1' or '0'. Depending upon whether the results of the test are true or false, one of two alternative instructions will be executed.
3 *Iteration structure.* A series of statements that repeats an instruction as long as the results of the condition are true. For example, statement B will be executed as long as condition X is always satisfied.

Systems flowcharts document the sequence and integration of processes that occur within an information system, and data and information input and output is of paramount importance. Flowcharts use formalised symbols (see Figures 5.3 and 5.4) to represent information flows and the related processing activities. Systems flowcharts depict the flow of documentation (and records) as inputs and outputs in an information system. The wider the symbol vocabulary the more articulate can be the analysis. Therefore, flowcharting is a graphic form of representing information flows within a business organisation.

Program flowcharts have a number of advantages in assisting in process analysis and the development of a process model. These advantages are as follows:

▶ Program flowcharts provide a structured framework for designing logical software programs which abide by certain design principles.
▶ Flowcharts are a useful graphical representation of a process that graphically shows the technical specialist and the business specialist the correctness and suitability of the process design.
▶ Flowcharts can be incorporated into any systems or end-user documentation as instructional or reference material for continued systems maintenance.

ACTIVITY **5.3**
••••••••••••

Flowcharting

Discuss the difference between systems flowcharting and program flowcharting and describe why such graphical flowcharting techniques are important in the activity of information systems analysis and design. In order to build effective information systems we need to be able to understand the operation of logical model building applying flowcharting techniques. Read carefully the following narrative which describes the decision-making activities of Gillian Baker in both physical and logical terms. (Remember you will need to separate out the logical aspects of the narrative in order to build a logical conceptual model.)

Gillian Baker met Steve Jones a few days before and Steve had said he would meet Gillian at the Abbey Conference meeting room on Friday afternoon at 3.00 pm. Gillian wanted to attend the meeting but was not sure if he was going to chair the meeting or whether it would be chaired by an outsider (in which case she would not attend). Anyway, Gillian was not sure whether she would be busy Friday afternoon and she certainly was not going to go along to the meeting if no one else was attending from her department!

Answer the following questions based on the above abstract:

1 Separate out the logical from the physical aspects of Gillian's job.
2 Break down the decisions into their component parts within the system.
3 Identify the decisions and label them '1' or '0' depending on whether the decision is 'yes' or 'no'.
4 Identify what action will be undertaken to acquire any further information for each decision in the decision chain.
5 Draw a flowchart to describe the decision-making activities of Gillian Baker.

Data flow diagrams (DFDs)

DFDs emphasise the structured nature of data processes. They assist in the construction of a logical system model, unlike flowcharts that often describe a system in terms of the physical files and documentation and storage mediums. Data flow diagrams are a graphical tool that show flows of data within an information system and the various processes that act upon (and transform) the data. DFDs are very important for defining the logical design of an information system. It is important to understand that data flows through a system can be manual or automated and involve human interaction. DFDs do not make any distinction because it is the logical aspects of the system that are investigated. There exists logical and physical independence. Data flow diagrams use a restricted set of symbols, which are shown in Figure 5.7. The data flow diagrams can be constructed using only four basic symbols. Data flow diagramming is a graphical technique that can be used as documentation of an information system or a communications tool between the technical and business specialists of a business organisation.

figure 5.7
Symbols used for data flow diagramming

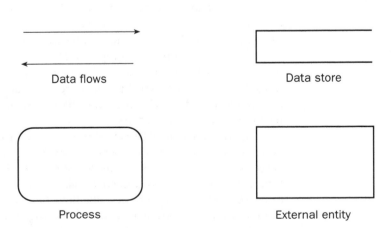

Data flows

Data store

Process

External entity

It can be seen that data flow diagrams can be constructed by using just four graphical symbols, as follows:

1   data flow
2   data process
3   data store
4   external data entity.

Data flow is represented by an arrow which points into or out of a data process; it indicates that data is moving from one process to another process and the direction of the flow. The nature of the data flow is uniquely labelled as it passes through the system. Data flows can be single data elements or multiple data elements. Data flows may consist of computer files, reports or other data representations.

Data processes indicate the tasks to be performed on the data flows. The data process is represented by a round-edged box. The process is an activity that transforms or alters the data in some way. For example, the data may be sorted, merged or verified. The round-edged box symbol usually has three compartments at the top, middle and bottom of the box. The top compartment contains a reference number for the process. The middle compartment contains the description of the process. The bottom compartment contains information on the location where the process occurs (see Figure 5.8). The data process box should usually have a data flow into the box and a data outflow from the box.

Data stores are represented by an open-ended rectangle which is uniquely labelled. Data stores are where data flows finally stop. A data store contains data from a process or stored data for retrieval to a process. Unlike flowcharts a data store symbol within a DFD does not indicate the type of storage media used; it can be a computerised file or even a manual handwritten list. The data store has two compartments, one for a reference code and the other indicating the name of the data store (see Figure 5.8).

External data entities are symbolised by a rectangle or square and represent an external source or destination of data (see Figure 5.8). Again this is where data may finally stop. External data entities may be external to the business organisation, such as customers or suppliers. They may also be another separate system within the business organisation. These external data entities are often referred to as data sources or data sinks. A source indicates data coming into a business organisation and a sink indicates data leaving an organisation and being received by an external entity.

The advantage of DFDs is that they use only four symbols and they are independent of the method of processing, so they can be used to describe either IT-based or manual systems. Figure 5.8 shows the DFD symbols being used for a typical business process known as *sales order processing*, which has been the example used previously to describe flowcharting. Within sales order processing there is an activity known as stock checking to determine whether a business organisation holds sufficient stock to meet a customer order.

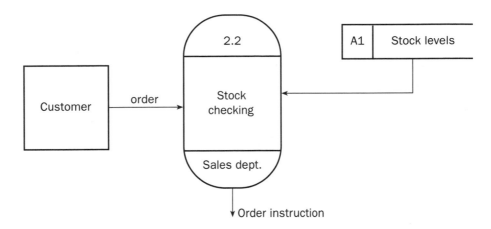

figure 5.8
**DFD symbols
(process of stock
checking)**

Data flow diagrams are constructed to visualise an information system at various decomposed levels of detail. The top level of detail can be broken down into deeper and deeper layers of detail. The very top level of symbolic representation is known as a *context diagram*. This is a general and broad representation of an information system. This context diagram can be broken into successive layers of detail. Therefore, the levels of a DFD are constructed using a top-down approach which begins with a context diagram and is broken down into level 1, level 2, level 3 and so on until the absolute level of detail is reached. The top level context diagram consists of the overall system being represented as a single process box, which alludes to the external entities. The data flows to and from the external data entities are represented by labelled arrows. The decomposition of the context diagram into further levels provides greater detail of the system being studied. This process of decomposition in the context of DFDs is known as *levelling*.

Figure 5.9 shows the top level, or context diagram, for a sales order processing system. The system is represented by a single process circle (or 'black-box') which alludes to the external entities of customer, storehouse and credit agency. This can be ascribed as level 0. Figure 5.10 shows this context diagram broken down to level 1, giving more detail of the processes of the sales order processing system.

figure 5.9
**Context diagram
(level 0) for a sales
order processing
system**

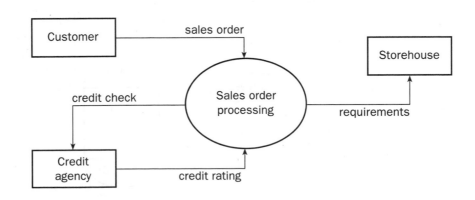

figure 5.10
**Level 1 diagram for a
sales order
processing system
(checking order)**

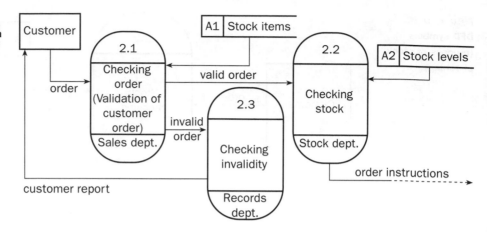

The level 0 diagram is known as the 'context diagram' because it shows the extent of the system boundaries. In Figure 5.9 the system's boundaries are shown by a circle bounding the system; in this case the 'sales order processing system'. The level 0 context diagram also should normally show all of the external entities (indicated by a square box), and the inputs and outputs (indicated by narrated arrows). Within sales order processing there is a sub-process known as stock checking where a customer's order is checked against existing stock items held by the organisation. If there are available items of finished stock, these will be dispatched to the customer, after all other checks (such as the customer's credit rating) have been made relating to the order. Figure 5.10 shows the process of 'checking order' and its related level 1 processes and data stores. Figure 5.11 shows a level 2 diagram revealing flows that exist *within* the process known as 'checking order'.

Within data flow diagramming the processes can be 'exploded' into greater levels of detail. In Figure 5.11 the process of checking order has been exploded down to three sub-processes of recording customer details, calculating customer bonuses, and generating invoices and reports.

figure 5.11
**Level 2 diagram for
a sales order
processing system
(checking order)**

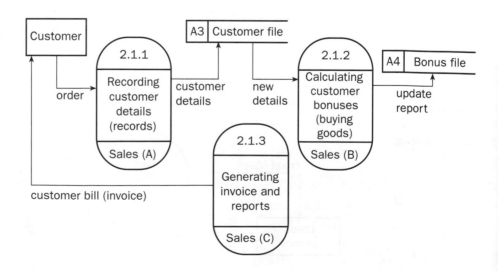

The DFDs can be refined and agreed by both the business specialists and the technical specialists until both are satisfied that the system has been correctly documented. The advantage of DFDs is that they are usually understood by business systems end-users with relatively little instruction. Collateral to the activity of levelling will be the activity of collecting details of each piece of data used in the DFDs. Details about each piece of data used in the data flows is contained in a *data dictionary* which contains information about the data flows and data stores in the DFDs. Data dictionaries provide information on all the data elements within an information system.

ACTIVITY **5.4**

Data flow diagrams

Discuss the role, purpose and function of data flow diagrams (DFDs) within process modelling and describe how DFDs are broken down into lower and lower levels of detail. Then explain what is meant by a context diagram and draw and annotate a context diagram to represent level 0 for a *purchase order processing* system.

Decision tables

Another tool which can be used to document the logic of process modelling is the *decision table*. This is a tool that facilitates the documentation of logical process modelling. The processes that are identified in DFDs are often described in written narrative. But sometimes this is not adequate for the purpose of describing complex actions which occur within a data process. What is required is a decision table to describe what is taking place in the process by defining the *conditions* and *actions* of the process. Decision tables are a tabular representation of complex conditions and actions that cannot easily be documented in written form. Decision tables can be separated into four separate quadrants with a format as follows:

Condition stub	Condition rules
Action stub	Action entries

The top line lists the conditions to be tested, whereas the bottom line lists the range of possible actions to be undertaken. The *condition stub* lists all of the possible conditions that can arise during a process, while the *action stub* lists all of the possible actions that can occur within a process. The *condition rules* contain a binary entry for each possible combination of conditions, for example, 'yes' or 'no', 'on' or 'off', '1' or '0'. The action entries indicate the action to be performed under specific and unique conditions. Decision tables are a way of representing the logic of a complex process where a number of actions can be undertaken given a finite set of conditions.

For example, consider a process within *sales order processing* known as 'validating customer order'. This process checks if a customer has a satisfactory credit rating or is an acceptable person to trade with for a business organisation. If the customer has a satisfactory credit rating, or is a regular cash payer, the order will

table 5.1
Decision table for validating a customer order

	1	2	3	4
Credit satisfactory	Y	Y	N	N
Cash payer	Y	N	Y	N
Approve order	x	x	x	
Reject order				x

be approved for goods to be sent to the customer. If the customer does not have a satisfactory credit rating, or is not a regular cash payer, the order will be rejected. Therefore, the two conditions are credit satisfactory or cash payer. Each condition will have an action entry of either 'yes' or 'no'. The two actions will be either approve order or reject order. The decision table is represented in Table 5.1.

There are obviously only four possible permutations for the conditions of credit satisfactory and cash payer (i.e. YY, YN, NY, NN).

ACTIVITY 5.5

Decision tables

The following is a process related to delivery charges for goods bought from Norman Payne Enterprises. For the purposes of determining price reductions (rebates) for buying in bulk, the business organisation divides customers into two categories; those who buy 500 or more units of a product at one time and those who buy less than 500 units at one time. If the number of units bought is equal to 500, or more than 500, the overall price is reduced by 15%. If the number of units sold is 500 or more and the customer has a Payne Enterprises Charge Card, the overall price is reduced by 25%. You are required to do the following:

1   Discuss why a business organisation would wish to charge customers a different price according to the amount bought and having a charge card.
2   Draw a flowchart to represent the decisions that need to be made regarding the different delivery charges.
3   Draw a decision table to reflect the conditions and actions to determine the different delivery charges according to sales region code.

Structured English

In addition to flowcharting, data flow diagramming and decision tables, another technique can be used to represent processes which is known as *Structured English*, which is a precise approach to process or procedure design that uses a restricted sub-set of the natural English language. Therefore, plain English statements rather than graphic symbols describe the processing stages and logic of the information systems activities. This is sometimes referred to as *pseudo-code*. There are a number of rules that underpin the use of Structured English as follows:

▶   Complex sentences and grammatical structures are broken down into logical parts.
▶   Use of statements that contain a precise verb and object (e.g. compute tax).
▶   Avoid all adjectives, adverbs and other words of vague meaning.

▶ Ignore words and sentences that are irrelevant to the process.
▶ Use unique terms to identify items of data within the process.
▶ Consistently use data terms found within DFDs and associated data dictionaries.

What decision tables, logic flowcharting and Structured English provide is a structured approach analysing processes which may assist the eventual technical systems programming or applications-based development. However, there is an obvious trade-off between wishing to maintain the user-friendliness of the graphical approach and the requirement to encourage structured program design and construction.

ACTIVITY **5.6**

Structured English

Define the term *Structured English* as used in the context of business information systems development and indicate its usefulness to the activity of process modelling. Then proceed to describe the rules that underpin the use of Structured English and explain why the technique is sometimes referred to as *pseudo-code*.

5.5 Tools and techniques of data modelling

The development of database technology and database management systems (DBMSs) has led to a greater emphasis within the modelling of business information systems on data and data structures. Data analysis techniques were initially developed to assist the construction and implementation of database systems. Therefore, this area is strongly related to issues of data storage and database structuring However, data modelling is now a useful and general technique used to analyse any data structures found within the business information systems environment. The main technique used in data modelling is known as *entity modelling*. The essence of entity modelling is to establish the *relationship* between data elements within a business organisation. An entity can be defined as a 'body' or 'object' such as a customer, supplier, employee or any other noun that is of interest to the business organisation. The data structures of an organisation can be graphically represented through the use of entity-relationship diagrams (ERDs), a design tool which represents all of the information requirements of a system. Entity-relationship diagrams use just three component objects to model data relationships within an information system. These components can be used to construct a model that reveals the data configuration and structures of an information system. The three component objects of the ERD are as follows:

1 the entity
2 the attribute.
3 the relationship.

The entity-attribute-relationship model is sometimes known by the initials EAR, or sometimes the E-R model for short. An *entity* is something about which data is to be stored. The key characteristic of an entity is that it is capable of independent existence within an organisation. For example, a customer, supplier, employee or product might be entities about which a business may wish to store information. These objects are of interest to the business organisation. Entities are usually represented as rectangles. An *attribute* is a fact that needs to be stored about an entity. For example, the attributes of the entity 'customer' may be name, address, unique customer number and credit status. Another example may be the entity 'employee' which may have the attribute's name, address, date of birth, employee number, and department name. Attributes can be considered properties of an entity. Within database construction an attribute is known as a field. Each entity should possess a unique attribute which is known as the *key attribute*. The key attribute is a separate and unique characteristic that is not duplicated within the overall data structure of an information system. For example, a unique 'customer number' could be a key attribute of the entity 'customer'. If this was the case, a unique customer number should identify only one customer of the business organisation and not multiple customers in order to be a key attribute.

Entity types within a business organisation may bear some *relationship* to one another within that business organisation. For example, there may be a relationship between the entities of 'customer' and 'order', or between the entities of 'employee' and 'department'. However, it may be the case that not all entities will bear relationships to all other entities within the business organisation. The relationship between entities is shown in an ERD by lines between the rectangular boxes. The relationship between entities is of particular importance to data modelling. The relationship between two entities will be addressed with some form of descriptive term which defines the relationship between the two entities. For example, within the relationship 'customer places order', the 'customer' and the 'order' are entities and the descriptive relationship name is 'places'. Another example might be the relationship between 'customer returns product', where 'customer' and 'product' are entities and 'returns' is the descriptive relationship term.

For example, in a typical business organisation the first task of data modelling would be to identify the entities of the organisation. Figure 5.12 shows four identified entities of 'employee', 'department', 'management staff' and 'technical staff'. It can be seen that there is a relationship between the employee and the department and employee and management staff (which might indicate the

figure 5.12
Entity modelling

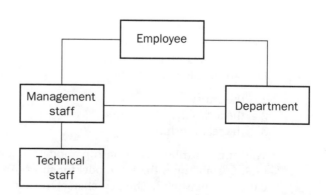

figure 5.13

Entity modelling with relationships

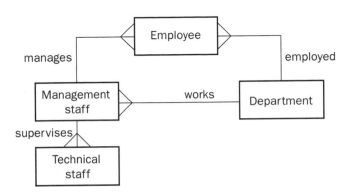

employee's line manager). However, no attributes have been defined for the entities in Figure 5.12. However, Figure 5.13 shows the same entity relationships with information on the attributes of each entity. The attributes should define the properties of the entity. Notice that an employee may only have one department, but a department entity may have many employees. Also, each department appears to have many managers. What has been revealed is the fact that there may be multiple relationships between entities. Data modelling using ERDs gives rise to three generic relationships as follows:

1   one-to-one relationship (denoted by the symbolic ratio of 1:1).
2   one-to-many relationship (denoted by the symbolic ratio of 1:*m*).
3   many-to-many relationship (denoted by the symbolic ratio of *m:m*).

These relationships are graphically shown in Figures 5.12, 5.13 and 5.14.

Figure 5.14 shows a one-to-one relationship between the two entities of man and woman. The descriptive relationship term is known as 'marries'. This one-to-one relationship will occur if one man is allowed to marry only one woman. If one man is allowed to marry many women, then the relationship will be described as one-to-many. The diagram also shows a one-to-many relationship, as when a customer places an order. The many-to-many relationship is represented by many customers buying many products (or many products delivered to many customers). There are four main stages to *entity analysis* within data modelling as follows:

figure 5.14

Entity relationships

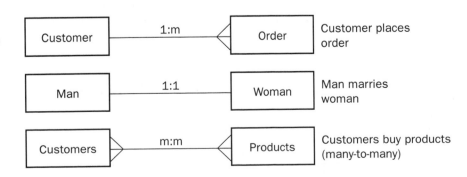

1 Define and set the boundaries for analysis.
2 Define the entities and establish the relationships between entities.
3 Establish the attributes and key attribute for each entity.
4 Normalise all of the entities.

ACTIVITY **5.7**

Entity-relationship diagramming

Define and explain the technique of entity-relationship diagramming to analyse a business information system, then create an E-R diagram to show the relationships between the entities 'supplier' and 'order', and between 'product' and 'order part'.

The E-R diagrams can be converted to a physical database, where each of the entities will become a table (sometimes known as a record) and each attribute will become a field on a table. In order to find the most effective database design a technique known as *normalisation* is used.

In order to establish a valid data model it must be fully normalised. This is the process of creating the most effective design for the data model. Normalisation aims to improve the logical design of entity-relationship models by making it free of redundant data, so that each fact is only recorded in one place, and to be flexible enough to allow future additions of entities, attributes and relationships without producing anomalies within the data model. Normalisation is a formalised technique for ensuring organisation within data structuring, so that updating a piece of data should only require adjustment in one place and deleting a piece of data should not lead to loss of other data.

The technique of normalisation developed as a response to the development of integrated database technology which shared common data files. The issue of insertion, deletion and updating of data becomes a more significant problem if many files are affected on an integrated database system. Normalisation attempts to rationalise data storage in order to simplify the process of insertion, deletion and updating of data. For example, Table 5.2 shows a sales-order relationship as a table.

In Table 5.2, customer name, product code and quantity ordered are attributes of the entity 'sales-order'. This is a simple form of entity-relationship model. Each row in a relation table is called a *tuple*. No two tuples should be identical in the entity-relationship model. In Table 5.2 the key attribute is customer name. However, in reality there may be more than one customer with the same name, so a unique customer number attribute would be more appropriate. This is shown in Table 5.3.

table 5.2
Sales-order relationship (three attributes)

Customer name	Product code	Quantity ordered
Khan	C443185	35
Morris	F429008	13
Smith	C329859	8

	Customer number	Customer name	Product code	Quantity ordered
	3456	Khan	C443185	35
	4469	Morris	F429008	13
	8995	Smith	C329859	8

table 5.3 **Sales-order relationship (four attributes)**

In Table 5.3 the key attribute is customer number. The table sales-order with the four attributes of customer number, customer name, product code and quantity ordered (with the key attribute of customer number) can be expressed in shorthand, notation as: sales-order (number, name, code, quantity). Normalisation can be used in its own right to structure any form of data in a business organisation, but commonly, it is done prior to the development of a computerised database system.

Later writers on normalisation, since Ted Codd, have suggested up to five levels of normalisation can be achieved. Under the original academic theory, achieving third normal form is considered satisfactory in practice and forms the basis of most data models.

In *first normal form* all the attributes are established at their most basic level and each attribute should have only one possible value. The aim of first normal form is to remove all of the repeated occurrences of attributes in the logical design, thus eliminating redundant data. In *second normal form* all the attributes that are not key attributes should be functionally *dependent* upon the key attribute. Therefore, all non-key attributes must be dependent on the key attribute. In order to convert to second normal form, any attribute which is not dependent upon a key attribute must be removed and placed in a different table along with the key attribute on which it is dependent. In *third normal form* all the non-key attributes should be functionally independent of each other attribute. Therefore, the aim is that there are no non-key attributes which are dependent upon any other non-key attributes. Once this level of normalisation is complete, the tables are referred to as fully normalised.

The aim is to make all the attributes in a relation table dependent upon the key attribute and nothing but the key attribute. For example, the key attribute of customer number (in Table 5.3) will probably have functionally dependent attributes of customer name and customer address. The customer name and customer address attributes should not be found anywhere else other than 'attached' and dependent upon the key attribute of customer number.

ACTIVITY **5.8**

Data normalisation

Define the term *normalisation* and explain why the process of normalisation is so important to the construction of physical databases. Then explain and describe the steps involved in first normal form, second normal form and third normal form. Once this has been done, indicate the significance of functional dependency whereby non-key attributes are dependent upon a key attribute.

5.6   Soft systems tools and techniques

Many of the techniques and tools so far discussed originate out of the traditional SDLC and other structured methods used to assist information systems development. However, when an information system is being developed at the management and executive levels of a business organisation the systems environment is often unclear or referred to as 'fuzzy'. In such environments it is suggested that less structured tools and techniques should be used. This is often known as a *soft systems approach*. The soft systems approach uses its own tools and techniques for analysing and designing the information systems environment. Three of the main techniques used are as follows:

1   rich pictures
2   root definitions
3   conceptual modelling.

All of these three techniques assist the analysis of information systems within the business environment. They originate from the soft systems methodology (SSM) of Peter Checkland (1981). The soft systems methodology will be studied in greater detail in the next chapter.

A *rich picture* should take into consideration all the issues related to the systems environment and boundaries. The rich picture should address people, organisation, technology and internal and external political issues. The rich picture may also include social roles and human behaviour present within the systems environment. The rich picture attempts explicitly to highlight conflicts of interest which are not considered, to the same extent, by other tools and techniques. A rich picture uses graphics and symbols to express the issues within a system's boundaries. It should be a *holistic view* of the role and purpose of the systems within a business organisation. It is essential that the rich picture is easily understood and requires little or no explanation. A rich picture should include both hard (objective) facts and soft (subjective) information about the business organisation. Since business is a human activity system, the rich picture technique is a useful way of analysing human to systems interaction. The rich picture can then be used as a communications tool to encourage users and systems participants to reveal their particular view of the systems environment.

A rich picture should set out to establish the elements of the system and then to look at the processes that are evident between the elements. The rich picture uses sketched objects that are linked by lines and arrows to indicate a relationship between elements. There is no universal set of symbols; any symbols or pictures that seem appropriate can be used. However, two symbols that appear to be used as standards within rich pictures are crossed swords and think-bubbles. A crossed sword indicates some form of conflict and the think-bubbles indicate the concerns of the participants within the system. Figure 5.15 is an example of a rich picture. There are five main advantages in using rich pictures as follows:

1   The act of putting pen to paper *focuses all participants* in the process of defining the systems environment.
2   Visual images are a more direct way of *eliciting the issues* of an information system than words or lengthy narrative.

figure 5.15

Rich picture (a university part-time course unit)

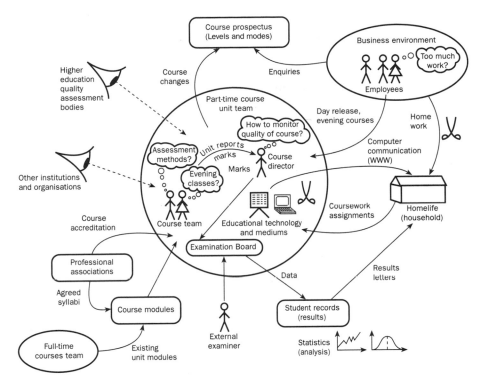

Rich picture key:

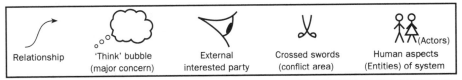

Relationship	'Think' bubble (major concern)	External interested party	Crossed swords (conflict area)	Human aspects (Entities) of system

Elements of the structure of the 'problem area' include:

1. Departmental and functional boundaries.
2. Types of activity.
3. Physical and geographical layout.
4. Types of product and service.
5. Processes, goals and actions (Determine 'what is going on').
6. Information flows.
7. Views of people within domains.

Aims of the rich picture

1. Include all relevant hard facts.
2. Include all relevant soft issues.
3. Express the problems, issues, conflicts, people ('actors') involved in the problem situation.
4. Identify issues and matters of concern.

3   It incorporates *human, social and political issues* to a greater extent than other tools and techniques of systems development.
4   It can be used as a *communications tool* between technical specialists and business specialists.
5   It encourages *participation* in the analysis and design of information systems by the end-users.

The rich picture should aim to highlight the primary purposes of the business organisation at the highest level. The secondary purpose is to identify the issues which matter and are of concern in the development of an efficient and effective information system. However, the technique does require a high level of individual freedom to allow political and human issues to be debated by all participants irrespective of their level and role within the business organisation.

ACTIVITY **5.9**
· · · · · · · · · · · · · ·

Rich pictures

Discuss and explain the technique of *rich pictures* and indicate why it is referred to as a soft systems approach to information systems analysis and design. Once the technique has been understood, draw a rich picture to describe the systems environment of a mail-order business and remember to highlight conflicts of interest.

A *root definition* is a concise description of the essential nature of an information system. The root definition is developed by considering six characteristics of an information system. The six characteristics are known by the mnemonic CATWOE which represents:

Client that is affected by the information system.
Actor is an agent of process transformation and change.
Transformation is the change that is taking place.
Weltanschauung is the established world view of assumptions.
Owner is the sponsor of the information system.
Environment relates to the wider system.

The use of CATWOE is a way of getting all participants in the system to agree and focus on a suitable root definition. By its nature the formulation of a root definition is a good way of exposing the different views of all the system participants.

DID YOU KNOW?
The term 'Weltanschauung' is a German word which refers to the idea that people and organisations are bound by a cultural, political and social view of ideas and attitudes.

A *conceptual model* shows how the various processes or activities of an information system are related and logically connected. It is a vital prerequisite to the design of an information system in that it establishes the foundations for the implementation of the information system. The conceptual model should ideally be understood and agreed by the business specialists and the technical specialists and should take its essential form from the *root definition*. The conceptual model should be sketched through a number of levels with each level describing the actions of a particular process or sub-system.

The conceptual model is an attempt to do things better and recognises that there may be more than one way to achieve a particular systems solution. The conceptual model can be compared with reality and is particularly useful in highlighting informal information flows within a business organisation. This is also true of rich pictures that look at both formal and informal information flows. It also serves as a tool for analysis and design, as a medium of communi-

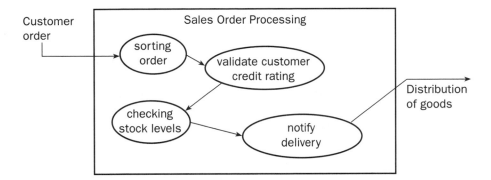

figure 5.16
Level 1 conceptual model

cation between the designers and client end-users, and as a set of instructions for the implementation of the information system. Figure 5.16 shows an example of a conceptual model sketch for a sales order processing system at one level of detail. Figure 5.17 shows the same conceptual model detailed down to level 2.

The conceptual model will be derived and drawn from the root definition. The root definition will form the overall mission statement for the business organisation, which will determine the shape and character of the required information systems.

The conceptual model is formed from the accepted root definition. The steps to forming the conceptual model should be as follows:

▶ Establish a holistic impression of the system as based on the root definition using verbs to describe the activities within the boundaries of the system.
▶ Determine the requirements of the system and outline aspects of monitoring and control of the various aspects of the system.
▶ Group together generic activities and logically connect each of these activities with arrows to indicate various flows of information.
▶ Finally, verify the model by comparing it to the real world problem situation.

The conceptual model should illustrate what ought to be happening within the information systems environment; it attempts to achieve the objectives established in the overall root definition.

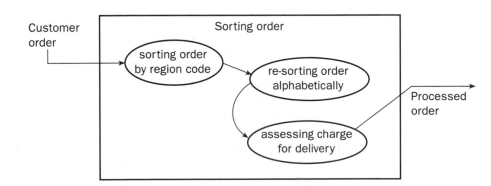

figure 5.17
Level 2 conceptual model

5.7   Chapter summary

Process modelling assists the activity of designing and constructing an information system by using structured tools and techniques which help bring the technical specialist and user views of the system into line. Process analysis modelling is particularly useful to the design of systems that are not stand alone, but are integrated with other systems, within a business organisation. In support of process modelling is data modelling which concentrates on establishing the relationships between components of data, which is a useful prerequisite technique for creating physical database systems. Both process modelling and data modelling requires a range of different tools and techniques. These various tools and techniques are used within an information systems development process to assist the analysis and design activities. It should be evident from this chapter that a fundamental theme of systems development is modelling information systems processes and activities within the business environment. Modelling is an essential exercise within the process of systems development. The modelling activity relies on a number of tools and techniques for describing business systems activity which can be separated into decision-making processes, information-based processes and functional processes. The following chapter will study how the tools and techniques covered are integrated into the fabric of various information systems development methodologies.

Short self-assessment questions

5.1 Briefly explain the difference between *process modelling* and *data modelling* in information systems development.

5.2 Define and explain the terms *tool* and *technique* and define the term *modelling* as applied in information systems.

5.3 Define and explain what is meant by the term *data modelling* and why such modelling is important to any business organisation.

5.4 Explain why the use of flowcharting may assist the analysis of decision making within a business organisation.

5.5 Outline the main advantages and disadvantages of using flowcharting within an information systems development project.

5.6 Outline three main advantages of using data flow diagrams and compare the usefulness of DFDs with other flowcharting techniques.

5.7 Define and explain when it is appropriate to use decision tables to describe and model processes within an information system.

5.8 Explain and describe the four quadrants of a decision table for recruiting part-time staff to a business organisation. (Remember you must identify your conditions and actions in order to complete the decision table).

5.9 Explain the terms of *entity*, *relationship* and *attribute* and provide three examples to describe a one-to-one, many-to-many and one-to-many relationship.

5.10 Outline the main advantages of using rich pictures and indicate why it is important to have a holistic view of a business organisation and its systems.

References
• • • • • • • • • • • • • •

Checkland, P. (1981) *Systems Thinking, Systems Practice*. Chichester, England: John Wiley. (*)

Codd, E.F. (1970) A relational model of data for large shared data banks, *Communications of the ACM*, 13(6) (*).

Further study and reading
• •

Books

Avison, D.E. (1992*) Information Systems Development: A Database Approach*, 2nd edition. Maidenhead, England: McGraw-Hill.

Corr, B. (1995) *Essential Elements of Business Information Systems*. London: DP Publications.

Curtis, G. (1989) *Business Information Systems*. Wokingham, England: Addison-Wesley

Date, C.J. (1995) *An Introduction to Database Systems*, 6th edition. Wokingham, England: Addison-Wesley.

Senn, J.A. (1989) *Analysis and Design of Information Systems*, 2nd edition. New York: McGraw-Hill.

Skidmore, S. (1996) *Introducing Systems Design*, 2nd edition. Oxford: NCC Blackwell.

An asterisk (*) next to a book reference indicates a *seminal text* which means it constituted a source for later developments.

Information systems methodologies

6.1 Introduction to information systems methods

The development of information systems within business organisations requires a framework, or method, to guide and control the development process. A number of information systems methodologies have been proposed and published since the early 1970s, to organise and coordinate the development of information systems within the business environment. Often a methodology is named after the individual, or group of individuals, that proposed or developed the methodology; these are often referred to as *proprietary methodologies*. Obviously not all methodologies are the same and it is a general principle that methodologies can be categorised as either 'soft' or 'hard'. A hard methodology will incorporate a greater amount of formal structure within the approach to development. Soft methodologies are as rigorous as hard methodologies, but they are not as formally structured as the hard approaches to information systems development.

This area of information systems development methods did not become a major academic research discipline until the late 1960s. Previous to this time, information systems were developed without the guidance of explicit methodologies. This was due to the nature of computing services and technology at that time, which was largely concerned with imperative programming, and the fact that computing services within a business organisation were often the sole preserve of specific and isolated corporate departments with their own trained systems analysts. Therefore, information systems were often developed *ad hoc* and determined by the abilities of a computer programmer or analyst in the computing department.

However, with the pervasion of IT throughout the whole business environment, there is now a need for information systems developers not only to be technically competent but also to possess good *human* communication skills. Information systems development is now an area that benefits from a rounded education, which includes the capability to communicate hard and soft systems problems to all stakeholders involved in the business systems environment.

There are a number of reasons why a methodology is a requirement for information systems development within business organisations. Some of these reasons are listed below:

▶ Information systems can be used to provide a *competitive advantage* to most business organisations.
▶ Systems should go through the process of rigorous planning, analysis and design and implementaion, as is the case with other major business projects.
▶ There is a need in most business organisations for an *integrated approach* to systems development rather than an *ad hoc* approach to the problem.

The aims (or objectives) of any information systems development methodology should encompass some or all of the following:

▶ To improve the *process* of information systems development.
▶ To permit the effective *monitoring* of the development process.
▶ To achieve accurate *analysis* of business and systems requirements.
▶ To permit the accurate *documentation* of the analysis and design process.
▶ To allow information systems to be delivered within a required *time* limit.
▶ To ensure that the *benefits* outweigh the cost of using the methodology.
▶ To improve the *efficiency* and *effectiveness* of the business organisation.
▶ To improve the *delivery* or achievement of business organisation objectives.
▶ To ensure that the *needs of the users* are fully satisfied.

An information systems methodology is usually based on a *philosophical view* of the development process, which leads to the use of specific tools and techniques which are deemed appropriate within the environment of the various development methodologies. Some methodologies are very structured and inflexible, while others are more expedient, and often place emphasis on the human aspect of end-user involvement in the process of systems development. Information systems development varies in the extent of structure present within the methodology. A number of development methodologies will be studied in this chapter which span the spectrum from hard to soft development approaches. Figure 6.1 graphically shows a spectrum of information systems methodologies, from hard to soft development approaches, indicating where each methodology resides on that spectrum.

ACTIVITY **6.1**
●●●●●●●●●●●●●

Systems methodologies

Discuss the difference between *soft systems* methodologies and *hard systems* methodologies within the information systems development context; then explain why a systems methodology is usually based on a *philosophical view* of the development process which leads to the establishment of the tools and techniques of the various

figure 6.1
Spectrum of information systems methodologies

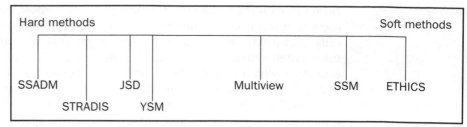

Key

SSADM	Structured systems analysis and design method
STRADIS	Structured analysis and design of information systems
JSD	Jackson Systems Development
YSM	Yourdon Systems Method
SSM	Soft systems methodology
ETHICS	Effective technical and human implementation of computer-based systems

methodologies. Once this has been thoroughly discussed and understood, proceed to search your college or university library for journal or magazine articles on *hard* and *soft* information systems methodologies. Construct a definition for both hard and soft approaches. Form into groups of five people and spend 20 minutes discussing with your colleagues the definitions you have constructed. At the end of the session, elect a spokesperson to deliver your findings in terms of a group-based definition of hard and soft systems methodologies. Did your individual definition change as a result of the group discussion?

6.2   Structured analysis and design of information systems

Structured analysis and design of information systems (STRADIS) is a highly structured approach to information systems development originated by Chris Gane and Trish Sarson. It is sometimes referred to as the 'Gane and Sarson approach'. The approach comes from their book entitled *Structured Systems Analysis: Tools and Techniques* which is cited in the references section at the end of this chapter. STRADIS is a *process-oriented* methodology that emphasises such tools and techniques as functional decomposition, data flow diagramming, decision tables and Structured English. (All of these tools and techniques were covered in detail in chapter 5.) The methodology was proposed in 1979 and encapsulated various work at that time into structured design processes and their application to information systems.

> **DID YOU KNOW?**
> The 'Gane and Sarson approach' to the analysis and design of information systems concentrates more on the tools *and* techniques *for a structured design, rather than in attempting the development of an all-encompassing methodology.*

The STRADIS approach emphasises the importance of decomposing systems functions and the use of data flow diagrams to structure the information systems problem. The approach does not restrict itself to large or small systems development projects. The approach proposes a number of detailed stages to systems development. The first stage is the *initial study* which can be equated to a feasibility study. It is at this stage that a decision must be made as to whether the benefits outweigh the costs of the proposed information systems project. The second stage is a *detailed study* which includes determining the potential uses and users of the system under investigation. It is at this stage that the potential users of the system are interviewed through formal questionnaires and other structured data collection techniques. Logical data flow diagrams (DFDs) are drafted which should have the additional effect of determining the systems boundaries under consideration. The STRADIS approach necessitates detailed data flow diagramming of the problem which is broken down into many sub-levels. The detailed study should normally include the following:

▶ a definition of the uses and users of the system
▶ a logical model of the current or proposed system
▶ a detailed statement of the costs and revenues accruing to the proposed system.

The third stage involves the defining and the designing of *alternatives* to the proposed system. This phase concerns the matching of the business organisation's objectives with the proposed information system's objectives; the two should be aligned for optimal business performance. It is at this stage that the proposed information system can be refined. The final stage is the *physical design* whereby the refined proposal is converted to a physical design, based on the current nature of IT, and it is ensured that the systems environment is satisfactory to users, in terms of the end-user interfaces and the application of information technology.

ACTIVITY **6.2**

STRADIS

Discuss with your colleagues why STRADIS is considered a *process-oriented* methodology and describe the types of tools and techniques that would be used within the STRADIS approach. Then construct a one-page executive statement for distribution to all employees in an organisation indicating the resources and time required to implement STRADIS in terms of questionnaires, interviews, and the use of various professional systems development tools and techniques. How would you justify time spent to build an information system with the benefits of that information system?

6.3   The Yourdon Systems Method

The Yourdon Systems Method (YSM) is another structured approach that is similar to STRADIS. It emphasises functional decomposition which is inherently a top-down approach to systems development. The Yourdon Systems Method was first proposed in the early 1980s and has undergone a number of version changes over time. This methodology uses most of the formal tools and techniques for documenting and describing an information system and considers both the systems requirements and the business organisation's requirements. For example, an entity-relationship diagram may be constructed for a section or department within an organisation but only part of it may be appropriate for the proposed system. Emphasis is placed on modelling both the business organisation and the system at the same time.

There are three main stages within the Yourdon Systems Method. The first stage involves a *feasibility study* that considers the current system and the information systems environment. The second stage involves constructing an *essential model* of the requirements of the proposed system. However, at this stage the Yourdon method does not consider any cost or technological constraints; it assumes unlimited resourcing and an absence of environmental constraints. The essential model is a representation of what is needed to satisfy the user's requirements and the modelling exercise involves:

▶ constructing an *environmental model* consisting of a statement of purpose, a context diagram and an event list of things to which the system must respond; and

▶ constructing a *behavioural model* which consists of data flow diagrams, entity-relationship diagrams, data dictionaries and process specifications, such as Structured English or decision tables.

The role of the environmental model is to define the boundaries of the system, taking into account the data flowing in and out of the system, whereas the role of the behavioural model is to indicate how the system behaves or deals with its environment over time, and can be equated to an entity life cycle. The third and final stage involves constructing an *implementation model* which activates the systems design process; it is at this stage that the ideal model developed at stage two is refined with regard to the limitations and constraints present in the environment. Such constraints include the performance and availability of information technology which may modify the essential model. It is interesting to note that Yourdon introduces the notion of modelling into the information systems environment. The allusion to modelling distinguishes the Yourdon approach from the Gane and Sarson approach to building effective information systems.

ACTIVITY **6.3**

Yourdon Systems Method

Outline and discuss the three main stages of systems development within the Yourdon Systems Method and suggest why the second stage does not consider any cost or technological constraints. Once this is understood, describe the essential modelling exercise of YSM and explain the use and purpose of each category of *model* used within the method. Do you think that the activity of modelling is a useful exercise within business information systems development?

6.4 Information Engineering

Care should be used when referring to Information Engineeering (IE) as there does not appear to be a standard information engineering methodology, but rather a generic class of IE methodologies. Information Engineering is a *data-oriented* systems approach that emphasises the nature and structure of data found within an organisation; it identifies data as being more stable than the processes that act upon the data. The IE approach uses diagramming to enable all stakeholders involved in the information system to understand the nature and role of the system. This approach, along with the STRADIS and Yourden approaches, uses standard and formal symbols for diagramming.

The primary information engineering model consists of three components of *data*, *activity* and *interaction* (of the data and activities). The IE approach usually utilises computer-aided software engineering (CASE) tools. The IE methodology can be separated into four layers as follows:

Information strategy planning where the aim is to construct an information strategy, or information architecture, that supports the overall and high-level requirements of the business organisation. The information strategy plan should consider the following four issues:

1 situation analysis of the business strengths, weaknesses, opportunities and threats
2 executive and managerial requirements analysis by individual or department
3 information and technical architecture definition of the system
4 information strategy plan which emphasises information priorities.

Business area analysis involving the end-users of the system dealing with the business areas identified in the information strategy plan. The business area analysis should consider the following five issues:

1 analysis of entities and functions
2 analysis of interactions between data and functions
3 analysis of the current system
4 verification and checking of results
5 definition of the design areas for consideration.

Systems planning and design which involves the internal and external design of business systems and the technical design. This layer involves the following aspects:

1 data structure design
2 system structure design
3 procedure design
4 verification and checking
5 technical design plan
6 data design
7 software design
8 conversion design
9 security and operations design
10 systems testing
11 planning for the implementation.

Implementation and changeover from old system. This layer involves the physical construction of the information system as follows:

1   construction of the IT environment
2   systems verification and testing
3   preparation for changeover
4   installation and conversion to new system
5   check consistency of systems use
6   evaluation of system
7   systems maintenance.

DID YOU KNOW?

James Martin, one of the founders of the IE approach, has set up a number of business enterprises to develop CASE tools to implement the IE approach. One of the best known CASE tools to support the methodology is known as the Information Engineering Facility (IEF), which James Martin built in cooperation with Texas Instruments in the 1980s.

It should be noted that the four layers mentioned above can often be undertaken in parallel and not necessarily in rigid sequential stages. Hence, the more appropriate term of layers rather than stages of development is used within IE.

ACTIVITY **6.4**

Information Engineering

Explain the significance of *information strategy planning* and *business area analysis* within the domain of information systems methods. Then, after discussion, indicate why the various components of IE are known as *layers* and not stages and describe some of the consequences of undertaking the development of various layers in parallel.

6.5   Structured systems analysis and design method

Structured systems analysis and design method (SSADM) is a highly structured approach used primarily to develop large-scale information systems for government departments in the United Kingdom. The approach was first used in 1981 and is a *data-oriented* methodology that emphasises data modelling tools and techniques. SSADM has gone through a number of versions, the latest being version 4.0 which was published in 1990 and includes greater consideration than previous versions of end-users within the process of development. The actual manuals and documentation for SSADM run into a number of thick volumes, each one prescriptively outlining how the methodology should be applied. Because of its prominence within the business environment, SSADM is probably the best known structured systems development approach. But it is only really applicable in the situation of major large-scale information systems development. SSADM version 4.0 lists seven stages to the development process (labelled 0 through to 6), which are outlined in Table 6.1.

Each stage of the SSADM life cycle is strictly defined along with the outcomes of each stage; these outcomes are often referred to as 'deliverables' within systems vocabulary. SSADM uses its own symbol terminology for data flow diagramming which is referred to as data flow modelling.

table 6.1
The seven stages of SSADM

0 Feasibility study
– defining the problem and selecting options
– creating feasibility report.

1 Requirements analysis: investigate current environment
– establish analysis framework
– investigate and define requirements
– investigate current processing
– investigate current data
– derive logical view of current services
– assemble investigation results.

2 Requirements analysis: business system options
– define business system options
– select business system options
– define requirements.

3 Requirements specification: definition of requirements
– define required system processing
– develop required data model
– derive system functions
– enhance required data model
– develop specification prototypes
– develop processing specification
– confirm system objectives
– assemble and construct requirements specification.

4 Logical systems specification: technical systems options
– define technical systems options
– select technical systems options
– define physical design modules.

5 Logical systems specification: logical design
– define user dialogues
– define update processes
– define enquiry processes
– assemble and construct logical design.

6 Physical design
– prepare for physical design
– create physical data design
– create function component implementation map
– optimise physical data design
– complete function specification
– consolidate process data interface
– assemble and construct physical design.

The *feasibility* stage involves using such techniques as interviews, questionnaires and data flow models of the flow of information documentation. The investigation of the *current environment* stage expands upon the feasibility stage by adding detail to the feasibility study. At the *business systems options* stage a cost–benefit analysis is carried out and only those systems options that show greater benefit to cost ratio will be continued and carried forward to the next stage. The *definition of requirements* stage establishes the full requirements specification and determines the following design stage. This stage is important in replacing investigation and analysis with specification and design. The question that needs to be asked is: 'what will be the requirements of the new or proposed system?'. This stage will normally involve entity modelling and normalisation of data relationships. Currently, within this stage in version 4.0 is a definition of user roles within the system. In addition, SSADM version 4.0 permits some element of *prototyping* to be carried out to assess the accuracy of user requirements, particularly in terms of user interface design.

The *technical system options* stage determines the software and hardware configuration of the IT to be applied to the information system; consideration is also given to the technical *constraints* that will impact on the final systems configuration. This stage is usually carried out in parallel with the logical design stage. Remember that chapter 2 outlined the importance of separating the logical from the physical systems model in order to ascertain the correct purpose and nature of the information system under development. The logical design stage incorporates user views of the proposed system in order to better establish the logical requirements of the system. Following this stage is the *physical design* stage which converts the logical design into a physical IS/IT environment. The main objective of this stage should be to establish a physical configuration that meets the user's requirements.

The rigour and structure of SSADM has enabled the methodology to become established in the information systems development arena. This has been assisted by the fact that SSADM, as a formal systems technique, is taught in many university departments, from business studies to computing, around the world.

ACTIVITY **6.5**

SSADM

Describe the systems development approach known as SSADM and outline the main difference of version 4.0 to previous versions of the method. Then proceed to define the term *deliverable* and outline the deliverables of each stage of the SSADM approach to building information systems. Suggest some of the main advantages and disadvantages to a business organisation of using the SSADM approach to information systems development. Do you think that the methodology is appropriate to large-scale or small-scale information systems development projects? Then discuss reasons why the use of SSADM may be highly inappropriate for small business organisations.

6.6   Jackson Systems Development

The Jackson Systems Development (JSD) approach is the last structured and 'hard' systems development methodology that will be reviewed. The methodology is named after Michael Jackson and is, therefore, another proprietary systems methodology. This methodology associates information systems development with the same techniques used for computer program language design; and the information systems project is effectively seen as a large computer program. Therefore, the methodology is useful in the development of large-scale software-based systems where the emphasis is on software rather than other issues of the organisation's overall startegic *business* requirements.

The JSD approach attempts to overcome the 'hidden path' problems between the initial specification and the final implementation by using what are termed *process scheduling* and *real-world modelling*. The three generic stages of the JSD approach are shown in Table 6.2.

The *modelling stage* requires that entities and events are identified and dynamic entity life cycles are created. The emphasis is as far as possible on modelling the 'real world'. An entity structure is then imposed and represented as a hierarchical JSD structure diagram which shows the sequence within the system's processes. Within this structure the timing and sequence of systems activities is considered; the *entity structure diagrams* represent a sequence of activities that are ordered in time from the beginning of an entity's life until its termination. The *network stage* includes an initial model step that is a simulation of the real world. For example, for each defined entity a sequential process is defined in the model to simulate the activities of the entity. This sequential process should be correspondingly implementable on a computer in the form of a program; this is referred to in JSD as structure text. The network stage also includes a function step that ensures that the required outputs are produced as a consequence of the occurrence of events. The final part of this stage is system timing which is concerned with the speed of execution of processes and their timing. There is a need to determine the lag times between receiving inputs to the various parts of the system and the timing of the resultant outputs. This timing information concerning the various parts of the proposed system is analysed in JSD by time markers which provide information on the timing and execution of processes. The *implementation stage* considers the physical systems specification assisted by the use of systems implementation diagrams that hierarchically show the scheduling of processes.

table 6.2
The three generic stages of JSD

1   The modelling stage
– entity action
– entity structure.
2   The network stage
– initial model
– function
– system timing.
3   The implementation stage
– physical system specification.

The advantages of JSD reside in its attempt to model dynamic real-world situations and, in order to achieve this end, JSD emphasises the importance of timing and scheduling considerations. The overall approach is process oriented rather than static data oriented.

ACTIVITY **6.6**

A

JSD

Briefly discuss and explain the relationship between computer program code structure and the JSD methodology and suggest two possible advantages of applying the structured technique of programming to information systems development. Suggest three advantages and disadvantages of using JSD to develop information systems within the business environment.

6.7 Effective technical and human implementation of computer-based systems

Effective technical and human implementation of computer-based systems (ETHICS) lies at the soft end of the methodological spectrum of systems development. The philosophy of ETHICS encompasses a *socio-technical* view of the systems development process. It is essential in this methodology for the technology to align closely with the social and organisational factors present within a business organisation. The human approach must consider such factors as the job satisfaction and quality of life of the human users of the system. The interests of the human users are paramount in the ETHICS methodology. The socio-technical view is based on a recognition of the interaction between technology, people and the organisation. The ETHICS approach is represented by two fundamental philosophical strands:

1   job satisfaction
2   user participation.

The ETHICS philosophy states that an information system will only be efficient and effective if it allows the system's end-user to have job satisfaction. To achieve satisfaction requires the system aligning the employee's aspirations and expectations of the job with what is required of the job by the system, which is known as organisational 'goodness of fit'. Job satisfaction can be achieved in a number of ways, for example, by increasing task variety, by job enrichment, through greater responsibility, and by job development through end-user suggested improvements to current methods.

> **DID YOU KNOW?**
> *The ETHICS methodology was proposed by Enid Mumford, at the Manchester Business School in the United Kingdom, and is in essence a socio-technical development methodology that is based on end-user participation within the systems development process. The methodology stresses the importance of the social and ethical aspects of information systems as well as the economic and technical aspects of information systems incorporated into the business environment.*

The second philosophical strand of the ETHICS philosophy is end-user participation in the system development process through the involvement of users in the decision-making exercises. The ETHICS definition of end-users is sufficiently broad to encompass direct and indirect users, such as managers, employees, suppliers and even customers. The decision making will often include hard and soft technical decisions motivated by the drive to use information technology to improve job satisfaction within the system's environment. Therefore, the *management of change* is a constant theme in the ETHICS approach along with the collateral drive to manage organisational conflict. Involvement has a purpose in that the end-users are often the most knowledgeable concerning their current job specifications and requirements. There is also a far greater likelihood of a system being accepted by the users if they were involved in decision making than if they were not involved in the decision-making process. The aim of the ETHICS approach is to ensure that the users are satisfied that their requirements are met by the information system. User involvement must be engaged at all stages of the generic development process from analysis and design through to implementation and evaluation.

Participation by end-users in the decision-making process of systems development possesses a number of benefits:

▶ Participation overcomes human resentment of the information system, thus reducing the risk of individuals working against the system or blaming the system for unjustified problems.
▶ Participation can reduce the cost of training or retraining in the use of the system because of the fact that the end-users already possess significant levels of knowledge from the development process.
▶ Participation increases the level of communication between employees at all levels of the organisation and, in doing so, publicises the overall strategic goals of the business organisation.
▶ Participation encourages and improves human–computer interface design. The quality of computer interfaces is measured in terms of visibility, simplicity, consistency and flexibility in meeting the end-user's needs.
▶ Participation engenders a feeling of empowerment within users that can lead to increased job satisfaction.

Participation must be real and a genuine collaboration between the users and the technical specialists. Within this scenario the role of the technical specialists is one of a *facilitator* to ensure the implementation of the user's requirements. The facilitator can be internal or external to the business organisation. Enid Mumford (1983) has suggested three levels of possible participation by the users as follows:

1 *Consultative participation*. This is the weakest and lowest form of participation, where users are merely consulted about change within the business organisation. This level of consultation may only take the form of user questionnaires and interviews.
2 *Representative participation*. This is a higher form of participation than consultative participation. In this scenario the users and the technical specialists form a team with users and technical specialists having an equal contribution within the decision-making process.
3. *Consensus participation*. This is the most significant level of participation with users driving the systems development process. Therefore, the end-users, rather than the technical specialists, are paramount in the design and development process.

Step 1	**Discussion of change** – reasons for change – SWOT analysis of change.
Step 2	**Identification of systems boundaries** – establish systems boundaries – assess impact on business activities – assess impact on business organisation.
Step 3	**Describe existing system** – establish current system operation – input-activity-output analysis – describe the design area activities.
Step 4	**Establish the key objectives, outcomes and tasks** – define the role and purpose of systems areas – define the functions of systems areas – define the variance between the current and proposed system.
Step 5	**Diagnosis of variances** – analyse the systemic variances – analyse the operational variances – analyse deviations from required standards.
Step 6	**Measure job satisfaction needs** – ETHICS questionnaire – formulate improvements to system.
Step 7	**Identify future changes** – analysis of future system needs – build flexible margins into the system.
Step 8	**Balancing systems efficiency with job satisfaction** – ranking of objectives – establishment of priority objectives.
Step 9	**Organisational design** – specify organisational changes – establish criteria for meeting the job satisfaction objectives – assess the organisational objectives.
Step 10	**Technical design** – specify technical hardware and software – merge the organisational and technical design options.
Step 11	**Detailed design** – define data flows and other relationships – confirm design with objectives and requirements.
Step 12	**Implementation** – implement the detailed design – coordinate the strategy for training and education – conversion of old to new system.
Step 13	**Evaluation** – check and test the system.

With the evolution of end-user systems development the issue of participation is becoming commonly accepted within competitive business organisations. However, participation can be restricted to a pre-defined boundary, with the role and remit of participation being stated at the outset. In order to build effective and efficient business information systems the participants should ideally possess equal knowledge. However, this may not always be possible, particularly where there are technical and non-technical specialists in a team with different experiences. Nevertheless, this team is often referred to as the *design group*. There are effectively 13 generic stages to the ETHICS design and development process. These are recorded in Table 6.3. It should be noted that these stages have never been formalised within the ETHICS approach and, therefore, the number of steps can vary from 13 through to 25 steps. The 13 steps in Table 6.3 are a generic collation of the main principles of the design and development process.

The ETHICS approach can be used to design small or large-scale business systems projects and the methodology is particularly useful in analysing, and establishing, the requirements of a business information system.

ACTIVITY **6.7**
· · · · · · · · · · · · ·

ETHICS

Discuss and describe the main benefits of end-user participation within the ETHICS methodology and explain the general importance of user participation in human–computer interface design. Dicuss the importance of a *facilitator* within the ETHICS approach in creating a suitable environment in which technical and non-technical users can equally participate in the systems development process. Finally, describe the three levels of possible participation by end-users within the ETHICS systems development process and explain what is meant by the term *design group*. What do you think the problems might be in selecting a design group of systems users?

6.8   Soft systems methodology
· ·

The soft systems methodology (SSM) uses many of the principles of general systems theory, discussed in chapter 2, and incorporates them into a practical methodology for business organisations. The SSM approach argues that business is often a complex human activity system where the individual components of a business system may react differently when examined individually than when those parts are seen in the context of the whole business system. One of the problems with traditional scientific analysis of systems is the insistence on decomposing a complex problem into its constituent parts by a process of decomposition to the lowest common denominator.

The SSM approach states that only the application of a soft systems methodology can provide the correct *insight* into business systems and human processes; which may lead to a better chance of achieving the most appropriate systems solution in

DID YOU KNOW?

The soft systems methodology (SSM) was developed by Peter Checkland at Lancaster University in the United Kingdom, from 1981 onwards, as a more appropriate and applicable method for developing information systems than the 'hard' and structured methodologies that were in use in the early 1980s. Checkland's original ideas are mainly encompassed in a book entitled: Systems Thinking, Systems Practice *(1981).*

the long term. SSM is the opposite of the structured and hard methodologies in that SSM argues that complex systems problems cannot be solved with rigid and deterministic methods. The SSM approach also implies that in addition to systems having goals they may more appropriately have *purposes* and *missions* that are not as simplistic as systems goals. The soft systems approach brings people together to determine the nature of a problem situation and attempts to search for a set of agreed *views* concerning the problem situation; this is referred to within the method by the German word 'Weltanschauung' which loosely translates as 'world view'. This world view establishes a set of beliefs and assumptions with regard to the system and its requirements. The world view sometimes materialises as a *mission statement* of the overall purpose of the system. For example, a university may have a world view that it should 'seek to provide the highest standard of education'. A business organisation may hold a world view that seeks 'to maximise revenue from overseas operations'. The principles that underpin the soft systems approach can be distilled into the following:

▶ Any system should be seen in its *holistic* systems context.
▶ Business systems problems are often *unstructured* and are not deterministic.
▶ Information systems problems are usually *specific* to a business organisation (such systems are normally not prone to the application of a single methodology).
▶ Normally business systems are *complex* and involve *human activity* components.
▶ Business systems problems are usually ill-defined or considered 'fuzzy' (these are sometimes referred to as soft problem situations).
▶ SSM recognises the importance of the various forms of organisation within business.
▶ SSM recognises that human activity is unpredictable within systems environments.

All the ideas of the soft systems methodology are incorporated in two books by Peter Checkland entitled *Systems Thinking, Systems Practice* (1981) and, with J. Scholes, *Soft Systems Methodology in Action* (1993). (These books are fully referenced at the end of this chapter.) There are seven stages to the SSM approach, some of which are referred to as *real-world activities* and some of which are referred to as contemplation and *thinking stages*. Checkland stresses that the stages need not be taken in sequence; he argues that a number of stages can be undertaken simultaneously and often stages will need to be revisited. Figure 6.2 indicates the framework necessary for applying SSM.

Stage 1: *The problem situation: unstructured* This stage is concerned with gaining an unstructured view of the problem situation. The term 'problem situation' is used by Checkland in preference to other terms that specifically relate to 'systems requirements'. This stage involves participation by all those concerned with the system under observation, and investigation, where the various views of the problem situation are gathered and acknowledged. This stage is undertaken to ascertain the channels of formal and informal communication within the system. Of interest is the fact that SSM looks at informal communications channels that fall outside of the formal organisational structure of the business organisation.

figure 6.2
SSM in action
(Checkland 1981)

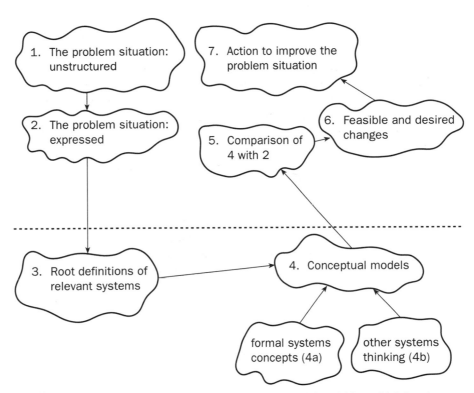

Note: The stages above the dotted line are the real-world activities which involve human interaction, that is to say systems practice; the stages below the dotted line are concerned with systems thinking.

Stage 2: *The problem situation: expressed* This stage takes the informal and unstructured picture of the problem situation, gathered in stage 1, and expresses the problem in a more formal and structured way. One of the tools used to achieve this is the creation of a *rich picture* of the problem situation. A rich picture uses visual symbols, pictures and drawings (with a minimum of text) to describe the problem situation (see Figure 5.15, pg 133). The rich picture should pictorially show the processes, actors and interaction of processes within the problem situation; it can be a useful tool for communication between the technical specialists and the non-technical specialists, and other users of the system. In drawing rich pictures the following principles are normally adopted:

▶ A rich picture should always use the terminology and vocabulary that is understood in the environment of the system under investigation and analysis.
▶ A rich picture should reveal problems and sources of conflict within the information systems environment.
▶ A rich picture is a tool of communication between the technical and non-technical system specialists.
▶ A rich picture should be used to identify problems and themes present within the systems environment.

▶ A rich picture should include the users, tasks, processes, internal and external agents affecting the system.

Stage 3: *The root definitions of relevant systems*   This stage involves the definition and naming of relevant systems. Often a number of options will be proposed and these will need to be evaluated to determine the most appropriate solution to the problem situation. The main activity of this stage is the formulation of a *root definition* for the relevant system. The root definition defines the problems and the system. The root definition should be a concise, tightly constructed description of a human activity system which states and defines the nature of the system. The root definition is created using a CATWOE technique which is a mnemonic for:

Client (the person affected by the system activity)
Actor (the agent of change who carries out transformation process)
Transformation (the change itself)
Weltanschauung (the world view assumptions)
Owner (the answerable authority), and
Environment (the wider holistic system).

Root definitions are a useful tool for clarifying the problems of a system and for exposing different viewpoints.

Stage 4: *The building of conceptual models*   This stage is undertaken when the participants in the system are satisfied that they have established a solid root definition. This stage requires the building of a conceptual model. The conceptual model is a diagrammatic representation of the activities and purpose of the system; it should give rise to debate in order to evaluate its application to the real world. The conceptual model should be drawn for each root definition and the models can be altered by a process of iterative changes, resulting from debate, by the participants using the methodology.

Stage 5: *Comparing the conceptual models with reality*   This stage involves comparing the rich pictures of the problem situation with the conceptual models. This stage should ideally lead to the formulation of recommendations regarding the necessary changes within the systems environment.

Stage 6: *Assessing the feasibility and desirable changes*   The recommended changes from stage 5 are analysed to ascertain which changes are feasible and desirable.

Stage 7: *Action to improve the problem situation*   This stage gives rise to recommended actions for a solution to the initial problem situation which gave rise to the activity of systems analysis and design.

Overall, the strength of SSM resides in providing a 'framework' for understanding a problem situation. However, a weakness is the fact that it is short on aspects related to implementation and evaluation of information systems. Significantly, SSM is different to hard methodologies in studying the softer human activity present within systems environments. Therefore, the SSM approach is often seen as an excellent method for *analysing* systems problems before adopting harder approaches for *implementing* a solution. In reality the majority of systems development projects within the business environment often assume a hybrid approach to solving systems problems, which may lead to adoption of tools, techniques and ideas from a range of development methodologies.

A ACTIVITY **6.8**
• • • • • • • • • • • • • •

Soft systems methodology

Outline and then discuss the main principles that underpin SSM and explain the problems of analysing 'fuzzy' systems within the business environment. Think about and discuss the term 'Weltanschauung', which loosely translates as 'world view', and indicate how this world view may constrain, or influence, the shape and form of information systems within a business organisation. Describe the process of developing a *conceptual model* and explain whether the use of conceptual models is a beneficial and appropriate way of defining the 'problem situation' facing a business organisation. Once you are happy with the ideas and thinking behind SSM, find a problem situation that occurs within business and use the soft systems method to analyse and solve the problem situation. Then prepare a report to your colleagues making recommendations regarding the problem situation and the required information systems solution.

6.9 Multiview
• • • • • • • • • • • • • • • • • • • •

Multiview is a systems development methodology that is a hybrid of a number of other methodologies and adopts various tools and techniques that are appropriate to the systems situation. Multiview is a soft systems development approach that borrows many of the ideas of SSM and ETHICS, but incorporates harder tools and techniques as necessary. It is a flexible approach which is often used for small-scale project development and to assist applications-based development. Multiview is a methodology that, as its name implies, takes a multiple view (or perspective) of a system's environment; it takes a view of the human, technical and organisational aspects of information systems. The five stages of multiview are listed in Table 6.4.

It should be recognised that the *analysis of human activity* stage is closely related to the SSM approach to analysing problem situations. Stage 2 involves *information modelling* to analyse the entities and functions of the system; this is done through the development of a functional model which decomposes the functions down to understandable levels. Data flow diagrams can also be used to show the sequence of events. This can then be augmented with the development of an entity model through the use of data modelling techniques. The third stage involves *analysis and design of the socio-technical aspects* of the system. This stage is influenced by the ETHICS approach to information systems development, particularly through user participation and systems stakeholder involvement in the development process; this stage assesses

DID YOU KNOW?
Multiview has been described as an exploration in information systems development. The main premise of the approach is that only particular systems techniques will be appropriate to certain business organisations, therefore a business should adopt different aspects of the various methodologies available as thought appropriate within its own systems environment.

table 6.4

The five stages to multiview systems development

Stage 1	**Analysis of human activity**
	– establish a Weltanschauung view
	– describe the systems requirements using rich pictures
	– establish root definitions
	– establish a conceptual model of activities
	– compare the conceptual model with the rich pictures
	– implement any changes through process of iteration.
Stage 2	**Information modelling**
	– develop a functional model
	– develop an entity model.
Stage 3	**Analysis and design of socio-technical aspects**
	– establish human requirements
	– establish organisational requirements
	– establish socio-technical goodness of fit
	– assess future socio-technical environment.
Stage 4	**Design of the human–computer interface.**
	– technical design of human–computer interface
	– establish the design of input and output mediums.
Stage 5	**Design of technical aspects**
	– design technical environment
	– implement a technical solution
	– system testing and evaluation
	– ongoing systems evaluation.

the socio-technical systems alternatives. The fourth stage involves *design of the human–computer interface* which is often one of the primary concerns of most systems users. The fifth stage involves *design of the technical aspects* of the system; this stage uses the entity models from stage 2 and the technical requirements from stage 4 to establish a technical design to implement, test and evaluate the system on a continuous basis.

 ACTIVITY **6.9**

Multiview

Discuss the role and purpose of *information modelling* within the multiview approach and suggest how this methodology might assist the design of human-to-technology aspects of business information systems. Then list and describe four main advantages and disadvantages of using a methodology that is a hybrid of a number of other methodologies.

6.10   Chapter summary

Information systems methodologies come in many forms, some relying on hard tools and techniques and others on softer approaches to information systems development. Therefore, there is no single universally adopted methodology for building business information systems. However, the aim of all systems methodologies is to develop the most efficient and effective information system for decision making within the business environment as is practicable and possible, given the environmental system's constraints.

It is essential that any student who studies information systems within the business environment is aware of the scope and flexibility inherent within the spectrum of information systems development methodologies. It is often the case in the business environment that information systems that are difficult to define call for a 'softer' approach to the analysis and solution to a business systems problem. On the other hand, many 'harder' methodologies, that are based on formal tools and techniques, are often inappropriate for analysing systems at higher levels of the organisational hierarchy above the transaction processing systems level of business. In the final analysis the adoption of a *methodological framework* should depend upon the nature of the organisation and its environment. It should always be recognised that human interaction within the systems environment is a significant factor that must be successfully addressed in order to achieve effective and efficient business information systems development. The eventual adoption of a methodology often depends upon the *systems philosophy* prevailing within the organisation and the design team and the effect on the ethos, or 'personality', of that business organisation.

Short self-assessment questions

6.1 List and explain the main reasons why a methodology is a requirement for information systems development within the business environment.

6.2 Describe the ideal *aims* or objectives that any information systems development methodology should encompass.

6.3 Define the methodology known as structured systems analysis and design of information systems (STRADIS) and explain its evolution as a systems development method.

6.4 Suggest some of the possible benefits to a business organisation of using a structured approach to information systems design and development.

6.5 Outline the four main stages of information systems development within STRADIS and explain the significance of each stage and its relationship to the traditional SDLC.

6.6 Define the Yourdon Systems Method (YSM) and describe the tools and techniques that would be used within the Yourdon method.

6.7 Define the information engineering (IE) method for developing information systems and describe the tools and techniques that would be used within the IE method.

6.8 Describe the four layers of IE and explain the purpose and function of each layer within the IE methodology.

6.9 Outline and explain the seven main stages of information systems development within SSADM.

6.10 Define Jackson Systems Development (JSD) and describe the main tools and techniques used within the JSD methodology.

6.11 Outline the three generic stages to systems development within the JSD methodology and explain the importance of *modelling* within the scope and remit of the JSD approach.

6.12 Define effective technical and human implementation of computer-based systems (ETHICS) and describe the two main *philosophical* strands present within the ETHICS approach to systems development.

6.13 Outline and describe the importance of user involvement in the ETHICS methodology and explain why job satisfaction and job enrichment are important aspects within its methodological framework.

6.14 Outline the 13 generic stages to ETHICS design and development and indicate the main principles of the development process.

6.15 Define soft systems methodology (SSM) and explain the use of the term 'soft' to describe the nature of an information systems development framework.

6.16 Outline and describe the seven stages to systems building using SSM and explain the difference between the *real-world activities* and the *thinking* stages.

6.17 Describe the use of *rich pictures* at stage 2 of SSM and outline the main advantages and disadvantages of using rich pictures to communicate the problem situation.

6.18 Explain the purpose and role of the *root definition* at stage 3 and describe the mnemonic CATWOE in defining a root definition.

6.19 Explain how multiview combines various system's ideas, tools and techniques into a holistic approach to systems development.

6.20 Describe the five stages of multiview and indicate the role of user participation within each stage of the systems development process.

References

Checkland, P. (1981) *Systems Thinking, Systems Practice*. Chichester, England: John Wiley. (*)

Checkland, P. and Scholes J. (1993) *Soft Systems Methodology in Action*. Chichester, England: John Wiley.

Gane, C. and Sarson, T. (1979) *Structured Systems Analysis: Tools and Techniques*. Englewood Cliffs, New Jersey: Prentice Hall. (*)

Martin, J. and Finkelstein, C. (1981) *Information Engineering*, vols 1 and 2. Englewood Cliffs, New Jersey: Prentice-Hall.

Further study and reading
••••••••••••••••••••••••••••••••••

Books

Avison, D.E. and Fitzgerald, D. (1995) *Information Systems Development: Methodologies, Techniques and Tools*, 2nd edition. London: McGraw-Hill.

Avison, D.E. and Wood-Harper, A.T. (1990) *Multiview: An Exploration in Information Systems Development*. Maidenhead, England: McGraw-Hill.

DeMarco, T. (1979) *Structured Analysis and System Specification*. Englewood Cliffs, New Jersey: Prentice-Hall.

Jackson, M. (1983) *Systems Development*. Hemel Hempstead, England: Prentice-Hall.

Martin, J. (1989) *Information Engineering*. Englewood Cliffs, New Jersey: Prentice-Hall.

Mumford, E. (1995) *Effective Requirements Analysis and Systems Design: The ETHICS Method*. Basingstoke, England: Macmillan.

Yourdon, E. (1993) *Yourdon Systems Method: Model Driven Systems Development*. Yourdon Press.

Journals

Mumford, E. (1983) *Designing participatively*. Manchester: Manchester Business School.

An asterisk (*) next to a book reference indicates a *seminal text* which means it constituted a source for later developments.

PART 2

The application of information technology (IT)

CHAPTER 7

Business systems activity

Objectives
··············

When you have studied this chapter you will be able to:

▶ define the role and purpose of planning, decision making and control within the business systems environment

▶ describe the environmental differences between the various systems found at each level of decision making within the business systems environment

▶ evaluate the nature of decision making within the business systems environment and understand how IT is incorporated into the decision-making process of business

▶ distinguish the characteristics and role of operational systems, management systems and strategic systems within the business environment

▶ understand the relationship and integration of transaction processing systems within the business environment.

7.1 Business systems and organisational decision making
··

The activity of *decision making* within the business systems environment involves undertaking two prerequisite activities of *planning* and *control*. The sequence of activity is (1) planning, (2) decision making and (3) control. Planning is the process of deciding, in advance, *what* is to be done, *how* it is to be carried out, *when* it is to be achieved and *who* is to achieve it. Therefore, planning is heavily dependent upon accurate information generated from reliable information systems. Planning is a means of providing a guiding steering mechanism for decision making; the activity of decision making is all about directing an organisation down a particular, desirable and chosen path. The activity of planning occurs throughout all decision-making levels of a business organisation. In chapter 2 we studied the nature and role of the three main generic decision-making levels of a typical hierarchical business organisation. At the bottom level of the decision-making hierarchy transaction processing systems (TPSs) are concerned with short-term planning, decision making and control; at the middle of the organisational hierarchy management information systems (MISs) are concerned with medium-term planning, decision making and control; and at the top of the organisational hierarchy executive information systems (EISs) are concerned with long-term and strategic planning, decision making and control.

The process of planning, decision making and control normally relies on the activity of modelling the information environment. Models can be graphical, numerical, symbolic, mathematical or algorithmic. The activity of modelling assists the planning process by allowing variables and alternative courses of action to be studied and manipulated at low organisational cost and with minimal business risk. The successful process of planning will enable the activity of decision making, and control of decision making, to be undertaken. The process of decision making involves selecting an approach and actioning a preferred plan. There are four main generic phases in the decision-making process as follows:

1 Investigating the occasions and conditions for decision-making activity.
2 Looking at and analysing a range of alternative courses of action.
3 Choosing and selecting a course of action and implementing the decision.
4 Evaluating and reviewing past decision choices and actions.

Like planning, the activity of recurring decision making is dependent upon reliable and accurate information which needs to be fed back into the decision-making systems environment from the established systems control mechanisms. Remember that in chapter 2 we studied the theory and practice of feedback and control models within information systems. The various decision-making levels of a business organisation exhibit different feedback and control time-frames. Decision making at the strategic level of an organisation will have a long time lag between the decision being made and the availability of feedback information to evaluate the initial decision. Such strategic decision making will also rely on a high level of human judgement which implies that strategic decision-making activity is prone to high levels of uncertainty and corrolated risk. However, at the transaction processing level of business, at the bottom of the typical organisational hierarchy, the decision-making activity will have an immediate time-scale between a decision being made and the availability of feedback information to evaluate that decision. Such operational decision making is made on a day-to-day, or ephemeral, basis and is characterised by structured and deterministic systems environments, with minimal human judgement or discretion involved in the decision-making activity. Within the decision-making and information feedback scenario the activity of *control* is concerned with the use of techniques and procedures to ensure that the decisions made, at each level of the organisation hierarchy, are implemented as required and according to the plan. There is normally within all business systems environments a planning, decision making and control *life cycle*. The overall cycle has the following steps:

► objectives setting
► planning strategies
► decision making
► directing and executing tasks
► obtaining feedback
► monitoring and control.

Information systems are essential in assisting the activities and processes of planning, decision making and control; they are part of the decision-making infrastructure and can also assist the decision-making process by providing information and support where and when required. In this chapter we will investigate the nature of the business systems environment and the types of information system used to support the planning, decision making and control activities found within the three generic levels of a hierarchical organisation. The information systems at each generic level of an organisation display a continuum of different characteristics which determine the goals and nature of each individual system used for decision making. We discovered in chapter 2 that operational systems operate under conditions of certainty and are deterministic to the extent that the inputs and outputs are known with certainty. The nature of the management information systems environment is different to that of the operational systems environment in that such systems operate under higher levels of uncertainty. The main goal of most managerial systems is to assist managers in their decision-making activities. Strategic information systems operate under business environment conditions of greater uncertainty than managerial systems, with the purpose of strategic information systems being to assist senior executives in making decisions that affect the long-term strategic direction of the overall business organisation.

At the operational level of the business systems environment routine decisions are made on a day-to-day basis, where much decision making is undertaken by computerised transaction processing systems. Management information systems aim to provide information for managers to take decisions regarding the allocation of resources, both human and technological, within the bounds of the organisation. Therefore, managers carry out the plans of senior executives by supervising, managing and coordinating the resources of the business organisation thereby fulfilling a role within the control systems of an organisation. Executive information systems aim to assist the senior executives in their task of guiding the long-term future direction of the business organisation. Executive decision-making is characterised by decision-making creativity and judgement and unstructured problems which are infrequent and difficult to define, often in environments exhibiting high levels of uncertainty.

DID YOU KNOW?
Operational systems, such as stock control, can be computerised to automatically reorder stocks of raw materials for the manufacturing process when the minimum stock levels have been reached. When stock levels are low, the computer automatically sends an electronic message or signal to the suppliers' computer system to place a reorder of stock, the suppliers' systems action the request and automatically generate a decision for goods to be supplied to its customer.

The quality of decision making will affect the performance of a business organisation. Therefore, planning, decision making and control are activities and processes that must be carried out thoroughly with regard to all relevant environmental factors.

An information system used to assist decision making, particularly at the management and executive levels of and organisation, will normally be characterised by performance of the following activities:

▶ Consider the full range of factors affecting the decision both formal and informal.
▶ Explore all the alternative courses of action available within the decision-making environment.
▶ Assimilate all the possible information related to the decision-making environment.
▶ Evaluate the risks, costs and benefits of a range of courses of action.
▶ Make detailed plans for implementing the various and available courses of action.
▶ Review the effectiveness of past decisions to assess the impact on current decisions.

The overall objective of the planning, decision making and control life cycle is to achieve the business goals and objectives of the organisation, and information systems are established in business organisations to support this activity.

ACTIVITY 7.1

Planning, decision making and control

Write a 500-word executive report to explain what is meant by the planning, decision making and control life cycle. Explain why these business systems activities are intrinsically related and suggest in the report whether there are any known phases or stages to the planning, decision making and control life cycle. Once this has been completed, outline seven reasons why the process of *planning* is considered difficult. Do you believe that a business organisation should invest human and technological resources into the activity and process of planning? Outline the main activities involved in the decision-making process of a business organisation and explain some of the different characteristics of decision making within the three main organisational levels of a typical decision-making hierarchy. Suggest why the process of control is a vital part of the planning, decision making and control life cycle and state the intended aim of management control within a typical business organisation.

ACTIVITY 7.2

The CAMPARI model

The creative use of business plans can determine whether an individual or business organisation receives any monetary backing for business ventures and projects. One method used by banks to judge the merits of a plan is known as the CAMPARI model. It stands for

Character
Ability
Margin
Purpose
Amount
Repayment
Insurance.

A review of the method can be found below.

Creative use of plans can bring in funds

by Derek Harris

Creative use of business plans for on-going monitoring of a firm's performance is one thing banks look for when assessing whether to give backing, according to David Lavarack, head of small business services at Barclays Bank.

He gave some tips on how to secure bank finance – including matching up to what is known as the Campari test – to an Institute of Directors' conference on financing company growth.

What worries Mr Lavarack is a lack of essential commercial skills among British managers in running their own businesses, underlined by some Barclays research. This showed only 54 per cent of businesses drew up a formal business plan, covering cash flow, budgeting, sales and marketing, production targets and staffing.

Only one in five understand that a business plan should be used as a living document to measure on-going commercial performance. This is because most businesses see writing a business plan primarily as a means of obtaining finance.

Two-thirds of businesses plan only a month ahead, with less than a quarter taking a one-year view.

Mr Lavarack said that, increasingly, Barclays bases its criteria for fundng small businesses on evidence of thorough planning and sound commercial acumen. Barclays has found nearly 40 per cent of plans contain no detailed marketing and sales estimates. With nearly two-thirds of businesses not fully understanding their costs, they underestimate the value of products and charge less than customers are prepared to pay.

A fifth of businesses without a plan have a delibrate policy of undercutting the competition, whereas only 4 per cent of those with a plan adopt this policy.

The Campari test covers assessments for character (of those running the business), ability (business skills levels), margin (the interest rate to be struck in relation to risk), purpose (the precise use of a bank loan which should be stuck to), amount (lending too little can be wrong), repayment, and insurance (in the sense of security for a loan).

(Source *The Guardian*, November 1993)

Write a brief 500-word report on the main strengths and weaknesses of the CAMPARI method for evaluating business plans and indicate other aspects that would need to be considered for the purposes of planning, decision making and control.

7.2 Transaction processing systems

Operational systems within the business environment are normally referred to as functional systems or transaction processing systems (TPSs) because they carry out basic day-to-day activities, transactions and functions within an organisation. Whether or not a business organisation sells products or services it will rely on a range of operational systems. The following is a list of the common transaction processing systems found within the operational level of a typical business organisation:

▶ sales order processing
▶ purchase order processing
▶ production planning
▶ production control
▶ stock (or inventory) control
▶ receiving and distribution
▶ payroll (wages and salaries)
▶ accounting (financial accounting and management accounting).

These operational systems are usually found within the environment of business organisations that manufacture or produce products. However, many of these operational systems will still be found within the systems environments of organisations that only sell or market services. Other information systems that are commonly found at the operational level and also at higher levels of an organisation are:

▶ personnel (or human resources)
▶ marketing

▶ research and development
▶ customer service (or customer support).

Transactions between the business organisation and its customers give rise to an exchange of money, therefore operational systems are essential to overall business prosperity in that they directly interact with an organisation's customers and suppliers.

A typical transaction processing system is characterised by the processing of large amounts of numeric and alphanumeric data and information and normally a transaction processing system will have four main *components*:

1 data input (e.g. keyboard, data scanner, voice input, data downloading, electronic data interchange)
2 data processing (e.g. mainframe or microcomputer processing)
3 data and information output (e.g computer screen, file transfer, reports, electronic data interchange)
4 data storage (e.g. computer disk, CD-ROM, mainframe storage, database).

Transaction processing systems are typified by a number of characteristics which are indicative of the routine and deterministic nature of the activity of operational systems within the business systems environment:

▶ large-scale alphanumeric data processing activities
▶ heavy data storage requirements
▶ high level of routine and repetition in the processing activity
▶ reliance on deterministic computation and mathematical algorithms
▶ frequent and routine operation on a regular day-to-day basis.

Transaction processing activities   Transaction processing systems usually involve the activities of data collection, data manipulation, data storage and data or information generation and output. Data *collection* is the process of collecting and collating all the data necessary for the transaction processing system. This data can be collected in a number of ways, such as, electronic or paper-based invoices, bar code readers, scanners and electronic point of sale (EPOS) terminals. Data *manipulation* is the process of data transformation by performing calculations on that data. This process may involve sorting, aggregating, classifying, summarising or calculation of the data. Data *storage* is the process of placing data in the correct and appropriate storage area once is has been through the process of data manipulation mentioned previously. Data or information *generation* involves outputting information in a form that can be used for immediate decision making or which can be used as the data input source of another related information system within the business systems environment. *Output* may take the form of a computer screen or hardcopy report or it may take the form of a data file which can be input into a related system via electronic data interchange

(EDI), which is concerned with the electronic transfer of data and information from one computer-based system to another computer-based system.

Transaction processing methods   When automated computerisation first impacted upon transaction processing systems in the early 1960s there was only one method available for data processing, known as *batch processing* because data was collated or grouped into batches which were processed together in one processing run. However, as information technology improved it was possible to achieve an alternative method of processing known as on-line or *real-time processing*. Such transaction processing involves dealing with transactions and processing transactions immediately as and when they occur. An airline booking system is an example of a real-time transaction system, where flight reservations are made on-line and the system immediately records and updates the central booking and reservation system. The majority of information systems within business are now real-time systems. However, the payroll (salaries and wages) function is still often dealt with by batch processing, particularly when the payroll system has been outsourced to an external body.

Transaction processing architectures   Transaction processing systems integrate a number of applications, the nature of which is dependent upon the type of operational system that is being used. However, many traditional operational systems included a master file and a transactions file; the master file represented a permanent storage of data (or information) on a storage medium such as a computer disk or CD-ROM. Examples of master files are customer data files, suppliers data files, or employee files etc. The data on the master files often remained locked in time until the file was updated. Related to such files were transaction files that contained activities or transactions that affected the master file. However, many modern day systems processing architectures utilise more sophisticated technologies that allow the automatic separation of master file and transaction file components.

The pervasion of computing and IT on the operational functions within the business systems environment has improved the efficiency and effectiveness of these systems by achieving the following outcomes:

▶   ensuring a high level of accuracy
▶   allowing security of data entry and output
▶   increasing the speed and productivity of operational functions
▶   encouraging alignment and integration of operational functions.

> **DID YOU KNOW?**
> An area of business that relies on large data storage and manipulation capacities is the trading and equities exchanges, such as the London Stock Exchange. For instance, in 1996 the London Stock Exchange, in cooperation with the Bank of England, introduced a new City of London share dealing system known as CREST.

Among the first business functions to be affected by computerisation and the proliferation of IT within the business systems environment were the activities of *sales order processing* and *purchase order processing*. The following sections will go into greater detail concerning the 12 functional systems outlined earlier in this section.

ACTIVITY **7.3**
· · · · · · · · · · · · · · ·

Transaction processing systems

Describe the main characteristics of a TPS and discuss why the payroll function of business organisations is considered an operational system and explain what is meant by *transaction processing activities*. Explain the term *transaction processing method* and provide two examples of a transaction processing method.

7.3 The sales order processing system
· ·

The sales order processing activity involves collecting and collating orders from a business organisation's customers. Customers usually place orders using a variety of communications mediums including telephone orders, fax orders, e-mail orders, and orders communicated directly from one business organisation's computer network to another organisation's computer network, known as *electronic data interchange* (EDI). With EDI a customer or client business organisation can place orders directly from its transaction processing system into the transaction order processing system of another organisation. Within the framework of EDI there are no constraints on the time that orders can be placed, since they can be efficiently and effectively placed any time of the day or night, with the advantage of immediate electronic acknowledgment of receipt of the order by the order processing system. Order processing systems can be either real-time or batch processing systems. Order processing systems normally generate the following *output* data and information:

▶ daily sales journal   (used as input to the accounting system)
▶ customer invoices   (sent to the customer who placed the order)
▶ stock order notes   (sent to the output stock system)
▶ sales reports   (used by the marketing system).

The connection between the sales order processing system and related systems is illustrated in Figure 7.1.

The *sales journal* information, which is sent to the accounting system as input data, usually includes customer information, products ordered (with product codes), any discounts offered and price information. The *stock order notes* are sent to the output stock system if there is a requirement for further stock to be

figure 7.1
**Sales order
processing system**

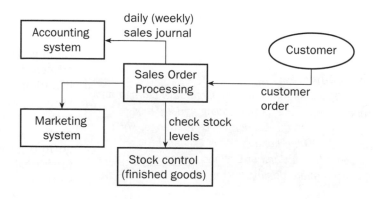

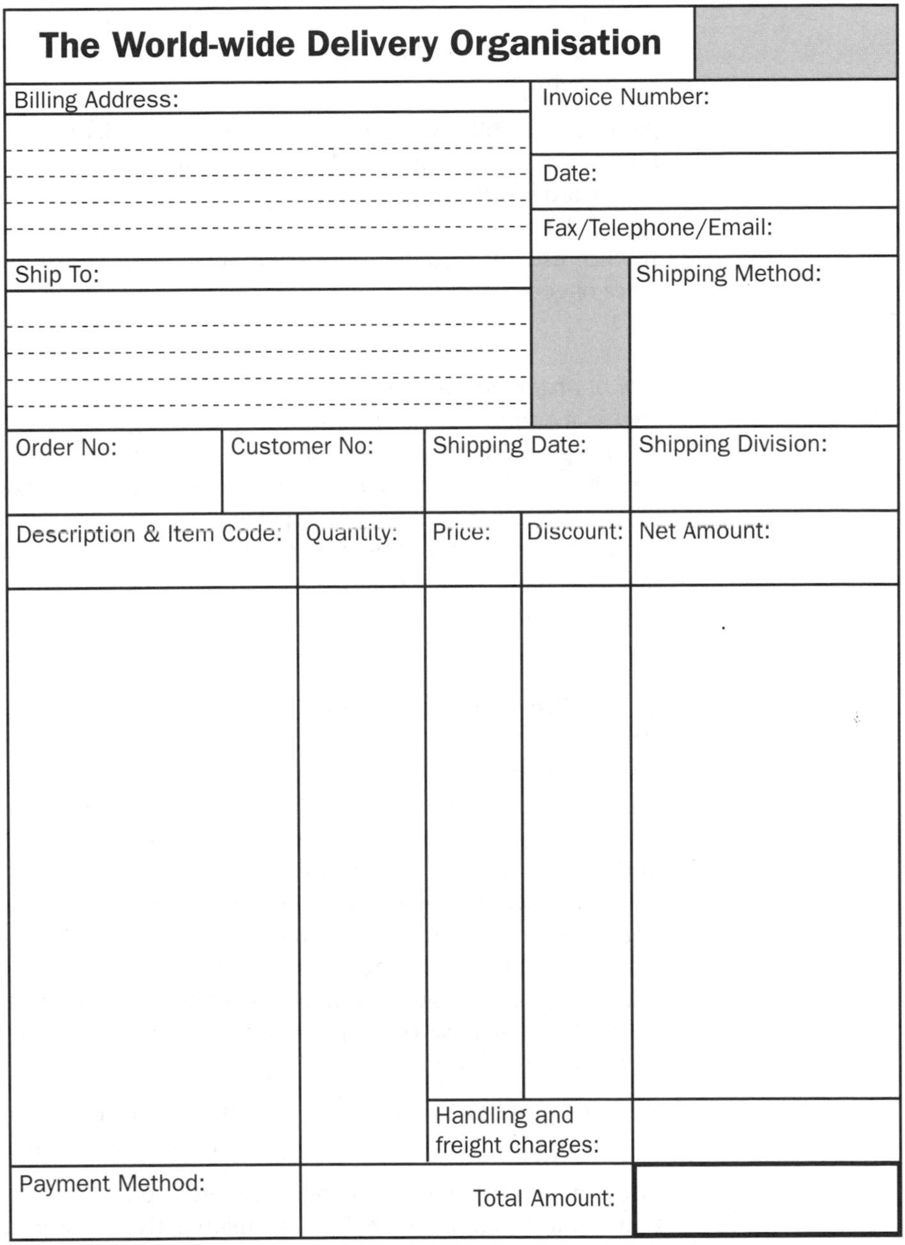

figure 7.2
Example of an invoice

The World-wide Delivery Organisation	
Billing Address:	Invoice Number:
- -	
- -	Date:
- -	
- -	Fax/Telephone/Email:

Ship To:		Shipping Method:
- -		
- -		
- -		
- -		

Order No:	Customer No:	Shipping Date:	Shipping Division:
Description & Item Code:	Quantity:	Price:	Discount:	Net Amount:
			Handling and freight charges:	
Payment Method:		Total Amount:	

accumulated. *Sales reports* can also be produced for the marketing system which analyse sales by customer, product line or by other demographic information. The usual sequence of events in a sales order processing system is as follows:

▶ A customer places an order with the system.
▶ The order processing system checks to see if the requested items are available in the current stock.
▶ If the stock is available, an invoice will be generated to the customer.

▶ If the stock is unavailable then the request becomes a back order and the order processing system sends a stock order note to the output stock system.

An *invoice* (or bill) is a record of the products or services a customer has ordered with the associated price and unique product line codes. Invoices are generated by the order processing system and sent as a factual record of activity to the customer. A typical example of a customer invoice can be seen in Figure 7.2. The invoice usually records information such as the customer name and address, price of goods and any discounts received on the goods.

ACTIVITY **7.4**

Sales order processing

Explain the term *electronic data interchange* (EDI) and discuss how EDI may be automated into the sales order processing system. List and explain three possible benefits of EDI and describe how a business organisation may use EDI to reorder stocks of raw materials from its suppliers. Discuss why a marketing information system may wish to receive sales reports from the sales order processing system and indicate how these reports may be used to determine market demand for goods and services.

7.4   The purchase order processing system

The purchase order processing system is responsible for purchasing, from external suppliers, all the raw materials, components and service requirements of a business organisation. This system is responsible for contract bidding for goods and services and for placing orders for raw material goods and services at the best available price. The purchase order processing system places orders with external organisations in a number of ways, such as by telephone, fax, e-mail or EDI. The system may also have the additional aim of maintaining a good relationship with its suppliers of goods and services in order to secure competitive prices from them. The purchase order processing system usually generates the following *output* data and information:

▶ daily purchases journal   (used as input to the accounting system)
▶ supplier orders   (sent to the relevant supplier).

The connection between the purchase order processing system and related systems is illustrated in Figure 7.3. The main activities of purchasing are to administer the purchasing of raw materials and equipment, maintain good contact with suppliers, keep track of new product developments, and negotiate suitable supplier contracts. The usual sequence of events in a purchase order processing system is as follows:

▶ A purchase order note is received from the input stock system.
▶ The purchase order processing system checks to see which suppliers need to be contacted for the requested items.
▶ A supplier order is generated and placed with the supplier.
▶ The purchase order system receives a supplier invoice.

figure 7.3
**Purchase order
processing system**

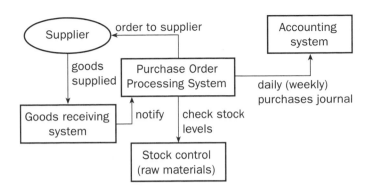

Every business organisation will have its own policies, practices and procedures for the purchasing of raw materials and equipment from suppliers. The purchase order processing system will usually possess vast stores of data and information on suppliers' goods and services. Purchasing is a major activity which can often absorb up to 75 per cent of the earned income of a large manufacturing organisation. Therefore, any cost savings can have a great effect on the overall profitability of a business organisation.

> **DID YOU KNOW?**
> *The aim of purchasing (which is sometimes known as procurement or buying) is to buy the right material, at the right quantity, of the right quality, at the right price, from the right supplier, with the right delivery arrangements, at the right delivery time and at the right payment terms.*

The increased use of information technology has given the purchasing function a broader and deeper access to information. For example, technologies like the Internet, and other on-line electronic consumer databases, have allowed purchasing managers to compare products and prices more efficiently and effectively than was the case previously. Furthermore, a business organisation's computerised purchase order processing system can be directly linked to the computer systems of its suppliers, to automatically reorder supplies through EDI channels; this has allowed business organisations to maintain low (yet adequate) raw material stock levels which in turn can provide reduced purchasing costs and a saving of time.

What has to be bought by the purchasing function will be determined by what is selling as a finished product. The minimum stock levels of raw materials stock (as with finished goods stock) is determined by the volume of sales (or customer demand) for the product. Stock levels are monitored and compared with the *minimum stock level* required for an individual raw material to determine when to buy raw materials and components for the manufacturing process. Therefore, although they are separate systems within a business organisation, sales order processing, purchase order processing and stock control are closely linked.

ACTIVITY **7.5**
•••••••••••••

Purchase order processing systems

Discuss how electronic data interchange (EDI) is automated into the purchase order processing system and describe how it benefits the relationship between a business organisation and its suppliers. Outline and explain the main aims and activities of the purchasing function of a business organisation and indicate the possible relationship of the goods receiving system and the stock control system within the overall purchase order processing system.

7.5 The goods receiving system and goods distribution system

The *goods receiving system* is usually responsible for physically taking possession of all the raw material goods coming into the business organisation. The receiving system is also responsible for inspecting the supplied goods and routing them to the input stock system. The receiving system should notify the purchase order processing system when items have been received (see Figure 7.3). The inspection application may take many forms, but it is primarily responsible for ensuring an acceptable level of *quality control*. Inspection procedures and automated practices can be established to monitor the quality of incoming raw materials and other equipment; any goods that fail the inspection can be sent back to the suppliers. The goods are usually delivered internally to the input stock system with a *stock received note*. Often, not all supplied goods are inspected, but rather a random selection of supplied goods are acceptance sampled. The goods receiving system often uses *sensors* and other control mechanisms to monitor the quality of goods incoming from suppliers.

The *goods distribution system* is responsible for shipping and delivering finished goods to the customer. The distribution system is responsible for implementing the most effective and efficient method of delivering goods to the customer. The distribution function is usually given the responsibility for physically packaging and delivering all products to customers. The delivery method can include mail service, truck and rail distribution or airplane distribution. The physical goods are usually accompanied with a *stock delivery note*. Many distribution systems are also responsible for keeping track of the location of goods during delivery. The function of getting goods from a business organisation to its customers is known as *logistics* and distribution involves logistical planning. Many software applications packages are available to assist in the logistical planning and coordination of the delivery of goods. Another application that is found within the distribution function is quality control of goods being dispatched to the customer. Many on-line distribution systems allow customers and clients to ascertain the status of their orders and products as they are in transit from the business organisation to the customer. Pause for thought 7.1 provides an example of a worldwide parcel delivery distribution system.

ACTIVITY **7.6**

The goods receiving system and goods distribution system
Discuss and describe the role that *quality control* plays within the two systems of goods receiving and goods distribution and suggest how information technology has affected these two business functions. Then describe the data and documentation that is an input and output of the goods receiving and goods distribution systems.

A worldwide parcel and package delivery system

To meet the demands of efficiency and effectiveness courier and package delivery organisations, such as Federal Express, DHL and United Parcel Service (UPS) have invested millions of pounds in information technology. Such investment is being used in two major ways:

Firstly, the global parcel and package delivery operators transact business on a global scale and the operational efficiencies of operating in many different countries are dependent upon increasingly sophisticated IT-based networks to hold them together.

Secondly, IT can enhance the relationship of the organisation with customers; and can, by doing so, provide a competitive advantage in a very profitable sector of the business environment.

The courier package and parcel delivery sector has changed from one based on mere transportation to one which is critically dependent upon information technology. In the 1990s, IT-based systems are used to schedule vehicle (and other types of transportation) fleets and to help plan and control the most efficient routes to delivery destinations. However, the global parcel and package delivery operators are faced each day with demands from customers to provide them with package and parcel tracking services, which entails the storage and retrieval of vast amounts of information, as and when required. Much of this information is gathered and transmitted to the customer organisations in order to augment their internal management information systems. For example, a business that has given responsibility for conveying a very valuable package or consignment will need to know at all stages its delivery status, from leaving until its arrival at its destination. Fast reporting of management information is vital to the reputation of a parcel and package delivery business.

For example, consider the case of UPS, a long-standing delivery business, that in the early 1980s operated a manual package handling system. Although this system was efficient, to a certain extent, it could not match Federal Express in terms of information technology provision and use, both internally and externally to the organisation. It was apparent to UPS that the leader in information management would be the eventual leader in package and parcel distribution and logistics. Therefore, UPS embarked on a heavy and directed programme of investment in information technology. It spent $50 million on a global IT-based information network; $100 million for a data centre to manage its data and information handling requirements; and $350 million for a delivery information acquisition system to track package and parcel consignments anywhere in the world. This major scale of IT investment was accompanied with investment among the workforce in terms of computerising their job tasks. For instance, hand-held computer facilities are installed into all forms of transportation for the drivers and operators; and throughout the processes of the delivery machine readable bar codes are used for tagging packages, in an effort to reduce reliance on paper-based information sources that are more vulnerable to error.

The delivery information acquisition system used by UPS allows two-way, and multiple, communication between drivers, operators and the source and destination depots. The system is used to collect details and to provide proof that deliveries have been made or where they are in transit around the world or nationally. The *cost of packages and parcels going astray, or being lost, has dramatically decreased because a parcel can be tracked from sending to receipt, whether by land, sea or air. UPS handles around 1 million to 2 million parcels per day on a global scale, a feat that would not be efficiently or effectively possible without investment in information technology in the requisite areas of the business. The technological investment has also led to competitive advantages in that UPS can additionally now offer a full 'business logistics service' that transcends national boundaries. For example, a manufacturing organisation based in Germany or France, that needs to be supplied with a network of material components from other business organisations from around the world (including any forms of trans-border authorisation or documentation) can outsource the logistical headache to an external organisation without the worry or cost involved in one-off, or specific, logistical projects. Therefore, a business organisation can have the whole of its logistical operations outsourced to a delivery services business without the worry or cost involved in one-off, or specific, logistical projects.*

7.6   The payroll system

The payroll system, sometimes known as the salaries and wages system, was one of the first transaction processing systems to be computerised within the business systems environment. Most payroll systems are still run through batch mode processing and payroll systems usually generate the following *output* data and information:

▶ wages or salary statement   (sent to employees as a record of work)
▶ payroll journal   (sent to the accounting system).

The *wages or salary statement* is sent to employees as a factual record of work activity. The statement usually contains information such as the employee name, department or location, the time period worked, tax and various other deductions. A typical example of a salary statement can be seen in Figure 7.4. Payroll systems are required to handle such variables as normal and overtime hours worked, holiday pay, national and local taxation and deductions, productivity and internal incentive bonuses. Most payroll systems have EDI applications that permit money to be electronically transferred from a business organisation's bank account to the individual accounts of its employees. It is often more costly for business organisations to pay employees in cash than it is to implement a direct electronic funds transfer system.

DID YOU KNOW?
Traditionally, the term salary *was applied to an employee payment made every month. Whereas, the term* wages *implied a payment made to employees on a weekly basis.*

Most payroll systems also produce a *payroll journal* which is used by the accounting system of a business organisation. The payroll journal usually records such information as employee names, departments where employees work, the total salary or wage paid to each employee by department, various deductions and other net pay calculations. The payroll journal can be used by the accounting system to produce a figure for

figure 7.4
Example of a salary statement

Organisation Name:		Period No.:	Department:	Employee Code:	Employee Name:
National Insurance Code:	Tax Code: 375L	Period:	Taxable Pay:	Division:	Pay Location:
Code & Payments	Hours:	Rate:	Period:	Code & Deductions:	Period:	Balance:	Net Pay:

Total Payments:

Total Deductions:

Amount Payable

total wages paid in any given period of trading operations. The aggregated wages information can be used as part of the external information reporting requirement to produce an organisation's *Trading and Profit and Loss Statement* and *Balance Sheet* which are published in the annual accounts of a business organisation. Many payroll systems are tailor-made for specific industries. Normally, payroll data is collected and collated using a range of sources and technologies, including time-cards, productivity measures and industrial sensors. Most payroll systems can handle overtime, holiday pay, variable and multi-rate salary structures, incentive programmes and commission fees and all the aggregated payroll amounts will appear in the *general ledger* of the accounting system.

ACTIVITY **7.7**

The payroll system

Explain the role of a wages or salary statement and describe the type of data and information included in such a statement. Indicate the types of data and information produced by the payroll system and suggest which other systems within a business organisation use payroll data as information inputs.

7.7   The accounting system

The accounting system is responsible for the collection and collation of financial data and information relating to all transactions that are internal and external to the business organisation.

The accounting system can be separated into the two distinct functions of financial accounting and management accounting. *Financial accounting* information is produced for individuals and other organisations that are external to the business organisation. Such information is contained in the annual accounts that a business organisation is required, by law, to produce for public scrutiny. *Management accounting* information is produced for internal management consumption in order to direct more efficiently and effectively the internal human and technology resources of the business organisation. There are three essential applications present within an accounting system as follows:

> **DID YOU KNOW?**
> The accounting system involves the process of identifying, measuring and communicating economic information to permit informed judgements and decisions by the users of the information.
>
> *(American Accounting Association)*

1   accounts receivable from customers
2   accounts payable to suppliers
3   the general ledger.

Accounts receivable usually takes the form of a statement of payment sent to the customer for goods (or services) previously supplied and invoiced to that customer. The bill sent to the customer usually includes information such as the customer's name and address, date of the order, product codes and description, allowances and returns, monetary amounts paid to date and monetary amounts receivable. It is this business function that receives money payment from customers for goods and services previously supplied. The accounts receivable data can be aggregated to determine the total *sales* (or demand) for a given period of business activity. Most business organisations can handle the payment for goods and services in a number of forms, including cash, bank cheques, credit card payment, or direct *electronic funds transfer* (EFT). The accounts receivable application of an accounting system allows a business organisation to collect money efficiently from customers. It also allows a business organisation to minimise losses by quickly identifying bad debt customers. Such information can be transmitted to the order processing system to blacklist bad debt customers and prevent them from ordering further goods until the bad debts are paid. The computerisation of the accounts receivable application has in most cases allowed business organisations to achieve better cash flows.

The *accounts payable* application of the accounting system aims to manage and control the outflow of money to the business organisation's suppliers. The activity involves issuing cheques to suppliers for materials and services purchased by the business organisation with the aim of providing control over the purchasing activity of the business organisation. The accounts payable activity checks that bills received are accurate and that the goods or services covered by the bill have been satisfactorily delivered. A typical report produced by the accounts payable activity is a *purchases journal* which summarises the business organisation's bill paying activities. Such information is important for a business to control its cash flows.

The *general ledger* is a large and aggregated list of all the transactions and internal business activities of the organisation. A computerised general ledger allows automated financial reporting and data entry. The reports that are generated include the following:

▶ Trading and Profit and Loss Statements
▶ Balance Sheets.

Examples of the above statements are illustrated in Figures 7.5 and 7.6. All business organisations will have an accounting system which will generate reports on the trading performance of that business. The reports are known in the United Kingdom as a Balance Sheet (showing assets and liabilities), a Profit and Loss Account (showing the gross and net profit of the business) and Cash Flow Statements (showing the movement in liquid or cash assets between two periods). Historical data can also be compiled from previous accounting periods in order to carry out an analysis of demand and supply trends for the organisation over time.

ACTIVITY **7.8**

The accounting system

Discuss and explain the three essential applications present within an accounting system and describe the function of each application. List two other business systems that supply information to the accounting system and describe how this information is incorporated into the general ledger application.

figure 7.5
**Example of a Profit
and Loss Statement**

**Elephant and Castle Ltd
Trading and Profit and Loss Account for the Year ending 31.12.96**

	(£ 000s)	(£ 000s)
Sales (revenue)		500
Less: Cost of sales		
opening stock	50	
stock purchases	300	
less: closing stock	(150)	200
Gross profit		300
Period expenses:		
Rent	50	
Wages	85	
Electricity	35	
Professional fees	25	
Depreciation	20	
Bad debts	15	(230)
Net profit		70

figure 7.6
**Example of a
Balance Sheet
(vertical format)**

**Elephant and Castle Ltd
Balance Sheet as at 31.12.96**

	(£ 000s)	(£ 000s)
Fixed assets		
Freehold buildings	100	
Plant and machinery	75	
Motor vehicles	75	250
Current assets		
Stock	75	
Trade debtors	50	
Cash in hand	25	
	150	
Less: current liabilities		
Trade creditors	(40)	
Bank overdraft	(25)	
	(65)	
Net current assets		85
		335
Capital and reserves		
Share capital	265	
Retained profits	70	325

7.8   The production planning and production control systems

An organisation that relies on manufacturing as the basis of its business activities will require two particular systems to deal with the manufacturing or production processes which are *production planning* and *production control*. Production planning is concerned with planning *when* to make a product. The role of production planning is to produce a *production schedule* that is used by the production control system in manufacturing to determine the next week, next month, or any other time period's production activity. *Production control* is concerned with managing and coordinating production resources, and configuring manufacturing machinery to carry out the instructions implicit in the production schedule. The aim is to produce finished goods through the most efficient and effective configuration of production resources; these resources being people, organisation and information technology.

Manufacturing organisations make products which require the use of raw materials, or other part-made components, as inputs to the manufacturing process. For example, a computer consists of microchips, disk drives and peripheral casing; often smaller clone-machine manufacturers assemble various parts and produce their own branded computers. Normally the most expensive part of any manufacturing organisation is the manufacturing process, which requires heavy investment in a location for production, employees, machinery and other peripheral equipment to carry out the manufacturing operation. Within IT-based manufacturing environments much of the manufacturing process is often automated with robots and other cybernetic technology undertaking the production control process.

Quality control checks are essential to the manufacturing process. These checks can be made for all items that come off the production process or just for a random selection of finished goods. The manufacturing process relies upon an *input stock system*, an *output stock system* and a *production planning system*. The relationship between these three systems is illustrated in Figure 7.7.

The systems of *input stock control* and *output stock control* are essential to the overall manufacturing process. Raw material stock must be kept at exactly the

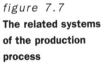

figure 7.7
The related systems of the production process

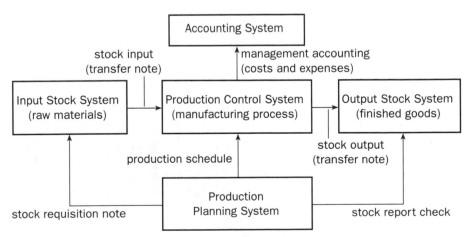

right levels. Too little stock would hold up the manufacturing process and too much stock would incur additional and unwanted costs of storage. It is essential for stock to be delivered into the manufacturing process at the exact time required and in the exact amounts, which is referred to as 'just-in-time' (JIT) manufacturing. The consumer food retail industry is a prime example of a business area that relies on an efficient and effective stock control system to increase profits and maintain a competitive edge over rivals. Within stock control systems technology, particularly within the retail sector, the use of *laser tills* has increased the efficiency of stock handling. A laser till uses a laser to scan bar codes on products or items of stock whereby the laser till is linked to a computer which recognises the product being scanned and carries out a number of data recording, updating and checking activities.

A key function of laser till technology is to capture retail sales data, update stock information and generate management level reports. The particular functions of laser technology are to read bar codes, update stock positions by product category, analyse sales demand by product category, calculate and monitor money through the till. Most of the large food retailers in the world have used information technology for many years for competitive advantage. Such technology allows managers to know which products are selling and how many are being sold, which provides an indication of product demand. If this information is not quickly and accurately available the products will go out of stock and sales may be lost. Most products that are sold in retail shops will have a bar code which details information concerning that product. Stock system technology also uses bar codes extensively. Most bar code numbers used in the United Kingdom are administered by the Article Numbering Association which uses unique numbers for individual products. Figure 7.8 is an example of a product bar code. The digits at the bottom of the bar code correspond to items of information about the product. Under the Article Numbering Association system the first two digits identify the number bank which issued the number. The next five digits are allocated to the company marketing or manufacturing the product. The following five digits are allocated to the particular size or variation of that product. The last digit is a computer check digit to make sure the bar code is correctly composed.

Laser till technology used in retail shops is normally referred to as *electronic point of sale* (EPOS) technology. Normally, the product which is being purchased by a customer is passed across a laser scanner built into the laser till technology.

figure 7.8
Example of a product bar code

The details of the scan are relayed to a computer system which sends back a description of the item and its price to the terminal, which is in turn then printed onto the customer's (or client's) receipt. There are a number of benefits in using EPOS technology in the retail sector as follows:

▶ increased checkout accuracy and more efficient checkout operation
▶ individual cashier performance assessment and customer analysis of buying habits
▶ efficient service including itemised receipts and bills
▶ efficient and effective stock level monitoring and marketing report analysis
▶ increase in product range held and reduced out-of-stock items
▶ improvements in store layouts and reduced stock storage areas.

Related to EPOS is a technology known as *electronic funds transfer at point of sale* (EFTPOS), which allows money to be immediately transferred electronically from a customer's bank account into that of the business organisation's bank account. In the retail sector, an EPOS terminal can also incorporate EFTPOS technology to cover electronic payment methods. For example, the electronic transfer of funds between accounts can be done through the use of a customer's *Switch card*. When a cashier at an EFTPOS till has totalled the bill for goods or services the customer may hand the cashier their Switch card. The card is scanned through a reader which interprets the customer's details from the magnetic strip on the back of the Switch card; the total value of the transaction is entered into the EFTPOS terminal and monetary funds can then be immediately transferred electronically. Unlike a credit card, the Switch card transaction does not provide periods of credit. This approach to payment has the advantage of being a direct payment method, eliminating the need to carry cash. A significant advantage of EPOS and EFTPOS technology is witnessed in various productivity improvements in retail store layout and reduced storage areas needed to physically contain stock. The food retail sector is a good example of an area of business that has benefited from reduced stock storage areas within its stores.

> **DID YOU KNOW?**
> *Laser till technology was first used in the early 1980s in the food retail sector and Sainsbury's became the first business organisation in the United Kingdom to link weighing scales to scanning terminals.*

Traditionally, the area within a shop set aside for stock storage was a wasted resource. The area given over to storage is unproductive related to the area that is set aside for products on display for customers to select and purchase. Figure 7.9 provides an example of two food retailers known as retailer A, who dedicates half the available shop area (50 per cent) to holding stock, and retailer B, who has eliminated much of the stock area to make the customer product purchasing area larger and in which just 10 per cent of the shop area is dedicated to stock storage. It is assumed that retailer B has a holding area for stock palettes, unloaded from lorries and awaiting stacking on shop shelves. By having stock palettes delivered just-in-time, as and when required, the store need not maintain large areas of its shop dedicated to warehouse storage.

From the example in Figure 7.9 it can be seen that retail store A has a storage area of 50 per cent and retail store B a storage area of 10 per cent. Assuming that each square foot of store area generates on average £5 income, then the following calculations can be made:

figure 7.9

An example of retail storage areas

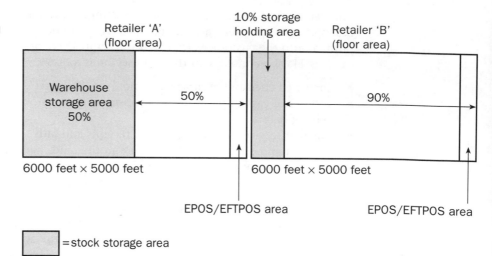

 = stock storage area

	Retail store A:	**Retail store B:**
Total floor space	= 30,000 square feet	30,000 square feet
Earning area	= 50%	90%
Earnings per store	= 50% × 30,000 × £5	90% × 30,000 × £5
	= £75,000	£135,000

Therefore, by dedicating a smaller area to stock warehousing, retail store B has earned an income of £60,000 more than retail store A. This is only possible if a retail shop receives stock just-in-time, as and when requested. Having the right stock levels is based on a number of simple rules related to maintaining minimum stock levels. A detailed study of the *stock control system* of business organisations will be undertaken in the next section.

ACTIVITY **7.9**
· · · · · · · · · · · · ·

Production planning and production control

Discuss the importance of an *input stock system* and an *output stock system* to the production control system and indicate why it is necessary to have raw material received just-in-time, as and when requested. Then explain the role and function of laser till technology for stock handling and product identification in the retail industry. Outline four possible events that may halt the manufacturing process and indicate what the consequences are of having either too much stock or not enough stock of raw materials passing into the manufacturing process.

7.9   The stock control system
· ·

Any manufacturing organisation which keeps stocks of raw materials or finished goods needs to operate a stock control system. Normally, stock must be controlled and coordinated to maintain the appropriate *minimum stock levels* across a range of goods. Stock systems should contain up-to-date information on stock quantity levels, prices, minimum stock levels and reorder levels. An efficient and effective stock system should automatically indicate when minimum stock levels have been reached. Stock control systems will also usually generate useful reports on sales patterns, stock flow through the manufacturing process, and early and late stock orders. The main effects of an automated stock control system are that a manager can quickly identify stock levels and the price of any individual stock item at any given time, usually at the touch of a button.

Stock refers either to the physical goods and raw materials that are bought in for the manufacturing process of the business organisation or to finished goods that are produced and waiting to be sold to customers. The central aim of a stock control system is to accurately monitor and control the flow of stock into and out of the production process. Therefore, stock systems can be divided into *input stock systems* and *output stock systems*, particularly where the business organisation is engaged in some form of manufacturing or production activity. The input stock system deals with the raw materials that have been bought into the organisation; these raw materials are held in stock until they are required to be used in the manufacturing process. The goal of the input stock system is to make the production activity more efficient and effective by placing just the right amount of raw material stock into the production control process. The output stock system is concerned with finished goods that are stored and waiting to be distributed to the customer. It should be remembered that the logical stock system should not be equated to the physical environment in which stock is stored. A warehouse for goods is merely the physical evidence of a stock system. The goal of the output stock system is to maintain and control the flow of stock from the manufacturing process out to the customer.

Various reports are produced by the stock system including *stock status reports* which indicate the levels of stock held in store, used by the production planning system to determine which particular set of goods or products need to be manufactured in a given production planning period. The stock status report assists the production planning activity to determine a *production schedule* for the manufacturing and production control system.

Minimum stock levels

Having the right stock level is based on some simple rules. Stock levels are dependent upon the movement of stock coming into or out of the warehouse storage area. The balance is indicated by the number in stock, which is constantly checked against the minimum stock level. The minimum stock level is calculated in the following way:

Minimum stock level (MSL) = (lead time × rate of use) + safety margin

The *lead time* indicates the lag time required for raw materials or stock to be reordered and delivered; the *rate of use* refers to the rate at which stock is consumed; the *safety margin* refers to the level of stock held in case of unforeseen circumstances and other contingencies. For example, if the demand (sales) for product A is 1000 units per day, the lead time is 5 days and the safety margin is 500 units, then the minimum stock level will be as follows:

Minimum stock level = 1000 (units per day) × 5 (days) + 500 (units) = 5500 (units)

figure 7.10
**Production planning
and decision making**

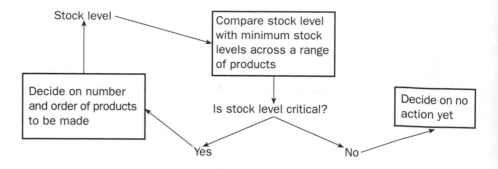

Therefore, the minimum stock level is 5500 units. The lead times, rate of use and safety margins will be determined by the nature of the individual product and in turn the nature of a product may be determined by trend analysis. For example, a supermarket store may perform a trend analysis on every product line in its stores taking into account changes in seasonal demand, marketing campaigns and special offers.

The complexity of the stock control system will depend upon the nature and range of products manufactured by a business organisation. Minimum stock levels can be affected by what is called 'shelf-life', which is the time it takes products to deteriorate or go off; any unused or soiled goods will be wasted after their shelf-life. This can constitute a cost to an organisation and is therefore of significance to the stock control system. In a manufacturing organisation the production planning system is activated by finished stock levels. The decision-making activity is revealed in Figure 7.10. The production planning system will make decisions on how many units to produce, the order in which they are to be made and the time-frame necessary for production. This information is contained in a production schedule which is passed to the production control system.

The aim of the production planning function is to achieve the goal of maintaining stock to meet demand at the lowest possible cost.

> **DID YOU KNOW?**
> *The production schedule must indicate what is to be made, how it is to be made and when it is to be made.*

ACTIVITY **7.10**

The stock control system

Discuss what information is required in order for the production planning system to produce a *production schedule* for the production control system. Explain the decision-making process necessary in determining the production schedule for a given time period and state the main aim of the production planning manager. Once this has been completed, assume that you have been appointed the production planning manager of a jam-making business known as PL Jams Limited. The stock control system maintains a record of what is in stock and the minimum stock levels required. Below is a pro forma *production schedule* for raw materials delivered to the business organisation. The information you have is that the supplier delivers 3000 units of raw materials on 21 March; the manufacturing process then draws 500 units on 28 March, 2000 units on 2 April, and a further 800 units are drawn on 7 April.

Date	Stock in	Stock out	Stock balance	Minimum stock level
2 March	2000	0	2000	1200
8 March	0	700	1300	1200
15 March	0	300	1000	1200
21 March	?	0	?	1200
28 March	?	?	?	1200
2 April	?	?	?	1200
7 April	?	?	?	1200

Fill in the gaps indicated by the question mark symbol given the above information on delivery and drawing of stock. Indicate at what point the stock became *critical*, which means it fell below the minimum stock level (MSL).

Figure 7.11 is an integrated illustration of the relationship between various functions within the business systems environment.

7.10   Management decision systems

So far this chapter has addressed operational systems within the business environment that rely on deterministic and routine transactions. The management information systems environment on the other hand normally deals with data and information which is both objective and subjective to varying degrees. Four particular systems that fall within the management information systems sphere are marketing information systems, customer support systems, research and development and personnel systems (human resources). The goal of all management information systems is to provide managers with information that allows them to plan, control and organise more effectively and efficiently the resources of the business organisation.

DID YOU KNOW?
The aim of management information systems is to provide the right information to the right person in the right format at the right time. Implicit in this function is the activity of planning, decision making and control of human, technological and other resources to achieve the aims and objectives of a business organisation.

Managers rely on formal reports generated by the various information systems of the organisation. These reports can be concerned with a number of internal activities such as resource scheduling, product demand and supply, and resource allocation. Such information is used by managers to control the medium-term direction of a business organisation and to keep it progressing in the appropriate and required direction dictated by the strategic level of the organisation. The information generated from internal information systems is normally just internally produced evidence of the functioning of the business organisation; external information usually forms only a minor part of the decision-making activity within the management information systems function.

figure 7.11
Integrated systems within a business organisation

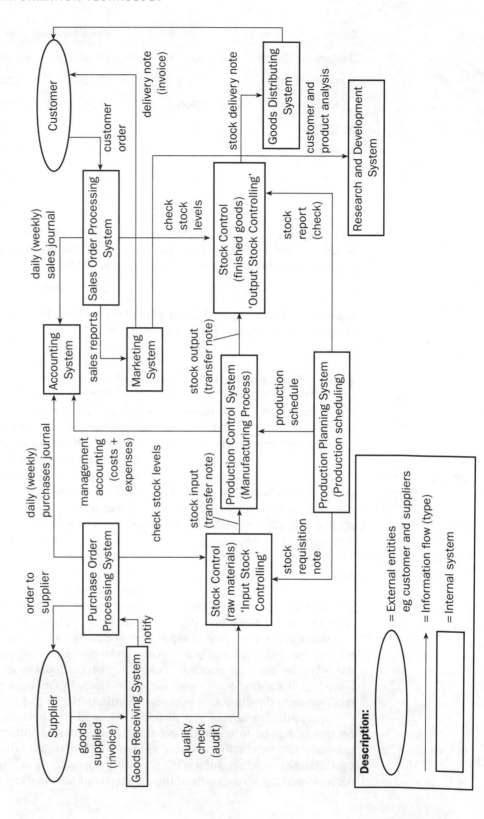

Therefore, management information is usually derived from internal data generated within the business organisation. Most management information reports rely on using past and present information which can be used to extrapolate or forecast the activities of the business for the next month, year or any time period between these two time-frames.

The marketing information system This system falls within the management information sphere and is concerned with supporting managerial activity in the areas of product development, customer distribution methods, pricing, promotion, advertising, and sales demand forecasting. There are two main functions within a marketing system as follows:

1 data and information collection and collation
2 advertising and promotion.

Often the two activities are confused within the umbrella term of marketing. It is commonly, but wrongly, assumed that marketing represents advertising. Marketing, more than most systems, relies on a significant amount of external as well as internal information. The marketing activities are usually determined by the overall strategic plan of the business organisation which may set sales targets that are influenced by the marketing activities of data collection and promotional advertising. The type of inputs to a marketing systems are as follows:

▶ *Sales reports.* These give an idea of customer demand for goods and services and can be used to forecast future sales activity or indicate areas of growth and decline in demand. Sales reports are generated by the order processing system.
▶ *Competition.* Information can be collated on competitor organisations such as new products being developed, pricing policies and advertising strategies.
▶ *Customers.* Information can be collected from customers in various forms including questionnaires, interviews, customer surveys and information collated by the customer support system.
▶ *Advertising.* Information and feedback from advertising campaigns can be used to produce different products or services or to modify the marketing strategy of an organisation.

The underlying premise of marketing is that long-term business growth can only be achieved if the needs of the customer are identified, anticipated and fulfilled. Therefore, the marketing system can provide a business with a competitive edge since marketing is concerned with the relationship between the business organisation and its external environment. Various models have been developed to make the activities of the marketing system more effective in achieving its goals. One of these is known as the '4-P Model' which represents:

Product
Promotion
Price
Place.

For a business organisation to be successful it must have the right product, with the right promotion, at the right price and placed in the right market area. The role of the market research function is to reduce uncertainty in decision making within the business environment. All products and services have a life cycle from being born into a market place until they expire due to changing tastes or the rise of more appealing substitute products. Figure 7.12 illustrates a typical product life cycle and indicates the characteristics and significance of each stage of the product life cycle.

ACTIVITY **7.11**

Management decision systems (1)

Provide four examples of the types of decision making undertaken by managers and describe the information requirements of a typical management information system. Explain four types of information inputs to a marketing system and further explain why it is important for a marketing system to appreciate the position and status of a product on the product life cycle.

The customer support system Customer support systems are vital in maintaining a good working relationship between a business organisation and its customers. This area is closely related to after sales care and after sales service, with the aim being to create a good and *continuous* working relationship between a business organisation and its customers; this will often encourage customer loyalty to a particular product or business organisation. The customer support system usually gathers information from customers, in the form of questionnaires and surveys, which can be used by either the marketing system or the research and development system. The marketing system can use customer information to focus advertising and promotion campaigns. The research and development system can incorporate customer views and preferences into the development of products that will appeal to customer tastes.

Research and development system This type of system usually concerns itself with researching the nature of products and attempting to develop new products that will be attractive to the customers of the business. Therefore, product research is a valuable exercise in identifying the features that customers desire in a product or service. For example, size, colour, composition, appearance, suitability and compatibility can be investigated to develop products and services that will be demanded by customers. The input data and information for research and development comes from the *marketing system* in the form of market research data and market reports generated from marketing analysis.

The human resources system The human resources system is concerned with contractual matters relating to the personnel (employees) of an organisation. People are the main resource of most organisations and as such need to be coordinated and guided by managers as a valuable resource. The main activities of the human resources system include employee hiring, employee contracts, maintaining employee records, employee analysis and employee evaluation.

figure 7.12
The product life cycle

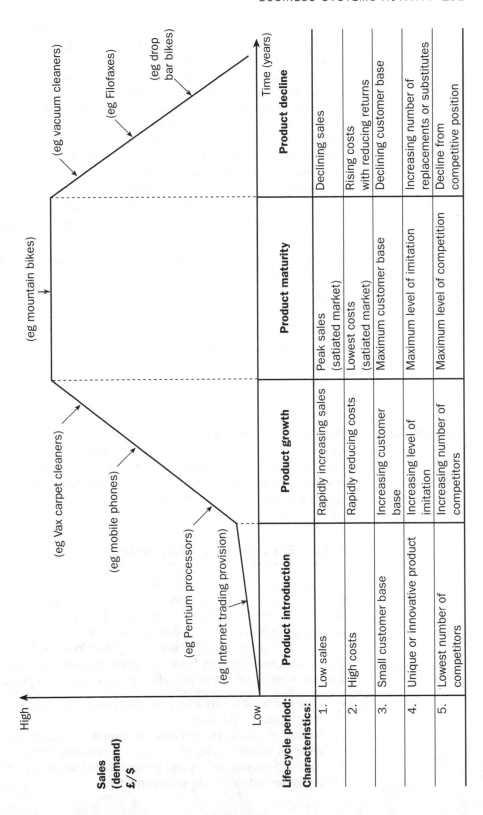

Life-cycle period: Characteristics:	Product introduction	Product growth	Product maturity	Product decline
1.	Low sales	Rapidly increasing sales	Peak sales (satiated market)	Declining sales
2.	High costs	Rapidly reducing costs	Lowest costs (satiated market)	Rising costs with reducing returns
3.	Small customer base	Increasing customer base	Maximum customer base	Declining customer base
4.	Unique or innovative product	Increasing level of imitation	Maximum level of imitation	Increasing number of replacements or substitutes
5.	Lowest number of competitors	Increasing number of competitors	Maximum level of competition	Decline from competitive position

Sales (demand) £/$

High

Low

Time (years)

(eg Internet trading provision)

(eg Pentium processors)

(eg mobile phones)

(eg Vax carpet cleaners)

(eg mountain bikes)

(eg vacuum cleaners)

(eg Filofaxes)

(eg drop bar bikes)

Inputs into the human resources system include payroll information, employee appraisal reports, personal employee data and employee work and employment status. The main activity of human resources is controlling the contractual obligations between the employee and the organisation which are usually determined on being hired by the business organisation. Most business organisations have computerised human resources information systems to store employee records. These systems can often be used to effectively match the skills of employees to particular projects and activities that arise on an intermittent basis. Output reports from the human resources system include human resource planning and coordination, job application review profiles, employee skills analysis and salary surveys. Effective human resources planning requires forecasting future demand for employees, matched by related skills, and anticipating future supply of skilled and able employees. Human resourcing systems usually include the following main activities:

▶ employee selection and recruitment administration and profiling
▶ maintaining employee records related to skills, training and employee development
▶ employee scheduling, placement and team composition profiling
▶ wages and salaries administration and related salary surveys.

The human resources system allows a business organisation to coordinate and direct human activity efficiently and effectively in order to better achieve the overall strategic goals of the organisation.

ACTIVITY **7.12**

Management decision systems (2)

Discuss the main information inputs and outputs of a typical human resources information system and explain the four main activities of a human resources system. Describe how a human resources system may be used to formulate working groups based on employee profiling.

7.11   Executive decision systems

Strategic decision-making endeavours to accurately predict the nature of business and the direction of the organisation into the distant future; the time-frames for strategic decision making may vary from 1–20 years. Such far-sighted decision making is not functional, nor deterministic, and normally relies on the marginal accuracy of various decision support applications used to assist the decision-making judgement of a high-level business executive. Executive decision support systems share a number of desirable characteristics as follows:

▶ ability to handle vast amounts of alphanumeric, textual, graphical and other multi-media information
▶ facility to handle, process and interpret data and information from very different sources, using different presentational formats
▶ ability to provide report and presentational flexibility which can be integrated into different output media

▶ facility to manipulate and analyse data and information through modelling and simulation and other *what-if* analysis.

Executive decision support systems are used by business organisations as a guidance tool for strategic decision making. Therefore, financial modelling and statistical software application packages are often considered part of the available set of decision support tools and techniques. Decision support systems can also cross over into the domain of expert systems which attempt to replicate the knowledge and decision-making ability of a professional expert in various areas. Executive decision support systems are characterised by user-friendly interfaces that are customised to an individual or select set of individuals at the executive level of a business organisation. The systems are usually tailored to the particular requirements of the executive level of the business organisation. There are four main models produced by executive decision support systems as follows:

1 *Financial models*. These analyse and predict the financial operations of the organisation, including cash flow analysis, investment analysis and rates of return analysis.
2 *Statistical analysis models*. These can provide statistics, trend analysis, statistical and econometric testing over a range of different variables.
3 *Graphical models*. These models can be designed to provide a visual picture of the underlying data and information held within the decision-making environment.
4 *Management models*. These models are developed to control and predict the management structure of an organisation and to guide any form of required project management to deliver the strategic aims of the business organisation.

Figure 7.13 illustrates the components that would be expected to be present within an executive decision support systems environment.

figure 7.13
Components of an executive decision support systems environment

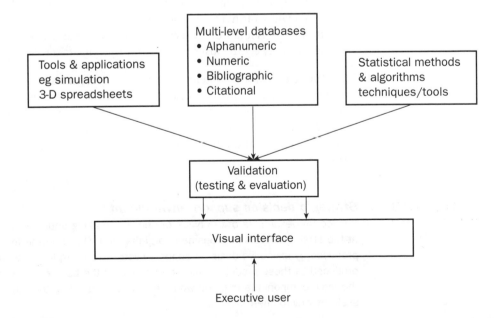

Executive decision support environments that assist strategic decision making bear a number of characteristics as follows:

▶ Strategic decision makers have to have access to a wide variety of information sources.
▶ The strategic decision-making environment is usually complex and highly uncertain.
▶ Strategic decision support systems are used to assist the evaluation of long-term decision making.
▶ Strategic information systems are end-user driven and customised to meet the needs of specific executive strategists.
▶ Strategic information systems are usually *multi-layered* and three-dimensional (e.g. possessing three-dimensional modelling applications).
▶ Strategic information systems are usually *multi-faceted* with an interface masking a relational database, modelling tools, decision simulation rules and algorithms.

Along with these characteristics there are usually a number of corresponding problems that need to be addressed when using strategic decision support systems as follows:

▶ Strategic decision making takes place in *dynamic* environments where information tends to be more subjective than objective.
▶ Strategic decision making relies on numeric as well as non-numeric (sometimes bibliographical) data and information. (e.g. socio-economic reports).
▶ There commonly exists an absence of information and *data validation*. Therefore, there is often an absence of data source testing and evaluation.
▶ Strategic decision systems often fail to test information and data sources, for example, in terms of the statistical characteristics of distribution (range and skewness) inherent in data sets.
▶ Often there is a failure to recognise or test for user-executive *risk psychology* (e.g. is the executive user risk neutral or a risk taker).

The strategic decision systems environment includes the hardware, software, procedures and support personnel required to assist the decision-making activities of the executive board of a business organisation. Ultimately, the strategic information systems environment must possess the capability to support strategic planning, control and decision making with regard to the whole organisation's resources.

ACTIVITY 7.13

Strategic decision support environments
Provide four examples of the types of decision making undertaken by executives at the strategic levels of a business organisation. Describe the four main models produced by executive decision support systems and explain how the information produced by these models would be used within the business environment. Discuss the main components that you would expect to find within the strategic information systems environment.

7.12   Chapter summary

We have seen from the evidence of this chapter that the *operational systems* of a business organisation perform the day-to-day activities of recording, processing and disseminating business transactions. These systems normally operate within information environments of certainty. The data and information that is produced by operational systems is often used at other decision-making levels of an organisation, for example, at the managerial or strategic levels. Management information systems are designed to select, analyse and produce useful information to enable managers to make decisions regarding the allocation of business resources. At the top decision-making level of the organisational hierarchy are systems to support executive or strategic decision making. These systems normally integrate various modelling facilities in order to predict or forecast the long-term effects of decisions that may influence the future direction of an organisation.

The following chapters will study the particular technologies, and their respective environments, found within the the main generic levels of the organisational hierarchy. In particular, aspects of *integrated office systems technology* will be covered in terms of the range of methods and procedures for using information technology such as databases, wordprocessors, spreadsheets, electronic networked diaries, electronic notice boards and electronic mail to improve the efficiency and effectiveness of business practices.

Short self-assessment questions

7.1   Define the concept of the planning, decision making and control life cycle and provide an example of the life cycle within any level of the organisational hierarchy.

7.2   Indicate why the decision-making environment is often described as either structured, semi-structured or unstructured.

7.3   Define and explain the term *transaction processing system* (TPS) and provide four examples of such systems within the business environment.

7.4   Define and explain the system known as *sales order processing* and indicate the sort of data that is input and output to the system.

7.5   Define and explain the system known as *purchase order processing* and indicate the sort of data that is input and output to the system.

7.6   Describe the systems known as *goods receiving* and *goods distribution* within the business systems environment.

7.7   Outline and explain the main functions and objectives of the goods receiving and goods distribution systems.

7.8   Define the system known as *payroll* and suggest why this business function was the first to be automated within most business organisations.

7.9   Outline the function of the *payroll journal* and describe the type of information typically included in the payroll journal.

7.10   Explain the role and function of the accounting system within a business organisation.

7.11 Describe the two main reports incorporated into the annual accounts of a business organisation that can be produced from the general ledger application.

7.12 Define and explain the terms *production planning system* and *production control system* within business organisations.

7.13 Describe the physical and information inputs and outputs of a manufacturing process and indicate which business systems are directly related to the production control system.

7.14 Define the two information technologies known as EPOS and EFTPOS and outline five main advantages of using EFTPOS technology.

7.15 Explain the system known as *stock control* and describe the difference between an *input stock system* and an *output stock system* in a manufacturing organisation.

7.16 Explain the role and function of maintaining minimum stock levels and describe the elements that are required in order to calculate the minimum stock level.

7.17 Describe a *marketing information system* and indicate the two main functions of marketing within the business environment.

7.18 Explain the function and role of the systems known as customer support, research and development, and human resources.

7.19 Describe the concept of strategic decision support and outline the main characteristics of such a strategic level systems.

Further study and reading
....

Books

Beer, S. (1966) *Decision and Control*. Chichester, England: John Wiley. (*)

Fletcher, K. (1990) *Marketing Management and Information Technology*. Hemel Hempstead, England: Prentice-Hall.

LaMoreaux, R.D. (1995) *Bar Codes and other Automated Identification Systems*. Leatherhead, England: Pira International

Rivett, P. (1994) *The Craft of Decision Modelling*. Chichester, England: John Wiley.

Silver, M.S. (1991) *Systems that Support Decision Makers*. Chichester, England: John Wiley.

Spaul, B. and Williams, B. (eds) (1991) *IT and Accounting*. London: Chapman and Hall.

Sprague, R.H. and Watson, H.J. (1993) *Decision Support Systems*, 3rd edition. Englewood Cliffs, New Jersey: Prentice-Hall.

Stair, R.M. (1995) *Principles of Information Systems*. Danvers, Massachusetts: Boyd and Fraser.

Turban, E. (1993) *Decision Support and Expert Systems*. New York: Macmillan.

Journals

Elliott, G. (1995) Applying statistical Evaluation Techniques in information retrieval to a company's business information systems to analyse performance and decision making, *Bulletin of the International Statistical Institute's 50th session*, Beijing, China, pp. 320–321.

Kleye, A. and de Korvin, A. (1989) A unified model for data acquisition and decision making, *Journal of Information Science*, 15, pp. 149–161.

Parkan, C. (1994) Decision making under partial probability information, *European Journal of Operational Research*, 79, pp. 115–122.

An asterisk (*) next to a book reference indicates a *seminal text* which means it constituted a source for later developments withi the academic discipline.

CHAPTER 8

The business environment

Objectives

When you have read this chapter you will be able to:

▶ describe the nature of the business environment and the forces that impact and constrain the business organisation

▶ evaluate and contrast the legal, economic, cultural and technological environments in which business organisations operate

▶ explain the implications of data protection and data privacy in the design of business information systems

▶ evaluate and describe the role and function of information technology within the business environment

▶ contrast and describe the impact of information technology on the banking and financial trading sectors of the business environment.

8.1 Introduction to the business environment

A business organisation is a *human activity system* that deals with, and is affected by, the *internal* and *external* forces found within the business environment; business organisations build systems to deal with these internal and external forces. A business organisation is an *open system* that builds information systems to deal with these internal forces, such as the organisation and its employees, and the external forces, such as its suppliers and customers. The role and nature of business systems is constrained, or governed, by four main forces present within the business environment. These component forces are outlined in Table 8.1.

Business is not an independent or solitary activity; the success of a business organisation will depend upon how well it integrates with the internal and external environment. The *legal and political environment* is concerned with government laws, business legislation and other directives that influence the activities of an organisation. The *economic environment* is concerned with the performance of national economies and international markets which are affected by taxation levels, trading quotas, inflation rates and national economic growth rates. The *cultural and global environment* is concerned with the way in which people relate to business activity and their conceptual ideas of business practice. Cultural factors are influenced by fashions, tastes, cultural behaviour and various other environmental and ethical considerations within

table 8.1

The components of the business environment

1	The legal and political environment.
2	The economic environment.
3	The cultural and global environment.
4	The technological environment.

the business environment. The *technological environment* has been one of the most significant considerations within the business environment because technology influences the competitive nature of an organisation.

ACTIVITY **8.1**

The business environment

Search your college or university library for magazine or journal articles on the use of information technology in the banking or finance sectors of the business environment. The article you select will be used as a unique *case study* and should be used to describe and communicate the importance of information technology to the banking and finance sector of the business environment.

8.2　The legal and political environment

The legal and political environment in which business operates will vary according to the country in which the organisation is located. Many countries and regions show a liberal attitude to business that encourages free market competition (known as *laissez-faire*), while other countries prefer to impose particular guidelines and constraints on business activity. The most direct way in which a country politically controls business activity is through taxation. Most countries also have laws that influence the way business activity is conducted and impose rules on the way that business activity is reported within the internal and external environment. In the United Kingdom the way companies collect, collate and disseminate information is governed by the *Companies Act* legislation which is updated every few years. Therefore, the government of a country or region can influence business activity in the following ways:

▶ direct state intervention through government agencies that control business activity
▶ economic and fiscal policy to control inflation rates and economic growth
▶ legislation affecting company law, contract law and employment law.

Legislation comes in a number of forms. The Companies Act in the United Kingdom defines various forms of business organisation (or incorporation) and prescribes the documentation that must be produced, and the format, of published information in the form of a trading and profit and loss statement and balance sheets. *Contract law* governs the use and nature of contracts between individuals and business organisations. A contract is an agreement that is enforceable under the law. Normally, business activity relies on formal and informal contracts between customers, suppliers and the organisations to which they relate. *Employment law* is concerned with protecting employees in their relationship with the business organisation; the legislation relates to matters of health and safety practice and the conditions under which employees and employers work within the business environment.

Data protection and privacy of information

Information is often said to be equated to power and influence. Therefore, any society should have a number of legal and statutory checks and balances in place to prevent the misuse of information. With vast amounts of information being publicly available and communicated around the world there is an ethical problem in ensuring the correct ownership of information and the proper use of information. A major consequence of the use of information technology is the increase in the handling of large quantities of information on employees, individuals and business organisations. Often this information is of a personal and private nature and the individual, or organisation, is reluctant for such information to be made available to the general public or other information agencies without their permission, knowledge or control. The main areas of primary concern on privacy and data protection are:

▶ that data and information should be *secure*
▶ that any private, personal or other data should be *accurate*
▶ that any data stored should not be *misused*.

The concern and fear that such private information could be used for purposes other than for which it was intended, and by people without the authority to use that information, has led to the introduction of policies and legislation to protect data and information. In the United Kingdom the *Data Protection Act* was passed in 1984 to provide greater legal protection for data held on individuals by organisations. The Data Protection Act set out to regulate the use of automatically processed information relating to individuals, and the provision of services in respect of such information. The Data Protection Act requires that all holders of computer-based records must register their databases with the *Data Protection Registrar*. The Act refers to individuals as the *data subject* and defines personal data as being data related to identifiable living individuals. Individuals also have the right not to have any information they supply to organisations kept in computer-based formats; individuals can opt to have the information kept in manual form. Most large organisations employ a person in the role of *Data Protection Officer* whose responsibility it is to deal with matters related to the Data Protection Act.

The Data Protection Act lays out seven main principles concerning data protection, which can also be considered as general data protection principles, as follows:

1 The data held for processing must have been obtained fairly and legally.
2 The data held must only be used for the specific purpose for which it was intended.
3 The data held must not be excessive but should be adequate and relevant for the purpose for which it was intended.
4 The data held must be accurate and up to date.
5 The data held must not be kept longer than is necessary for the specified purpose.
6 The data must be protected and held securely against unauthorised access, alteration or disclosure.
7 The data must be available to the data subject on request and the individual data subject has the right to have the data corrected and/or erased.

Certain categories of data are exempt from the Data Protection Act. The main categories of data that are exempt are as follows:

- ▶ data held for National Security
- ▶ medical and Social Service records and information
- ▶ data held by the Customs and Excise and the Inland Revenue
- ▶ data held by the police for the detection and prevention of crime
- ▶ data held for personal, family or household use.

For example, data held by the Inland Revenue (the body responsible for taxation in the United Kingdom) which is used for the purposes of collecting taxation is exempt, and so is information held by the police for the specific purposes of preventing crime and prosecuting criminals.

DID YOU KNOW?
It is the responsibility of the Data Protection Registrar to consider complaints against data users and to determine whether there has been any infringement of the principles of the Data Protection Act.

The Data Protection Act attempts to give protection to individuals against personal information being misused or inaccurately recorded. The Act requires anyone who intends to keep information about individuals on a computer to be listed in a register. Organisations (or individuals) that wish to keep information about individuals are known as *data users*. This register is open to public inspection and data users must only operate within the limits of the entry in the register.

ACTIVITY **8.2**

Data and information protection

Discuss the role of the Data Protection Registrar and provide two examples of how the registrar can protect the privacy and interests of consumers, or other individuals, with regard to personal information held on information systems. Select a banking application (e.g. loans, mortgages, electronic funds transfer, share dealing etc.) and explain, in the form of a report, the following: the purpose and nature of the application you have chosen; the advantages of IT to the application; identify three pieces of personal customer information that may be stored by the bank; describe the methods used to ensure data security; state two examples of data that are exempt from the Data Protection Act.

8.3　The economic environment

The fundamental aim of all business activity is to make money. The economic environment can be divided into micro-economics and macro-economics. *Micro-economics* is concerned with the nature of individual business organisations and their activities such as pricing, cost evaluation and competitive behaviour, whereas *macro-economics* is concerned with the aggregated effects of individual business activity on the national or regional economy. Therefore, macro-economics is concerned with national growth rates, inflation rates, the cost of government borrowing, international trade balances and the value of national currencies.

The major economic impact of information technology on society has been on labour force working patterns which have affected the type of work available in society and the *nature* of working practices and conditions. In economic terms, technology has caused the creation of jobs and at the same time the loss of some jobs, and a change in the nature of general working patterns. The rapid pace of change in information technology affects the skills requirement of society and means that the work force has to train and retrain more frequently than ever before during their working life as the jobs they previously did are superseded or replaced by other working practices, or altered by advances in IT. The economic cost of technological training and retraining has become a growing and major expense to many competitive business organisations.

The highest incidence of job losses in modern information societies has occurred in the production and manufacturing sectors where human labour has been replaced with computer-aided manufacturing and computer-based production robotics. However, it is often the pace of change and not technology change itself which leads to job losses; if new information technology is incorporated into society or organisations at a steady and manageable rate then there is assimilation time available to deal with labour force retraining or redeployment. Under such circumstances job losses can often be managed by labour force contraction due to natural employee wastage (e.g. retirements and normal movements of labour between jobs). It is the impact of instant or sudden changes in the application of new information technology that leads to job losses, as a mismatch develops between the availability of new jobs in information technology and the available pool of retrained or re-educated labour.

> **DID YOU KNOW?**
>
> *Studies have shown that in the long term more jobs are created than lost by the introduction and use of information technology, which can often lead to new business opportunities in terms of products or services. For example, parcel courier services, which deliver business parcels between clients, use internal IT for 'tracking' the location of a parcel from leaving one client to receipt by another client. This internal tracking service, provided by IT, is sold on to the clients at an additional cost so that the client organisation can keep track of its own set of parcels being delivered around the world.*

In economic terms information technology is adopted because it is beneficial to an individual or a business organisation; it may enable an organisation to achieve a higher profit than by merely operating manual systems. If this potential increase in profit is multiplied across all organisations in a national economy the national increase in economic wealth can be significant. It is claimed that one of the reasons for Japan's great economic success, in the second half of the twentieth century, is due to the development and adoption of all forms of information technology on a national scale. Japan and other technologically advanced countries and regions use information technology to increase the general per capita (per person) wealth of the nation. Ultimately, the bulk of jobs created in technological economies are in areas related to information technology.

ACTIVITY 6.3

The economic environment

Discuss what is meant by micro-economics and macro-economics and suggest how each economic force influences the nature of business activity. Provide two examples of jobs that have disappeared and two examples of jobs that have been created as a result of the growth of information technology. Then investigate sources of published business information and list all the possible users and uses of the various business information sources. Your starting point should be to investigate the published *annual accounts* of a large business organisation. Analyse and describe whether the sources of business information you have found are required, or influenced, by legislation.

8.4   The cultural and global environment

The cultural environment is influenced by people and the way in which people relate to business activity. Therefore, the cultural environment in which business activity takes place is influenced by customers, suppliers, employees, the general public, politicians, shareholders and other stakeholders. All business activity relies on individuals acting as customers, suppliers and employees. In addition, the cultural environment is also affected by fashions and trends influenced and encouraged by population masses. All business activity systems are influenced by environmental, social and ethical considerations. For example, the way in which business organisations treat their employees and the way in which an organisation relates to the environment in terms of dealing with waste and pollution.

DID YOU KNOW?

As health and welfare have improved over the centuries the population has grown as the death rate has decreased. The world population was estimated to be approximately 300 million in AD 1000. But by the year AD 2000 it is projected to be 6000 million (or 6 billion). This represents a potentially significant pool of customers within the business environment.

One of the major cultural changes within business activity has been the growth of telecommuting or working from home. *Telecommuting* involves an employee being established at home with all the facilities of the traditional integrated office environment. For example, a networked personal computer with electronic mail (e-mail) and Internet facilities, all linked to a modem and telephone/fax machine, can permit certain categories of employee to carry out their work as efficiently and effectively as being located physically within the office environment. Therefore, telecommuting can remove the need for attendance in the office of workers in secretarial, administrative, and some executive related areas. It can also often lead to more productive work because the employee does not have to commute into work and can often allow their work activities to complement their social activities (e.g. collecting children from school and dealing with maintenance problems in the home). Telecommuting may also result in less days lost through illness and personal responsibilities which may lead to an increase in employee morale. The main disadvantage is the loss of social and personal contact between staff which often requires a work culture adjustment within the individual and the organisation. Some employees also may find it difficult to appropriately separate the work role and home role, instead favouring a two-site approach to their life.

The social effects of the application of information technology have been widespread throughout the business environment. Many types of manual jobs have been eliminated or automated, thus reducing the need for human labour. However, an advantage of the application of information technology is that many unpleasant and dangerous jobs are now carried out by robotics automation. Whatever the role and remit of information technology, it is indisputable that it has altered the workplace environment. Many laborious and deterministic tasks can now be carried out more quickly and more efficiently than ever was the case before. However, those that relate to IT are often required to spend long hours sitting in front of a computer screen or other peripheral technology which can cause a number of health problems, for example, poor posture and eye-strain. Some of these problems are being overcome by greater research into *ergonomics* which is the study of the interaction of human to machine relationships and is particularly concerned with the design of human to computer interaction.

The growing sophistication of communications technology permits people to meet and interact in forms not previously possible. *Teleconferencing* is an electronic form of meeting which allows a number of people to confer using telephone, e-mail and other types of groupware-based communications applications. This allows geographically dispersed individuals to meet and communicate as if in the same physical location. *Videoconferencing* includes the type of technology used in teleconferencing with the additional advantage of video technology which allows the participants in an electronic meeting to see one another (on screens) as if in the environment of a face-to-face meeting. Both teleconferencing and videoconferencing let people communicate ideas and thoughts in a meeting forum without the cost and time factors involved in transporting people from one geographical location to another, which is an important consideration for organisations that do business on a global scale. There is an additional benefit in that such technology allows the 'globalisation' of ideas to flourish within the business environment.

ACTIVITY **8.4**

The cultural and global environment

Describe the *cultural environment* and explain how attitudes and beliefs (*Weltanschauung*) affect business activity and business systems. Discuss all the possible categories of people who might interact with the internal and external environment of a business organisation and explain how people influence the nature of business activity systems. Now read Pause for thought 8.1 and outline ten significant aspects of telecommuting within the business environment. Write a report discussing whether the trend of telecommuting is likely to increase in the future and what implications there are on the contractual obligations between an employee and a business organisation. Discuss the ways in which telecommuting affects the nature of interaction between humans, technology and the organisation.

PAUSE FOR THOUGHT **8.1** | *Telecommuting: the advantages and disadvantages of working from home*

The Information Age will reach most individuals and organisations through the Internet, electronic commerce and various other forms of information technology. Households can now conduct business, purchase goods, play computer games and keep in contact with agencies, organisations and individuals through electronic mail. A natural consequence of this information technology is the ability to work from home because the technology allows an individual to work unrestricted by geographical or physical location.

Business organisations are constantly seeking access to information technology that will help employees complete their jobs more effectively and efficiently. With the development of 'knowledge working' within the business environment, telecommuting (or working from home) seems to fit the knowledge worker model of activity. Knowledge workers develop and exchange information to complete their job functions. However, the need for information is not limited to the physical confines of a corporate headquarters or regional office. Even when away from a physical office, home workers can access data, information and software applications when and as they need these resources. Therefore, what are the benefits and drawbacks of telecommuting?

Employees will often view telecommuting as a convenient, flexible aspect of an otherwise rigid environment, such as being confined for 35 hours per week in a particular office location. Business organisations believe that telecommuting is a clever way of extending the working week at no extra cost, while reducing overhead costs such as rent, lighting, heating and electricity in one physical office location. Telecommuting may also attract strong and able staff by providing a flexible and independent working environment. Often telecommuting is the only viable alternative for sole traders or small businesses that cannot afford luxury office space.

Many companies do not have defined policies towards telecommuting and many are still psychologically unfavourable towards the concept, believing that it may lead to a loss of organisational control over employees. Many regions of the world, particularly in the United States, have legislation (such as clean air acts) that encourage telecommuting. In order to effectively deal with telecommuting many business organisations are going through the difficult process of evolving policies and organisational structures to deal with issues of telecommuting.

One major drawback of telecommuting is often the lack of the correct and appropriate computing infrastructures to support a teleworker's demands. For example, many telecommunications networks are often slow or difficult to access, which may lead to a loss of time and revenue. Also, there is a need for a good local area network to be available in the home to deal with peripheral equipment such as scanners, printers, and telecommunications modems. Other drawbacks include the loss of personal contact between individuals that may lead to a feeling of social isolation.

Whatever the advantages and disadvantages of telecommuting, it is often the case that telecommuting can provide tangible benefits to a competitive business organisation; as long as the prerequisites of a suitable contract and appropriate environment are present within a business organisation.

8.5 The technological environment

Information technology is an integral part of everyday human life. Information is considered an important business and human asset and so is the technology that enables the storage, processing and communication of information. The technological environment has greatly influenced the nature and practice of business activity systems; it has increased the efficiency and effectiveness of business systems and in turn improved the way business organisations operate within the business environment. Table 8.2 outlines some of the important technological developments, which have influenced business activity and business systems, over the last 200 years.

The incorporation of technology into the business environment is not a new concept. In 1890 Herman Hollerith who worked for the Census bureau in the United States invented an automated punch card machine known as a Pantograph Punch and Electrical Tabulator. The mechanical device was invented to allow quicker and more accurate processing of census results through punch card technology; the handwritten data obtained from printed census forms was transferred on to punched cards that were placed through a tabulator which sorted and processed the information more rapidly than previous manual methods. Hollerith's automated machine allowed the 1890 census to be completed in only three years compared to the seven years it took to complete the 1880 census. In 1911 punch cards were used in the British census for the first time. In the United States, tabulators were used up until the 1960s when advances in electronics and computer technology allowed smaller, cheaper and more reliable machines to be built.

> **DID YOU KNOW?**
> *The development of technology to perform specific tasks automatically can be traced as far back as 1804 with the invention of the Jacquard card-controlled loom. Joseph Marie Jacquard was a French textile manufacturer who used a punch card system to control the weaved pattern on a loom. Jacquard's loom allowed complicated patterns to be woven automatically.*

> **DID YOU KNOW?**
> *Herman Hollerith, who used punch cards to input census data into a tabulation machine in the 1890s, went on to become one of the founders of the business organisation known today as IBM.*

Information technology has had a significant impact on society as a whole because of the rapid developments since the 1940s in electronics, integrated circuitry, semi-conductors, silicon microchip technology and telecommunications. Information technology has had an impact on individuals, business organisations and society. By far the biggest impact of information technology has been in the business environment. Some of the earliest applications were in the processing of clerical or what is known as operational business data for payroll and stock control. Such operational systems have been described previously in chapter 7. Information technology then gravitated into the management sphere and is today mainly used to assist management and executive decision making.

In the manufacturing sector information technology tools and techniques, such as computer-aided design (CAD), computer-aided manufacture (CAM), robotics and artificial intelligence are used to improve products and manufacturing performance. Such technology is particularly prevalent in the research and development operations of the business environment. *Computer-aided design* allows design models to be created on a computer screen; the structure of the designs can normally be easily altered and simulated to achieve different design concepts. One of the advantages of CAD is that it saves time over manual methods; ideas can be sketched on a computer screen and can be saved, recalled or modified. The sketches are usually three-dimensional and can be tilted, rotated and reshaped as required. CAD is used in the design of large structures such as cars, ships, buildings and small structures such as microprocessor circuits and electronic items. CAD systems usually allow simulation criteria such as stresses and forces on buildings to be tested and compared safely in the design department.

table 8.2
Historical developments affecting business systems and technology

	BC	
	c. 2000	The Senkereh Tablet found near Babylon lists numbers in cuniform writing.
	c. 650	An Indian Hindu named Brahmagupta invents decimal numbers.
	c. 500	The Egyptians and Greeks use simple abacus to record financial information.
	AD	
	c. 876	Indians use *zero* as a place holder in written numbers.
	c. 1000	The Arabic decimal notation makes its way to Europe (Arabic or Hindu-Arabic numerals).
	c. 1300	Early evidence of business systems and record keeping by an Italian business organisation trading in Provence.
	1492	An Italian named Pelacci claims to have invented the decimal point.
	1494	A Franciscan friar named Luca Pacioli produces the first textbook on accounting systems called 'Sumna de Arithmetica, Geometrica, Proportioni et proportionalita'.
	1694	Von Leibnitz produces a calculating machine to perform multiplication.
	1725	A Frenchman named Bouchon in Lyons uses a silk loom controlled by the positions of holes in a paper roll.
	1804	A Frenchman named Joseph Jacquard uses a fully automatic loom where the pattern is controlled by punch cards.
	1814	George Stephenson (British engineer) constructs the first successful steam locomotive.
	1822	A Britain named Charles Babbage demonstrated a Difference Engine.
	1825	The first passenger railway between Stockton and Darlington (in England) was opened.
	1833	Charles Babbage begins work on an Analytical Engine (unfortunately the project ran out of funding before being built).
	1842	Lady Lovelace writes 'punch card' programs for Babbage's Analytical Engine.
	1850	An American named Parmalee patented a calculator with numbered keys.
	1877	Thomas Edison invents the phonograph and contributes to the development of the electric lamp and other electrical devices.
	1890	Herman Holerith of the United States invents a series of machines to process census data.
	1911	Punch card technology is used in the British census.
	1920	A British company invents a machine that prints alphabetic data from punch cards.
	1936	Alan Turing (a British academic) proposes the concept of digital computer.
	1945	Von Neumann of the United States writes a report detailing the characteristics of computer processing.

Information technology applications in production and manufacturing often take the form of factory automation. *Computer-aided manufacturing* techniques are used to replace human intervention in the factory assembly line process. Information technology is used to control intricate or precision machine tools. Industrial components can be cut and shaped to higher standards of accuracy and consistency than through manual control processes. Such systems are appropriate for repetitive, precision tasks. The actions of the machine tools are determined by comparison with a design pattern (of size and shape specifications) stored in the computer. The CAM system can be alerted to any variations or deviations from the computer design pattern and the system will often adjust as appropriate. This is known as computer-aided quality assessment.

The other main area of CAM is the application of industrial *robotics* that replace human activity within the manufacturing process. An industrial robot often consists of manipulative arms with articulated joints to allow flexible movement. The actions of the robot are determined by pre-specified programs stored on the computer. Robots sometimes operate within certain bounds of sensitivity and are often fitted with sensors that detect the immediate environment around the robot. For example, robots can be programmed to detect and differentiate between shapes and sizes, whereby the robotics may be programmed to only pick up certain shapes or sizes that fall between two bounds (e.g. to retrieve particular shapes measuring between 20cm and 45cm). The increased use of robots has led to the decrease in manual work by employees which has been replaced by supervision and control of technology. Usually information technology will be adopted where there is a need to improve the efficiency and effectiveness of a process or work task. For instance, information technology may allow some tasks to be carried out which would be impossible to do manually. In the nuclear industry radioactive materials in the centre of atomic reactors are handled remotely by machinery, such as robotic arms, controlled by workers sitting at computer terminals.

ACTIVITY **8.5**

The technological environment

Discuss the *technological environment* and outline the most significant technological developments over the past 200 years which have affected the business environment. Define the concepts of computer-aided design and computer-aided manufacturing and describe three possible uses of robotics within the manufacturing systems process.

Information technology has had a significant effect within the business environment in the way in which an organisation relates to its customers and suppliers, which can loosely be called the customer or consumer environment. Information technology in the consumer environment is most obvious in the retailing and banking sectors of the business environment. In recent years the use of cheques, as a medium of payment, has been largely replaced by the use of credit card payment and other forms of electronic payment. A credit card allows a customer to buy goods and pay for them later after a period of time. Credit cards offer credit to a pre-set limit and each month the cardholder receives a statement listing the outstanding balance and the transactions for that month. No interest is charged if the cardholder settles the full amount of the balance. However, a cardholder need not settle the full amount but may pay off a proportion of the outstanding balance; there is usually a minimum amount that has to be paid each month. Alternatively, a debit card automatically transfers money out of a customer's bank account to another bank account when the card has been processed through an appropriate EFTPOS terminal.

Many of the large retail food distributors (e.g. Tesco, Sainsbury's, Asda in the United Kingdom) use information technology extensively within their business operations and activities in relation to both its suppliers and customers. All large supermarkets now have cash tills that are connected to bar code optical laser scanners, which is known as EPOS (see Chapter 7) technology. Such technology automatically decodes and registers information on a central computerised system; the information is used to reconcile the items sold with the money spent on the items and to update the stock records to reorder items that have been consumed down to their minimum stock requirement levels. EPOS technology can also analyse individual cashier performance and provide sales analysis reports for managers.

Many advanced societies are becoming to a large extent cashless societies. One of the advantages of a cashless society is the elimination of the need to withdraw large sums of money from the bank whenever a person needs to make an expensive purchase of goods. However, one disadvantage is that societies may become dependent upon credit rather than paying for goods immediately. One of the consequences of a cashless society is the requirement for tight data accuracy and data security controls to prevent fraudulent misuse of funds. Banks were one of the first industry sectors to make use of information technology to assist in dealing with their customers. Banks have used IT as a competitive weapon to gain an advantage over their banking rivals to the extent that banks are always looking for information technology to provide new services for customers and to increase employee productivity. In the 1980s banks introduced *automated teller machines* (ATMs) as a customer service. ATMs are cash service tills that are usually situated outside banks and in other areas of high population movement, such as airports and shopping centres. These tills are also known as *cash dispensers*. ATMs allow customers to draw out money, check their bank balance, or order cheque books and statements. The tills are normally available 24 hours a day and seven days a week (provided the money in the tills has not run out!). The ATMs are networked to a central computerised system where any cash withdrawals or transactions are recorded and individual customer accounts are adjusted.

Data and information accuracy is therefore of importance within the business environment. For example, business organisations rely on data being accurate in order to carry out appropriate and correct decision making; organisations often model data to present a range of decision-making scenarios. The best scenario option will be selected by the company after consideration and deliberation of each option. If the information is inaccurate then the business organisation is prevented from choosing an optimum decision scenario and may lose potential income as a result of choosing an inferior decision option. Therefore, data accuracy is essential to the smooth application and working of information technology in the business environment. For instance, ATMs dispense money to account customers when the correct PIN (personal identification number) is keyed in on the ATM machine. The system will compare the keyed number with the one that has been allocated to the card. If the keyed number is inaccurate the user will have a further two opportunities to enter the correct PIN number. If after three attempts the inaccurate number, or numbers, is persistently keyed in then the card will be retained by the machine. It is essential in order to achieve the confidence of the consumer that information technology treats data and information with integrity. Well built information systems usually incorporate checking routines to detect data input and output errors; these systems should include safeguards to prevent data being corrupted by unforeseen faults.

Modern banking practices also use information technology to transfer money from one place to another, a process known as *electronic funds transfer* (EFT). The electronic processing of cheques and money transfers saves time and paperwork. International banks use EFT to transfer funds from country to country where the funds will earn the highest international interest rate. In 1971 a system known as the Society for Worldwide Interbank Financial Telecommunications (SWIFT) was established to provide secure and reliable international communications between European and American banks. SWIFT is based in the Belgian capital of Brussels and is essentially a message switching system where the messages contain instructions and advice about funds transfer, but the system does not actually move money into and out of bank accounts. The main problem of passing information through telephone lines is security.

ACTIVITY **8.6**
··············

The banking environment

Discuss how advances in information technology are used by high street banks to gain a competitive advantage over their rivals. Then investigate the banking organisation in the United Kingdom known as 'First Direct'. Is First Direct associated with any high street bank that you know? Discuss how First Direct differs from other retail banks in the way that it uses information technology and interacts with its customers. Write a report on your findings. Your headings should include (i) background intelligence on the business organisation, (ii) how First Direct is different to other banks, and (iii) the use of IT within First Direct. Do you know of any other organisations that are moving into the banking domain from another area of business?

PAUSE FOR THOUGHT **8.2** *Information technology in the Bank of England*

The Bank of England, founded in 1694, is the central bank of the United Kingdom. Most countries have a central bank; for example the Federal Reserve System in the United States; the Deutsche Bundesbank in Germany; the Banque de France; and the Bank of Japan.

The Bank of England makes extensive use of information technology (IT) in all aspects of its business. The bank was using punch card systems in the 1930s for handling data input and these were replaced by the first modern computer systems in the 1960s. Today, the use of information technology is regarded as a normal and accepted part of the bank's day-to-day activities. The bank's IT-based development is linked closely with that of other financial institutions, both British and international. This kind of systems interconnectivity requires close cooperation between a number of financial organisations to plan and develop new and improved ways of taking advantage of IT.

One of the earliest IT-based systems initiatives was called CHAPS (Clearing House Automated Payments System) which conveys guaranteed payments between banks. This was followed by the CGO (Central Gilts Office) which is a transfer and settlement system for gilt-edged securities. More recently this has been augmented with the CMO (Central Moneymarkets Office) which deals with certificates of deposit. This systems interconnectivity has led to the development of various ·communications systems linking all of the European central banks. Such interconnectivity relies on efficient and effective IT systems and telecommunications networks.

The Bank of England's business is conducted from a number of separate sites, including London, Gloucester, Birmingham, Bristol and Leeds. The main site is in the City of London (in Threadneedle Street). The Bank keeps a constant watch on developments in IT. Throughout the 1970s and 1980s, many services were provided through centrally operated mainframe computers, with most of the systems being operated and developed by the Bank's own in-house IT staff. However, responsibility for the development and operation of some IT-based systems started to be devolved to end-users and specific business areas, by the late 1980s, with central IT resources only providing support. This trend was fuelled by the introduction of an increasing number of PCs into the fabric of the Bank's operations. By the early 1990s there was a deliberate strategy by the Bank to move away from centralised, shared services, towards distributed or departmental processing. This has led to separate IT programmes being pursued in different areas of the Bank, as appropriate to the localised needs of areas and users. A greater reliance has been placed on the use of standard commercial applications software, accompanied by some degree of localised development and tailoring of applications package software.

Most of the Bank's IT activities take place in the London premises. For commercial operations the Bank uses a number of platforms such as UNIX and PC environments. Systems such as CMO, CGO and CHAPS, which serve the financial markets, and for which system failure is unacceptable, operate on fault tolerant processors. These systems are also supported by 'stand by' systems in case of major disasters. The areas of the Bank which carry out the Bank's supervisory role (of financial markets) and those which specialise in economic analysis use mainframes and networked desktop computers. The Bank also has an interest in document image processing and uses DTP (desktop publishing) software applications packages for producing a range of reports, bulletins and other documents produced by the Bank. The Bank's bank note printing works in Essex, United Kingdom, operates a largely self-contained and networked IT system with extensive use of local area networking (LAN) technology. An integrated office system is prevalent throughout the Bank (with extensive use of electronic mail (e-mail) using LANs supported by the various IT platforms of the Bank.

The Bank of England is using IT as comprehensively as any other institution and behind its traditional facade in Threadneedle Street lies an organisation with its feet firmly in the Information Age.

8.6 Expert systems within the business environment

An expert system (ES) mimics the expertise and knowledge base of a human expert by using a process of heuristic, or random, induction to arrive at findings and conclusions. Expert systems are in use in a wide range of business environment areas to assist business activity and decision making. For example, many banking and financial institutions use expert systems to assist managers in the decision of whether or not to make financial loans to customers. Expert systems are often used to assist human decision-making processes and as such fall into the realm of decision support systems. An expert system is usually comprised of three main components as follows:

1 *knowledge base* represented by deterministic rules and semantic networks
2 *inference engine* which seeks information relationships from the knowledge base
3 *user interface* which acts as an interrogation window for questions to the user.

The *knowledge base* is not merely comprised of deterministic rules but also structures the information relationships that exist in certain knowledge fields. The knowledge base captures and stores the knowledge, experience and reasoning of an expert; the knowledge bases are usually assembled by establishing the knowledge of many experts in a particular field. However, the obvious problem in this scenario is that some experts are more knowledgeable than other experts(!), which is a consideration when building a knowledge base. The relationship between information is referred to in expert systems as the *semantic network*, which is concerned with the way in which knowledge, or information objects, are stored and related in a particular knowledge field. Semantic networks (or 'semantic nets' as they are commonly called) are logical hierarchical relationships between information objects that are based on inherited characteristics.

The *inference engine* aims to seek information and understand relationships from the knowledge base to provide answers to enquiries. The inference engine attempts to find the correct and logical information, rules and interpretations from a knowledge base in order to deliver a correct answer to an enquiry. The *user interface* allows the system to be interrogated by a human user; the intention of the user interface is to be as user-friendly as possible and permit an inter-relationship between the user and the expert system. The emphasis is on creating a clear communications channel between the human user and the expert system.

Expert systems possess a number of advantages that benefit their use in the business environment. Firstly, they provide decision-making support which allows an individual to call on the knowledge and experience of an expert, as and when required, without the constraints of time and availability of the comparative human expert. Secondly, expert systems can be used at the highest levels of the decision-making hierarchy within a business organisation; strategic goal setting through the life cycle of planning, decision making and control can be assisted with reference to an expert system or set of expert systems. Thirdly, an expert system is useful when knowledge is required in a number of different locations (e.g. branches of a bank) where it would normally be too costly to place multiple human experts because of the demographics of the branch region. Some of the disadvantages of expert systems revolve around the issues of a

THE BUSINESS ENVIRONMENT **213**

knowledge base being only as good as the experience and knowledge of the human expert underpinning the system.

Expert systems are normally developed in group cooperation between the *field expert*, the *knowledge engineer* and the systems *end-user*. A field expert is an individual, or group of individuals, with an expertise that needs to be captured within an expert system; a knowledge engineer is the individual that has the responsibility for analysis, design, implementation and maintenance of the expert system; the end-user is the individual, or select group of individuals, who use and benefit from the expert system. Traditionally, expert systems were developed by technical specialists; however, IT has advanced to a stage whereby it is possible and practicable for expert systems to be developed by cooperation between the field expert and the end-user. This has been made possible by *expert system shells* and other products available within the business environment which remove much of the programming burden and allow end-users to develop their own expert systems.

An expert system shell is a collection of software tools and techniques that permit end-users to analyse, design, develop and maintain an expert system. A number of pre-designed and pre-built expert shells can be purchased commercially from software vendors. For example, the shell called Financial Adviser® can be used to analyse financial investment in a business's fixed assets, such as the purchasing of factories, machinery and other major equipment. The expert system shell known as Leonardo© is a flexible facility to create a range of expert systems in the business environment such as are found in marketing and competitor analysis. There are a number of advantages of using expert system shells as follows:

> **DID YOU KNOW?**
> *Knowledgepro® is a commercially available expert system shell that allows the integration of other software applications, such as databases and spreadsheets, to allow organisations to build expert systems using existing datasets and modelling applications.*

- ▶ Shells are normally user-friendly and utilise high-level programming environment tools and techniques.
- ▶ Expert system shells normally comprise established rules and knowledge matrices that can readily be applied to a knowledge field.
- ▶ Expert system shells can be used by field experts and end-users to build systems rather than relying on a knowledge engineer to convert an understanding of the problem into program code.

Expert systems can be used for a number of purposes from providing services to business planning, quality control and business diagnosis. Expert systems are increasingly becoming a tool that permeates throughout the whole business environment. Table 8.3 outlines examples of some available expert systems and application areas.

Table 8.3
Examples of expert systems application areas

MYCIN	Medical expert system used to diagnose diseases.
ACE	An expert system used to manage and maintain telephone networks.
CLUES	Loan underwriting expert system to determine credit worthiness.
CARGEX	An expert system used for logistical management and goods distribution.
ExpertTax	Tax profiling expert system for optimal tax evaluation.

8.7   Artificial intelligence within the business environment

Allied to the design and use of expert systems is the use of artificial intelligence (AI) in the business environment. Artificial intelligence systems do not necessarily possess a knowledge base, but they do possess the capability of mimicking human thought processes, particularly human reasoning and learning from past experience. The most advanced chess computers are a good example of the differences between artificial intelligence and expert systems. The most sophisticated chess computers use both expert system and artificial intelligence techniques. A chess computer possesses a knowledge base in order to understand the moves and rules of chess. However, the most advanced chess computers have the additional capability to apply human reasoning to a given situation; with the ability to learn from past mistakes and experience by adding knowledge and experience to its internal memory and knowledge base.

Artificial intelligence is found in many areas of the business environment from manufacturing robotics through to various business decision-making environments. The following is a list of just some of the aspects of AI found within business organisations:

▶ *Robotics* of mechanical and other manufacturing processes, such as production assembly lines and quality control systems, that utilise computer-aided manufacturing techniques.

▶ *Sensor and perception systems* incorporate AI to provide the systems with an ability to sense the immediate environment such as human vision and hearing. This is particularly useful for systems that need to recognise patterns of size and shape of manufacturing components.

▶ *Neural networks* is an advanced idea that attempts to build systems that are modelled on the neural processes of the human brain. The goals are to understand and develop systems that possess human 'thinking', although what is human thinking is still a much researched and debated problem.

▶ *Intelligent agent software* is an area of computing and IT concerned with the development of software to act on behalf of a human user to search for information and assist humans to define their individual information needs. For example, the Internet (which will be studied in chapter 11) can utilise intelligent agent software to search for information sources and define information requirements by automatically and routinely searching the Internet. Such software acts like an employed agent on behalf of a human user of a system.

The area of expert systems and artificial intelligence is innovative and important to business organisations in that such technology applications allow organisations to compete more effectively and by doing so add value to a business organisation.

ACTIVITY 8.7

Expert systems and artificial intelligence

Outline the three main components of an expert system and explain how these components fit together in an expert system. Discuss the concept of *expert system shells* and describe the role and function of shells in the development of expert systems within the business environment. Discuss the role and function of artificial intelligence systems within business organisations and outline five application areas of the business environment that utilise the tools and technology of artificial intelligence.

Expert systems and artificial intelligence add intrinsic value to a business organisation by making the decision-making actions of an organisation a more effective process. However, this relies on the creative understanding of technology to appreciate its usefulness to new and different business application areas. For example, one of the largest threats to the stability of the banking sector is credit card fraud. Banks and other financial institutions spend much time and expense on finding innovative ways to combat fraud. A typical fraud may involve a credit card being stolen and used to buy goods up to the card's credit limit. Most credit card providers receive information reports on card transactions up to two or three days following the transaction. These *usage reports* are not timely enough to immediately detect fraudulent card usage; often a credit card provider is only aware of a problem when a card is reported stolen by a customer. However, expert systems can be used to detect and combat fraudulent credit card usage by profiling customers and applying many hundreds of rules to credit patterns and credit transactions. The expert system analyses transaction patterns related to particular categories of customer and provides a warning of unusual or suspicious credit card usage. Such an expert system is usually programmed to routinely, for example, on a daily or hourly basis, retrieve credit card transaction data from a central data bank source and automatically search for variations and deviations from standard *customer profiles*.

A customer profile that indicates a rare dependence on drawing cash on the credit card would automatically be alerted to a transaction that withdrew a large amount of cash from an ATM. The expert system assigns a 'fraud likelihood score' to each transaction and alerts either the credit card provider or credit card customer to determine the legitimacy of the unusual transaction. This form of expert system has saved credit card providers a large amount of money by detecting irregularities and fraud.

Two of the largest and most successful sectors of the business environment that utilise IT for competitive advantage are banking and food retail. However, by being successful in the use and application of IT for business purposes, both of these sectors have the potential to move into other areas of business activity. The late 1990s has seen a motivation in many large business organisations to offer an ever increasing range of services and products that were traditionally not found within the boundaries of the business organisation. For example, food supermarket chains are offering credit card and banking services that were traditionally the domain of retail banks. The banking sector in turn offers financial services that were traditionally offered by specialist business organisations. The growth of expert systems technology and artificial intelligence has made this

DID YOU KNOW?
From 1997 Sainsbury's, the largest supermarket chain in the United Kingdom, is to become the first supermarket chain to open a bank and offer banking services as part of its overall supermarket activities. Sainsbury's will offer full banking services to its 12 million customers.

process possible by making expertise and knowledge more widely available within the business environment.

By offering its customers the services of the banking sector Sainsbury's hopes to create for itself a competitive edge in the food retail sector. The Sainsbury's bank will offer current accounts, deposit accounts, loan facilities and credit card services. It will also eventually offer mortgages to home buyer customers. Like the First Direct bank it will transact all business with customers through telephone banking. Sainsbury's possesses the technology infrastructure to offer banking services and merely requires authorisation under the UK Banking Act from the Bank of England. Sainsbury's already has the technological base and the customer base to immediately begin banking activities as and when it wishes.

ACTIVITY **8.8**
........•.......

Technological expertise within the business environment

The following are two quotes regarding the development of banking in Sainsbury's. One quote is by David Sainsbury, which is in favour of the scheme to offer banking services, and the other quote is by a financial analyst, which is unfavourable to Sainsbury's banking services scheme.

> Our customers tell us they want good, efficient and reliable banking services. In Sainsburys Bank customers will have the reassurance of a name they know and trust, coupled with the banking expertise of the Bank of Scotland. Together we are committed to providing our customers with the most up-to-date and efficient direct banking service in the UK.
>
> (David Sainsbury, *The Times*, 26 October 1996)

> The scheme might help to tie in the loyalty of existing customers, but that is about it. Who will close their accounts with Lloyds Bank or Midland Bank? They might use it as a subsidiary account.
>
> (Financial analyst, *The Times*, 26 October 1996)

Form into groups of three or four students and discuss your understanding of each quote and suggest five advantages and disadvantages of supermarkets offering banking services to their customers. Present your advantages and disadvantages in the form of bullet points which can be presented to the other groups.

8.8   Integrated electronic office systems
....

Information technology is common in most areas of administrative office work within the business environment. An integrated office system aims to automate office methods and procedures using information technology such as databases, wordprocessors, spreadsheets, electronic networked diaries, groupware, electronic notice boards and electronic mail (e-mail). The overall aim is to improve efficiency and effectiveness in administrative office practices. An example of the electronic office is where e-mail is used to communicate notes and memoranda between systems users both internal and

DID YOU KNOW?

The Internet is a network of thousands of computer networks and systems that allows computers to communicate with one another on a global basis; a network is a system that connects computers together to permit the sharing of resources and information.

external to the business organisation. E-mail reduces the amount of paper copy produced in the office environment. The use of e-mail, often in conjunction with the Internet and access to the 'information highway', has changed the communication system environment in many organisations.

Within the business environment the Internet allows an individual to connect to other systems on a worldwide basis and in doing so allows the user to 'surf the net', which is the process of accessing and searching areas of the Internet where billions of pages of information are available on over 50,000 computer networks. Therefore, it is important to understand the nature of the Internet within an integrated office systems environment. The uses of the Internet by business organisations are many and varied, but the main uses are as follows:

▶ *Sending and receiving e-mail.* The largest use of the Internet is in the sending and receiving of e-mail along Internet pathways to users in other business organisations.
▶ *Transferring information between networked systems.* The Internet forms an electronic library where information can be accessed, stored or retrieved without leaving the safe confines of the user's computer system.
▶ *Searching and accessing information sources.* A number of software applications are commercially available which allow a user to browse the information on the Internet. Commonly used search services include Gopher, Veronica, or WWW (World Wide Web).
▶ *Groupware and multi-user participation.* Those with an interest in a certain topic can communicate with other interested groups and individuals through the medium of leaving messages on bulletin boards or developing direct contacts through e-mail.

The integrated electronic office is the general term used to describe a technologically feasible office environment which makes maximum, or optimum, use of information technology. Typical integrated electronic office technology includes the following:

▶ Information technology with associated software applications for wordprocessing, database applications, spreadsheet applications, graphics, desktop publishing and multi-media information support, and other applications to carry out the day-to-day activities of a business.
▶ Input and output technology in the form of optical, text and graphical scanners (known as OCR for optical character recognition software) and monochrome or high-resolution colour printers for text and graphics.
▶ Communications technology such as facsimile transmission and e-mail through hardwired or modem technology using standard telephone, satellite or other network media.
▶ Electronic data interchange (EDI) using terrestrial (wire or fibre optics) or extraterrestrial (radio and microwave) technology to electronically transmit and receive data and information between computers and computer system networks.
▶ Multi-media technology supported by high-storage memory devices such as CD-ROM (compact disk-read only memory) technology and local and remote on-line information databases and information highways such as the Internet.

▶ Teleconferencing and more sophisticated videoconferencing technology which allows numerous people to be simultaneously connected in vision and sound even though they may be in remote locations and many hundreds or thousands of miles apart.

Such technology was once referred to as the office of the future. It is now the reality of the present and an essential part of the competitive business environment.

ACTIVITY **8.9**

The integrated electronic office

Discuss the concept of the integrated electronic office system and indicate the main role and responsibility of such systems within business organisations. Explain four possible uses of the Internet for business organisations and suggest the category of information an organisation may wish to send and receive. Indicate the advantages and disadvantages of using e-mail over non-electronic means of communication such as surface mail.

8.9 Chapter summary

The use and application of information technology pervades the whole business environment. The legal, economic, cultural and technological forces that impact on the business environment need to be appreciated in order to understand their effect on the building of information systems within business organisations. It is often the case, in many business organisations, that there exists an overlap between technologies found in the business environment because of the penetration and spread of advanced IT, such as expert systems and artificial intelligence. For example, a transactions processing system can be enhanced to provide information for management decision making, which in turn could be integrated into decision support systems to assist the management and executive decision-making functions of an organisation. Therefore, an understanding of expert systems and artificial intelligence in the realms of supporting the process of decision making is a fundamental step in appreciating and applying IT to information systems found within the business environment. From this vantage point, the following chapter will study various business information technology applications and will concentrate on developing a further understanding of the integration of IT applications within the business environment. However, the emphasis will be on the *modelling* of decision making using a range of information technology applications.

Short self-assessment questions

8.1 Outline and explain the four main component forces of the business environment.

8.2 Explain why legal and technological factors may affect the way information systems are designed and operated within the business environment.

8.3 Define and describe the political environment and explain how national legislation affects business practices and working patterns.

8.4 Describe three ways in which the government of a country can influence business activity within the business environment.

8.5 Explain the term *telecommuting* and suggest three possible advantages and disadvantages of telecommuting from the point of view of the individual employee and the business organisation.

8.6 Identify two types of job that could be done by telecommuting and discuss the attributes that make telecommuting appropriate to certain jobs.

8.7 Define the term *ergonomics* and explain the significance of ergonomics to the design of human–computer interfaces.

8.8 Suggest some of the main health hazards that can arise when IT is badly configured, with little regard to human considerations present within human–computer interaction.

8.9 Describe the gravitation of information technology from operational systems into management and executive information systems within the business environment.

8.10 Describe the consumer environment and explain how the methods that consumers use to pay for goods and services has changed with advances in information technology.

8.11 Explain the significance of IT to the retail and banking sectors and provide two examples of technologies that have altered the way customers interact with retail shops and high street banks.

8.12 Describe ways in which information technology has allowed banks to offer services on a 24-hour basis which would not have been possible without advances in IT.

8.13 Explain the main areas of primary concern on privacy and data protection within the business environment.

8.14 Outline and explain the significance of the Data Protection Act in terms of its main principles and discuss why the Act was introduced.

8.15 Describe ways in which the Data Protection Act affects how business organisations collect and store data and explain how this impacts on the design of information systems within the business environment.

8.16 Describe the use and importance of PIN numbers in the retail and banking sectors of the business environment.

8.17 Suggest three security techniques which may reduce the possibility of data and information being wrongly accessed or incorrectly recorded.

8.18 Define the terms *expert system* and *artificial intelligence* and contrast the differences between the two definitions as found within the business environment.

8.19 Provide two examples of the use of expert systems within business and suggest five reasons why expert systems provide useful assistance for decision making within the business environment.

8.20 Explain the relationship between the *field expert*, the *knowledge engineer* and the *end-user* in the development of expert systems within the business environment.

Further study and reading

Books

Durkin, J. (1994) *Expert Systems Design and Development*. New York: Macmillan.

Egner, F.E. (1992) *The Electronic Future of Banking*. Maidenhead, England: McGraw-Hill.

Feigenbaum, E. and McCorduck, P. (1985) *The Fifth Generation: Artificial Intelligence and Japan's Computer Challenge to the World*. Wokingham, England: Addison-Wesley.

Forrester, J. (ed.) (1989) *The Information Technology Revolution*. Oxford: Blackwells.

Giarratano, J. and Riley, G. (1994) *Expert Systems, Principles and Programming*. PWS Publishing.

Mockler, R. (1992) *Developing Knowledge Based Systems Using an Expert Systems Shell*. New York: Macmillan.

Scharr, H. and Rappaport, A. (1989) *Innovative Applications of Artificial Intelligence*. Cambridge, Massachusetts: AAAI Press.

Zuboff, S. (1988) *In the Age of the Smart Machine*. Oxford: Heinemann.

Journals

Yoon, Y., Guimaraes, T. and O'Neal, Q. (1995) Exploring the factors associated with expert system success, *MIS Quarterly*, 19(1).

CHAPTER 9

BIT applications and information modelling

Objectives

By the end of this chapter you should be able to:

▶ define and describe the nature, function and role of BIT applications within the business environment

▶ evaluate the integration of BIT applications and the incorporation of such software-based applications within the business systems environment

▶ contrast and compare a range of applications tools and techniques for data and information modelling

▶ describe and recommend the use and integration of various BIT applications to model the decision-making environment of a business organisation

▶ advise on presentational methods and communications mediums for conveying information within the business systems environment.

9.1 Introduction to information modelling

In chapter 5 the concepts of data modelling and process modelling were introduced. This chapter will look at information modelling in terms of the infrastructure of IT-based software systems and their integration for the purposes of delivering information for decision making. Software applications can be categorised into seven broad areas as follows:

1 wordprocessing applications
2 spreadsheet modelling applications
3 desktop publishing applications
4 database applications
5 programming applications
6 multi-media applications
7 communication architectures.

Information modelling is concerned with the output from an information system and the use of that information for the purposes of business decision making. This chapter is less concerned with the structuring of data but more concerned with the modelling style and delivery of information for decision making within the business environment.

9.2 Modelling information within the business environment

Decision making involves the handling of data and the conversion of data into usable information; such usable information will often be the basis on which a business makes critical organisational decisions. Therefore, how this data is collected, collated and presented is of paramount importance within the business systems environment. The need for information has existed since the birth of mankind. The need for systematic handling of facts has evolved as human beings have developed more sophisticated ways of living and interacting with one another; the development of interwoven societies, trade and commerce has led to an increased need for information to be handled and processed efficiently and effectively.

Today the amount of information in the world grows proportionately year by year. We read in chapter 1 that this deluge of information and the need for knowledge has led to the late twentieth century being referred to as the Information Age. Information provides a person with knowledge, and knowledge in turn empowers a person to make *optimal* decisions. However, as human decision makers, we do not have the individual capacity to cope with the deluge of information that is available within the business environment; so we depend upon IT-based data and information handling systems to assist with this process.

The modern process of business information modelling can be traced in a number of ways to the American space programme of the 1960s. In that decade the National Aeronautics and Space Administration (NASA) mission, outlined by President John F. Kennedy in 1960, was to put a man on the moon by the end of the decade. This feat required vast amounts of information to be collected, processed and stored. Therefore, new information technologies were required to accomplish this feat. For instance, the need to effectively and efficiently handle data and information led to NASA scientists developing the first computerised storage systems known as databases to manage and coordinate vast banks of information.

However, before information can be modelled, data must first be selected, obtained and structured. This process can be sequentially separated into ten stages of development from converting raw data into information. Table 9.1 shows these ten stages of data acquisition, handling and delivery.

table 9.1
Stages of data acquisition, handling and delivery

Stage 1	**Selecting** the data	(Data selection)
Stage 2	**Collecting** the data	(Data capture)
Stage 3	**Organising** the data	(Data structure)
Stage 4	**Inputting** the data	(Input method)
Stage 5	**Searching** the data	(Data interrogation)
Stage 6	**Manipulation** of data	(Data management)
Stage 7	**Retrieval** of data	(Output method)
Stage 8	**Delivery** of data	(Communications medium)
Stage 9	**Presentation** of data	(Data format)
Stage 10	**Information for decision making**	

ACTIVITY **9.1**
••••••••••••• *Modelling information within the business environment*
Discuss the main role and function of data and information modelling within a
business organisation. Explain why modelling is such an important exercise within
the business environment.

9.3   Data and information capture
••

Before any form of business data processing can occur, the data or pre-processed
information, must first of all be selected and obtained. Initial data selection
involves searching and finding data that is relevant and suitable to the requirements of the business user and appropriate to the decision-making environment.
There are many and various sources of business data and other information.
Information can be obtained in computer readable format, such as a computer
floppy disk, CD-ROM or a range of other hardcopy formats that can be scanned
(or digitised) into an IT-based information system. Another method of obtaining
data is by the use of *data sensors* which monitor and acquire information. An
example of data sensoring is the scanning of bar codes on products sold in shops;
a laser scanning device reads the bar code and records the item and the price of
the item within its EPOS system; the data is then recorded and stored for future
reference. The data acquired from sensors can be stored and maybe at a later
stage input into a database application in the required organisational format.

A popular method of information acquisition is through the design and use
of *data capture forms*, which can either be paper-based or in electronic (screen-
based) format. For example, if a new video hire club opens, it will need to have data
capture forms to be completed by all applicants wishing to become a member of
the video club. Figure 9.1 shows a typical data capture format for a video hire
club, in this case Lillington's Video Hire Club.

figure 9.1
**Example of an
electronic data
capture format for a
video club**

Lillington's Video Hire Club – Leeds Branch		
APPLICATION FORM FOR MEMBERSHIP		
Membership number:	(Form: A4New)	
SURNAME:	VIDEO CATEGORY	
FIRST NAMES:	PREFERENCE	
	(Please tick box)	
Address: _____	Adventure	
_____	Comedy	
_____	Drama	
_____	Horror	
Postcode: _____	Thriller	
Telephone (Home):	Science Fiction	
Telephone (Work):	Children's	
Comments:	Other (specify)	
Type of proof of identity shown:		
Date of Application:		
Signature of Applicant:		
Signature of Branch Manager:		

ACTIVITY **9.2**
·····••••·····

Information and data capture

Discuss the main role and function of data capture techniques and suggest three types of data capture format found within the business environment. Outline four methods of capturing data and indicate types of data that would be collected and the use of such data to a decision maker within the business environment.

9.4 Data and information structuring
·····································

Before the establishment of database technology and database management systems, a business organisation stored its captured data in file systems that were organised into a number of files. Each file contained a collection of records, and each record was composed of a number of fields which referred to the basic facts being stored. In order to uniquely identify a record in a file, one of the fields would be designated a *primary key* field which must be unique. This form of hierarchical data organisation is shown in Figure 9.2. The process of data structuring is similar to the entity-relationship diagram (ERD) discussed in chapter 5. Remember that ERDs were composed of the three elements of entity, attribute and relationship. Therefore, ERDs can be used as a tool and technique for data modelling within the business environment.

Within a hierarchical data structure, a *file* refers to the overall subject of the data to be stored; a file is defined as a collection of related records of data. For example, a file might be concerned with personnel information in a human resources system or market research data within a marketing information system. Each file would consist of a collection of *records* which contain a sub-division categorisation of data within the file. A record is divided into a number of *fields*, each of which relates to an item of information found within the record. A field is often referred to as an *attribute* and a record as an *entity*. Records may contain as many fields as required by the user of the information. The sub-division of files into records and the sub-division of records into fields can clearly be seen from Figure 9.2 below. In the Lillington's Video Hire Club example of a data capture format, Figure 9.1, if this was to be transferred to a hierarchical database structure then the *file* would be all the members of the video hire club. Each member would have their own personal *record* and the *fields* would comprise the information contained in the data capture form (e.g. membership number, surname, first names, postcode, telephone number).

figure 9.2
**Traditional
hierarchical data
organisation**

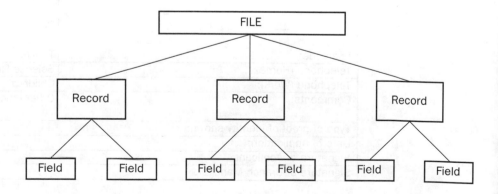

Records in a file can have fields of either fixed or variable length. The length refers to the number of alphanumeric character positions allocated to a field. The combination of letters of the alphabet and numerals is known by the term *alphanumeric*. A combination of letters and numbers is known as an alphanumeric string (e.g. ABC123). If the fields are of fixed length then each field has a maximum set number of character positions. If the fields are of variable length then the number of characters in each field will not be the same for every record. Again, referring to the example of Lillington's Video Hire Club in Figure 9.1, an example of a fixed length field would be the postcode since these are of a specified length determined by the Post Office. The format of these postcodes are a maximum of four characters followed by three characters (e.g. SE34 5XD). This is also an example of an alphanumeric field. The surname field could be of fixed or variable length. For example, a maximum length of 30 characters could be used to hold the surname. However, since most surnames are considerably shorter than this it would seem to be a waste of storage space to use a fixed length field.

However, how would the structuring of data occur in business practice? Table 9.2 illustrates a typical structure of a company personnel database as may be found within an application of a business organisation's payroll system. The personnel data shows a record for each employee; each record has seven fields (or attributes), reading across the page from employee name to salary. For example, the record for Davies, F. shows fields for employee number, employee name, gender, department, age, grade and salary.

Each record within a file will always have a field that uniquely identifies that record. This type of field is often referred to as the *primary key*. In the personnel database in Table 9.2, it might be assumed that a specific record could be identified and located by the employee's name. However, this is not possible if employees have the same surname! In reality some personnel files contain multiple employees with the same name; in order to ensure that a record can be uniquely identified each employee would be assigned a primary key field that is unique to that employee's personnel record. In this example, the primary key field is employee number. However, if it is only necessary to retrieve a group of records that fulfill a wider search criteria, then *secondary keys* may be used. For example, a company may wish to retrieve all the records related to grade 2 employees, in order to establish salary differences at that grade. The secondary key for 'grade' would then be used to search and retrieve all the records which matched 2 in the field (or attribute) of the key 'grade'.

table 9.2
An example of data structuring

Employee no.	Employee name	Gender	Department	Age	Grade	Salary(£)
9056497	Smith G.R.	M	Sales	54	2	31,000
9315649	Jones M.T.A.	M	Accounts	23	5	12,000
9543287	Evans W.	F	Accounts	29	4	15,000
9567845	Khan C.	M	Marketing	31	4	15,000
9647825	Davies F.	F	Personnel	43	3	21,000

However, there are a number of problems and disadvantages associated with the traditional hierarchical file system approach as follows:

▶ *Data redundancy*. The traditional file system encourages duplicate files to be kept because separate applications may use the same categories of data across a business organisation.
▶ *Data inconsistency*. The same data may occur on many files but be updated at different times which causes reduced control over the data and reduced data accuracy at a given time point.

Overcoming data redundancy and data inconsistency was covered in detail in chapter 5 with an analysis and discussion of data *normalisation*. Advances in IS/IT, and particularly database technology, have allowed data to be stored in more user-friendly structures and technological environments. A database is an organised collection of data which can be accessed by many users and for many purposes. There are three main types of database structure found within the business environment:

1   *hierarchical* database structure
2   *relational* database structure
3   network database structure.

Commercial *relational database* applications have become the norm in most business organisations, for example, DBase® and Microsoft Access®. There are a number of advantages of database technology over traditional computer-based file systems as follows:

▶ A reduction in wasted storage capacity and reduced data redundancy. A database is controlled and structured to avoid data duplication and wasted capacity.
▶ A database encourages data standardisation and security by maintaining unique standards of data structuring, storage and user access within a database environment.
▶ Databases are easier to maintain and expand than traditional computerised file systems.

The coordination and control of a set of databases is usually assisted by a *database management system* (DBMS), which carries out the functions of storing, searching, retrieving, maintaining security and information integrity, and providing facilities for the manipulation of data within the database framework. In many ways the DBMS acts as a user-friendly front-end interface tool between the end-user and the database. The ultimate aim of database structuring is normally to organise, control and make data accessible to the systems end-user so that there is available reliable, accurate and timely information for business decision making.

ACTIVITY **9.3**

Information and data structuring

Describe the main disadvantages associated with the traditional hierarchical file system approach and outline the main advantages of relational database systems within the business organisation. Discuss the relationship between the files, records and fields of traditional hierarchical file design and the use of entity-relationship diagrams (ERDs) as a tool for structuring data.

9.5   Data input and data modelling

Having organised and applied a logical structure to the data it then has to be input into the relevant database application. The most common method of *data input* is by using a normal QWERTY keyboard connected to the computerised system or data storage device. Inputting can also take a range of other forms, such as voice recognition input, scanning text and pictures, and electronic downloading and uploading of computer files from other local or remote on-line applications. With the growth of multi-media technology, and the Internet, pictures, graphs, sounds and movies may also now form part of a database application.

> **DID YOU KNOW?**
> *The term QWERTY arises from the first five letters on a standard keyboard. The QWERTY configuration was originally designed to slow down the typist to prevent the hammers of the old manual typewriter from jamming. Today, research is being carried out to find a more efficient and appropriate configuration of letters for the typist.*

Once data is stored in a database application it may be interrogated and edited. Interrogation is the process of accessing the data records within a database to extract information for users in their decision-making activities. Information editing has two main activities as follows:

1   *Database editing and data maintenance.* This is the activity of adding or deleting data within a database application. For example, if an employee moves home, then their new home address would have to be changed in their individual personnel record within an application of the human resources system.
2   *Database interrogation.* This is the activity of accessing a record to validate the information contained in a particular record, but not to alter the record. For example, the personnel record of an employee may be referenced to check the age of that employee and their current salary level.

9.6   Information output and search patterns

Databases can be sorted, merged and integrated with other applications across a range of systems within the business environment; this area is often known as *data manipulation*. For example, data can be sorted into ascending or descending order, as required by an end-user, or merged by interleaving the data from two or more files to produce one large database application. Table 9.3 illustrates a worked example of database sorting and merging techniques. In this example there are two files in a database labelled 'File A' and 'File B'. File A contains five records and File B contains seven records. Both files have records with the same number and type of fields (or attributes).

table 9.3

Data and information manipulation

FILE A

Record no.	Name	Department	Age	Salary(£)
20543	Davies T.	Sales	54	28500
25765	Evans G.D.	Accounts	23	14000
22359	Francis P.A.	Accounts	29	15500
31527	Evans C.	Marketing	31	18000
25980	Jones D.F.	Personnel	43	21500

FILE B

Record no.	Name	Department	Age	Salary(£)
21337	Ghandi A.G.	Accounts	24	14000
29879	Evans D.A.	Sales	24	14000
22341	Smith C.	Sales	37	20000
23336	White G.D.	Personnel	21	13500
27614	Jones S.B.	Buying	47	24000
25601	Brown C.	Accounts	58	30500
25753	Carter V.M.	Marketing	32	23500

If File A and File B are sorted by the primary key field of 'Record no.' in descending order, then the following listing would occur:

FILE A (sorted)

Record no.	Name	Department	Age	Salary(£)
20543	Davies T.	Sales	54	28500
22359	Francis P.A.	Accounts	29	15500
25765	Evans G.D.	Accounts	23	14000
25980	Jones D.F.	Personnel	43	21500
31527	Evans C.	Marketing	31	18000

FILE B (sorted)

Record no.	Name	Department	Age	Salary(£)
21337	Ghandi A.G.	Accounts	24	14000
22341	Smith C.	Sales	37	20000
23336	White G.D.	Personnel	21	13500
25601	Brown C.	Accounts	58	30500
25753	Carter V.M.	Marketing	32	23500
27614	Jones S.B.	Buying	47	24000
29879	Evans D.A.	Sales	24	14000

If File A was *merged* with File B to create File C, and sorted by the field 'Record no.', then the following result would occur:

FILE C (Files A and B merged and sorted by Record Number)

Record no.	Name	Department	Age	Salary(£)
20543	Davies T.	Sales	54	28500
21337	Ghandi A.G.	Accounts	24	14000
22341	Smith C.	Sales	37	20000
22359	Francis P.A.	Accounts	29	15500
23336	White G.D.	Personnel	21	13500
25601	Brown C.	Accounts	58	30500
25753	Carter V.M.	Marketing	32	23500
25765	Evans G.D.	Accounts	23	14000
25980	Jones D.F.	Personnel	43	21500
27614	Jones S.B.	Buying	47	24000
29879	Evans D.A.	Sales	24	14000
31527	Evans C.	Marketing	31	18000

Finally, if File A was merged with File B (to create File C) and sorted alphabetically by the field Name, then the following result would occur:

FILE C (Files A and B merged and sorted alphabetically by Name)

Record no.	Name	Department	Age	Salary(£)
25601	Brown C.	Accounts	58	30500
25753	Carter V.M.	Marketing	32	23500
20543	Davies T.	Sales	54	28500
31527	Evans C.	Marketing	31	18000
29879	Evans D.A.	Sales	24	14000
25765	Evans G.D.	Accounts	23	14000
22359	Francis P.A.	Accounts	29	15500
21337	Ghandi A.G.	Accounts	24	14000
25980	Jones D.F.	Personnel	43	21500
27614	Jones S.B.	Buying	47	24000
22341	Smith C.	Sales	37	20000
23336	White G.D.	Personnel	21	13500

In many circumstances the users of data files require the information listed and printed out in formats similar to those for File C. Databases can be searched and data ordered into various output formats, which in turn can be downloaded to other applications within the business environment.

Boolean logic   Databases can be searched using search term alphanumeric strings or by using Boolean logic. Boolean logic operators are 'and', 'or' and 'not'. By using such operators a subject or topic area can be searched and the relevant records retrieved from the database. For example, a manager of a business organisation may wish to retrieve all the records in a database system relating to employees on grade 3 or 4. Then the *search pattern* may be as follows: 'employee and (grade 3 or 4)'. Note that in Boolean logic the terms in the brackets will usually be linked and the operation carried out before other terms in the search pattern.

One of the ways of presenting data is in the form of *reports* to be read by a manager or executive, or to be presented to a manager or executive of a business organisation. The report will need to be narrated with headings and titles and presented neatly for the report end-user. The content and the report itself should be clear, visual and purposeful.

ACTIVITY **9.4**
....

Information output and search patterns

Norman Payne Enterprises operates a *purchase order processing system*. The business organisation requires you to advise and recommend improvements to the current system. Using a database application of your choice set up a database to manage and coordinate the ordering of raw materials from various suppliers. (Remember chapter 7 outlined the role and purpose of a purchase order system.) The record structure should include such data and information as the supplier's name and address, product category, supplier product codes and descriptions. Indicate the data and information requirements of the purchase order processing system for Norman Payne Enterprises. Design a suitable data capture format to record the above information required for the system and state whether it is numeric, alphabetical string or alphanumeric. Set up a suitable database application to hold the above information for the purchase order processing system. Furthermore, advise the business organisation on the implications of too much or too little data within a business information system.

9.7 Spreadsheet modelling
....

One of the most popular BIT applications used to model data is an electronic spreadsheet. A spreadsheet is an application programme which lays out an analysis sheet of rows and columns. The spreadsheet is based on the traditional accountant's lined analysis sheet, used for financial calculations. In an electronic spreadsheet the rows and columns make up a matrix of *cells* which can be uniquely identified by a number (row) and letter (column). Text, numbers or formulae can be entered into the cells of the spreadsheet and each cell will have a unique alphanumeric code; for example, the first cell in the top left-hand corner of a spreadsheet is identified as A1. Most electronic spreadsheets have at least 63 columns and 254 rows, making 16,002 available cells! The power of the spreadsheet lies in the ability not only to do calculations in single cells, but also to be able to recalculate the whole spreadsheet each time one or more changes are made to any

DID YOU KNOW?

One of the earliest commercially available spreadsheets was a package called VisiCalc produced by VisiCorp Inc. in the United States. Since then numerous other packages have come on the IT market. Two very popular spreadsheet packages in widespread use today in the business environment are Lotus 1-2-3® and the Microsoft Corporation's Excel® spreadsheet applications. Spreadsheets are some of the most widely sold of all BIT applications packages in the business environment.

figure 9.3

Example of a cash flow budget modelled in a spreadsheet application

Summary cash budget for a six month period
(Example of management planning and control)

	Jan (£)	Feb (£)	Mar (£)	Apr (£)	May (£)	Jun (£)	Six month total
Opening bank balance	3435	4685	4935	4585	3085	1535	
Total receipts	3900	3000	2500	1450	1500	3000	£15,350
Less: total payments	2650	2750	2850	2950	3050	3150	£17,400
Net receipts	1250	250	-350	-1500	-1550	-150	-£2,050
Balance carried forward	4685	4935	4585	3085	1535	1385	
Bank overdraft limit	1500	1500	1500	1500	1500	1500	£9,000
Overdraft margin	3185	3435	3085	1585	35	-115	

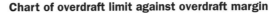

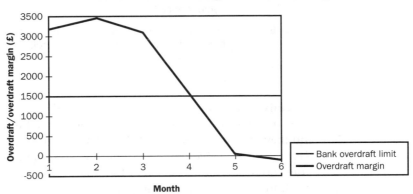

Chart of overdraft limit against overdraft margin

individual cell. The recalculations can be performed almost instantaneously. Thus, spreadsheets lead to a reduction in clerical and intellectual effort and an increase in data modelling efficiency. Figure 9.3 illustrates an example of a spreadsheet application showing a summary *cash budget* and its corresponding graphical presentation.

Electronic spreadsheets were originally designed for use by accountants. However, an electronic spreadsheet can be used in any subject area where there is a need to model and manipulate information. The uses of the spreadsheet are limited only by the imagination of the modeller.

Spreadsheet methods   Spreadsheets recognise and manipulate four types of data or information. *Text* which is often used for column or row headings; *numbers* which are the numbers used for the calculations; *formulae* which are used to calculate results in certain cells from information contained or referenced in other cells; and *operators* which use arithmetic signs, usually + for addition, − for subtraction, * for multiplication, / for division, and ^ for raising to a power.

table 9.4

**Examples of
spreadsheet terms
and definitions**

Active cell	This is the cell which is currently waiting to receive data. It is indicated on the screen by the cursor.
Cell	A cell is identified by a column number and a row letter (e.g. A1). A cell is empty until it receives some type of data.
Command bar	This appears either at the top or the bottom of the worksheet. It indicates the options available to the user.
Display window	This is what is actually seen on the screen. It may only be a portion of a large worksheet.
Entry line	This can appear either at the top of the screen or the bottom of the screen. It is used to input and display the commands or data to be placed into a cell.
Scrolling	This is the term used when moving around the worksheet over a number of cells.
Status bar	This bar appears either at the top or bottom of the screen. It keeps the user informed of each cell's status (e.g. text, numbers or formulae).

Spreadsheet layout   Spreadsheets can be *formatted* so that columns sizes can be altered and the data within cells either justified to the left, right or centred, and they have the facility to add or delete columns from the worksheet. A *worksheet* is the name given to the area of rows and columns which are being used to store and record numbers, text or formulae. A user can move around the spreadsheet, from cell to cell, by using the cursor (or arrow) keys (< >) located on the keyboard. The cursor is often indicated on the spreadsheet by a flashing line or by one cell being highlighted more than the other cells. Before progressing further it is important to build up a vocabulary of common spreadsheet terms. Table 9.4 lists and defines some of the commonly used spreadsheet terms.

All spreadsheet applications have a command menu bar which appears at the top or the bottom of the spreadsheet screen which provides useful general command options for the user, such as saving a worksheet, loading a worksheet, inserting or deleting rows or columns, and creating pictorial displays of data such as graphs, charts and diagrams. Many spreadsheets are far too large to be viewed on a single screen and so a portion of the worksheet must be chosen for viewing at any one time. The computer screen may be regarded as a *window* which can be used to view any portion of the spreadsheet.

Spreadsheet functions   One of the advantages of spreadsheets is that formulae may be entered and stored in cells. The mathematical formula allows a cell to be recalculated if a number is changed in a related cell; a related cell is one that is affected by the formula. A formula can be either simple or complex, depending on the situation and what is being modelled. Most spreadsheet applications have *formulae functions* built into the spreadsheet applications package. A function is a special kind of formula which has been prepared in advance to perform a variety of chores. Most functions carry out some action on a cell value or group of cell values in order to produce another value. A simple example is

AVERAGE	Used to find the average of a row or column.
IF	Tests the value of a cell and does one thing if the test is positive (true) or another thing if the test is negative (false).
MIN	Used to reveal the lowest number in the selected cells.
MAX	Used to reveal the highest number in the selected cells.
PI	Provides the number for pi (3.1415926536).
SUM	Used to find the total in a row or column.
SQRT	Used to find the mathematical square root of a number.

table 9.5
Examples of common spreadsheet functions

the function known as SUM, which is a frequently used function to total rows and columns. For example, the function formula SUM(C3-C9) is informing the spreadsheet to add together all the values in cells C3 to C9. The form and sequence of alphanumeric characters, or the syntax, of the command formulae may vary slightly from package to package. Table 9.5 lists and describes some common functions that are built into spreadsheet applications.

ACTIVITY **9.5**

Spreadsheet modelling theory

Discuss the role and function of spreadsheet applications for the modelling of decisions within the business environment. Provide two examples of the use of spreadsheet modelling of accounting applications and information modelling within a marketing information system. Describe the information requirements for a decision regarding the purchase of an additional factory to support a business organisation's manufacturing process and discuss the way you would go about building a spreadsheet model of the decision-making environment.

9.8   Modelling techniques

Modelling is at the heart of problem solving and eventual decision making within the business environment. A model is a representation of some aspect of reality. Models attempt to recreate in a controlled manner the *systems* that exist in reality. In modelling, the term system is used to mean all the features of reality the model is attempting to explain. Models can be categorised into three types:

1   physical models
2   logical (mathematical) models
3   mixed logical and physical models.

An example of a *physical model* is the use of wind tunnels to model the effects of wind patterns and vortices of air flowing over the frame of an airplane or even a racing car. The wind tunnel model would be physically built to be as realistic as possible. Physical models such as this are built and tested because it would be too expensive, and often too dangerous, to build and test a full size airplane or racing car. Another example of a physical model is the building of small engineering models of tall buildings to test the stresses and other forces exerted on the frames and main supports of the building. Such modelling is essential within the construction sector of the business environment. Again, a model would be built because it would be too costly in time and money to build an untested actual size building.

Logical models are theoretical and are made up of statements of principles, logical assumptions and numerical calculations. The process of logical modelling is the forming of concepts about everyday reality within domains of the business environment. Such models are appropriately designed using IS/IT data analysis and logical analysis techniques. Logical and mathematical models are ones that lend themselves easily to computer-based analysis and implementation. A spreadsheet applications package is ideal for building logical models because the logical assumptions and numerical calculations can be readily structured, and usually such packages are supplied with in-built mathematical functions. For example, a model can be built using logical assumptions of demand and supply to extrapolate or predict the sales of products and services. However, other statistical analysis and modelling packages may be used as appropriate (e.g. Genesis Model Building® or Witness®). By using a BIT modelling application a user may analyse, experiment and test any model of business systems reality.

Mixed logical and physical models use logical modelling techniques which are applied to a built physical model. For example, a flight simulator program run on an ordinary home computer. A user (or player!) by using a joy-stick can simulate the flying of an airplane. The flight simulator computer program is designed and written using theoretical, logical and mathematical principles of flight. The user is able to interact physically (by using the joy-stick) to fly the airplane. An ideal mixed modelling system is the commercial flight simulators built and designed to train commercial airline pilots. The simulator 'box' is a physical model and all movement and flight is attained by computer programs using logical (and mathematical) modelling. The commercial package Witness® can be used, for example, to model client calls coming through a telephone switchboard to analyse the number and type of calls made and related user-support activity resulting from these calls. The idea is to build the most efficient telephone user-support system to deal with client enquiries.

The bounds of what can be modelled is only limited by the imagination, or inspiration, of the modeller. Most models are based on theoretical principles and logical assumptions. It would be very rare to find a model that perfectly represented reality. However, the role of a model is to represent, as far as possible, some degree of reality. A model enables a user to predict, test or explain a representation of reality. Often no two managers or executives will carry out a model-building exercise in the same way; there is plenty of scope in modelling for individuality of thought and approach. However, within modelling there are standard concepts and guidelines on development stages to assist the model builder. Any model should be developed methodically and systematically. Table 9.6 outlines eight generic stages in the process of designing and developing a model for the business environment.

table 9.6
Stages of model building

Stage 1	Determine which **system** of reality is to be modelled.
Stage 2	Formalise the **specifications** of the model.
Stage 3	Establish the **assumptions** and **variables** of the model.
Stage 4	Prepare a **proposal** for the building of the model.
Stage 5	Carry out **data collection** and **data modelling**.
Stage 6	Create user **documentation** for the model.
Stage 7	Carry out a **validation** of the model.
Stage 8	Put the model into **use** and **update** the model as required.

Stage 1 of any model building exercise begins with the establishment of which *system* of reality is to be modelled. Once an area of interest has been established by the model builder then, in stage 2, the *specifications* of the model should be formally laid out. These indicate the bounds of the modelling environment. The specification indicates which particular aspects of reality are to be modelled; it defines the *boundary* of the model system. Stage 3 of the model-building exercise requires the establishment and description of the model's *assumptions* and *variables*. The assumptions of any model summarise the simplifications and limiting principles made in identifying the system to be analysed; the assumptions also state and describe the relationship between components of the system. The variables of the system identify the quantifiable components, also referred to as the entities, of the system. The model builder should always list and describe all the variables in the system model and the relationship between the variables. This relationship between variables can often be reflected in simple or complex numerical formulas. In any model there are usually one or more *decision variables* in the list of total variables. A decision variable is controlled by the modeller and is fundamental to the modelling exercise. These control variables are sometimes referred to as the control *parameters* of the model.

The fourth stage of the model-building exercise is to prepare a *proposal* for the building of the model. The proposal should determine how the model is to be built, what is to be used, and whether it is to be a physical, logical or mixed model. The proposal should also indicate the type of information technology to be used to construct the model or assist in the modelling exercise. The fifth stage of *data collection* and *data modelling* is central to the model-building exercise. Once the assumptions and variables have been determined, then the data to be analysed needs to be collected and quantified. It is at this stage that the data can be modelled, based on the assumptions and relationships between variables established in previous stages. In logical models the modelling will involve establishing mathematical formulae for the relationship between variables.

The sixth stage of the modelling exercise is to *document* the model to explain the purpose and function of the model. The documentation should also be written to explain to new users how to operate the model. It is often the case that a model may be developed by one person only to be updated and used in the future by another person. The seventh stage of the modelling process is *model validation.* This is an important part of the modelling process. The model is tested to verify that it is true and accurate. Models can often be validated by testing them against known or observed data. Validation involves determining the accuracy of the model within certain pre-defined modelling parameters. For example, a model that determines the required braking distance for a vehicle at various speeds could be validated by setting up a practical experiment with vehicles braking at certain speeds then recording the data. The real data recorded for braking distances can then be matched against the braking distances established by the model.

The final process of the modelling exercise is to put the model into use and to *update* the model in the future to incorporate any changes in the model's constraints. For example, a spreadsheet model could be set up to determine the amount of monthly interest received by an investor who deposited his money in a bank at the existing interest rate. The spreadsheet would likely include a column recording the 12 months of the year, a column for the interest payment and a column for the resulting amount including interest. If the interest rate changed in the future, then the new rate could be input into the model and the new amount of interest payable could then be ascertained.

An explanation of all the concepts found in the development stages of modelling can be found in the following example of a spreadsheet application, Table 9.7, modelling the number of products sold by Miss Coady, a sales agent for Norman Payne Enterprises.

In the spreadsheet in Table 9.7 the *system* being modelled is Miss Coady's monthly salary and bonus for working as a sales agent. The bonus is related to the number of products sold each calendar month. The *variables* of the model are Miss Coady's bonus, the number of products sold, the month of the year and Miss Coady's monthly salary. The *relationship* between variables is embedded in the column formulae of the worksheet. Miss Coady's bonus recorded in column

table 9.7
Spreadsheet application example – Miss Coady (Sales Agent)

	A	B	C	D
1	Month:	Products sold:	Salary(£):	Bonus(£):
2	Jan	42	84.70	21
3	Feb	27	79.45	13.5
4	March	34	81.90	17
5	April	19	80.15	14.5
6	May	23	78.05	11.5
7	June	40	84.00	20
8	July	31	80.85	15.5
9	Aug	17	75.95	8.5
10	Sept	33	81.55	16.5
11	Oct	32	81.20	16
12	Nov	18	76.30	9
13	Dec	54	88.90	27

D is calculated by the formula (B2*0.5). This indicates that for every poster sold, Miss Coady receives 50 pence as a bonus. Therefore, there is a relationship between column B and column D. Miss Coady's monthly salary is calculated by the formula ((£100+D2)*(0.7)). This indicates that Miss Coady receives a fixed salary of £100 plus the bonus pre-calculated in column D. This total is then multiplied by 0.7 (or 70 per cent) to work out the salary after taxation. This makes the *assumption* that the taxation rate is 30 per cent. Obviously, this assumption can be varied to model the effects of any taxation rate.

What makes this example a model, and not just a representation of a situation, is the existence of *decision variables*. In this example the decision variables are the bonus rate (e.g. 50 pence), the basic salary of £100 and the taxation rate (e.g. 30 per cent). A decision variable is a variable that is controlled by the model user and forms the basis of any experimentation carried out on the model. The variables are sometimes referred to as the parameters of a model. Certain parameters can be fixed in order to establish a *sensitivity analysis* of the altered variables. For example, the bonus rate of 50 pence per product could be changed to 60 pence per product. The model user would merely have to change the formula in column D to indicate 0.6 rather than 0.5 and the whole spreadsheet could be recalculated to ascertain Miss Coady's new salary situation. The model could be used to predict what salary Miss Coady may receive in the future or what Miss Coady's salary would have been had the bonus been 60 pence and not 50 pence. The worksheet would be established by *data gathering* of information on the number of products sold by Miss Coady. This could be done by looking through sales order invoices processed by the sales order processing system. Therefore, data gathering is an essential exercise in the model-building process.

It can be seen from Miss Coady's model that it is important to *document* the model in some way. For example, a new user would have no idea of the origin of the percentage rates used for the bonus in column D (e.g. 0.5) or the origin of the after taxation rate used in column C (e.g. 0.7). Any documentation of the model should include the basis of the technique used for data gathering and the items of any formulae used or embedded into the model. Finally, the model should be *validated* by testing the worksheet to determine if the variables are being calculated correctly. The spreadsheet can also be *updated* and used in the future to incorporate any changes such as Miss Coady receiving additional bonuses for selling other products.

Sophisticated calculations can be performed in spreadsheet applications by writing program *macro* to perform certain operations. A macro is a complex set of formulae that is akin to a short computer program. Macros allow laborious spreadsheet operations to be undertaken methodically and to a more sophisticated extent than is possible by merely using inbuilt functions. Macros can also be written to link different BIT applications within the business environment. For example, Microsoft VisualBasic® is a useful fourth generation language programming tool for empowering and integrating BIT applications within MicroSoft's overall suite of software applications. For instance, data from a database can be automatically transferred into a spreadsheet, like Excel®, and then again automatically output to a graphical package to produce useful reports. This level of package 'empowerment' can only be achieved by writing macros to perform and implement various operations.

ACTIVITY **9.6**
• • • • • • • • • • • • •

Spreadsheet modelling practice

Provide a definition for three categories of model and explain the characteristics, function and purpose of each category of model. Describe the role and function of *macros* in empowering software applications and outline three benefits of using fourth generation programming languages to integrate BIT applications within a business organisation. Once this has been achieved, use your understanding to do the following:

A photographic shop owned by Hill Photos Limited charges £250 for taking pictures at weddings. It also charges £12.50 for each film of 24 exposures that it uses. Reprints are charged at £3.50 for a 6" by 4" photograph, £3.70 for a 7" by 5" photograph, £4.00 for a 9" by 6" photograph, £5.50 for a 12" by 8" photograph and £15 for a 24" by 16" photograph. (Note that 17.5 % VAT is added to all purchases). You are required to establish a spreadsheet model for the business organisation so that the number of reprints of each size of photograph, and the number of films used, once entered, creates a breakdown of the total cost which can be presented to the customer as a bill and indication of the estimated cost.

9.9   Information communication and presentation
• •

Wordprocessing is one of the most widely used BIT applications in the information technology domain, particularly in integrated electronic office systems. Wordprocessing and desktop publishing can be used to communicate and present information that has previously been modelled using database and spreadsheet applications. Wordprocessing can be defined as the automatic manipulation of natural language text. The modern day computer-based wordprocessing technology is a direct descendant of the earliest manual typewriters which emerged over 100 years ago. Progressive improvements have been incorporated over the years from the days of heavy manual typewriters through to fast and light electronic typewriters, which allowed limited levels of text manipulation, to today's highly manipulative computer-based wordprocessing systems. However, certain features of wordprocessing have not changed with the progress of technology. The standard QWERTY keyboard used today to input alphanumeric data has changed relatively little over time.

DID YOU KNOW?

In the United Kingdom, one of the first mechanical typewriting tools was patented by Henry Mill in 1714. Commercial typewriters were first manufactured on a large scale in the 1870s and the first semi-automatic typewriters, which used punched paper rolls as input, were manufactured in the early 1930s. The first machines to incorporate facilities to actively manipulate text were produced in the 1940s.

In 1943 the International Business Machines Corporation, now known as IBM, won a contract from the government of the United States to produce an automatic machine to produce personalised letters to be sent to the next of kin of war casualties. The contract required the machine to be capable of inserting sections into, or omitting sections from, a standard text prepared on paper tape. In the 1960s IBM produced a commercial typewriter called the Selectric which was known as a 'golf-ball' typewriter and enabled a typist to manipulate the golf-ball to achieve different type styles on the same machine. Rather than keys, the Selectric had a golf-ball shaped printing device that was more efficient in printing individual letters. Further advances in the 1960s included the capability for text justification, high quality printing and typewriters with magnetic memory features. All these advances were incorporated into the fast and lightweight electronic typewriters of the 1970s and 1980s. However, electronic typewriters were soon overtaken by the expansion of computer-based wordprocessing packages.

Wordprocessing applications allow text to be corrected and modified more easily so that letters or documents do not have to be rewritten each time an alteration is required. Wordprocessing applications can be integrated with other applications such as databases and spreadsheets. Using wordprocessing technology, letters and documents can be personalised, edited, stored and eventually printed to specific formats. However, a distinction must be made between *textprocessing* and *wordprocessing*; textprocessing is primarily concerned with presentation while wordprocessing is concerned with the mechanics of communicating a message. However, with advances in information technology the limits of these two areas are becoming blurred; often it is the case that wordprocessing applications contain extensive desktop publishing (DTP) features to incorporate the handling of both textprocessing and wordprocessing.

9.10   Principles of information presentation

Wordprocessing applications allow alphanumeric text and numbers to be input, edited, manipulated, stored in memory, and eventually printed to a computer screen or paper printer, or downloaded to another software application. Wordprocessing improves the efficiency and effectiveness of people who undertake the task of producing high quality text documents. Above all computer-based wordprocessing applications save time and reduce the repetitive nature of letter writing and document preparation. Wordprocessing application packages can be either menu driven or command driven. Menu-driven applications allow the user to select functions and features, such as page set-up and printing, by selecting a particular menu option and sub-option. With command-driven applications the user must remember the commands that are required for a particular function. Most wordprocessing applications have additional tools such as a spell checker, grammar checker, thesaurus (to enable the user to search for synonyms or words with similar meanings), word counting and general help facilities. Figure 9.4 illustrates the usual features and functions of a WP/DTP application found within the business environment.

Most wordprocessing packages are WYSIWYG (**W**hat **Y**ou **S**ee **I**s **W**hat **Y**ou **G**et). Text and numbers are input through a keyboard and the text appears on the screen. Any changes to the text are seen on the screen as they are being undertaken. The alterations to text can be made by using various keys on the keyboard or highlighting the particular areas of text using a hand-held *mouse*. By using the cursor keys or a mouse the pages of text can be moved into view or out of view on the screen which is known as *scrolling*. When completed, letters and documents can be given a name and saved to a file which can be recalled to screen as and when required. The functions of entering, editing, formatting, saving and outputting text files are usually performed by marking (or highlighting)

figure 9.4
The WP/DTP environment

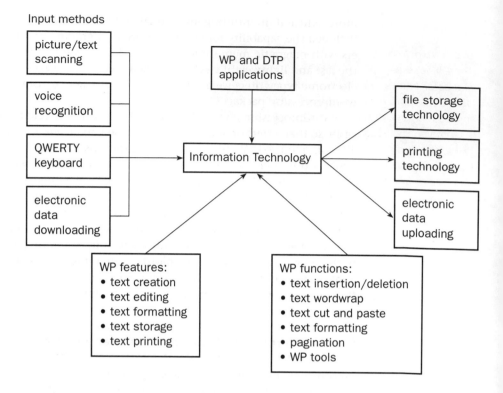

the beginning and end of the particular block of text and then using the various function commands to carry out the command operation. These commands can be initiated either by using a combination of keys on the keyboard or by highlighting the menu option if the system is attached to a mouse. Most word-processing applications enable graphics, pictures, text and diagrams to be imported into the current document.

Many wordprocessing applications have a facility known as *mail merge* which enables a user to import data from another file into the current document file. For example, a typical letter file may be merged with a file containing data such as names and addresses of the customers of a business organisation. The two files can be combined so that standard letters can be personalised with different names and addresses. The common *functions* of wordprocessing (e.g. pagination, justification, text size, text status, tabulation etc.) can be used to emphasise certain aspects of the text document. Usually, most of these functions related to formatting of text can be carried out by using page set-up commands. Most systems are set up with default (existing) parameters, such as margin size and text font, which can be altered by the user to suit their requirements.

Printers Once the text document has been formatted it can be saved to an electronic file either on the hard disk of the computer or to a floppy disk. The document can then be sent to a printing device or downloaded to another application within the business systems environment. The main types of printer in use today are dot-matrix printers, laser printers and ink-jet printers. Dot-matrix printers do not give high quality printouts, but they are quicker than either laser printers or ink-jet printers, and with advances in technology the gap is narrowing. The best output results are achieved by using laser printers which provide greater text resolution, around 300 dpi (dots per inch), and a greater range of fonts than dot-matrix printers. For instance, the Apple LaserWriterII® has numerous available fonts, 2 Mbytes of memory and can be networked to multiple computers. A laser printer works by scanning a laser beam across a charged xerographical drum to build up an electrostatic image of the text. High quality photocopying paper can then be passed over the surface of the drum and the toner is transferred to the paper. Ink-jet printers transfer text to paper by spraying a series of precision ink dots.

> **DID YOU KNOW?**
>
> *The Chinese as early as AD 600–700 were using porcelain character blocks to reproduce images on paper. As early as the eleventh century AD the Chinese were using movable character printing blocks that could be assembled and reassembled for different printing tasks. In Europe in the 1450s a German goldsmith named Johann Gutenburg pioneered the development of movable type made from cast metal characters. The print characters were arranged in wooden trays, inked, then a piece of paper was placed on top and pressed using a hand-operated press.*

Desktop Publishing   Textprocessing is concerned with the presentation of a document and not merely with the production of short documents such as letters. This area of textprocessing is referred to as *desktop publishing* (DTP). It has become more affordable to all types of business organisation and is no longer the exclusive domain of professional typesetters. DTP can be used to produce newsletters, in-house magazines, publicity materials, business forms, presentation materials and a range of other applications where good design and layout is an essential feature of the material. A desktop publishing application enables the incorporation of text, pictures, graphs, tables and diagrams into a unified form that allows more complex and visually meaningful information to be produced.

> **DID YOU KNOW?**
>
> *In Europe in the Middle Ages much copying out of written work was done by monks, usually in the Latin or Greek language, on calfskin or sheepskin called vellum. The people who copied out written works were known as scribes. The books produced were beautiful and decorative examples of typography; the works were embellished with flowing capital letters and decorated borders.*

Desktop publishing has its roots in the art of typography and printing. In the Middle Ages, chronicles and written works were laboriously done by hand-crafted penmanship. Those with the ability to read and write were very few; usually they were members of religious establishments or the nobility. In 1884 Ottmar Mergenthaler of the United States invented a machine called the linograph which enabled a complete line of text to be cast at one time. In the 1980s typesetting ideas, along with graphics, were introduced to DTP technology. The advances in information technology have led to DTP becoming more commonly available within the business environment at an affordable cost. Usually, DTP makes extensive use of WIMP technology (**W**indows, **I**cons, **M**ouse and **P**ointers). A window is viewed on the monitor and a user can put a number of windows on the monitor's screen at the same time. An icon is a small picture that represents a facility (e.g. an application package, or a wastepaper basket to represent a bin for deleting files!). A mouse can be used to direct a pointer on the screen to a particular icon. For example, an icon can be highlighted with the pointer and the window can then be activated by click-ing the mouse button. The configuration of a desktop publishing system ideally includes the following IT products:

▶ microcomputer with DTP applications
▶ large high-resolution colour screen monitor
▶ high quality laser printer
▶ text and image scanner
▶ computer-aided design (CAD) tablet and pen.

Page layout and design   When undertaking a DTP exercise there are a num-ber of initial technical considerations that have to be addressed and understood. Firstly, what sort of text layout will be adopted? Secondly, what sort of typeset-ting will be adopted? Text may be displayed on a document in block format or in *snaking columns* where the text flows from the bottom of one column to the top of the next until the page is filled, then it flows on to the next page. (The index at the back of this book is an example of snaking columns). The use of multiple columns can be used to create a number of effects to achieve a more infor-mative appearance. There are many thou-sands of different *typefaces* in professional and general use with DTP systems. Each typeface has its own characteristics of design and form. Typefaces can be divided into two broad groups (1) serif and (2) sans serif. Serif typefaces have a fine line either at the top or bottom of a text character and make sentences easier to read because they make the eyes flow over the line of print. Serif typefaces are used when typesetting books and news-papers. Sans serif typefaces on the other hand are modern and functional in visual appearance.

> **DID YOU KNOW?**
> *A typically used example of a serif typeface is 'Times', not surprisingly used on* The Times *newspaper! A typical example of a sans serif typeface is 'Helvetica' which is a Swiss designed typefont, the name coming from the Latin name for Switzerland which is Helvetica.*

The sort of typefont adopted will depend upon the purpose of the material produced on a DTP system; the typefont that is used must be appropriate for its intended purpose. For example, the typefont used on business conference mate-rial may be produced to look elegant and eye-catching. However, the typefont used for motorway signs should not be decorative, but instead should be clear, informative and functional. Often the range of typefonts available will be deter-mined by the capability of the DTP system. Take for example, the Apple LaserWriterII® (working with a print application known as PostScript®). This printer makes available some of the following typefonts: Athens, Avant Garde, Bookman, **Chicago**, Courier, Geneva, Helvetica, Monaco, New York, Palatino, Times and *Zapf Chancery*. The size of each typefont can be adjusted to a different point size which is the basic unit of measurement in typesetting. A point is nor-mally 1/72nd of an inch and is used for measuring spaces as well as typefonts. The decisions related to spacing and point size are as important in DTP as is selecting the appropriate typefont. The appearance of a font may vary greatly depending on the size of typefont adopted. The point size of a typefont is the distance between the base line of a line of text and the base line of the line of text directly below. Traditionally the point size was based on the size of the metal

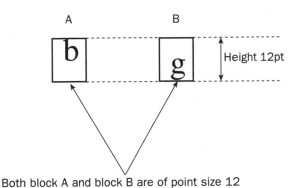

figure 9.5
**Point size type
measurement**

A   B

Height 12pt

Both block A and block B are of point size 12

body on which the character was cast for printing purposes. Figure 9.5 shows an example of point size measurement. The character ' b' has an ascender which goes to the top of the block and the character 'g' has a descender which goes to the bottom of the block.

There are other typefonts that are used for specific purposes. For example, 'Symbol' is a special typefont that is used for creating scientific or mathematical documents where Greek letters and mathematical characters are required to produce formulae. The following is a representation of the Symbol characters from a to z:

a b c d e f g h i j k l m n o p q r s t u v w x y z
α β χ δ ε φ γ η ι φ κ λ μ ν ο π θ ρ σ τ υ ϖ ω ξ ψ ζ

Spacing is another very important aspect of DTP. Spacing can be used not only between words and lines, but also between characters of a word. The spaces between characters in a word are often closed up to achieve more pleasing and visually consistent letter spacing. This process is called *kerning*. Important in the preparation of documents with multiple pages is the use of *pagination* which is concerned with the setting of page lengths. If a document has multiple pages then the page breaks must be set to ensure that there are no awkward breaks in the body of the text. For example, it would look untidy if a sub-heading for a paragraph lay isolated at the bottom of a page; the separation of a sub-header from its text or images is a bad page break. It would have been preferable to have set the page break above the sub-heading, thus carrying the sub-heading forward to the next page. The terms *widow* and *orphan* are used to refer to loose items of text that get detached from the main body of a paragraph when the text is carried across a page break. The orphan is the text that gets left behind at the bottom of the page whilst the main body text gets carried over to the next page. The widow refers to single words or part of a sentence that gets carried over to the next page. However, what is considered a good page break is a matter of visual perception and judgment by the page designer!

There are numerous graphics application packages available that enable illustrations and artwork to be prepared for importing into a WP/DTP system. Also available are clipart and icon libraries of ready made images that can be customised and imported into a DTP system for graphical illustration of text. Graphical application packages usually incorporate *painting* and *drawing* facilities. Painting packages allow the user to produce bit-mapped images in black and white or colour. Drawing packages usually have additional facilities for producing geometrical shapes and lines of the type used in technical drawing. Most packages allow the designer to use paint and draw facilities.

9.11 Chapter summary

Information empowers systems end-users to make informed judgements and reasoned decisions upon that information. For information to be useful to the end-user's needs, it must possess certain good qualities and characteristics which were outlined at the beginning of this book. The availability of systems to be modelled in the business environment is only limited by the imagination of the model builder; models can be set up using various data gathering techniques. The operation of modelling itself can also take many forms from robotics (cybernetics) modelling to data modelling using spreadsheets. However, a good model should be appropriate to the circumstances of the problem situation and should reveal a breadth of understanding of the problem scenario.

The emphasis within the business systems environment should be on integrating applications into a configuration that allows modelling activities to be undertaken. This will normally require a high level of understanding of software applications environments, to the extent of using languages (such as VisusalBasic®) to script macros to integrate and extend the capability, and usefulness, of a software applications package. For example, the MicroSoft Office® suite of applications (normally comprising a spreadsheet, presentation package, database and wordprocessing application) can be empowered, customised and integrated with other MicroSoft® applications through the use of macro programming.

Short self-assessment questions

9.1 Outline the ten generic stages of data acquisition, handling and delivery, and indicate the importance of these stages to data and information modelling.

9.2 Explain the main role and function of data structuring techniques and suggest why it is important to impose organisation on business data and information.

9.3 Outline the three main facets of traditional data file design and suggest why this approach has largely been replaced by relational database technology.

9.4 Define the term *database management system* (DBMS) and explain the main role and function of a database management system.

9.5 Describe and explain the use of Boolean logic for information retrieval and describe two other search and retrieval techniques found within the business environment.

9.6 Outline and describe three types of report formats and explain how and why such report formats would be used within a business organisation.

9.7 Explain the process of sorting and merging files within a database application and provide an example of such data manipulation within a marketing information system.

9.8 Describe the role of spreadsheet functions in the construction of decision-making models and provide an example of the use of logical and mathematical functions.

9.9 Explain eight generic stages in the process of designing and developing a model for the business environment.

Further study and reading

. . . .

Books

Brown, J. and Caldwell, E. (1990*) The management of Information Systems Technology*. Oxford: Alfred Waller.

Date, C.J. (1995) *An Introduction to Database Systems*, 6th edition. Wokingham, England: Addison-Wesley.

Hussain, D.S. and Hussain, K.M. (1993) *Information Management*. Hemel Hempstead, England: Prentice-Hall.

Inmon, W.H. (1996) *Building the Data Warehouse*, 2nd edition, New York: John Wiley.

Jones, G. and McNamara, T. (1988) *Information Technology and the New Accounting*. Maidenhead, England: McGraw-Hill.

Richards, C. (1996) *Using Lotus Notes 4: Special Edition*. Que Corporation.

Spurr, K., Layzell, P., Jennison, L. and Richards, N. (eds) (1994) *Software Assistance for Business Re-engineering*. Chichester, England: John Wiley.

Wright, P. (1995) *The Beginner's Guide to Visual Basic 4.0*. Chicago: Wrox Press.

CHAPTER 10

Telecommunications and BIT networks

Objectives
. . . .

When you have read this chapter you will be able to:

▶ define the nature and role of IT-based communications networks found within the business environment

▶ evaluate the most appropriate configuration of telecommunications technology to meet the requirements of a business organisation

▶ describe the advances in terrestrial and extra-terrestrial communications and understand the characteristics and function of local and wide area networks

▶ explain the range of communications software and hardware requirements of networked business environments

▶ evaluate the effectiveness of networked IT environments and be able to formulate a strategy for communications requirements within the business environment.

10.1 Introduction to telecommunications
. . . .

The previous two chapters described information technology in terms of how it could be used for modelling the information requirements of an organisation and the use of BIT for the purposes of decision making. This chapter takes that technology one stage further to incorporate *telecommunications technology*. The term information technology (IT) assumes not only the presence of computing technology but also the organisation of information systems into networks, through the application of telecommunications technology. It is the development of sophisticated electronic telecommunications technology which has led to the IT revolution within the business environment.

Electronic telecommunications technology is concerned with the transmitting of data and information between computer systems over *local* or *remote* networks via *terrestrial* or *extra-terrestrial* (satellite) communications channels. Telecommunications systems can transmit numeric or alphanumeric text along with graphics, voice or video information; which is referred to as multimedia information. The following chapter will further discuss, in detail, the Internet and its role and utilisation within the business environment, to reveal the importance of telecommunicated information to both business and the competitive environment in which business organisations operate. The use of telecommunications to link IT networks across the world is colloquially known as the *information superhighway*. The race to service, own or dominate the worldwide business telecommunications sector is one of the most competitive of the late twentieth century. Telephone and telecommunications organisations, such as British Telecom, AT&T in the United States, and other national telecommunications industries, are competing to

DID YOU KNOW?
The term telecommunications *is defined as an electronic means for sending and receiving data and information over a distance.*

build and control a vast web of electronic networks delivering information for business, education and individuals. These networks form an information highway as influential to business organisations as the first railways were to business activity at the start of the nineteenth century.

Telephone and telecommunications business organisations are able to exploit the information superhighway because they already have in place an extensive global network of *wire-based* and *wireless* telephone communications channels. These channels are now being used to communicate multi-media data and information from network to network. Telephone and telecommunications organisations have invested heavily in research and development of information technology. Consequently, these business organisations now provide communications channels and services that can allow some or all of the following tasks:

▶ transmission of pictures, images and videos
▶ transmission of facsimile text, graphics and sound
▶ provision of teleconferencing and videoconferencing facilities
▶ provision of home–office and telecommuting facilities
▶ provision of on-line telebanking and teleshopping.

To provide all of these services it is essential that telephone and telecommunications organisations increase the transmission capacity of their telecommunications technology. This can be achieved by applying either of the following two approaches:

1 Improving the efficiency of existing communications channels (by physically enhancing the wire-based or wireless networks).
2 Installing additional communications capacity.

The first can be achieved by replacing current *coaxial wire* channels with improved technology such as *fibre optic* cables. The second approach can be achieved by purchasing or merging with other telephone and telecommunications organisations. The information superhighway not only connects business organisations, but also connects business organisations to universities, research institutions and various other profit making and non-profit making organisations.

Twisted wire transmission is a relatively unsophisticated and slow transmission medium that is often prone to communications interference. However, *coaxial cables* consist of thickly insulated copper wire that allows faster and more reliable data communications; interference is greatly reduced because of the plastic insulation surrounding the wire. *Fibre optic* technology has superseded wire-based communications channels. Fibre optics are strands of glass fibres fitted together into cables; the cables transmit pulses of laser light rather than electronic pulses. The laser light pulses represent data signals which can be transmitted at much faster rates than conventional electronic pulses. However, fibre optic cables are less robust than wire-based cables and require correspondingly more care in installation (see Figure 10.1). Table 10.1 describes some of the available telecommunications hardware found within the business environment and the telecommunications capacity of each form of *communications medium*.

All of the telecommunications channels so far described are tangible and terrestrial in that the communications technology channels are Earth based. However, there are other forms of telecommunications channels that transmit data signals through the atmosphere. For instance, *microwave* communication

figure 10.1
Fibre optic cable

methods transmit high frequency radio signals through the air waves with no need for physical cabling. Microwaves travel in straight lines through the atmosphere, without regard for the curvature of the Earth. However, the development of satellite technology has allowed microwaves to be bounced off satellite receiving and communications devices high in outer space, often up to 25,000 miles above the Earth, thus making microwave communications more practicable. Satellites not only receive microwave signals, but amplify those signals and transmit them back to relevant reception centres back on Earth. The advantage of satellite technology is in globalising data communications between computer networks that span the Earth. The disadvantage of satellite technology is the time delays present in transmitting data signals thousands of miles into space and back again to Earth. Therefore, satellite-communicated global conferencing facilities are often prone to voice and visual time delays. For example, this is why people experience delays on long distance telephone calls.

table 10.1
Telecommunication channel hardware

Terrestrial transmission:

1	**Twisted wire cables**	Capacity of 10 megabytes per second.
2	**Coaxial cables**	Capacity of 200 megabytes per second.
3	**Fibre optics**	Capacity of up to 10 gigabytes per second.

Extra-terrestrial transmission:

1	**Microwaves**	Capacity of 100 megabytes per second.
2	**Satellites**	Capacity of 100 megabytes per second.

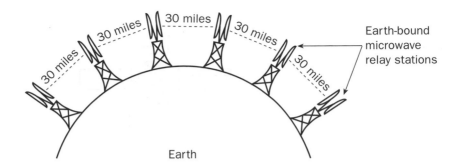

figure 10.2
Satellite communications (a) Terrestrial transmission

In deciding on an appropriate telecommunications medium consideration must be given to the relationship between cost and performance. For example, satellite communications can cost more than other mediums, but the flexibility and global nature of the medium may outweigh the costs for a globally trading business organisation. Figure 10.2 illustrates the relationship between satellite technology and the business environment. Many international organisations do not relay through government satellites, but rather through private satellite communications systems; such satellite systems are often known as *very small aperture terminals* (VSATs) which can be located within the physical confines of a business organisation's buildings anywhere in the world.

Terrestrial transmission   Microwaves are a form of cableless transmission using high frequency radio signals to send data and information through the air. Microwaves can be transmitted using terrestrial stations or communications satellites. However, with terrestrial relay the Earth-bound relay stations can only be approximately 30 miles apart to send and re-broadcast signals (Figure 10.2a). This is because microwaves travel in straight lines and the 'line-of sight' between the transmitter and receiver must be unobstructed. Therefore, microwave relay stations are usually located on the tops of high-rise buildings in built-up urban areas, or at the peaks of hills and mountains in more rural areas. Microwaves can carry thousands of channels at the same time.

However, the preferred method of microwave transmission where data and information is required to be sent over large distances unobstructed is satellite transmission. A satellite is fundamentally a microwave relay station located in outer space. The satellite orbits the Earth. Normally, the satellite orbits approximately 22,000 miles above the Earth. The communications satellite acts as a relay station that receives signals from one relay station on Earth and re-broadcasts that signal to another Earth-bound relay station.

DID YOU KNOW?
Parcel and package delivery businesses equip their trucks with VSATs. These receivers allow the business and its drivers to be in constant contact anywhere, any place and any time. (See Pause for thought 7.1.)

Satellite transmission   A satellite is any small body that orbits a larger one, either natural or artificial (Figure 10.2b). A natural satellite is the moon which orbits the Earth. Artificial, or man-made, satellites perform four main purposes: (1) scientific research, (2) weather forecasting, (3) military applications, and (4) communications. The first artificial satellite was launched into orbit around the Earth by Russia in 1957. It was called Sputnik1.

figure 10.2
**(b) Satellite
transmission**

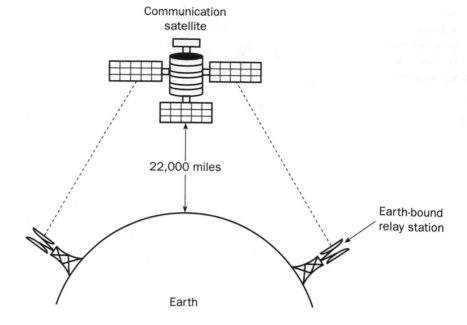

figure 10.2
**(c) VSAT satellite
communication
system**

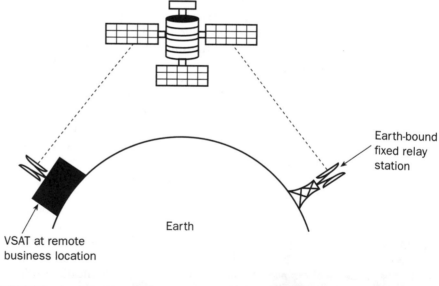

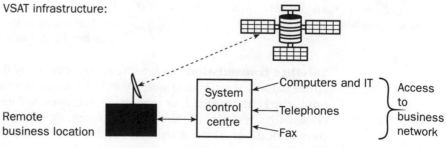

In the 1990s many business organisations are using their own satellite for internal telecommunications. Of growing importance are VSATs (very small aperture terminals) which are part of the networking infrastructures of an increasing number of organisations. A VSAT is a relatively inexpensive satellite Earth station with an antenna with a diameter of under one metre. VSATs can be mobile and located in remote areas (Figure 10.2c).

ACTIVITY **10.1**

Telecommunications networks

Search your college or university library for journal or magazine articles on terrestrial and extra-terrestrial communications technology. Prepare a business presentation, as if to the Board of Directors of a business organisation, to advise on the advantages and disadvantages of terrestrial and extra-terrestrial communications. Particularly, emphasise the effect on data security of each form of telecommunications. Then proceed to explain why telephone and telecommunications organisations are able to exploit the information superhighway. Discuss the advantages and disadvantages of using satellite technology to communicate data and information within the business environment.

10.2   Telecommunications components

Computing is no longer solely concerned with the defined technology of the computer, or the central processing unit (CPU), as it was often referred to in computing science. Today the computer is a component of computerised and integrated information systems and the computer exists alongside other equally sophisticated telecommunications systems and techniques. Nevertheless, it is important to realise that the proliferation of telecommunications technology within the business environment is computer based; an understanding of computing technology is essential to an understanding of how to build IT-based telecommunications systems within the business environment. A telecommunications system will normally comprise the integration of computer hardware, computer software and communication technologies. These may be referred to as the three components of a telecommunications system which are outlined in Table 10.2.

table 10.2
The three components of telecommunications system

1 **Computer hardware**	Mainframes and microcomputers (central or distributed processing units)
	Input and output devices (scanners, printers, voice, keyboard)
2 **Computer software**	Programs and instruction code (control and direct input and output communications activity)
3 **Communication technology**	Communication channels (wire, fibre optic or coaxial cables, satellite)
	Communications processors (modems, front-end processors, multiplexers)

Components of a networked system

A computer can be defined as a device which operates under the control of software programs that automatically input and process data to produce information as an output. The central processing unit (CPU) manipulates inputted data (of the form numeric, alphanumeric and symbolic) into more useful forms and controls other aspects of computer technology. In addition to the CPU is the arithmetic-logic unit (ALU) which carries out the necessary arithmetic and logical instructions upon the data. The two are not physically separated, but the functions are different. The CPU is often contained on an individual semi-conductor silicon chip. A silicon chip allows millions of circuit elements to be etched (or embedded) into its surface, without significant error or redundancy. The silicon chip is a component of information technology largely responsible for the miniaturisation of hardware found internally within a computer.

Primary storage (or main memory storage) stores primary instructions and the related data for instructions to be carried out. Whenever data or program instructions are placed in primary storage they are assigned to bytes. A byte represents a single character of stored data. A byte will possess a unique address so that is can be located when necessary. Therefore, primary storage consists of data and instructions held until they are required. The instructions dictate actions to be taken on the data. The results of the action will then be held (stored) until needed for output. Secondary storage (which is often referred to as backing storage) is used to assist primary storage in storing data and instructions (e.g. magnetic disk, CD-ROM and optical disks). Each physical computer will have a *control function* which retrieves instructions from the primary storage and interprets the instructions. The control function issues the necessary instructions to the components comprising the computer. The control function is responsible for directing the hardware operations of the computer by reading stored program instructions, usually sequentially, and directing the computer to perform certain tasks and operations. Information between functions and devices is transferred by means of *buses*.

Storage and speed of processing are major considerations of using computers within networked architectures. Computer processing consists of two component *machine cycles*. One is the instruction cycle and the other is the execution cycle. In the instruction cycle an instruction is received from primary storage and decoded. In the execution cycle a data address is located, an instruction executed and the results of the execution are stored locally or remotely. During processing the computer mechanistically reads a computer program (known as computer software) and carries out operations, many of which are transferred to storage. One of the important considerations of a networked system is speed of data communications and processing power. Therefore, storage capacity is of essential importance to computing. Memory storage capacity can be of two main types – RAM (random access memory) and ROM (read only memory). RAM is used for short-term storage of data or program instructions. The contents of RAM can be read and changed when necessary. ROM is a permanent storage of program instructions. The storage capacity of a computer can be determined by the extent of RAM available on the computer system. Table 10.3 describes the terminology used to gauge computer network storage capacity.

Whether computers are used in isolation or coupled together to form a network they represent data in what is known as *binary data* form. Information and data is normally communicated across networks in binary format. All symbols, words, pictures and other data forms can be converted into binary digits. Binary means having only two states and *binary logic* is the fundamental basis of electronics and computing. A binary state can be 'yes' or 'no'; 'on' or 'off'; 'dark' or 'light'; '1' or '0'. Binary numbers are represented by just two symbols, 1 and the 0. The 1 and 0 that comprise the binary system are referred to as **binary bits** (bits).

Within the electronic circuitry of a computer the binary state is represented by electronic charges being 'on' or 'off'. A conducting (charged) state in a semiconductor circuit represents 1, while a non-conducting state represents 0. Magnetic storage media works on the same binary principles. A magnetic field can be positively charged or negatively charged, the direction of the field representing either 1 or 0.

DID YOU KNOW?

Deoxyribonucleic acid (DNA) represents the nucleic acid found in the nuclei of all cells. It is considered as a gene. The chemical structure of DNA is characterised by sequences of four nitrogen bases (known as adenine, thymine, guanine and cytosine). The sequence of bases on a gene constitutes a code which determines the nature of characteristics conferred on an organism.

Even within the human body the genetic coding for human characteristics, such as eye colour, hair colour and other features, are determined by 'switches' being either 'on' or 'off' within a strand of DNA (deoxyribonucleic acid).

DID YOU KNOW?

Storage capacity is measured in bytes where the base measure is the kilobyte which equals 1,024 (or 2^{10}) bytes.

Within binary logic the position of the 1s and 0s is significant. For computing purposes, binary coding schemes must be able to represent not only numbers, but also letters of the alphabet and symbols (for example %, $, £, &). The two most common binary coding systems are Extended Binary Coded Decimal Interchange Code (EBCDIC) and American Standard Code for Information Interchange (ASCII). EBCDIC is an 8-bit coding scheme, whereas ASCII has an 8-bit version and a 7-bit version. Each binary string of code is known as a *byte*, with each byte representing a single and unique letter, symbol or number. For example, the letter C within the ASCII coding system is represented by the 8-bit string of code 0100 0011. Table 10.3 describes the terminology used to classify computing storage capacity.

Processing speed can be similarly determined to judge the time it would take to implement instructions, across a network, in terms of machine cycle time. The benchmark of judging the performance of processing speed is in millions of instructions per second (MIPS). Table 10.4 describes the terminology used to classify levels of processing capacity.

table 10.3 **Networked computing storage capacity**	Kilobyte	Approximately one thousand bytes	(1,000 storage positions)
	Megabyte	Approximately one million bytes	(1,000,000 storage positions)
	Gigabyte	Approximately one billion bytes	(1,000,000,000 storage positions)
	Terabyte	Approximately one trillion bytes	(1,000,000,000,000 storage positions)

table 10.4
Networked computer speed and processing capacity

Millisecond	One thousandth of a second	(1/1,000 second)
Microsecond	One millionth of a second	(1/1,000,000 second)
Nanosecond	One billionth of a second	(1/1,000,000,000 second)
Picosecond	One trillionth of a second	(1/1,000,000,000,000 second)

Networked systems performance is dependent upon the speed and capacity of the microprocessor technology employed within the network architecture. The three major aspects of microprocessor architecture are (1) word length, (2) bus width, and (3) clock speed. The term *word length* refers to the number of bits that may be processed together as a block. Words may be subdivided into bytes, which normally correspond to the storage capacity of a single character. A byte is normally taken to be equal to 8 bits. For example, a 16-bit chip can process 16 bits in a single machine cycle (or operation), compared to an 8-bit chip which can only process 8-bits in a single machine cycle. A 32-bit chip will be faster than an 8-bit chip because it takes fewer machine cycles to transfer data between storage and the processor. A 32-bit machine can transfer four 8-bit characters in a single machine cycle, compared to an 8-bit machine which can only transfer one set of 8-bit characters. Therefore, a 32-bit machine can be said to be four times faster than an 8-bit machine.

Computer performance is further constrained by *bus width*. Buses within computing are physical connections that allow the transfer of data within a networked system. The bus width refers to the number of bits that can be transferred in a single operation between the central processing unit, primary storage and other devices within the computer. Buses can be of various widths. A 32-bit machine with only an 8-bit internal bus would have its performance reduced by the fact that data would be processed in 32-bit blocks, but would only be able to be transferred in 8-bit blocks between the central processing unit, main storage and external devices. There are three kinds of buses that connect the CPU, primary storage and other devices of the computer. The three buses are: the address bus, the data bus, and the control bus. The *address bus* carries signals used to locate a given address in primary storage. The *data bus* carries data to and from primary storage, and the *control bus* carries signals indicating the read/write commands for changing specified addresses in primary storage or peripheral devices.

The third performance indicator is *clock speed*, which is related to the rate at which the processor receives pulses from a special digital clock built into the computer. Clock speed is a measure of machine cycle time which in turn is concerned with the speed at which a processor transfers data to and from main storage. The clock speed governs the pacing of machine cycles by emitting millions of pulses per second which are received by the processor. Clock speed is measured in megahertz (MHz) which represents one million cycles per second. For example, a computer performing with a clock speed of 30 MHz will be three times faster than a computer performing at 10 MHz.

The speed and efficiency of microprocessing within networked architectures can be increased by the incorporation of advanced processor chips that allow reduced instruction set computing (RISC). The microprocessor chips used in

RISC have only the most frequently used instructions embedded within them, rather than ordinary processors that have infrequently used instructions embedded within the chips. This makes processing more efficient and increases the speed of the networked system. The efficiency of the network can also be improved by techniques of *parallel processing* which is the activity of processing more than one instruction at the same time, within the physical domain of a computer. The instruction set is divided up into sub-instructions which are sent to separate processors which simultaneously tackle the problem. This is often made possible by networking computing systems. Parallel processing can be achieved by linking multiple computers together via a communications network so that the processing activities can be divided up between mainframes and microcomputers undertaking the processing of activities cooperatively.

ACTIVITY **10.2**

Networked systems performance

Discuss how binary data representation affects the computing environment and explain the two main systems used for binary coding. Describe the three major aspects of microprocessor technology being the word length, bus width and clock speed and explain the relationship of the three for gauging networked systems performance. Explain how the speed and efficiency of networked systems can be increased by the incorporation of advanced processor chips that allow reduced instruction set computing (RISC).

Telecommunications technology can be divided into an analysis of *communication channels*, which is concerned with the physical technology required to transmit data and information, and *communications processors*, which are responsible for providing support functions for data and information transmission.

Communication channels   These are the links via which information is transmitted between sending and receiving devices within a telecommunications network. These communications channels can be either tangible, such as wire-based, fibre optic or coaxial wire cables or intangible, such as, satellite, microwave or wireless-based communication. Communications channels act as conduits for various types of voice, sound, picture, graphics, video, numerical or text-based information being transferred between receiving and sending devices. For

example, a telephone network is a system by which voice information may be transferred between human beings. However, a telephone network may also be used to communicate data or information via wire-based or wireless-based communication; to do so requires a *communications processor* such as a modem. A modem is a device that allows a telephone channel to be connected to a computer or network of computers to transfer various types of information.

Communication processors   These provide support for data or information transmission activities across a network. The modem acts as an agent technology allowing an existing telephone network to be connected to a networked telecommunications system. A modem is a simple gateway connection between networked systems. However, there is often a requirement to dedicate a single central processing unit (or separate computer) to the function of communications management. This is known as a *front-end processor* because a dedicated processing function is acting as a networked front-end interface support to a host computer. A front-end processor removes most, if not all, of the burden for management of communications from the main computer system within a network. A *multiplexer* is a communications tool that transmits data from multiple sources through a single communications channel; this performs the function of controlling the flows of information within a networked information system. A *concentrator* performs a similar communications management function by storing data messages to be forwarded together as a set, at times that allow optimal communications efficiency.

Processing hardware is supported by *telecommunications software* that performs the following four main functions within a networked information system:

1   network management
2   transmission control and access
3   error detection and correction
4   data integrity and security.

The rules by which one networked system sends and receives data signals with another networked system are known as *protocols*, which determine the underpinning rules of communication and indicate how one networked system 'handshakes' with another networked system. Protocols perform the actions of identifying, verifying and checking data message transmissions between computer systems and related peripheral input and output devices. The physical hardware used for transmitting data across telecommunications channels may determine the speed, efficiency and performance of data communication. Telecommunications performance is measured in bits per second. This measure is often referred to as the *baud rate* and represents an electrical charge of either positive or negative through the communications channel.

ACTIVITY **10.3**

Telecommunications components

Describe the three components of a telecommunications system and indicate the two main categories of communications technology. Define the term *communications software* and describe the four main functions performed by telecommunications software within a networked information system.

10.3   Telecommunications systems management

The most basic operating systems allow one user to run one application, or operation, at one time. However, most operating systems, particularly ones that are windows based, permit the user to run or activate more than one job or application at a time. Networked systems advance to a higher level of sophistication by permitting more than one user to activate an application, or set of applications, at the same time; referred to as a multi-user system. This is possible through the networking of computers. There are a number of advantages of networking technology. Firstly, data and information can be shared by computers and also a business organisation's employees in local or remote geographical locations; secondly, a more equitable distribution of computing, task allocation and processing activities is made possible; and thirdly, more rapid and effective communication of data and information for decision making is available.

A telecommunications system consists of communications media technology and collateral software required to connect two or more computer systems. Computer networks may be restricted to the local confines of a room or building or can span the entire globe, as with the Internet. Networks that are confined to a room or single physical environment are referred to as *local area networks* (LANs) and networks that are not physically confined are referred to as *wide area networks* (WANs). Computer networks can in turn be connected to other computer networks creating a global web of information flows. At LAN level, networks can be used to share hardware, such as servers, scanners, printers, and software applications. At WAN level the technology can even be used to direct the international operations of a globally trading business organisation.

Telecommunications networks are managed by *communications software* which forms the instructional base for data and information transmission. The rules that dictate the methods and procedures used in transmitting data and information over a network are known as protocols. The software and protocol requirements of a networked communications system is usually handled by a *network control program* (NCP). In the main, communications software performs a number of functions as follows:

▶ permits interconnection between various computers and computer systems
▶ ensures coordination of hardware devices
▶ performs error checking and security control
▶ monitors network use and applications activities.

In addition to communications software there is a need for *network operating system software* which allows desktop computers and other hardware devices to be connected in a network with telecommunications devices. Such networked systems software controls the computers and peripheral devices on a network and allows the various devices to communicate. A network operating system normally performs the same types of function for the network as operating system software does for an individual computer. NetWare® by Novell™ and Windows NT™ are examples of network operating

systems software for PC-based networked environments. Other software tools and utilities are also available which act as *network management software* which assists the monitoring of computers and peripheral devices on a network, scans for viruses, and ensures compliance with software licenses and company policy. Network management software usually provides functions to establish fault logging and evaluation of network system performance, analysis of usage by node and type of data traffic, passwords and access control.

The protocols act as standards to ensure communications among networks using different technology bases and platforms. Historically, in the 1970s, the United States government pioneered the development of the Transmission Control Protocol/Internet Protocol (TCP/IP) to connect its defence research departments. This is still used but has often been replaced with the Open Systems Interconnection (OSI) standard. In addition the X.400, X.500 and X.25 protocols are also still in use with many business organisations. However, with the explosion of the Internet and the need to communicate multi-media data, such as text, pictures, sound and videos, there is a need for a more advanced technological standard. Asynchronous transfer mode (ATM) technology may overcome some of the problems of using separate networks for voice, picture and data transmission, as it incorporates the possibility of multi-media transmission using one standard technology.

ACTIVITY 10.4

Telecommunications systems management

Discuss the use, role and function of network management software and suggest three possible advantages to a business organisation of using networked management software to control the information resources of a business organisation. Define the term communications protocol and outline the types of communications protocols in use within the business environment.

10.4   Network topologies

As with the building of information systems the building of networks requires first logical and then physical design. There are several ways of logically arranging the computers and devices within a network; this is often referred to as connecting the *nodes* on a network. A node is a point of connection on a computer system or device on a network. The arrangement of nodes is referred to as the network topology and there are five main logical topologies used to describe how networks are organised. All of these topologies are illustrated in Figure 10.3, the five main topologies being:

> **DID YOU KNOW?**
>
> *Network topology is concerned with network structure, configuration and the way in which telecommunications devices are organised into an inter-related network of components.*

1   ring network
2   bus network
3   hierarchical network
4   star network
5   hybrid network.

A *ring network* (or loop network) contains computers and other peripheral devices placed in a logical ring or circle. The connecting metallic wire, coaxial cable or

figure 10.3
Network topologies

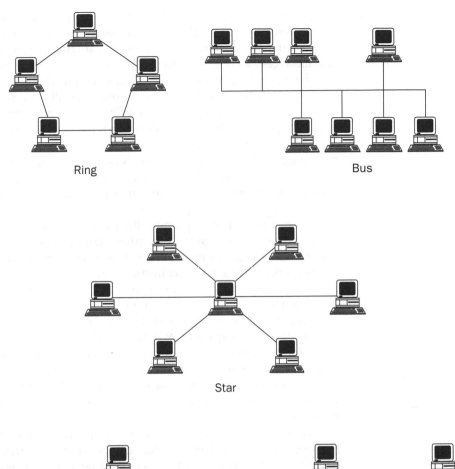

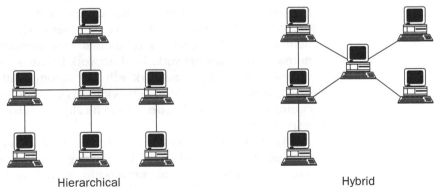

fibre optics form a closed loop which permits each computer to communicate directly with another computer in the network. Data and information is passed along the ring in one direction only, passing from one computer to another, but each computer processes its own applications independently of the other computers. Therefore, there is no central or main computer and information flows around the ring with equality of participation within the overall network.

A *bus network* is a metallic wire, coaxial cable or fibre optics cable with computers and devices attached to it. This type of network architecture connects the computers and other peripheral devices through a single communications channel. Therefore, the network consists of computers and other devices attached on a single line. All communications messages are transmitted to the entire network and messages can flow in both directions along the cable line. Each device can communicate directly with all other devices on the network. If one computer on the network fails it does not affect the other devices and so the configuration is far less vulnerable to total network failure. Therefore, this is a robust form of architecture because the various devices on the network are independent and are unaffected by single computers or devices failing on the network. However, the configuration is slow for data intensive applications, particularly when a large amount of data traffic is being handled. However, the bus network operates best for applications such as e-mail and the sharing of resources such as printers and scanners.

A *star network* is characterised by a central host computer connected to a number of smaller computers and other peripheral devices such as printers. It is the central host computer which controls and coordinates the messages through the network. This form of architecture is useful when there is a requirement to centralise many aspects of the system. All communications are required to be relayed through the host computer. However, a failure of the central host computer will automatically close down the entire network. Therefore, it is more vulnerable than other forms of network topology. The star network topology is useful for business organisations that wish to maintain some form of centralised control over data and information. The star network allows master files stored on the host computer to be downloaded to local computers for processing but with the necessity of uploading back to the central host computer when the task has been completed.

A *hierarchical network* uses a tree-like configuration; the data and information messages are passed from the top computer down through the connecting branches to the relevant computer or other device. However, a hierarchical network does not require a centralised host computer to control the communications of the network. Total network failure is less likely because a failure of one branch of the network will not automatically affect the whole network. Overall, a hierarchical network forms a system in which control and processing functions are allocated hierarchically and often by means of supervisory responsibility.

A *hybrid network* is simply a combination of one or more of the topological configurations described earlier. The topology adopted by a business organisation will be dependent upon that organisation's needs and network objectives on a local and wider geographical scale.

The above descriptions of network architectures used the terminology of computers, terminals and peripheral devices. Sometimes terminals are referred to as being 'dumb' terminals or 'intelligent' terminals. The difference lies in whether or not the computer terminal possesses its own microprocessing capability. Today microcomputers with very effective processors pervade the whole of business; therefore, most network computer components contain powerful, independent processing capabilities. It is becoming increasingly rare to find networks comprised of only dumb terminals without any local processing capability.

Network topologies

Explain the five main logical topologies used to describe how networks are organised within a business environment. Contrast the five main types of network topology and suggest which type of configuration is most suitable to small desktop computer-based environments.

10.5 Local area networks

A local area network (LAN) connects computers and devices together usually in a single building, or a departmental floor or office suite within a building. The classification for local is dependent upon the physical distance between nodes on the network. The networked devices are usually connected by either metallic or fibre optic cabling. A local area network is usually characterised by a ring, star, hierarchical or hybrid topology. LANs are normally used to link desktop computers and other peripheral devices so that they can share information. The local area network is a popular network-based solution for many business organisations because it can be built independently of a central computing system. It is also suitable for numerous server-based applications within the business environment.

LANs are used within the business environment to allow desktop microcomputers to share information and have access to expensive peripheral devices such as laser printers, image/text scanners and central servers. A central *file server* is usually a powerful microcomputer, with large memory storage capacity, that is used to store operating programs, software applications and provide access to peripheral devices that are available to all microcomputers on the local area network. A file server allows other computers and devices to share files and programs. The server will transfer the necessary programs, data and other applications to the user's computer. The file server often contains the software programs used to drive and manage the LAN. Some local area networks are sometimes connected to other external networks through a *network gateway* which may connect a LAN to the telephone network or other networks across the globe; a network gateway connects the LAN to public networks in the external environment. The main four LAN technologies for connecting networked technology are as follows:

1   Ethernet™   (developed by Xerox, Digital Equipment Corporation (DEC) and Intel)
2   AppleTalk™   (developed by Apple Computer Corporation)
3   Token Ring™ (developed by IBM and Texas Instruments)
4   Arcnet™   (developed by Datapoint)

Local area networks can be built around desktop microcomputers or mainframe computers. When a desktop microcomputer is connected to a local area network, a network interface card is usually required to be placed in the computer's expansion slot to enable it to communicate within the network. For example, an Ethernet card is required to be placed in a microcomputer for it to be able to communicate over the Ethernet. The Ethernet® is a common communications protocol often used within LAN environments. The Ethernet® standard is adopted for LANs that use a bus topology which allows users to connect to a common communications line to share network facilities and other resources. A LAN can also be represented within a ring topology which is often used for e-mail and the sharing of on-line BIT software applications. Figure 10.4 shows a typical example of a ring topology for a LAN with associated peripheral devices.

The capability of a LAN is determined by the network operating system that is employed. The network operating system can reside on every microcomputer on the network, which is the case for AppleTalk™, or it can reside on a single designated computer that acts as a server for all devices on the network. There are a number of commercially available LAN management software programs that come with a microcomputer operating system or can be added to a microcomputer operating system. For example, Apple Computer's AppleTalk©, Microsoft Corporation's Lan Manager© and Novell's NetWare©. These LAN management software applications may operate within a number of physical LAN communications and transmission channel technologies such as the Ethernet (DEC) and AppleTalk (Apple Computer Corporation). There are also a number of other communications channel technologies that compete in what is a competitive network software market. Local area network technology offers three main advantages:

1   *Resource sharing.* A LAN can be economical as hardware and software can be shared by many devices and locations. It also allows expensive hardware and software applications to be purchased with the cost evened out over the total number of users on the network.

figure 10.4
Example of a LAN ring topology

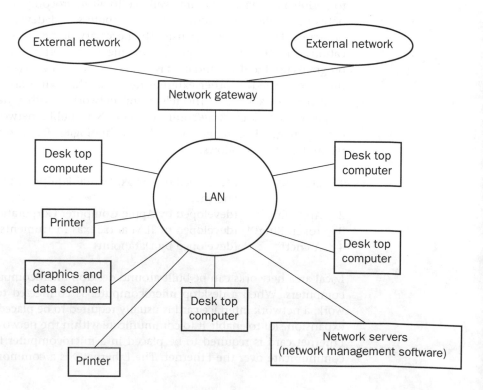

2 *Organisation*. LAN technology may allow greater organisation, standardisation and consistency in a network within the business environment.

3 *Integration*. The LAN allows disparate components and resources of a business organisation to be administered and managed with greater control.

10.6 Wide area networks

A wide area network (WAN) usually spans a broad geographical area on a national or international scale. Such distances are usually covered using microwave and satellite transmission or standard ISDN (integrated service digital network) telephone lines. Wide area networks are usually provided by what are known as common carriers, which in the main refer to private or government owned telephone and telecommunications organisations, for example, AT&T in the United States and British Telecom in the United Kingdom. The common carriers typically determine the transmission rates and the connection between lines. WANs normally require the process of communications *switching* which involves routing messages through a range of network architecture gateways and transmission mediums. At each gateway the data message may be decoded and made more appropriate before being switched through the network. Data messages are often transmitted over networks in bundles which require coding and decoding at each gateway connection between systems, which is often known as *packet switching*.

Networks that link systems together between countries are sometimes referred to as international networks or, commonly, global area networks (GANs). International networks give rise to a number of problems concerning transborder data flow. Many countries have restrictive laws governing the movement of information and data across international borders. Nevertheless, for large international business organisations the use of WANs and GANs are essential for the coordination of global enterprise.

DID YOU KNOW?

A wide area network (WAN) is a telecommunications network that links geographically dispersed users across the globe.

The largest WAN today is the Internet which connects over 35,000 individual networks across the globe. The Internet was originally established to transfer academic papers between scientists. However, today it is used by anyone with the appropriate connection hardware and software and is becoming a major tool for all competitive business organisations.

A *value added network* (VAN) is an alternative to business organisations managing their own networks. A value added network is a multipath data-only network that is normally managed by a private business organisation which operates the network for a fee. Individual organisations pay a fee to be permitted access to the network; the fee can be in the form of a rental charge or a network connection charge. For example, a business organisation may control a particular network which uses ISDN telephone lines, or microwave and satellite technology, which a small organisation is unable to afford outright. Such telecommunications technology can be made available to that organisation for a fee; this allows the small organisation access to advanced technology that it could otherwise not afford through its own hardware investment. The advantage of VANs is that client users do not have to invest in expensive network equipment or provide internal technical support for managing the network. The costs of using the network are usually shared among many users so resulting in economies of scale. Example of VAN suppliers are Compuserve, BT Global Network Services and Tymnet.

ACTIVITY **10.6**
················

Wide and local area networks

Define the term *local area network* (LAN) and describe the role and use of *file servers* and *network gateways* within a LAN environment. Discuss the main advantages of local area network technology within a business organisation and suggest some of the possible costs and benefits of operating a LAN. Describe the use and function of communications switching to transfer data between networks within the business environment.

10.7   Client-server computing
···

The sophisticated developments in network hardware and software architectures has led to a new model of networked computing known as *client-server computing* which divides processing tasks according to whether they are appropriate to the client or server functions of a network. Client-server computing has evolved because of the increasing performance of desktop microcomputers that have replaced dumb terminals within computer networked environments. In the client-server model some tasks are processed by the file server whilst other tasks are processed by the connected microcomputers that act as clients to the main file server. Each function within the network is assigned on the basis of efficiency to optimise network resources. Therefore, microcomputers on the network are assigned tasks that they are capable of performing to reduce some of the burden on the main file server. This model of networking, where the client computer takes responsibility for certain tasks, is only possible if the client hardware has the capability to process tasks independently within the overall network. The client microcomputer may store independent user-interfaces, applications and instructions, while the main file server has the task of implementing large data storage or processing functions. The client machine often appears to be independent but empowered by increased applications handling and processing capabilities.

Most client-server networks encompass communication facilities that permit messages and data to be transferred between microcomputer users through file servers and across networks. The increased performance capabilities of microcomputers have led to client-server network architectures being a direct threat to mainframe computing facilities. The advantages of client-server technology are as follows:

▶ less expensive than mainframe computing for many network functions
▶ more flexible than mainframe computing in terms of network architecture
▶ more appropriate in distributed business computing environments.

The disadvantages of client-server technology are as follows:

▶ May require higher end-user involvement and training.
▶ Some client/server architectures are not as reliable as mainframe computers.
▶ There is a need for increased standardisation of use and configuration.

Each device on a client-server network is assigned appropriate and suitable functions; given the configuration of the network, therefore, different hardware devices can operate on the same problem. In the client-server model some processing tasks are handled by the servers, while others are handled by the client computers. The aim is to apportion the functions to the computers and devices that are best at performing that function. Client-server technology allows greater end-user systems participation within the business environment by allowing user-friendly access to databases and software applications with the ability to download data and information to be used on the client computer.

ACTIVITY **10.7**

Client-server technology

Discuss how client-server computing shares characteristics with the ideas of a mainframe computer linked to a number of terminals and suggest reasons why advances in IT have allowed client-server technology to flourish in the business environment. Then write a resumé indicating how client-server technology has affected the way information resources are dealt with in a business organisation. Prepare a ten-minute presentation to communicate when it is appropriate or inappropriate to use the client-server model within networked business environments.

10.8   Open systems standardisation

It is often the case that computer networks are required to connect to dissimilar networks. Therefore, there is a need for rules of engagement between networked systems. These rules were described earlier in this chapter as network protocols. Such protocols will only be effective if there is *standardisation* among computer network architectures and communication channels. This is essential in an age when there is a restricted amount of hardware and software standardisation within the configuration of networks. Standardisation is an issue that is closely related to *open systems*. There are a number of existing standards that influence network communications and architectures. For instance, standardisation within international and national telephone networks have existed for some time and have been produced by the Consultative Committee for International Telephone and Telegraphy (CCITT). This body has produced a number of standards for telecommunications, ranging from series X1 to X25, that have influenced data communications.

Governments, industries and commercial organisations with vested interests are constantly meeting to create standardisation within networking and telecommunications. However, because of the rapid change in computing technology, and the large amounts of money invested in certain technologies, it has often been difficult to agree on common standards. The following three standards are important for a knowledge and understanding of networked environments:

1 open systems interconnection (OSI) reference model
2 transmission control protocol/Internet protocol (TCP/IP).
3 Integrated Services Digital Network (ISDN).

The open systems interconnection (OSI) reference model was formulated by the International Standards Organisation (ISO) in 1978 and has formed the basis for standardising functional layers of control within networked systems architectures. The intention was to permit any computer on a network to be able to communicate with a computer on another network irrespective of the particular vendor-specific hardware and software being employed. The OSI reference model set standards for functional layers within global networked systems. The OSI standard established seven layers to a networked architecture, whereby a data message sent from one networked system would be required to sequentially progress down the seven layers on being received by another networked system. The seven layers of communications architecture are as follows:

1 **physical control layer** (responsible for electronic signal transmission of data in raw binary form)
2 **data link layer** (data transferred in packets with control protocols to check correct transmission)
3 **network layer** (routes and relays data packets over a wide area network)
4 **transport layer** (checks and ensures correct end-to-end delivery between host computers)
5 **session layer** (establishes connections and manages dialogue between host computers)
6 **presentation layer** (provides data transmission formats and layouts)
7 **application layer** (user applications control and determine data to be transmitted).

The user on one networked system would begin the activity of sending a data message at the *application layer*. This would be fed down to the *presentation layer* which would convert the data message into a format suitable for transmission. The *session layer* then initiates communication between hosts before the data message is passed to the *transport layer* to be addressed. The data message is then passed on to the *network layer* to be split into appropriate data packets for transmission. These data packets are then checked and corrected through protocols at the *data link layer* and the data messages are then finally sent through the *physical control layer* in raw data form over suitable transmission channels.

The transmission control protocol/Internet protocol (TCP/IP) is a model that divides the telecommunications process into five stages that perform similar functions to the OSI model. This model is prevalent within certain operating systems environments such as UNIX. The Integrated Services Digital Network (ISDN) is a common standard for communications through national telephone networks. ISDN permits the communication of digital data, voice and video information from computer to computer through standard telephone networks. In a similar way the asynchronous transfer mode (ATM) protocol permits video, voice text and other data, that come from different technological backgrounds, to be integrated into commonly acceptable packets of information. Despite the various standards for layering networked systems architecture and for standardising communications processes, the first interface between the user and the networked system is at the applications human end-user interface layer.

Data and information can be transferred through the physical paths of networks in many and various ways. Consideration must be given to (1) the preparation mode of data transmission and (2) the coordination of transmissions to make the most efficient use of pathways through networks. The three main forms of transfer modes within the business environment include:

1 packet switching
2 frame relay
3 asynchronous transfer mode.

Packet switching involves grouping the data message and transmitting it in manageable segments called packets. This allows data messages to be broken up into packets and sent along a number of communications pathways, rather than transmitting the data message in total over one pathway. Network routers, which determine the flow of messages between computers, will normally transfer the data packets from the sending computer to the receiving computer, which reassembles all the packets into the original data message. *Frame relay* is a faster and more economical form of transmission that uses wideband communications to transmit data messages over networks. Frame relay involves packet switching, but without the requirement for the packets to be held up for routing information and error checking routines to be performed. Frame relay packets include already routing information which increases the speed of transmission.

Asynchronous transfer mode (ATM) is a high-speed transmission technology that provides for multi-media data and information in the form of voice, sound, graphics and video to be transferred through the same communications channel. ATM uses wideband communications media to speed data transfer. ATM uses cells to carry digital signals; each cell is 53 bytes. In using a standard size cell ATM can switch data using only hardware and not resorting to software to implement the routines of switching. This speeds transmission and allows many types of data, in various multi-media forms, to be switched between users over a network. The majority of common carrier telephone operators use the *Integrated Services Digital Network* (ISDN) which has become an international standard; because ISDN is used by the major telephone utilities it comprises a ready-made network for communications.

ACTIVITY **10.8**

Open systems standardisation
Discuss the term *open systems standardisation* and explain why open systems are important for efficient and effective data and information communication within the business environment. Explain what is meant by the open systems interconnection (OSI) reference model and outline the seven OSI layers to a networked architecture in a networked computing environment.

10.9   Networking principles

There are a number of network principles to consider when deciding on the network topology, type, and transfer mode to be adopted by the business organisation. The network adopted must support the business organisation's goals. Therefore, the business organisation needs to consider the following principles:

▶ *Reliability of the network.* The performance of a business organisation will depend upon the reliability of the network adopted; above average failure will adversely affect business performance. Reliability may be related to the complexity of the network design.

▶ *Security and data integrity.* The network must be protected from illegal or improper use. Users will often wish to maintain private files of information and the network manager may have to impose varying levels of privilege on access to individual data files and other applications. It is essential for data to be protected from corruption through multiple use and access to information files.

▶ *Performance.* This can be measured in terms of response time to transmit and receive data messages. The actual performance of a network will depend upon a number of connected factors including speed and capability of computers and other devices, the network controllers that govern the coordination of devices, and the amount of data traffic the network is required to carry.

▶ *Vendor support.* Choosing the correct network and configuration must be allied with appropriate vendor support to overcome problems quickly and effectively; it is important that the vendor has a track record of service and delivery. This can only be gauged by looking at the previous history of the vendor in supplying networks to other business organisations.

▶ *Flexibility and compatibility.* The network should be flexible enough to cope with changes and adjustments. It should also be expandable enough to cope with the inclusion of additional computers and devices. The network should be expected to meet current and future standards for information technology hardware and software; it should also meet all expected telecommunications standards.

▶ *Privacy and ethical factors.* The privacy and control of data is important in networked business environments where there is shared access to information. Freedom of information must be balanced with the need to protect data and information from improper use and communication.

▶ *Technological infrastructure.* It is important that a network is suitable to a business organisation's technical infrastructure. Having to upgrade the physical environment of a business organisation may increase the cost of establishing a network; this is particularly true if a network adopts fibre optic technology rather that more robust coaxial cable and wire technology.

It is important for a business organisation to weigh up the factors involved in establishing a network. It should be a business requirement to create a *network plan* before embarking on the purchase of information technology to establish a telecommunications network.

ACTIVITY **10.9**

Networking principles

Discuss the various networking principles that a business organisation will need to consider when adopting a networked information system to support the business organisation's goals. Outline the importance of a _network plan_ before embarking on the purchase of information technology to establish a networked computing environment within a business organisation.

10.10   Chapter summary

A core strand of the discipline of BIT involves an understanding of networked telecommunications environments. The successful integration of business information systems through the use of telecommunications can enhance the performance of a business in meeting its overall goals and objectives. Information systems integration requires an understanding of networking standards and procedures; it also requires a higher strategic understanding of the role, nature and effects of networking within the business environment. Networked systems allow levels of homogeneity across markets and products that were not previously possible without networking. For example, in the early 1990s the Ford Motor Company made a strategic decision to no longer operate business enterprises that designed and built cars for specific geographical markets. Previously, Ford Motors in the United States designed and built cars for the American market and Ford Motors in Europe designed and built cars for the European market. The business recognised that there was an overlap of the design, building and other business functions on a global scale. The Ford Motors' solution was to isolate business functions to unique geographical areas based on functional specialisation. Now, the whole of Ford's car design function is based in the United States, which designs cars for all global markets. Ford business organisations across the world no longer compete with one another, but rather now compete as one business organisation on a global scale. The centralisation of functions, such as design, by global region is only possible if there exists appropriate telecommunications technology to overcome distances and to make these functions appear part of the physical fabric of a business, irrespective of its geographical location.

Short self-assessment questions

10.1   Define the term _telecommunications_ and explain the difference between terrestrial and extra-terrestrial communications channels.

10.2   Describe the difference between _wire-based_ and _wireless_ communications channels and suggest five possible services offered to a typical business organisation via these communications channels.

10.3   Outline two ways in which telephone and telecommunications organisations can increase the transmission capacity of their telecommunications technology.

10.4 Describe the types of physical hardware used for transmitting data across telecommunications channels and indicate the benefits and drawbacks of coaxial and fibre optic communications hardware.

10.5 Define the term *networking* and suggest three possible benefits of a communications network for a business organisation.

10.6 Explain the difference between local area networks (LANs) and wide area networks (WANs) within networked computing environments.

10.7 Outline the possible advantages of computer networked environments for business organisations that carry out business activity on a global scale.

10.8 Explain the main functions of communications software and describe the role and purpose of a network operating system within a business organisation.

10.9 Define the term *network topology* and explain the meaning of connecting nodes on a telecommunications network.

10.10 Outline the main advantages of wide area networks (WANs) within the business environment and suggest some of the possible costs and benefits of operating a WAN.

10.11 Define the term *value added network* (VAN) and describe the use and benefits of such value-added to a typical business organisation.

10.12 Define the term *client-server computing* and describe the main characteristics and differences of the client-server configuration as compared to other forms of networked environment.

10.13 Outline the main advantages and disadvantages of the client-server model of networking within the business environment.

10.14 Explain how client-server computing allows greater end-user participation within a business organisation.

10.15 Discuss why the asynchronous transfer mode (ATM) protocol is so important to the communication of multi-media data and information in the business environment.

10.16 Discuss why one of the most important layers to the end-user is the applications human–computer interface layer.

10.17 Describe the three main forms of data transfer modes found within the business environment.

10.18 Explain the reasons why the Integrated Services Digital Network (ISDN) used by common carriers has become an international standard.

Further study and reading
....

Books

Bakman, A. (1995) *How to deliver Client/Server Applications that Work*. Manning Publications.

Friedman, R. (1996) *International Telecommunications Handbook*. Norwood, Massachusetts: Artech House.

Kalakota, R. and Whinston, A.B. (1996) *Frontiers of Electronic Commerce*. Wokingham, England: Addison-Wesley.

Moore, M.L. (1995) *ISDN Strategies: A Survival Guide for Corporate Managers*. IDG Books Worldwide.

Tanenbaum, A.S. (1996) *Computer Networks*, 3rd edition. Englewood Cliffs, New Jersey: Prentice-Hall.

CHAPTER 11

The Internet and business activity

Objectives
··············

By the end of this chapter you will be able to:

▶ understand the history and development of the Internet and its commercial impact within the business environment

▶ describe the nature and use of software for browsing and searching the Internet and the use of such front-end technology within business organisations

▶ explain the nature of the World Wide Web (WWW) as a tool for transacting commercial ventures and business activity

▶ understand the advantages and disadvantages of using the WWW within the business environment

▶ contrast the use and application of the Internet as a medium for business activity and commercial practice.

11.1 Introduction to the Internet
···

The Internet has emerged from the academic research world to become one of the most significant driving forces behind business change and innovation. It is estimated that there will be between 100–200 million users of the Internet by the year 2000; which offers the possibility of households and business organisations, with the appropriate information technology, being connected across a vast international information network that truly offers a global economy. The Internet with the additional attractive and exciting features of the *World Wide Web* (WWW) is inspiring entrepreneurs, business organisations and consumers with equal intensity. The importance of the Internet to business practice can be gauged by the following quote:

The real promise of the Internet for entrepreneurs and consumers alike lies in its potential for electronic commerce: transaction conducted through computer networks

FT a–z of the Internet (Financial Times Guide, 1996)

The Internet provides consumers and business organisations with a global communications facility that acts as a vehicle for electronic commercial transactions. The use of the Internet is assisted by the development, and application, of various user-friendly software for searching or browsing the Internet's enormous information resources. The act of searching or browsing the Internet is often referred to as 'surfing the net'. It is an appropriate analogy given the vast ocean of information that is available for anyone with a suitable search engine (or 'surf board'!). Therefore, it is in the interests of all business organisations to understand and utilise the Internet in order to remain competitive within the commercial business environment.

11.2   What is the Internet?

The Internet is a global network of millions of smaller computer networks linked by terrestrial and extra-terrestrial communications channels. The most popular business use of the Internet is for sending and receiving national and international electronic mail (e-mail). E-mail provides a direct cost saving to a business in that the cost of e-mail is independent of how far the message travels. This can mean a significant cost saving to an organisation that relies on global communication between individuals and business organisations. The Internet, which is often referred to by the shortened term 'net', can also provide an important facility for cheaper videoconferencing and other interactive telecommunications. However, the most significant business promise of the net lies in the potential for global electronic commerce in the shape of transactions conducted through the millions of computer networks that make up the Internet. The consumer market for a business organisation's products and services is potentially vast. The Internet is a relatively inexpensive business resource that permits small organisations to compete with large organisations because of the absence of any major cost or competition constraints of using the web.

The first major recipients of profit from the growth of the Internet was the computer industry through its provision of software and telecommunications hardware used to access and handle the facilities of the web. For example, Sun Microsystems®, a manufacturer of powerful desktop, and UNIX-based mini-computers has witnessed its profits growing through the manufacture and provision of computer *servers* used to handle and store the telecommunications infrastructure needed to interact with the Internet. Likewise, Cisco Systems® and Bay Networks® have earned significant profits throughout the 1990s through the provision of network *routers* that enables data and information traffic to be directed across the Internet. However, it is the suppliers of Internet *software*, for searching and browsing the web, that have been the beneficiaries of the most dramatic increases in profit achieved by providing Internet facilities. Two business organisations that have benefited significantly from the provision of software for searching the Internet are Yahoo!® and

DID YOU KNOW?
Marc Andreessen, the co-founder of Netscape Communications with Jim Clark in April 1994, was a multimillionaire at the age of 24 when the business was placed on the United States stock market in August 1995.

Netscape Communications®. For instance, Yahoo's profits rose very quickly from its birth to a level where after only two years of business activity the organisation was quoted on the United States equity market in 1996. The Netscape Communications organisation markets a net software browser called Netscape Navigator which was a commercial development of an earlier net browser known as Mosaic. Netscape Navigator 2.0 was marketed in early 1996 to incorporate the facilities of e-mail and multi-media applications written in the *Java* programming language developed by Sun Microsystems. The Netscape Navigator browser became the Internet standard in 1996 with over 75 per cent of Internet users employing the application to access the web.

The widespread dissemination of marketing information and advertising across the web is the most obvious sign of the commercialisation of the Internet. In order to meet this advertising growth through the Internet, a number of business

table 11.1

Advertising and the Internet (in US dollars). First quarter of 1996.

Top recipients of advertising revenue (by site):		Top advertisers (by company):	
Infoseek	$3,107,500	IBM	$1,528,300
Lycos	$2,622,200	Microsoft	$1,010,900
Yahoo!	$2,190,000	Netscape	$929,000
Netscape	$1,908,500	Cellnet	$612,300
Cellnet	$1,330,500	AT&T	$606,700

(Source: 'Techwatch', *Time*, 1 July 1996)

organisations offer services in the creation of attractive *web sites* and Internet-specific advertising. A web site is a set of linked information pages which forms a unique home location for a user on the Internet. Individuals and organisations can create their own web sites of information to reflect their own business needs. Table 11.1 indicates the level of advertising revenue in the first three months of 1996 accruing to the top five *recipients* of advertising revenue and the top five *advertisers* within the Internet market.

Advertising on the Internet not only provides a source of information, equipping consumers with the knowledge to make informed decisions, but also offers the possibility of allowing consumers to interact with the product or service in the same way that a user interacts with a computer game. Although advertising is extensively available on the net, the *consumer* is in control of the nature and extent to which he or she interacts with the advertising; whereas with other forms of advertising, such as on television, the *advertiser* is in control of the advertising message and delivery to the consumer. Therefore, by interacting with the web the consumer has more control over the influ-

DID YOU KNOW?

Yahoo! was founded in 1994 and became one of the spectacular share issues of the financial year of 1996 when its value doubled in the first three hours of trading on the over-the-counter shares market in New York, USA. The shares rose from an opening price of $13 to $26 on the first day of trading! The issue made instant multimillionaires of its two founders, Jerry Yang and David Filo. Their holdings on the first day of trading were worth $140 million each.

ence of advertising, which forces organisations to become more competitive and creative in the way they try to market and sell products and services to consumers.

Another significant potential use of the Internet is the provision of on-line shopping from the comfort of a consumer's own home, which is still in its infancy in the 1990s. Home shopping through the net has the potential to be one of the most generally accepted commercial activities of the Internet in the future. Already, a number of electronic 'shopping malls' exist which allow a consumer to travel through a *virtual* shopping centre adding virtual products to a virtual basket. The only major obstacle to mass electronic shopping at present is the relative insecurity of paying for goods on-line using credit or debit card mediums of payment. When the consumer's fear of insecurity of payment is overcome, electronic shopping will explode as a medium for purchasing goods and services. In order to accomplish mass global electronic shopping the three major credit card organisations (MasterCard, Visa International and American Express) agreed to collaborate in the mid-1990s to establish a standard method of *encrypting* credit card numbers as they are transmitted over the Internet.

Encryption is the activity of coding data to protect its privacy, particularly when being transmitted over networked telecommunication links. Electronic commerce through the web can only prosper when encryption is a widespread and reliable tool for commercial electronic communications traffic. Networked communications are particularly vulnerable to interception and although encryption cannot prevent interception it will render the data unintelligible and useless to the interceptor. Traditional encryption techniques use a secret *key* to encode data that is privileged only to the sending and receiving systems. The method and permutation of encoding is held within a *cipher*. As long as the key to the cipher remains secret then the code will remain secure and enable relatively risk-free telecommunications. Commercial ciphers normally rely on a two-key system; one is a public key which is available to anybody and the second is a private (secure) key known only to the recipient.

The development of advanced encryption technology is essential in alleviating the fear of consumers in communicating personal and private data such as credit or debit card details. Confidential data transfer over the Internet is a prerequisite for creating consumer confidence in using the net; related to this is the need for business organisations to abide by national and international standards on data protection and privacy. For instance, in the United Kingdom the Data Protection Act (1984) requires organisations that process *personal data*, through information technology, to ensure that it is safe from access from unauthorised users; an organisation is legally bound to show an individual what information is kept on them by an organisation. The Data Protection Act also covers the case of information on individuals gathered and collated over the Internet. The practice of data collection on individuals is carried out extensively by organisations using the Internet to indicate demographic preferences and other marketing information.

The Data Protection Act became law in 1984 and is therefore lacking in many regulations regarding the Internet. For example, it is possible for an organisation to put images from surveillance cameras on the net without the permission of those being filmed. Such a case occurred in July 1996 when an organisation broadcast live over the net the movements of people in and out of the UK Secretary of Defence's private residence in London. A clear breach of personal privacy without legal redress. A 1995 European Commission Directive on Data Protection provides greater protection in that it directs that data should only be sent outside of the European Community (EC) to countries with adequate data protection laws. Future European Community legislation is likely to further concentrate on data protection on telecommunications networks including the Internet.

ACTIVITY **11.1**

The growth of the Internet

Discuss why advertising on the Internet not only equips consumers with the knowledge to make informed decisions, but also offers the possibility of allowing consumers to interact with the product or service in the same way that a user interacts with a computer game. In terms of 'trading on the Internet', outline the various business functions, such as marketing, sales, distribution, that could benefit from the Internet. Once these tasks have been completed, read through Pause for thought 11.1 and discuss some of the advantages and disadvantages of marketing products and services over the Internet.

PAUSE FOR THOUGHT 11.1 *Commercial transactions on the Internet*

The Internet and the competitive environment of business

The explosion of the Internet has brought on-line information services to millions of businesses and customers around the world. The Internet is changing the way that businesses communicate with their customers, suppliers, agents and within their own organisations. For many commercial activities the Internet equates to profit-making opportunities. However, some organisations are still unaware that the Internet will inevitably affect established business patterns and practices. All business organisations will eventually find themselves challenged by the new developments of the Internet.

Businesses can benefit from the Internet, but also be victims of the Internet. For example, paper-based publishers of academic journals may be affected by libraries and colleges opting to find research papers through the Internet, rather than subscribe to paper-based journals. Likewise, businesses involved in telecommunications, such as British Telecom, may be challenged by Internet-based communications using voice communications software. The attitude of 'back-bone' telecom providers is to join the Internet revolution, rather than be left behind, or competitively challenged by the technology. For instance, Internet users normally pay local call rates, irrespective of the call distance. This is a challenge to the price-per-distance approach used by telephone providers.

A significant advantage of the Internet is that it allows small organisations to compete effectively with large organisations because the cost of entry to the technology is low. For instance, the Internet allows a business organisation to provide a cut-price commercial transactions mechanism that new entrants can use without building a tangible infrastructure of high street branches, thus reducing the overhead costs associated with starting a new business. In such a dynamic competitive environment, banks and financial institutions are wise to get involved in the Internet. In 1995 the Security First Network bank, a US-based savings and loan group, was the first financial institution to offer on-line banking over the Internet. There are now a range of other banks that offer Internet based services. In a similar respect to banks, the traditional stock brokering areas of advanced commercial societies are developing on-line securities trading services. One of the first was the US-based E*Trade Securities which provides share trading on-line.

In 1995 there were approximately 60 million users of the Internet worldwide, making the Internet a significant and growing business asset. Often, business success goes to organisations that recognise consumer trends and have a knowledge of the technology required to satisfy demands. For example, the Lotus organisation, which provides groupware applications, has entered the Internet market in order to protect its 'Lotus Notes' groupware from the competitive pressure of using the technology of the Internet as an 'intranet' within business organisations. Intranets are internal corporate networks using similar software technology and communications standards as the Internet.

Many paper-based national newspapers now offer on-line, web-based, electronic formats. Some are available free, whilst others are available through subscription. Advertising revenue through on-line newspapers has benefited the news and media sector of the business environment. Many organisations market and sell their products and services on-line. For example, the 'Amazon' organisation (amazon.com) claims to be the largest on-line book shop in the world, although there are competitors such as the United Kingdom based Internet Bookshop. The Amazon bookshop can offer books at reduced costs because it can buy directly from publishers and does not have the large overhead costs of staffing and running shops in high streets.

Ultimately, the Internet offers the opportunity to challenge existing thinking on how, when and what to sell; the Internet has challenged traditional models of interaction between individuals and business organisations. Therefore, creativity of business practices, using the Internet, will now offer many business opportunities within competitive business environments.

11.3   The World Wide Web

The World Wide Web (WWW) is a global collection of pages and sites on the Internet. It encompasses advanced information technology facilities that make it a user-friendly way of storing, handling and accessing information on the Internet. Individuals and organisations can create their own unique set of information pages, known as a *web site*, with each page being uniquely identified to a user or location by a *web address* on the Internet.

The World Wide Web, which is often referred to merely as the 'web', was first developed by the European Council for Nuclear Research's (CERN) European Laboratory for Particle Physics. CERN is located near Geneva in Switzerland. It attracts and employs some of the best academic physicists, mathematicians and computer scientists from around the world. The main activity at CERN is to implement experiments into sub-atomic matter using atomic particle accelerators. Such leading edge scientific research requires extensive use and application of computing and information technology. The web was first developed as an academic publishing tool to enable scientists to distribute academic papers to fellow colleagues. To achieve this end, the web was conceived in 1989 to provide a common communications facility to deal with the various hardware platforms and software languages being used by the geographically disparate research staff connected to CERN.

The main advantage of the web is that it provides a common front-end interface that can be used on different hardware platforms and IT environments, with the additional innovation of *hypertext* tools and techniques which allow the contents of a document to be linked and cross-referenced by embedding a unique web address into pages of information which can in turn be called up by someone browsing the information. A hypertext link can be marked by highlighting a key word which can be clicked on with a mouse to link to a related document or information page. The web was developed, through the leadership of Berners Lee and a team of associated researchers at CERN, and introduced to the Internet in 1990. The web's suitability, regardless of the IT platform or environment in which the user worked, made the web instantly recognisable as a useful communications interface. A further advantage of the web is that it offers interactive *multi-media* features such as photographs, graphics, icons, sound and video which can be incorporated and embedded into textual web pages.

Individuals and business organisations can register a web site which can be available to anyone searching or browsing the Internet. Commercial web sites range from simple product lists to elaborate multi-media presentations incorporating 3-D (three-dimensional) images, sound and video. In order to achieve the hypertext and multi-media context of the web the scientists at CERN developed two specialist software language applications known as *hypertext mark-up language* (HTML) and *hypertext transmission protocol* (HTTP). HTML permits users to design web pages, and other documents, with all the necessary hypertext links to other pages

> **DID YOU KNOW?**
>
> *Ted Nelson, a computer scientist, is reputed to have originated the term 'hypertext' in 1972. He wrote a book entitled* Dream Machines *in 1974 which conceived the idea of a global hypertext network. He called the theoretical network Xanadu.*

and documents. The links can be local or over global networks. The linked documents are retrieved and sent in plain text format to speed the transmission process and the *browser* software program (such as Netscape Navigator) interprets the HTML on to the user's screen. The HTTP application deals with the *communication* of documents and overcomes the need for a user to link to other networked computer systems in order to achieve communication with another network.

In order to interact with the Internet a user needs to use a *browser*. The most popular application is the Netscape Navigator, but other browsers include Infoseek, Mosaic, HotJava, and Microsoft Explorer. The tools and technique of hypertext allow a web user to travel across a global array of networks connected through a set of visually obvious, but not technologically obvious, links on a web page. The user-friendly nature of browser applications has persuaded some organisations to replicate and incorporate the wider techniques of browser technology into the internal information systems of the business domain. For instance, the visually attractive and user-friendly front-end interfaces of browsing software can be duplicated to access the integrated information systems that are internal to a business organisation; such application of web technology into the fabric of a business organisation is known as an 'intranet', rather than 'Internet', because the scope of the technology is restricted to the physical confines of a business organisation. Such intranet systems offer the flexibility of browser applications technology with the additional advantage of security; due to the fact that the intranet is restricted to internal use and control within a business organisation.

ACTIVITY 11.2

The World Wide Web

Hypertext is the term used to describe the technique of linking electronic multi-media documents together over a network. Key words, images or icons within one document can be highlighted and linked to other documents and information sources. These can be used by a human browser to retrieve linked pages and the information contained on these pages, which may in turn be linked to other related information pages. Theoretically, there is no end to the linkage possible, which may even be infinite based on the fact that pages of information are continuously being added globally by the second!

Discuss with your colleagues the benefits and drawbacks of hypertext links (often referred to as hyperlinks) and suggest whether there is any danger of loss of control of information if it is possible for a *linked* web site to be outside of the control of other web sites to which it is linked or associated. Therefore, discuss whether you consider that the Internet should be regulated to restrict certain information being publicly available on the web. Locate a newspaper article that refers to any form of regulation on the Internet and use it as the basis of an argument for or against regulation of the Internet.

PAUSE FOR THOUGHT 11.2   *Share dealing on the Internet*

A number of electronic on-line share dealing services are available that exploit the flexibility of the Internet. One of the most well known in the USA is E*Trade Securities (etrade.com) which allows customers to buy and sell shares (securities) over the Internet. Normally, the dealing costs per transaction are lower with on-line share trading. All that is needed is a home computer, suitable modem, and access to an on-line share dealing service. The costs of trading are lower because, unlike traditional share dealing brokers, the electronic brokers do not require expensive office buildings and numerous staff.

There are often additional on-line services that provide financial information for investors in stocks and shares. For example, a potential investor may use an on-line newsgroup such as the Silicon Investor (techstocks.com) where knowledge about businesses can be exchanged. In order to deal in shares with an on-line broker, an investor needs an account with an on-line brokering business. Normally, no money changes hands over the Internet, only the share trades are recorded over the open lines. But in order to trade a customer must first of all open an account, often with cash or some other form of securities (like an existing portfolio of shares). Most Internet brokers allow customers to monitor their 'positions' or their own portfolios and retrieve up-to-date market information. It is important to recognise that with on-line brokers the transactions are normally on an execution basis only. That is to say, there is no brokering advice attached to a share deal. The customer is on their own and largely responsible for their own actions. On-line share brokers do not specialise in advice and personal service.

With the proliferation of such electronic commerce, national governments are often concerned to legislate against misuse of the Internet. Often, if financial institutions are to remain competitive they must embrace all the regulatory uncertainties that go along with the Internet. One of the main problems is maintaining a balance between protecting investors and protecting the interests of financial institutions. In the United Kingdom, the Centre for the Study of Financial Innovation set up eight working groups to assess the implications of the Internet for the financial sector. The groups covered regulation, crime, security, personal finance, retail banking, equity (share) trading, payment and settlement systems, and insurance. Ideally, a web site provider should have to comply with all systems of law worldwide. For instance, should there be laws to prevent an overseas business setting up web sites that comply with their own domestic laws but not with the laws of other countries? In the United Kingdom the Financial Services Act (1986) prohibits an unauthorised person from issuing an investment advertisement in the UK unless it has been approved by an authorised person.

It is important for any business organisation looking to set up a web site to ensure that all possible steps have been taken to protect against foreign enforcement action or to block access to anyone without an authorised password. An organisation should ensure that its web site complies with commonly agreed standards of fairness and accuracy as well as the laws of the countries towards which the web site is aimed. Many countries, such as Malaysia, are reluctant to regulate the Internet (beyond ordering the blocking of some web sites) because they believe that their commercial future hangs on Internet technology. For example, in 1996 the Malaysian government launched a scheme to attract foreign media, software, information technology and manufacturing organisations to a 'Multimedia Supercorridor' in an area of 750 square kilometres near the Malaysian capital, Kuala Lumpur. It was hoped that the laws that prevail in the Supercorridor would be more liberal than those in other countries related to the multi-media of the Internet.

Business success relies on a suitable balance between national regulation, to protect investors and users of the Internet, and freedom to exploit the Internet to its full advantage within the global business environment.

11.4   Business and commercial activity on the web

The Internet offers small business organisations the potential opportunity to trade alongside large business organisations on an international scale which is not possible through conventional business trading mediums based on financial muscle. The potential growth of all forms of *electronic commerce* is enormous and only limited by the imagination and creativity of the individual and the organisation. For instance, electronic data interchange (EDI) over the Internet is on average half as costly as traditional EDI mediums. The Internet allows individual customers to personally interact with a business organisation and to select aspects of information relating to that organisation which are specific to the inquiry or user of the web. Despite the problems of security, standardisation and consistency of approach by business organisations, the financial services domain is a major business sector that appreciates the importance of the Internet. Nearly all financial services organisations around the world have their own tailored web sites offering access to various technology-supported services, such as knowledge-based decision support systems relating to loans, mortgages, pensions and other personal investment plans that can be tailored by the customer to their specific needs. However, the inter-networking of systems using different communications protocols presents a problem in terms of consistency of network performance and mechanisms to guarantee delivery of commercial transactions. For example, international commodities trading is only possible with consistency of telecommunications and the avoidance of time-lags in the trading process which may jeopardise the operation of perfect market environments.

Despite insecurity of payment medium through the web, the use of on-line electronic shopping is gaining significant popularity to become the main method of retail shopping if business organisations can guarantee the efficient and effective distribution and delivery of goods to the customer. On-line shopping from home is enhanced by the visual nature of the web which permits a customer to view the goods on offer in addition to a textual description. General research into on-line shopping suggests that it encourages impulse buying which is often influenced by the nature and attractiveness of the web site and product.

The banking sector is one area of business that stands to benefit greatly from a universal and secure web environment. The first specialist Internet bank, known as Security First Network Bank, was established in 1995 and offers personal banking services to customers. In addition, it promotes its own security system known as Secureware which can be utilised by any other banks to provide Internet banking services. As security becomes prevalent on the Internet, so a whole host of banking and other financial services will be traded without fear of the possible security breaches of privacy.

> **DID YOU KNOW?**
> One of the most popular web shopping sites in the United Kingdom is operated by Barclaycard Visa and is known as 'BarclaySquare'. It is typical of the type of electronic shopping mall available on the Internet. A customer can browse virtual stores to purchase goods and services such as flowers, books, records, clothes, electrical goods and various other products on a list too long to record. The goods can be paid for on-line and delivered to an address specified by the buyer.

ACTIVITY 11.3

Business activity on the web

Using a web browser, such as Netscape Navigator or Mosaic, search the Internet for incidences of 'shopping mall' web sites. If you cannot readily locate such a site, then use the following unique URL indicated by the italicised characters: *http://www.barclaysquare.co.uk/* (URL is shorthand for Uniform Resource Locator which identifies network locations and enables navigation of the Internet). Write a review of the web site you have found, highlighting the following considerations:

▶ ease of use and relationship between the related web pages
▶ logical and physical design characteristics
▶ payment medium process and characteristics
▶ advantages and disadvantages of shopping on the Internet
▶ security measures employed to guarantee the integrity of using credit cards.

Discuss the social and economic consequences of shopping from the comfort of a consumer's home or office and suggest how shopping on the web may develop in the future.

11.5 Registering a web site

There are many millions of pages of information on the web. In order for a business to utilise the advantages of using the web it must register a *web site*. A number of Internet provider companies have arisen to deal with applications from organisations to establish commercial or non-commercial web sites. There are four main stages to establishing a web site. Firstly, the business organisation must register a *domain name* for its site. In the United States business domain names end with the extension '.com' indicating that the site address belongs to a company. In the United Kingdom the domain name ends in the extension '.co.uk'. The following lists an example number of *domain site* names for various organisations:

http://www.the.times.co.uk	(*The Times*)
http://www.telegraph.co.uk	(*The Telegraph*)
http://www.timeinc.com	(*Time* magazine)
http://www.oracle.com	(Oracle)
http://www.microsoft.com	(Microsoft Corporation)
http://www.ibm.com	(IBM)
http://www.apple.com	(Apple Macintosh Computers)
http://www.twa.com	(Trans World Airlines)
http://www.bbc.co.uk	(BBC Television)
http://www.whitehouse.gov	(The White House Presidential Site)

The second stage to establishing a web site involves a business organisation deciding between having the site based in-house or serviced externally by an outside supplier or web provider. This choice may be dependent upon the size of the organisation and the availability of IT and web-literate staff in the business organisation. This stage will determine whether the web pages are developed internally or externally to the business. There are a number of web service providers who will use their specialist expertise to design and create an organisation's web site pages. One of the considerations at this stage is the ease of maintainability of the site by the business organisation, because it is normally an ongoing requirement for business organisations to update their web pages on a regular basis, particularly to meet the changing requirements of dynamic business environments.

The third stage involves selecting a *scripting language* to construct the web pages for the site. The commonest form of scripting language application is HTML which is a simple tool for creating web pages, with the advantage of being accessible to the majority of browsers. However, a number of other more user-friendly web publishing tools exist to ease the process of establishing a set of web pages for a web site, for example, Microsoft's PageMill®, which automates much of the process of converting ordinary files for publication and use on the web.

The fourth stage should determine the logical relationship of the site in relation to customers and competitors. The decision to be made concerns the purpose for which the site will be used. For example, the web site pages can be used merely as an information board or for more sophisticated commercial activity involving levels of interaction with the user or client. The *logical* purpose of a web site will determine the design nature and complexity of the web pages and their associated hypertext links to other sites. Any form of business or commercial activity through a web site will inevitably necessitate the purchase of encryption software to secure and protect customer details within the working environment of the web site.

ACTIVITY **11.4**   ***Registering a web site***

Evaluate, through discussion with your colleagues, the significance of electronic commerce using the Internet and explain some of the benefits and drawbacks of using EDI to pass data over the Internet. Provide examples of two sectors of the business environment that stand to benefit from using the Internet for electronic commerce. Discuss and record some of the problems of creating a web site that has a range of hypertext links to other web sites within the Internet domain.

11.6 The Java language environment and the Internet

Java is a programming language developed by Sun Microsystems which, in the 1990s, is becoming a standard for the Internet, largely because it is a *cross-platform language*, which means that it can be used with a variety of operating systems from MS-DOS to Unix and across a range of computer platforms from AppleMacs to IBM-compatible terminals. The advantage of Java lies in the fact that it is a dynamic, rather than static, language which can extend the scope of the Internet beyond its use as a mere information retrieval system. A business that records, and handles, information or products on the web usually describes them in static form. Therefore, every time the information changes the web must be updated manually. However, within the Java environment the information changes can be extracted from a normal database; the web pages will reflect the database files and change as and when the database files change. Hence, Java permits information on web pages to be dynamic rather than static. Microsoft and IBM have licenses to incorporate Java into their various hardware platforms and, as such, promote Java as a standard language for Internet communications.

ACTIVITY **11.5**

The Java language environment and the web

Explain the significance of the Java language and its use within the environment of the Internet and outline three main advantages of using the Java language environment in connection with the Internet. Suggest and describe some of the ideal characteristics a programming environment should possess to be beneficial and appropriate for use on the Internet.

11.7 Networking and communications on the Internet

Networking and the Internet have liberated the stand-alone personal computer from its existence as a very localised business support tool into an exciting *interface* to the external business environment. Eventually, the personal computer may be replaced by a new generation of scaled-down, but performance powerful, desktop machines that merely act as network technology; many such machines already have network support and inbuilt network connection software incorporated within their architectures.

The Internet is largely a network of computer networks linked by telephone connections. Internet communications are largely conveyed by backbone telecommunications carriers, such as British Telecom or AT&T, and a number of smaller relay carriers of data traffic. For example, in the United States in the 1990s the Internet comprised five main communications traffic carriers which normally used communications systems constructed by fibre optics; the five backbone carriers in the United States are NSFnet, Alternet, AT&T, Sprintlink and PSINet. In the European Community most countries rely on national telephone and telecommunications networks to convey data and information across the Internet. However, these are largely linked by a European-wide system known as Ebone.

The Internet telecommunications networks are characterised by transmission management systems known as *routers* and *servers*. Internet routers provide a means of data traffic control; the aim of routers being to direct data traffic along the most efficient and effective telecommunications path over the network. The main rules of transmission are governed by the Transmission Control Protocol-Internet Protocol (TCP/IP). This protocol allows different computer hardware systems to communicate with each other, or as it is known, to 'handshake' between different systems. In the long term it will be a requirement to improve the existing communications protocols to include multi-media transmission through one common transmission route. The most effective method of multi-media transmission is through asynchronous transfer mode (ATM) technology which permits the combination of voice data and video data on the same transmission path. Within the Internet communications architecture, servers act as a storage area for information and software. Such servers on the Internet supply documents and web pages for users and some carry vital search engines that allow users to access and retrieve information. The future direction of communications over the Internet is to have more active servers that include *search agents* to automate the process of searching information sources for users.

Many business organisations are also integrating telephony software into their Internet systems. Telephony applications can often include a capability for audioconferencing and videoconferencing. The main advantage of telephony, using transmission paths, over the Internet is the relative cost reduction in making international calls because the callers in a conversation are only charged for connection to the local Internet site, irrespective of the distance of the call. However, a disadvantage lies in the fact that there is often a voice time delay which makes Internet telephony inferior to normal telephone connections.

ACTIVITY **11.6**

Networking and communications on the Internet
Describe the role and purpose of Internet transmission management systems known as routers and servers. Discuss why, in the long term, there is a need to improve communications protocols to include multi-media transmission through a common transmission route. Explain the benefits of multi-media transmission using asynchronous transfer mode (ATM) technology which combines voice data and video data on the same transmission path.

11.8 Ethics and etiquette on the Internet

The Internet is a relatively new and largely unregulated environment which has remained untamed by national and international legislation. There are four main issues related to ethics and etiquette on the Internet as follows:

1   security of data and information flow
2   privacy of the individual and organisation user
3   censorship and free speech
4   ethical obligations of users.

Many of the *security* issues have been dealt with in earlier references to encryption software with regard to business and commercial activity over the Internet. Current legislation by national governments has mainly concentrated on dealing with possible breaches of decency over the Internet. However, the level and form of national legislation varies from country to country. The main body of existing national legislation has concerned blocking or restricting the distribution of pornography and other forms of indecency over the Internet. However, most on-line Internet access providers are policing their own affairs by providing *filtering software* to prevent access to sites deemed unsuitable. For example, in July 1996 the government of Singapore ordered Internet access providers to block out sexually oriented and other forms of sensitive material. In Singapore the government is firm in regulating web pages and controlling access to users based in foreign countries that might undermine public morals, political stability or religious harmony. However, with such national legislation there is often much debate concerning decency versus freedom of information. Singapore is not isolated in intervention legislation that affects the use of the Internet; other governments have also been instrumental in restricting communications access within and without their national borders and jurisdiction. In most Internet-literate countries there have been two main schools of thought; one favours consistent regulation and the other favours total freedom without government influence or regulation. However, one fact that is clear to all users of the Internet is that it is the most participatory form of mass speech yet developed and as such requires ethical consideration.

In February 1996 the government of the United States introduced the Communications Decency Act to deal with on-line, offensive and indecent material. However, in June 1996 the new law was mitigated by a federal judicial ruling that declared the law unconstitutional as it did not recognise the First Amendment of the US constitution which guarantees free speech. The ruling declared the Internet:

A medium of historic importance, a profoundly democratic channel for communication that should be nurtured, not stifled.

(*Time*, 24 June, 1996)

The ruling continued to state that 'the Internet deserves the highest protection from government intrusion.' What is apparent is that legislation varies from country to country.

One of the significant ethical issues involves dealing with users who use the Internet to defame or smear the reputation of individuals and business organisations. An organisation that strives hard to maintain a competitive reputation must ensure that no other Internet user can lay claim to that reputation or attempt to besmirch that organisation's reputation. The following lists a code of etiquette that the majority of users abide by in their dealings over the Internet. The rules of etiquette are often referred to as 'netiquette'. The *netiquette code of conduct* lays out some standards of courteous behaviour that should be commonly acceptable on the Internet as follows:

▶ Never send any electronic message, or commercial transaction, that you would not want publicised or to be used in the public domain. The rule to acknowledge is that what you would put on a postcard you would not mind being seen in the public domain.

▶ Never engage in the sending of abusive, threatening, harassing or bigoted electronic messages or creating web pages that threaten another individual or organisation.

▶ Avoid smearing the reputation of others and avoid the creation of shadow identities on the Internet that besmirch the reputation of an individual or business organisation. Such shadow identities can misinform and mislead the Internet user.

▶ On a technical level, try to avoid creating web pages that require an enormous amount of memory space to run. This will slow down the transmission rate and may prevent users with inferior technology being able to access the relevant web pages.

 ACTIVITY **11.7**

Ethics and etiquette on the Internet

Explain the four main issues related to use, ethics and etiquette on the Internet and suggest aspects of Internet use that are of particular importance to business organisations. Provide four reasons why national governments may wish to monitor or control the use of the Internet by individuals and business organisations.

11.9 Business communications technology

In 1991 the Commercial Internet Exchange (CIX) was established to accommodate business organisations in connecting to the Internet. Since then various organisations have adopted the Internet with the purpose of meeting their respective business needs. The largest use of an Internet facility is through the incorporated e-mail applications found within the web domain. The Internet is used for many purposes ranging from sending and receiving business orders to information storage and retrieval, and business applications of the Internet are only limited by innovation barriers and the imagination of the organisation. However, the following is a list of some of the common business uses of the Internet:

▶ Information storage and retrieval through the establishment of web pages and the use of Internet search engines.

▶ The sending, receiving and distribution of e-mail messages to individuals and groups of individuals internal and external to the business organisation.

▶ The sending and receiving of documents around the globe and responding to suppliers and customers through EDI links on the Internet.

▶ The acquisition of business intelligence through the establishment of web page links to keep an organisation abreast of competition and social, political and economic developments on a global scale.

▶ Collecting and collating market research information and publishing tenders for contracts and other competitive bid work.

▶ Keeping up to date in current research and development through the publication and dissemination of research articles via the areas of government, business and academia.

▶ Acquiring and downloading commercial software applications that are relevant to the business environment and the interrogation of various help and assistance sites.

Rapid, reliable and effective telecommunications are essential to competitive business organisations. Telecommunications are essential for organisations that trade over a wide geographical area or across continents. Business organisations have access to a number of communications applications that speed the transmission of information.

Voice mail is a system where a spoken message is digitised and transmitted over a telecommunications network to be stored for later retrieval. The message is then converted to audio and listened to by the recipient. Voice mail allows users to leave, receive and store verbal messages from anyone connected to the system across the globe. Voice mail facilities also allow the sender of a voice mail message to send the message to a single recipient or to multiple recipients. For example, the manager of a sales team that is dispersed around the world can leave a voice mail message and, through the attachment of a code to the message, have it copied to all personnel in the manager's sales team. The advantage of voice mail lies in the fact that it does not involve typing text, as is the case with e-mail, and it incorporates more meaning in the tone and modulation of the sender's voice.

Facsimile (or fax) technology permits users to transmit text documents, pictures and graphics electronically over a standard telephone line from one location to another distant geographical location. The sending fax machine digitises the text, graphics or pictorial image and transmits it to a receiving fax machine where the text, graphics or pictorial image is reproduced as a facsimile (or duplicate) for the recipient. The facsimile is reproduced in hardcopy form by the receiving fax machine.

Electronic mail (e-mail) is a computer-to-computer exchange of text-based messages. E-mail is a cost-effective alternative to using the standard telephone for business communications. E-mail makes it possible for a text-based message to be sent from one microcomputer to another connected (or networked) microcomputer. There is often the facility to attach lengthy documents to an e-mail message. The receiving computer is informed that there is a message waiting and this can be accessed through windows-based (or other) communications software on the recipient's computer. Therefore, it is a popular form of business communication with the majority of organisations possessing an e-mail address. There are a number of windows-based communications software programs for dealing with the sending and receiving of e-mail; three common and popular programs are:

1 Eudora
2 Pine
3 PopMail.

E-mail is often the preferred medium of communication to many business organisations, particularly, with the development of the Internet which can incorporate e-mail facilities into standard web pages. Figure 11.2 shows a typical screen image of the Eudora e-mail program being run within an AppleMacintosh microcomputer environment.

E-mail has many advantages in terms of speed, accuracy and the ability to send, receive or forward messages to individuals or groups. However, within written language it is often difficult to interpret the sender's mood and accent on certain pieces of text. For example, should the text be read as a joke, sarcasm or a serious unembellished remark? In order to add tone to e-mail a special set of symbols has become standard in the conveyance of mood and meaning. These are often referred to as *emoticons*, or 'smileys', which is a play on the words 'emotion' and 'icon'. Table 11.2 lists some examples of emoticons and their meaning. Look at each emoticon at a sideways angle and you will perceive the visual meaning.

figure 11.2
Eudora working in a Macintosh environment

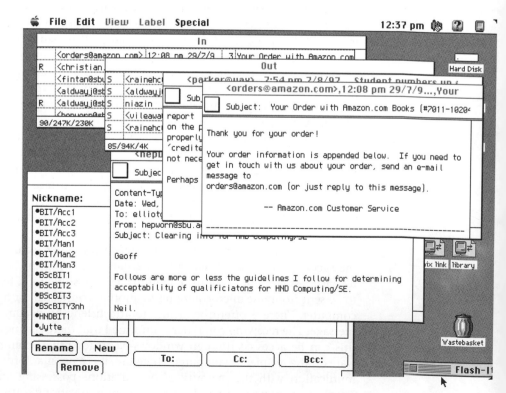

table 11.2 **The meaning of emoticons (or smileys)**	:-)	happy
	:-(	sad
	;-)	wink
	:-ll	angry
	:-0	amazed!
	:-P	poking out tongue
	:->	sarcastic remark
	:-l	indifferent attitude

Emoticons indicate emotions within the body of a message or other form of communication. It is important that electronic communications, such as e-mail, should be clear and concise and eliminate any misunderstanding. Good communication avoids misunderstanding and any tool or technique that assists in that pursuit is important within the domain of information technology in the business environment.

ACTIVITY **11.8**
·············

Business communications technology

Provide four reasons why the acquisition of business intelligence through the establishment of web page links to other users on the Internet allows a business organisation to keep abreast of competition and social, political and economic developments on a global scale. Discuss the effectiveness of voice mail, facsimile (fax) and e-mail as communications mediums in the business environment.

11.10   Chapter summary
·······································

Efficient and effective communications are essential for business activity; information is only a powerful resource if its communication is timely and accurate when conveyed through an appropriate telecommunications medium. The Internet offers all business organisations, both large and small, the opportunity to compete globally, and on equal terms, irrespective of the size and nature of the organisation. Once the current barriers of insecurity of data transfer are overcome then the Internet will be a significant medium for various business activity. Unlike many business opportunities in the past, the financial barriers to entry do not exist in any significant form on the Internet; to establish a web presence is a relatively cheap exercise. Therefore, business organisations are likely to become more competitive and rely on the knowledge, wisdom and creativity of those individuals and teams that specialise in delivering Internet products and services. The intelligence and creativity of such Internet professionals will increasingly provide the competitive advantage of organisations in the future business environment.

Short self-assessment questions

···

11.1 Define the term Internet and suggest three possible commercial uses of the Internet for business activity.

11.2 Explain why a major obstacle to mass electronic shopping is the insecurity of paying for goods on-line using credit or debit mediums.

11.3 Describe the techniques used by business organisations to try to ensure the security of data when customers purchase goods using a credit or debit card.

11.4 Define and term *World Wide Web* (WWW) and explain why the web was developed as a useful business communications tool.

11.5 Explain the significance and function of *hypertext* in providing hyperlinks to other documents and areas on the web.

11.6 Define the term *multi-media* and describe the characteristics and possible uses of multi-media information in the business environment.

11.7 Evaluate the differences between the Internet and the intranet and suggest four advantages to a business organisation of operating an intranet user interface.

11.8 Describe the role and function of the hypertext mark-up language (HTML) and hypertext transmission protocols (HTTP) within the Internet domain.

11.9 Outline the role and purpose of the European Commission Directive (1995) on data protection and suggest possible reasons why data should only be sent outside of the European Community to countries with adequate data protection laws.

11.10 Explain why in order for a business to utilise the advantages of using the web it must register a web site and describe the four main stages to establishing such a web site.

11.11 Explain why electronic commerce through the web will only prosper when encryption is a widespread and reliable tool for commercial electronic communications.

11.12 Evaluate the significance of traditional encryption techniques using a secret key to encode data that is privileged and describe the method and use of cyphers.

11.13 Describe the commonest form of medium used to transmit (or 'carry') data and information traffic over the Internet.

11.14 Explain how filtering software may prevent breaches of decency occurring over the Internet.

11.15 Define the term *netiquette* and outline the main points of etiquette that should be present when using the Internet.

11.16 Define the technology known as e-mail and suggest three possible advantages and disadvantages of using electronic mail.

11.17 Outline three main business uses of the Internet and describe why these uses may be essential for business activity in the twenty-first century.

11.18 Define the term *emoticon* and describe how emoticons may reduce misunderstanding that often occurs by using other informal text-based communications mediums.

Internet terminology

Attachment Text or other file that is attached to an e-mail message.

Browser Software program displaying images and text which provides and interface to Internet and WWW documents.

Bookmark Means of marking a user's location on the WWW.

Cybernaut A person who actively browses and searches through the Internet.

Download To transfer data from a remote site to a user's computer system.

E-mail An electronic message that is sent between users on a network.

Emoticon Character graphics used in e-mail messages that represent emotions.

Eudora Windows based e-mail management program.

FAQ Shorthand term for 'frequently asked questions'.

FTP File transfer protocol for transferring messages across the Internet.

GIF Graphic interchange format file extension that indicates the file contains a graphics image.

Home page The first or main index page of a user or location linking and pointing to a series of other pages.

Hyperlink Hypertext link marked by the highlighting of a key word which when clicked on with a mouse will link to a related document.

Netiquette A code of conduct for users of the Internet.

Netscape Hypertext-based browser program used for locating WWW information.

Pine Menu-based e-mail management program.

Popmail An e-mail management program.

Protocols The rules that govern how software and hardware communicate on a network.

Telnet A program for connecting and logging on to computer systems on a network.

Upload To transfer a data file from a user's computer system to a remote system on a network.

URL Shorthand for uniform resource locator which identifies network locations and enables navigation on the Internet.

WWW World Wide Web global collection of pages and sites on the Internet.

Web address Unique identification of user or location on the Internet.

Web page Single screen page on the WWW.

Web site Unique location for a user on the Internet.

Yahoo Search program for locating information pages and sources on the WWW.

References

Financial Times (1996) *The FT A–Z of the Internet*. London: Financial Times.

Further study and reading
••••••••••••••••••••••••••••••••

Books

Cronin, M.J. (1995) *Doing more Business on the Internet*. New York: Van Nostrand Reinhold.

Cronin, M.J. (1995) *Global Advantage on the Internet*. New York: Van Nostrand Reinhold.

Ellsworth, J.H. and Ellsworth, M.V. (1996) *The New Internet Business Book*. Chichester, England: John Wiley.

Langford, D. (1996) *Practical Computer Ethics*. London: McGraw-Hill.

Manger, J.J. (1995) *The International Internet Information Guide*. London: McGraw-Hill.

Negroponte, N. (1995) *Being Digital*. London: Hodder and Stoughton.

O'Leary, T. and O'Leary, L. (1996) *Internet*. New York: McGraw-Hill.

Vacca, J. (1996) *Internet Security Secrets*. Chicago: IDG Books.

CHAPTER 12

Norman Payne Case study

Information Systems analysis, design, implementation and evaluation within the BIT environment

Objectives

After you have studied this chapter you will be able to:

▶ work in groups and solve information systems related problems within the business environment

▶ develop as students of BIT a confident knowledge of the scope of networked and integrated IS/IT environments

▶ competently manipulate, manage and advise on IS/IT configuration within a business information systems environment

▶ develop a knowledge of information systems theory, project management and group dynamics within the business environment

▶ demonstrate an ability to analyse complex problems and professionally convey appropriate IS/IT solutions.

12.1   Introduction to the case study

The basis of a programme of study in BIT is the integration of a number of discrete business, computing and IS/IT disciplines. This chapter sets out to integrate the various academic disciplines and skills, set out in the previous 11 chapters, into a holistic project unit. The modern emphasis within business information systems is on end-user information systems development, which eliminates the historic need for specific task-related intermediaries such as proprietary programmers and business systems analysts; these two roles are often merged into one role within the business systems environment. Careers and job descriptions within the business environment have, through business evolution and technological change, seen an increasing movement away from demarcation in computer-based tasks. National economies as a whole require better trained and educated BIT specialists who possess a broad vision of how IS/IT integrates into an organisation and have the ability to adapt to dynamic internal and external forces within the business environment.

This case study unit should be used by the reader to gain expertise in the analysis, design, implementation and evaluation of information systems and information technology within business organisations. Students of BIT should develop an understanding of the integration of business software applications, information technology, and information systems theory, into a body of knowledge capable of delivering IT solutions to general or specific business systems problems. This necessitates not only an understanding of information systems but also the application of information technology to solve a systems problem. The student should see this case study unit as an IS/IT project with the aim of expressing an understanding of the various BIT skills and disciplines studied throughout this book.

12.2 Student remit and requirements

Students using this case study should be aiming to deepen their understanding in the development and integration of a number of BIT areas as follows:

- information systems (IS)
- information technology (IT)
- networked business systems environments
- information systems development frameworks and methodologies
- information systems theory and practice
- information systems and information technology (IS/IT) integration and strategy
- software and hardware application within fourth generation development environments
- project team management and group dynamics
- information systems and technology literacy.

The integration of BIT disciplines should be focused on achieving a given business goal or set of business objectives. For the purposes of this case study a student should take on the role of a business information technology specialist or *consultant* brought into an organisation to solve a number of 'hard' and 'soft' business information systems problems as elicited by the case study. This will entail careful reading and absorption of the case study to achieve the following end product:

- Review the position of the company within the business environment.
- Analyse specific and suggested 'hard' and 'soft' IS/IT problems.
- Recommend solutions to achieve company bound objectives and goals.
- Use a development methodology to analyse and design appropriate business systems.
- Use a development framework and tools to implement and evaluate systems.
- Recommend and integrate software applications and IT to meet user requirements.
- Present findings as if delivered to the business organisation's Executive Board.

The evolution of the project should use a systems development methodology, as a guiding framework, such as the traditional information systems development life cycle (SDLC), rapid applications development (RAD), prototyping or another related methodology. However, a student must be careful to justify the use of the methodology chosen in terms of its appropriateness and suitability to the case study scenario.

It is recommended that the case study be undertaken in groups of two, three or four students. However, if the case study is used as an individual activity this is still appropriate, although the final outcome will not be able to fully address issues of group dynamics and group management. Any more than four students would dilute the meaning and purpose of the project exercise. If the case study is tackled in groups, then it is strongly recommended that additional skills such as minute taking and apportionment of team member roles and responsibilities be established. The case study could then be used as a vehicle for assessing group dynamics and other softer group-based communication skills. These skills are a valuable asset to any computer-oriented professional working in the business environment where human and technology communication skills are of paramount importance. Pause for thought 12.1 outlines the importance of good communications skills for career progression within the business environment.

The formation of working groups is a prevalent situation in the business world. Working groups are often formed to achieve a specific or desired outcome that cannot be achieved by an individual's isolated effort. The successful operation of group dynamics is an essential feature of the BIT domain. Therefore, part of the assessment criteria can have regard to the way a group manages and controls the evolution of the case study. Groups with a common objective offer an enriched learning experience and, on the basis of the systems theory premise that the '*sum is greater than the parts*', it can enhance the group's overall knowledge and understanding of the subject matter. Therefore, the ability to collaborate to achieve a given objective is an important skill to acquire. In addition to working in groups, the ability to provide technical advise and expertise, and to communicate ideas and solutions to a BIT problem, are essential qualities in the profile of any business information technology specialist.

The case study project groups can, if desired, be required to make a team presentation in the presence of any other project groups undertaking the same project. It is suggested that the presentations should be of a finite 15 minutes in length, and groups should be encouraged to use relevant communication and presentation techniques (e.g. slides, handouts, OHPs, screen show, graphics tables etc.). However, the presentations should be delivered as if to the client's Executive (or strategic) Board of Directors.

PAUSE FOR THOUGHT 12.1   *Are you ready for IT?*

The Guardian, Saturday 1 February 1997

After years of cutbacks in graduate recruitment there are definite signs that companies are once again courting students. And one of the most buoyant areas is in Information Technology. BT has doubled its graduate intake in 1996 from 250 to 500, and this year plans to expand to 750.

The type of companies offering IT jobs now include not only the traditional software and hardware companies but pretty well every other type from advertising to super marketing and from tourism to publishing. Although there are plenty of vacancies it seems that not enough people with the right skills are putting themselves forward.

The Association of Graduate Recruiters, which represents 500 of the country's leading employers, closely monitors the situation. AGR's chief executive Roly Cockman says the market is competitive for students who have what the employer wants, and that doesn't just mean a degree in Information Technology.

'The larger IT employers are looking for academic ability from a broad range of disciplines, and just as important, a good portfolio of personal skills. The demand for these graduates is reflected in salary terms too. The average starting salary in 1996 for a graduate going into IT was £15,250 as opposed to £14,900 for someone starting in general management.'

South Bank University's Sue Edmonds has found that her own figures reflect this increasing demand for students to go into IT.

'Eighteen months ago 40 per cent of all vacancies notified directly to us were IT related, today it is 80 per cent. These jobs fall into two categories. On the one hand smaller software companies are asking very specific questions about our IT courses and students; do we for instance cover neural networks? On the other hand there are the larger employers who like to train their own graduates in IT. There is an employer perception that IT graduates are non-communicative and that IT skills can be grafted on to a graduate from another discipline.'

The IT Systems sub-committee of the Association of Graduate Careers Advisory Services, AGCAS, is looking into the whole area of what employers want and what students expect. Tom Franks, careers adviser at Birmingham University, says that there is a popular misconception among many undergraduates that an IT job means having an IT degree and being tied to the computer screen when the majority of jobs are people jobs. 'When company recruiters are interviewing students, apart from looking for general nous they also ask themselves would I let this person loose on a customer, and would I choose to have dinner with this person?'

This is confirmed by ICL which takes on up to 150 UK graduates a year. The company has three core values for all its employees: putting the customer first, it's "one ICL", and teamworking. Most people in the company work with customers, and the ability to get on with them is paramount. The company has supplemented its traditional job-specific training scheme with a programme called Challenger which seeks to develop these important personal skills during a new entrant's first 18 months. Ann Allen of ICL's Consultancy service manages the project. 'Challenger shows graduates that ICL has a serious commitment to their long-term future by helping them to develop their inter-personal skills and business awareness. It also helps us to develop future leadership within the company.'

AGCAS's own research suggests that employers agree there is an under supply of really good people in the system. At the same time there is increased recognition by IT employers that good graduates can be found in all universities not just in the older established ones. What counts is focus, enthusiasm, and transferable skills.

A 1995 report by AGCAS on Skills for Graduates in the 21st Century identified why these good graduates were not coming forward during their final year: firstly under-graduates are having to work much harder academically: secondly students are more hard-pressed financially and have to take on part-time work leaving them little time to consider their future: thirdly the forms that companies are sending out are becoming more complex, often requiring up to six hours to complete, time the students simply don't have available.

IBM failed to fill all its vacancies at its first attempt last year and had to launch a second campaign during the summer. The company hopes to avoid this in 1997 and meet its target of up to 300 trainees by establishing better links with more university departments. IBM is unusual in that it tries to build links with undergraduates by running a number of pre-university schemes, giving students a chance to work with the company for a year or two prior to going to university.

Not surprisingly many students who've been on this scheme choose to apply to IBM when they graduate. They also uniquely run a computer science degree programme in conjunction with Portsmouth University, taking up to 20 undergraduates every year.

The reason for this level of investment according to Chris Micklethwaite, who coordinates the undergraduate programmes, is that by catching people early they are more likely to show company loyalty.

Students who have taken a sandwich degree, and therefore have a year's work experience to offer, have a definite advantage over other graduates when it comes to securing a place on a graduate recruitment scheme.

Their technical skills will have been advanced by the experience, but they also develop other personal skills that help them in the world of work. They are often offered first refusal by the employer they worked for during their placement, and overall have a higher success rate in gaining employment than other graduates.

But universities are now starting to seek alternative ways of making sure that all their graduates are equipped with the sort of non-academic skills that companies are now demanding. The Department of Education and Employment has awarded contracts to three institutions to develop skills programmes.

Chris Phillips from the University of Manchester and UMIST Careers Service is the project manager for one of these programmes in Career Management Skills. 'Over a two-year period, 12 departments will be developing these skills as an assessable 12-week module of their degree programmes.

'The Maths department at Manchester and the Computation department at UMIST are the first to be involved.

'We are teaching skills such as negotiation and listening through a combination of traditional teaching and resource materials. And by bringing in people from industry to help both in the delivery of the course and in developing course materials we are convincing the students that what we're trying to do will enhance their career prospects.'

The lessons of this programme eventually will be passed on to other colleges, but in the meantime students need to try to establish just what employers are looking for by talking to as many companies as possible. They need to recognise what their non-academic skills are, and understand that these may count for just as much as their academic ones.

12.3 The integration of BIT theory and practice

The case study should act as an integrating assignment, incorporating the knowledge acquired over the previous three chapters. The Norman Payne Enterprises case study acts as an intelligence report containing aspects of the following information on the business organisation:

▶ business history
▶ trading interests and market characteristics
▶ information and communication infrastructure
▶ management and systems structure
▶ existing manual and IT-based information systems
▶ corporate plans and future requirements.

It is suggested that the written report should have the following structure (which should only be used as an indicative guide): (1) preamble or abstract, (2) project specifications, (3) business systems and user requirements, (4) problems and conflicts, (5) analysis and design, (6) implementation and evaluation, and (7) recommendations and conclusion.

The nature of downsizing and decentralisation within the business environment has led to more information systems related activities being undertaken through the formulation and management of task-specific project groups. Consequently, the softer skills of project team management, control and coordination are central to the ethos of BIT. The Norman Payne case study attempts to abstract a real-world situation which is characterised by hard and soft information requirements. The idea of project teams being created to achieve IS/IT solutions is fundamental to the BIT philosophy; as is the recognition of the importance of group-based development activities.

The Norman Payne case study aims to develop a capability to identify, analyse and solve a set of business information technology problems that are characteristic of the type facing large and small organisations within the business environment. It is suggested that the project should be developed with reference to the '5-I Model' which can be used to assist the development of the case study project. The 5-I Model attempts to convey to those studying BIT the fact that most business systems problems require inspirational thought and creative ideas. Business systems problems cannot usually be solved by the application of inflexible or prescriptive solutions. Therefore, the application of BIT principles and disciplines within the business environment requires a significant level of innovation. The strands of the 5-I Model are as follows:

Independence	(of project management)
Identification	(of BIT problem areas)
Integration	(of BIT disciplines, tools and techniques)
Implementation	(of the project and delivery of outcomes)
Inspiration	(of thought and attitude to solving a BIT problem)

(The '5I-Model' was developed by Geoffrey Elliott and Susan Windmill and is copyright of South Bank University ©).

The case study project is intended as a means of integrating various theoretical and practical material and to provide a vehicle for developing skills in business information systems engineering.

12.4   Case study outcomes

The case study aims to provide a flavour of the knowledge and skills set required for a rounded understanding of the use and application of IS/IT within the business environment. An understanding of business information technology will necessitate acting as a conduit between the disciplines of IT and business, translating the information requirements of the business environment into usable business systems. We understand from a socio-technical perspective that business information systems involve people, organisation and technology. Therefore, those engaged in applying business information technology theory and practice will need to be able to accomplish some or all of the following:

▶ To work with a variety of information technology and understand the environments and disciplines necessary for the development of integrated business information systems.

▶ To effectively communicate and understand the requirements of different business activities and sector specific procedures and practices.

▶ To analyse, design, implement and evaluate IT-based business information systems within different commercial or organisational constraints.

▶ To understand the business environment and the range of disciplines necessary for the development of software-based information systems.

▶ To establish information systems within the business environment for strategic, managerial and operational decision making.

▶ To manage, control and coordinate IT-based information systems projects and other related business resources.

▶ To recommend, plan and apply appropriate hardware and software applications within a business organisation and to provide advice on the connectivity and integration of information technology.

▶ To perform a knowledgeable liaison role, effectively linking the business domain to the computing and IT domain within the business environment.

▶ To evaluate and determine areas where information systems and information technology (IS/IT) might be used to achieve a competitive advantage within the business environment.

▶ To establish information requirements for an organisation and to develop a specification for business information requirements within a business.

12.5 Management and human decision-making behaviour

The fundamental premise of BIT is that business is a 'human activity system' which relies on decision making of all forms and at all levels of the organisation. Decision-making activity within the business environment is normally supported by information systems. The effectiveness and efficiency of these information systems allow an organisation to compete and, in many cases, can often provide a competitive edge within the environment in which business activity and decision making takes place.

The process of making decisions can be separated into three generic stages. This process of decision making is illustrated in Figure 12.1. Earlier chapters have stressed the importance of understanding the nature of decision making within the three generic levels (operational, managerial and strategic) of the organisational hierarchy. The rigidity of an organisational structure will depend upon the culture (or ethos) of the business organisation. For example, Figure 12.2 shows

figure 12.1

**The process of
making decisions**

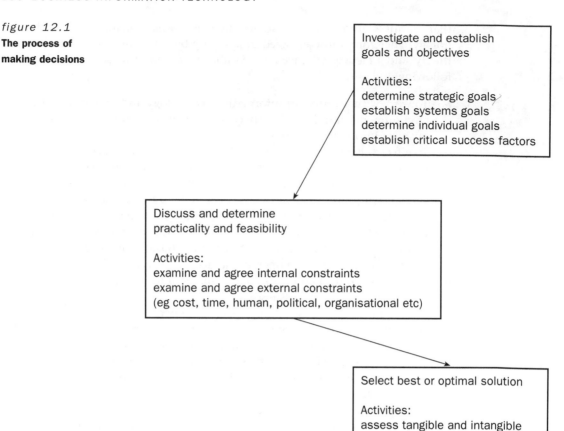

Investigate and establish
goals and objectives

Activities:
determine strategic goals
establish systems goals
determine individual goals
establish critical success factors

Discuss and determine
practicality and feasibility

Activities:
examine and agree internal constraints
examine and agree external constraints
(eg cost, time, human, political, organisational etc)

Select best or optimal solution

Activities:
assess tangible and intangible
costs and benefits

The process of making decisions can be separated into three generic stages. The decision-making philosophy that pervades a business organisation may span the spectrum from autocratic to democratic. Nevertheless, it is essential that the underlying decision-making process concludes with selection of the best, or optimal, solution. It is then important to follow decision making by putting into place within the business environment the control mechanisms to deliver the decision.

the hierarchical management structure that operated in the Bank of England in 1995; the organisational schema shows the lines of authority and also indicates the functional specialisms that exist in the Bank of England. Organisational structures need not be as rigid as that for the Bank of England; nevertheless, organisational structure often affects the way in which IS/IT is incorporated into the business environment.

The decision-making philosophy that pervades a business organisation can be autocratic or democratic. Nevertheless, it is essential that the decision-making process concludes with selection of the best solution. It is then important to put into place the *control mechanisms* to deliver the decision. The effective application of management is essential in order to control an organisation's three main resources of people, technology and organisation. Therefore, the activity of *management* is concerned with coordinating and directing the human, technological and financial resources of an organisation. Some of the earliest academic

figure 12.2

The management and organisational structure of the Bank of England

The organisation of the Bank

The Bank is governed mainly by the 1946 Bank of England Act, under which it was nationalised. The Act provides for the appointment, by the Crown, of the Governor, the Deputy Governor and the 16 other members of the Bank's board, which is known as the Court of Directors. Governors serve for a term of five years, and Directors for four years; both can be renewed. Up to four of the Directors may serve as full-time executives of the Bank. The Non-Executive Directors represent a wide range of interests in the City and industry. Court sits weekly and is responsible for all the affairs of the Bank. The present operational structure of the Bank is shown below.

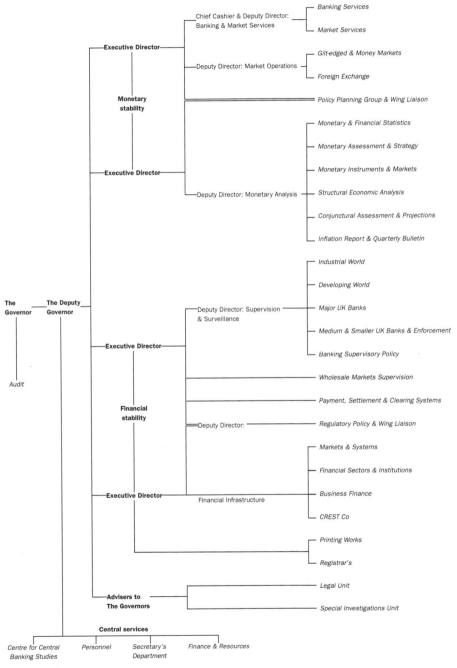

© Bank of England

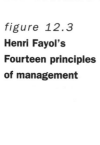

figure 12.3
Henri Fayol's
Fourteen principles
of management

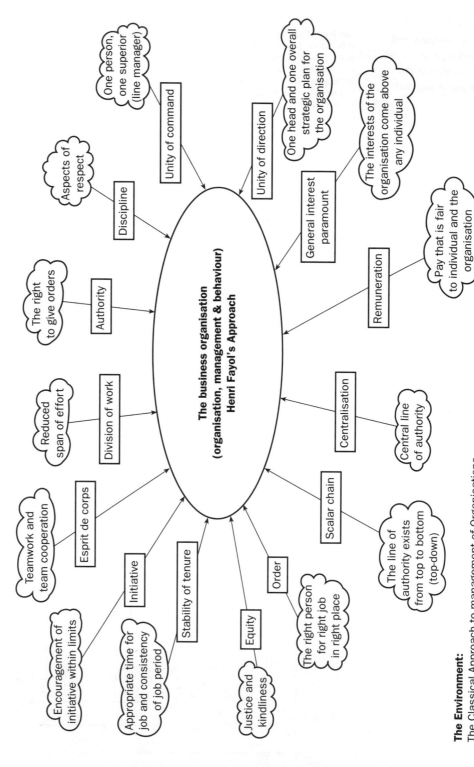

The Environment:
The Classical Approach to management of Organisations

work in the area of management science and organisational behaviour was by a French industrialist named Henri Fayol. Fayol was one of the founding fathers of modern management science. Fayol's definition of management is still used as the fundamental basis of modern management science and the foundation for many academic courses on management.

Henri Fayol derived 14 general principles of management which were concerned with management lines of authority and organisational behaviour. These principles are outlined in Figure 12.3. These principles can be utilised and absorbed into all aspects of management and control within the business environment. For instance, the ideas of Fayol form the basis of the the planning, decision making and control life cycle studied earlier in this book. Fayol's principles are a classical approach to management within organisational boundaries. However, not all of these principles are recognised as desirable within the context of modern business organisations, particularly the notion of rigid structure for lines of authority and the division of labour. Many organisations operate within flatter (non-hierarchical structures) which devolve much responsibility for decision making to individuals, rather than maintaining a centralised authority. Also, many of the classical principles ignore the humanistic aspects of modern IS/IT within business organisations. Modern approaches to management often highlight the human relations aspect of business and recognise the fact that business is a human activity system.

INTELLIGENCE REPORT
· ·

NORMAN PAYNE ENTERPRISES Plc

Mr Norman Payne established Norman Payne Enterprises in 1984. In 1996 the company went public and now shares for the company are quoted on the UK Stock Market. The shares currently trade at 133p each. In 1990, Mr Payne was awarded the honour of 'Businessman of the Year' by the Confederation of British Industry (CBI). Norman Payne Enterprises has branch offices in Rome, Paris and Lagos, Nigeria. A strategic review of operations in 1995 suggested that any future expansion of the business organisation would only take place by targeting overseas customers. However, it is the view of Mr Payne that the Marketing Division of the company has failed to attract overseas customers because of its outdated marketing methods and techniques. Mr Payne believes that the development and integration of an improved, IT-based **Marketing Information System** may address some of these apparent underlying problems.

In a major strategic review of operations, in 1995, the following areas of concern were highlighted:

The Marketing Division was failing to target a suitable level of customers and to meet its performance standards. However, what these performance standards were is a matter of debate! Furthermore, the company operates a hierarchical

Case study:
Norman Payne Enterprises

NORMAN PAYNE ENTERPRISES

100 Enterprise Buildings
Free Trade Road
Southwark
London

BIT Consultants
Techno-Centre
Farsighted Road
London

21st February

Dear Consultant,

We are inviting your firm of BIT consultants to submit a proposal for the development of the following systems and procedures within our international organisation:

1. An IT-based Human Resources System.

2. An IT-based Marketing Information System.

We would also like you to carry out an investigation and analysis of the following:

1. The cost and benefit of a weekly Company Newsletter.

2. Improved logistical distribution system.

3. Improved Sales Order Processing and Purchase Order Processing System.

Our company has been trading since 1984 and the number of staff employed by our organisation has increased from 4 to 504, employed in four countries including the UK. We now feel that our present systems are inadequate to meet the needs of our continually expanding organisation.

Your proposal should include detailed system and technical specifications, as well as the associated development and equipment purchase costs. The proposal should also include a review of the organisation's business systems to ensure that the business is operating efficiently and effectively.

Attached to this letter are details of our business activities and current trading position. You will see that our income is quite healthy, but our associated costs and expenses are significant.

Your response should reach our offices no later than 1st March. Please do not hesitate to contact me if you require further information.

Yours sincerely,

Mr Norman Payne
President and CEO
Norman Payne Enterprises Plc

organisation structure, with few responsibilities devolved to divisional heads. The term business information systems is used here to describe a variety of information systems such as transaction processing systems, management information systems and decision support systems.

The business organisation known as Norman Payne Enterprises has two main trading strands that overlap in certain areas. Business strand one involves the buying, selling and fitting of shop fixtures and fittings, including the supply of refurbished business machines and other business organisational equipment. Business strand two involves the auctioning of bankrupt office equipment and fixtures and fittings from premises in Kent, England.

Despite the recession the organisation has succeeded in remaining marginally profitable, although profit margins have been squeezed by the high level of cost incurred in the organisation's trading operations. The business is computerised in certain areas but not in other areas and there is a concern that the systems that exist are not fully integrated within the business organisation. Furthermore, the use and understanding of IT within the business organisation is limited. The sales order processing system and purchase order processing systems were updated and computerised in January 1993. The payment of staff salaries has been computerised since 1985.

In August 1992, the organisation recruited a marketing consultant from a top City of London advertising firm. The initial improvement in the marketing operations widened the customer base of the organisation on a global scale. However, most areas of the organisation do not have the benefit of IT and still rely on old manual systems and procedures. These systems have fuzzy boundaries and often staff are employed in various areas as and when required with little need for task specialisation. In an attempt to keep all his employees informed of the organisation's practices, procedures and future direction, Mr Payne believes that the organisation should have an Employee Newsletter of facts and figures. The type of information requirements of the Newsletter have yet to be solidified. However, Mr Payne has suggested that the Newsletter should not be 'chatty', but should be factual and distributed to all employees around the world on a weekly basis (an obvious logistical headache!).

In a major review of operations with his Executive Board, Mr Payne highlighted the following areas of concern within the organisation (see letter on page 304):

▶ The Human Resources system
▶ Telecommunications between international branch offices
▶ The dissemination of information between branch offices
▶ The distribution of material and goods between branch offices
▶ General integration and linkage of systems within the organisation
▶ Failure to exploit marketing opportunities and other business advantages.

The establishment of an organisational newsletter may help to unite the international divisions, and publicise overall business strategy. The function of marketing within Norman Payne Enterprises is concerned with the planning, promotion, and sale of products in existing markets, and the development of new products and new markets to better serve present and potential customers. Thus, marketing performs a vital function in the operation of the business organisation. Strategic, tactical, and operational information systems assist the marketing managers in product planning, pricing decisions, advertising and sales promotion strategies and expenditures, forecasting market potential for new and present products, and determining channels of distribution. Collateral reporting systems support the efforts of marketing managers to control the efficiency and effectiveness of the selling and distribution of products and services.

The Human Resources System

Business organisations keep details of their employees, whether they employ only one or two staff or have thousands of employees. Norman Payne Enterprises Plc requires an IT-based Human Resources System to be developed covering all divisions within the organisation on a global scale. The exact content of personnel information varies from one business organisation to another but there are a number of items which are always present (e.g. name, address, telephone number, details of next of kin, unique employee number). Other items are required in most business organisations so that they can complete forms required for government departments (e.g. number of registered disabled employed). Such a system is necessary because Norman Payne Enterprises is legally bound to keep details of pay, income tax and other information for all staff.

A brief study of Norman Payne Enterprises, in December 1993, found that individuals kept some records of their own for the staff for which they were responsible. These, however, would not be the same as those kept by the personnel department and, in some cases, the personnel department would not keep the same details. For example, the person responsible for booking training courses would keep full details of all courses attended by any member of staff while the personnel staff would only record the dates and titles of the courses. Discrepancies of information flows need to be sorted out quickly to reduce data redundancy in the organisation.

The **Human Resource Management** function involves the recruitment, placement, evaluation, compensation, and development of the employees of an organisation. Originally, businesses used computer-based information systems to (1) produce paychecks and payroll reports, (2) maintain personnel records, and (3) analyse the use of personnel in business operations. Many business organisations have gone beyond these traditional functions and have developed **Human Resource Information Systems** (HRIS), which also support (1) recruitment, selection, and hiring, (2) job placement, (3) performance appraisals, (4) employee benefits analysis, (5) training and development, and (6) health, safety, and security.

Human Resource Information Systems support the concept of human resource management. This business function emphasises (1) **planning** to meet the individual needs of the business, (2) **development** of employees to their full potential, and (3) **control** of all personnel policies and programmes. The goal of human resource management is the effective and efficient use of the human resources of a company.

The particular system within Norman Payne Enterprises has one central office with only 35 members of staff located there and all the other staff (500 at present but increasing) working in the various other branches and sites around the world. The personnel office currently finds it very difficult to arrange meetings of various groups of staff as the central office does not normally keep information about holidays with the exception of breaks of one or more weeks. As it is not always possible to speak to staff during normal office hours unless they contact the central office during the day, it sometimes takes three or four days before a meeting can be finalised. It has recently become important that the staff at the central office may be able to identify qualified (trained) staff as quickly as possible to fill areas with a skills short-fall. It was suggested that the human resources system should have the following information requirements: (i) provide the necessary links with the existing payroll system; (ii) provide details of training courses attended (and planned) as part of individual staff development programmes. Certain activities can cause extra strain on the human resources system at particular times of the year. One example of this would be salary reviews and, as these tend to occur towards the end of March each year, a change would be expected for each employee at about this time. The system should require minimal staff internal re-education or training. Training may have to be **outsourced**.

Some of the major applications of information systems that support human resource management are: (1) **Staffing**. Record and track human resources through personnel record-keeping, skills inventories, and personnel requirements forecasting. (2) **Training and Development**. Plan and monitor employee recruitment, training, performance appraisals, and career development. (3) **Compensation**. Analyse, plan, and monitor policies for employee wages, salaries, incentive payments and fringe benefits. (4) **Governmental Reporting**. Reporting to government bodies concerning equal opportunity policies and statistics, employee health, workplace accidents and hazards, safety procedures, and so on. Changes in job assignments and compensation, or hiring and termination, are examples of information that would be used to update the personnel database.

Personnel requirements forecasting assures that a business organisation has an adequate supply of high-quality human resources. This application provides information required for forecasts of personnel requirements in each major employment category for various company departments or for new projects and other ventures being planned by management. Team composition must have regard not only to the skills set of each member, but also the personality and softer attributes of each member of the team. Efficient and effective information systems help managers plan and monitor employee recruitment, training, and development programmes by analysing the success history of present programmes. They can also be used to address the career development status of each employee to determine whether development methods such as training programmes and periodic performance appraisals should be recommended.

It was suggested that with the introduction of a computerised human resources system the organisation could keep one central personnel record for each member of staff. However, because it is possible to **network** many terminals to the computer used in the personnel section, other members of staff could also use the information without having to remove it from its central location. It was suggested that a specialist BIT consultancy firm be employed to advise on the establishment of an effective and efficient human resources system. The nature of **data security and privacy** also needs to be addressed. It was also suggested that a large business organisation will often have many terminals connected into the system and staff will have been given user numbers and passwords to allow them to use the section(s) of data related to their jobs while, at the same time, they will not be allowed to look at (view) or update data which is not related to their job function. Other functions such as word processing, electronic mail and diary arrangements can easily be linked into this system as well as the more normal links to other business information systems. This is known as systems integration.

The methods used for such IT network links will depend largely on the location of the various members of staff as some firms have all (or most of) their staff located in one office block while other firms have their staff located in many separate offices which could be in many parts of the country. There is a need to investigate the appropriateness of **local area networks** (LANs) and **wide area networks** (WANs) within the organisational boundaries of Norman Payne Enterprises. When staff are located in many separate sites across the globe the major advantages of a central integrated system are easily seen as information can be obtained very quickly and collectively.

The Newsletter

Mr Payne requires the Newsletter to be short and to the point. However, it must contain a balance of hard facts for operational purposes along with personnel news (such as promotions, staff training courses, social events etc.). The Newsletter will be used as a vehicle to communicate facts to the divisions within the UK and abroad. This will save time and money spent communicating general information on an individual basis. The Newsletter should be linked to the organisation's human resources system. However, Mr Payne would accept advice on the exact relationship of the Newsletter within the organisation's integrated information systems as a whole. The hard information requirements would be along the following lines:

1 Delivery dates and times for overseas divisions.
2 Work scheduling details.
3 Staff scheduling and task changes.
4 Reporting structures.
5 Information on strategic direction.

Mr Payne suggests that a newsletter with colour graphics would be preferable to a text newsletter, as long as the benefits outweighed the costs. Norman Payne is also excited about the prospect of possibly putting the newsletter on the **World Wide Web (WWW)**. Many of the competitors of Norman Pane Enterprises already have their own web pages. Could Norman Payne Enterprises transact business over the Web?

Improved Distribution System

Currently, Norman Payne Enterprises ship goods to overseas divisions using various sea and air carriers. They have use of their own cargo plane to ship goods around the UK and France. They also use a fleet of seven long-distance container trucks. Road haulage is the dominant mode of transport used by most business organisations and Norman Payne Enterprises is no exception. Such systems consider:

1 Vehicle route/load-planning systems.
2 Fleet management systems.
3 Tachograph analysis.
4 On-board computers.
5 Fuel management systems.
6 On-board communications.

Business organisations are often faced with the problem of optimising the use of a vehicle fleet to meet a given delivery workload. Determining the optimum route for each vehicle is only a very small part of this problem. It also involves determining which deliveries are allocated to each vehicle. This normally means taking account of the weight and volume of goods for each delivery, as well as its location. Frequently there are also other **constraints**, such as specific agreed times or 'bookings' for particular deliveries, or early closing days. Finally, not all organisations aim for service levels requiring all available orders to be delivered each day, so that a separate decision has to be made on which orders to include on loads today, and which to defer. Road network databases are now available for most countries in the developed world, and certainly for most countries in western Europe. Transport operators can pay separately for a license to use most such databases. However, it is far more common for them to buy or rent a route-planning package including the use of the relevant road network databases.

Norman Payne Enterprises would like to link some of the functions of distribution into its proposed web site. For example, the monthly auction catalogue will be placed on the web site for customers to browse and view the items to be auctioned. Could the site utilise **EFT** and **EDI technology** to conduct business transactions?

Norman Payne Enterprises is also considering automating the **sales function**, particularly with regard to its team of 50 sales agents within the UK and abroad. In many business organisations the sales force are fitted out with laptop computers, hand-held PCs, or even pen-based tablet computers. This not only increases the personal productivity of sales people, but dramatically speeds up the capture and analysis of sales data from the field to marketing managers at company headquarters. In return, it allows marketing and management to improve the support they provide to their sales people.

Therefore, many business organisations are viewing sales force automation as a way to gain a strategic advantage in sales productivity and marketing responsiveness. For example, sales people use their desktop PCs to record sales data as they make their calls on customers and prospects during the day. Then each night sales reps in the field can connect their computers by **modem and telephone links** to the mainframe computer at company headquarters and upload information on sales orders, sales calls, and other sales statistics, as well as send electronic mail messages and other queries. In return, the host computer may download product availability data, information on good sales prospects, **e-mail messages**, and other sales support information.

Product managers need information to **plan and control the performances of specific products**, product lines, and brands. Computers can help provide price, revenue, cost, and growth information for existing products and new product development. Information and analysis for pricing decisions is a major function of the sales and marketing system. Information is also needed on the manufacturing and distribution resources proposed products will require. Computer-based models may be used to evaluate the performances of current products and the prospects for success of proposed products. Marketing managers need information to help them achieve sales objectives at the lowest possible costs for advertising and promotion. Computers can be used for analysing market research information and promotion models to help (1) select media and promotional methods, (2) allocate financial resources, and (3) control and evaluate results of various advertising and promotion campaigns. For example, a marketing analyst may develop an electronic spreadsheet model to analyse the sales response of advertising placed in a variety of media.

The basic functions of sales **forecasting** can be grouped into the two categories of short-range forecasting and long-range forecasting. Short-range forecasting deals with forecasts of sales for periods up to one year, whereas long-range forecasting is concerned with sales forecasts for a year or more into the future. Managers use market research data, historical sales data, promotion plans, and statistical forecasting models to generate short-range and long-range sales forecasts.

A **marketing information system** often provides marketing intelligence to help managers make more effective marketing decisions. It also provides marketing managers with information to help them plan and control the market research projects of a business organisation. IT often assists the market research activity collect, analyse and maintain an enormous amount of information on a wide variety of market variables that are subject to continual change. This includes information on customers, prospects, consumers, and competitors. Market, economic, and demographic trends are also analysed. Data can be purchased in computer-readable form from external sources, or from gathering data through telemarketing and computer-aided telephone interviewing techniques. Finally, statistical analysis software packages help managers analyse market research data and spot important marketing trends.

Marketing managers use computer-based information systems to develop short-range and long-range plans outlining product sales, profit, and growth objectives. They also provide feedback and analysis concerning performance-versus-plan for each area of marketing. The use of variances is an important area of **Management Control**. Computer-based marketing models in decision support systems and expert systems are also being used to investigate the effects of alternative marketing plans. In addition, the fast capture of sales and marketing data by sales force automation systems helps marketing management respond faster to market shifts and sales performance trends and develop more timely marketing strategies.

The following summarises the goal of six particular information systems found within Norman Payne Enterprises. However, there is concern that the goals and characteristics of these business systems may change if the business organisation applies a drastic **business process re-engineering (BPR)** approach to the holistic integration of business information systems within Norman Payne Enterprises.

Sales Order Processing is an important transaction processing system within Norman Payne Enterprises which captures and processes customer orders and produces invoices for customers. This data is needed for sales analysis and **stock control**. In many business organisations, it also keeps track of the status of customer orders until goods are **delivered**. Computer-based **Electronic Data Interchange (EDI)** of the sales order processing system provides a fast, accurate, and efficient method of recording and screening customer orders and sales transactions. EDI is also used to automate the **Purchase Order Processing** system. Norman Payne Enterprises is trying to establish whether it is possible to merge the two business functions of sales order processing and purchase order processing within one IT-based structure.

Stock control systems process data reflecting changes to items in stock. Once data about customer orders is received from an order processing system, an IT-based stock control system records changes to stock levels and prepares appropriate shipping documents. Then it may notify managers about items that need reordering and provide them with a variety of inventory status reports. Computer-based inventory control systems thus help a business provide high quality service to customers while minimising investment in stock and **stock holding costs**.

The **accounts receivable** process is part of the **financial accounting system** which keeps records of amounts owed by customers from data generated by customer purchases and payments. The system produces monthly customer statements and credit management reports. IT-based accounts receivable systems stimulate prompt customer payments by preparing accurate and timely invoices and monthly statements to credit customers. They provide managers with reports to help them control the amount of credit extended and the collection of money owed. This activity helps to maximise profitable credit sales while minimising losses from bad debts.

The **accounts payable** process keep track of data concerning purchases from and payments to **suppliers**. The system prepares cheques in payment of outstanding invoices and produces cash management reports. IT-based accounts payable systems help ensure prompt and accurate payment of suppliers to maintain good relationships, ensure a good credit standing, and secure any discounts offered for prompt payment. The system provides tight financial control over all cash disbursements of the business organisation. It also provides management with information needed for the analysis of payments, expenses, purchases, employee expense accounts, and cash requirements.

The **payroll** process receives and maintains data from employee time cards and other work records. They produce paychecks and other documents such as earning statements, payroll reports, and labour analysis reports. Other reports are also prepared for management and government agencies. IT-based payroll systems help businesses make prompt and accurate payments to their employees, as well as reports to management, employees, and government agencies concerning earnings, taxes, and other deductions. They may also provide management with reports analysing labour costs and productivity.

The **general ledger** consolidates data received from accounts receivable, accounts payable, payroll, and other accounting information systems. At the end of each accounting period, they 'close the books' of a business and produce the general ledger trial balance, the income statement and balance sheet of the firm, and various income and expense reports for management. IT-based general ledger systems help business organisations accomplish these **accounting tasks** in an accurate and timely manner. They typically provide better **financial controls** and management reports and involve fewer personnel and lower costs than manual accounting methods.

In general, business information systems support all areas and hierarchical levels of Norman Payne Enterprises through a variety of IT-based operational, management and strategic information systems.

Further study and reading

Books

Burke, R. (1993) *Project Management: Planning and Control*, Chichester, England, John Wiley.

Cooper, B. (1978) *Writing Technical Reports*, London: Penguin Books.

Corbitt, T. (1992) *Information Technology and its Applications*, 2nd edition. Harlow: Longman.

Ennals, R.T. and Molyneux, P. (eds) (1993) *Managing with IT*, Springer-Verlag.

Taylor, K. (1991) *Computer Systems in Logistics and Distribution*, London: Kogan Page.

Appendix: Example of a formal questionnaire

IT OUTSOURCING STUDY QUESTIONNAIRE

1. COMPANY INFORMATION

Company name _____

Address _____

_____

Tel no: _____ Fax no: _____

Name of participant _____ Position _____ Reporting to: _____

How many people does your company employ?

In total within the UK _____

In IT _____

What is the core business of your company? _____

Are you directly responsible for outsourcing strategy? YES/NO

Are you currently using outsourcing for any IT functions? YES/NO
(IF NO – GO TO QUESTION 11)

2. EQUIPMENT TRANSFERRED
Please identify the equipment type and how currently used:
Please tick the appropriate items

	Mainframes	Servers	Workstations	Other (specify)
Ownership transferred but run on your site				
Ownership transferred but run on your site as a service centre for other customers				
Work transferred to provider's site				
Ownership retained by company				

3. APPLICATIONS

Which applications are involved? (please circle)

Accounting	CAD/CAM	EPOS
Order processing	Production control	Electronic mail
Stock control	Process control	Other (specify) _____

_____

_____

4. SERVICE DESCRIPTION AND QUALITY (please tick as appropriate)

	Service	Service quality					Trends		
	Delivered	Very poor	Poor	OK	Good	Very good	Improving	Worsening	Static
Processing									
Hardware maintenance									
Software support									
Application development									
Systems conversion									
Network management									
Project management									
Performance review/ reporting									

5. THE OUTSOURCING DECISION

Who made the justification for the move to outsourcing?
(please enter as appropriate)

In-house   *Consultants*

Position _____   Company name _____

What were the objectives? (please circle)

Cost reduction	Service improvement	Technical improvement
Space reduction	Control and accountability	Other (specify) _____

Has the implementation met its original objectives?   YES/NO

If no, which have not been met? (circle as appropriate)

Cost reduction	Service improvement	Technical improvement
Space reduction	Control and accountability	Other (specify) _____

6. CHOICE OF SUPPLIER

Reasons for choosing current supplier (please circle as appropriate)

Reputation   Recommendation   Technical knowledge

Sales effort   Cost   Other (specify) _____

What selection procedures did you use? (please circle)

Detailed service specification produced   Responses rated by a points system

Evaluation by steering committee   User community involved in decision

What is the length of the current contract? _____

When is the next date for contract review? _____

Do you feel 'locked in' to your current provider?   YES/NO

If yes, why? (please circle below)

Technical knowledge   Cost of change   Other (specify) _____

Termination conditions

7. CHANGING SUPPLIERS

Have you changed suppliers since starting outsourcing?   YES/NO
(IF NO – GO TO QUESTION 8)

If yes, why did you change? (please circle as appropriate)

Cost saving   Performance dissatisfaction   Technical capability

Specific skills and experience relating to new initiatives

Other (specify) _____

What was the length of the initial contract? _____

Did it run its full term?   YES/NO **If no, what was the reason?**

_____

Are you using more than one supplier at the same time?   YES/NO

If yes, what is the reason? (please circle)

Performance trials   Specific skills in one supplier for a particular service

Dissatisfaction with the existing supplier

Other (specify) _____

Has the initial contract been – (please circle)

Returned to in-house operation   Awarded to the original supplier

8. FUTURE PLANS

What are your future plans for outsourcing? (please circle)

Change supplier   New applications

No change   Additional supplier

What is your timescale for change?

This year   Next year   Later (specify) _____

What do you see happening to the outsourcing budget over the next three years? (please indicate)

Reduce   Increase   No change

9. PERSONNEL ISSUES

How effective would you rate the handling of the employee communication and transfer process? (please indicate)

	Excellent	Good	OK	Poor	Very poor
Initial employer information about intentions					
Communication from the selected supplier before the date of transfer					
Efforts of supplier to deal with the fears and reservations of employees					
Absorption of employees into the supplier's culture and ways of working					
Overall, has the transfer benefited the employees					
Overall, how successful has the transfer been					

10. SERVICE LEVEL AGREEMENTS

Are service level agreements in operation between your company and the supplier? YES/NO

How are the performance measures structured? (please indicate)

In computing terms, e.g. hours of availability

In terms of the business objectives of the users

Other (please specify) _____

11. FOR THOSE WHO HAVE NOT YET IMPLEMENTED OUTSOURCING

Are you considering using outsourcing? YES/NO
If YES which equipment types will be involved?

Mainframes   Servers   Workstations   Networks

Other (IT) _____   Other (non IT) _____

What type of processing service will you require? (please circle below)

On own site   On supplier's site   With other customers on a customer site
No change

What outsourcing services are you likely to take up? (please circle)

Processing   Hardware maintenance   Software support

Application development   Systems conversion   Network management

Project management

What are the objectives of the change? (please indicate below)

Cost reduction   Service improvement   Technical change

Space reduction   System migration   Accountability

Other (specify) _____

When will this be implemented?

This year / Next year / Other (specify) _____

THANK YOU FOR COMPLETING THIS QUESTIONNAIRE

Reproduced with the permission of Brian V. Maurice, the Institute of Data Processing Management (IDPM) Outsourcing Group.

BIT Glossary

A

Access. To obtain data from the computer. This may be stored inside the CPU or on a remote backing store.

Access time. The time interval between the instant at which data is called for from a storage device and the instant delivery begins.

Accounting system. An internal (management) and external (financial) transactions system used for collecting, collating, recording and publishing data and information using a monetary base (e.g. £, $, Yen).

Ada. A programming language developed for the Department of Defense in the USA to be open and portable accross all military hardware and software. Now also used for commercial applications.

Adaptive system. One that senses, monitors and reponds to changes in its systems environment.

Address. An identification as represented by a name, label or number, for a location in a storage medium.

Algorithm. A set of rules which gives a sequence of operations for solving a problem.

Alphanumeric. Letters of the alphabet A to Z and numbers 0 to 9.

Analysis group. A team of people given the task of analysing a system.

Application. As in application software package. A program designed to perform a particular task or set of functions (e.g. a database, wordprocessor, spreadsheet, DTP).

Applications generator. A software tool used in high-level development environments to create and generate appropriate applications codes from natural language instructions of an end-user.

Arithmetic-logic unit (ALU). A component of the CPU that carries out arithmetic and logical operations on data.

Array. A linearly ordered set of data items, such as a table of numbers.

Artificial intelligence (AI). A branch of computing concerned with systems which mimic the characteristics of human intelligence and thinking.

Artificial intelligence shell. Programming environment of an AI system.

ASCII. A method for coding data in which eight binary bits can be combined to represent the characters on a keyboard. The acronym stands for American Standard Code for Information Interchange.

Assembler language. A computer program which performs the task of assembling a symbolic program to machine language code.

ATM (Automated Teller Machine). A machine in the walls of banks that dispenses cash to authorised holders of a cash dispenser card.

ATM (Asynchronous Transfer Mode). A multi-media high-speed network that allows the transmission of voice, vision, pictures, text and graphics data.

Attribute. Data concerning an entity. Used in entity-relationship context diagrams.

Automated number identification (ANI). Telephone system technology used to identify and display the number of an incoming telephone call.

B

Backup file. A copy of a file which is used in the event of the original file being corrupted.

Bandwidth. The range of frequencies on a particular telecommunications medium.

Bar code. An array of black and white lines used on products and other physical items to be electronically read by OCR scanning technology.

BASIC. A high-level programming language. An acronym for beginners all-purpose symbolic instruction code.

Baud. The rate data is transferred along a communications line. Usually 1 bit per second.

Binary. A state of only two possible conditions (e.g. 'yes' or 'no', 'on' or 'off', 1 or 0). Binary code has a base of 2, using either 1 or 0.

Binary digit. In binary notation either the digits 1 or 0.

Bit. Binary digit 0 or 1.

Bit mapping. Video graphics technology environment that allows each pixel on a screen to be addressed and organised by a computer.

Boolean logic. A set of logical operators for expressing logical relationships.

Buffer. Temporary storage location for data as it is transferred from one device to another.

Bug. A mistake or error in a computer program or computer system.

Bus. An electrical connection between the components of a computer system along which data is transmitted.

Bus width. The number of bits that can be transferred at one time between the CPU and other related peripheral devices.

Business environment (BE). The total of all conditions and aspects of the environment that affect or impact on business activity.

Business functions. The generic tasks or activities necessary for an organisation to undertake business activity (e.g. sales order processing, purchase order processing or stock controlling).

Business organisation. The inter-related set of human, technology and systems resources that are managed and coordinated to achieve certain objectives and goals.

Business process re-engineering (BPR). A drastic information systems development approach that looks at the overall goal of an organisation and the inherent nature of the processes needed to support that goal.

Byte. A set of bits (usually eight) which is used to represent one character.

C

C. A common programming language used within the business environment.

CAD (computer-aided design). The use of computer applications to produce technical drawings.

CD-ROM (compact disk-read only memory). An optical disk storage technology.

Cellular telephones. Mobile telephones using radio waves to transmit voice and other data.

CPU (central processing unit). The area, or unit, of a computer system that includes the main storage and the circuits controlling interpretation and execution of instructions that control other parts of the computer system.

Character string. A sequence of alphanumeric characters joined together.

Chip. An integrated circuit that is etched on to a small piece of silicon.

Client-server computing. A model of computing that divides the processing tasks to be performed between client and servers on a network. Each machine is given the tasks that it performs the most effectively.

Coaxial cable. A telecommunications transmission medium of insulated copper wire.

COBOL. A high-level programming language used mainly in business situations.

Communications software. Software used to communicate data over a telecommunications network.

Compiler. A program that converts a high-level language into a low-level language or machine code.

Computer literacy. Knowledge and understanding of computing and IT, its role and application.

Configuration. The various pieces of hardware and software integrated to complete a computerised system.

CPS (characters per second). A measure of the speed of data transfer between hardware devices.

Cursor. A blinking square or character which appears on the VDU screen to indicate the position of the display.

D

Data. The raw facts that can be processed to produce information.

Database. A series of files structured and stored for the storage and manipulation of data.

Database management system (DBMS). The software application that acts as an interface between the database and the user. It assists the user in interrogating and manipulating data within a database.

Data capture. The technique of collecting data by using various devices and procedures.

Data channel. A path along which data can flow electronically.

Data dictionary. The part of a DBMS that stores definitions and characteristics of data items.

Data flow. The movement of data and information within an information system.

Data flow diagram (DFD). A graphical tool used for documenting the logical design of an information system.

Data Protection Act. A law which restricts the way personal information is stored and processed using a computer.

Data redundancy. The existence of duplicated data within a database or storage file.

Data retrieval. The process of extracting data from a database.

Data security. The process and techniques for preventing unauthorised access to computer systems.

Debug. To detect, locate and remove mistakes and errors from a program or computer system.

Decision support system (DSS). An IT-based system used to assist human decision making within an organisation.

Demodulation. The process of converting analogue signals to digital signals.

Desktop publishing (DTP). A software application package for producing professional quality reports and documents incorporating text, graphics and pictures.

Directory. A list of the names of programs and files stored on a disk.

Disk. A magnetic storage device.

Distributed database. A database that is used and maintained in more than one location.

DOS (disk operating system). Usually used with 16-bit microcomputers. A standard for IBM-compatible microcomputers.

Dot-matrix printer. A robust key-impact printer used for printing documents from a computer system.

Downsizing. The miniaturisation of software, hardware technology and the movement of computer tasks towards smaller technology and multiple task end-user environments.

E

Edit. To modify the form or format of data.

EDI (electronic data interchange). The automatic electronic transfer of data from one computer system to another computer system.

EFT (electronic funds transfer). Communicating and transferring monetary transaction details along telephone wires, satellites and other transmission mediums around the world to transfer money.

EFTPOS (electronic funds transfer at point of sale). The transmission and transfer of money electronically usually at an EFTPOS terminal in a retail shop (at the point of sale).

E-mail (electronic mail). Process by which letters are transferred from one computer to another through telephone lines to appear on the VDU screen at the letter's destination.

End-user. The individual that has responsibility for using information and developing the systems to support the processing and delivery of that information.

Entity. An object or item on which information is maintained.

Executive information system (EIS). An information system used at the top strategic decision-making level of a business organisation.

Expert system (ES). A system that mimics the knowledge, reasoning skills and professional decision making of experts in particular areas. (e.g. medicine, geology and financial advice).

F

FAX (facsimile). A technology that transmits documents containing text and graphics over standard telephone lines.

Feasibility study. A formal analysis of whether something is possible and practicable given the internal and external constraints within an environment.

Feedback. The process of obtaining output and then feeding it back into another process or the same process.

Fibre optics. A transmission technology medium which uses clear glass fibre to transmit data through the use of pulsing laser beams of light.

Field. An area on a record which contains a single string of information.

File. A collection of related records treated as a unit.

File server. A computer which acts as a repository of data and applications, that allows other computers on a network to share files and applications software.

Fixed disk. A computer storage disk which is permanently fixed to the computer system.

Floppy disk. A portable memory storage medium, which can be rigid or 'floppy'.

Font (or fount). A style and size of typeface character.

FORTRAN. A high-level programming language used mainly for mathematical and scientific applications. An abbreviation for FORmula TRANsaction.

Fourth generation development. The tools and techniques used to develop information systems with little or no involvement from technical specialists. Such development environments are more user-friendly and encourage end-user development.

Fourth generation language (4GL). A programming language that uses a high level of natural language rather than mathematical symbolism.

Freedom of information. The right of individuals and organisations to have free access to available data and information kept by organisations.

Fuzzy logic. A concept used in AI and ES to recognise the fact of uncertainty within strategic and managerial decision-making environments.

G

Gateway. A computer system's interface between two computer networks which may have various access controls.

Geographic information systems (GIS). Applications that produce two- or three-dimensional maps and graphics, used for modelling.

Gigabyte. Computer storage measurement equal to approximately 1,000 million bytes.

Graphical user interface (GUI). The computer interface environment of screen icons, cursor and other visual aspects of interaction.

Graphics. Diagrams, charts, pictures or graphs produced using a computer system.

Graphics tablet. An input device which allows diagrams to be input into a computer.

Groupware. Software that assists the activity of project development and team-based activities (e.g. scheduling meetings and sharing ideas).

H

Hacker. A person who tries to break into secure or restricted computer systems.

Hardcopy. Printed output from a computer system that can be taken away and studied.

Hard disk. The term used to indicate the rigid recording surface used for bulk storage of computer data.

Hardware. The physical and electronic components that make up a computerised system.

Heuristic program. A computer program that has the facility for self-learning.

Hierarchy. The arrangement of individuals in an organisation according to rank or authority.

High-level language. A user-friendly programming language that uses natural language (e.g. English, French, Chinese).

Host computer. The main responsible computer on a network.

Hypermedia. A network of nodes or connections across a set of various data and information

I

Icons. Symbols and pictures displayed on a screen often in the form of menu pictures.

Implementation. The process of converting a systems solution into a tangible product or outcome.

Index. A series of identifiers each of which characterises a piece of information.

Indexed file. A file that includes an index directory to facilitate random processing.

Index term. A word or phrase used to classify a document or item in a database.

Inference engine. The rule base of an expert system.

Informatics. The study of information and its handling especially by means of information technology. The term is derived from the French word 'informatique'.

Information. The result of processing data for use and meaningful decision making.

Information retrieval (IR). The process of recovering specific information from stored data (e.g. databases).

Information science. The study of all aspects of storage, processing and dissemination of information.

Information system (IS). Inter-related components working together to collect, store, process and disseminate information for decision making.

Information technology (IT). The creation, processing, storage and dissemination of pictorial, vocal, textual and numerical data/information by means of computerised and communications technology.

Information theory. The study of the problems and processes of the *transmission* of information.

Ink-jet printer. A printer that works by spraying ink on to the paper to make up the shapes of type characters.

Input. Data or information received by a computerised system from outside.

Input device. An item of equipment which permits data or instructions to be entered into a computer (e.g. keyboard, scanner or sensor).

Integrated circuit (IC). A miniaturisation of electronic circuits so that thousands of components are formed on a small chip of silicon.

Integrated software. The composition of two or more software applications packages (e.g. spreadsheets, databases and wordprocessors).

Intelligent agent. A program application that performs services or functions on behalf of a user (e.g. intelligent agents for searching information on the WWW).

Internet. A network of computer networks spanning the globe.

ISDN (Integrated Services Digital Network). A standard transmission technology used by common telephone service carriers.

Iteration. To repeat a procedure with data derived from the last run of the procedure (i.e. using feedback) in order to obtain a more accurate value.

J

Job. A specified group of tasks prescribed as a unit of work for a computer system.

Justify text. To adjust the positions of words on a page of text so that the margins are regular. Type can be aligned on the left, or the right, or centred.

K

Key field. A field within a data record to identify the record.

Keyboard. An input device consisting of standard typewriter keys, numerical keys and often special function keys.

Kilobyte. A measure of microcomputer storage capacity (equal to 1,024 bytes).

Knowledge. The set of concepts and cognitive frameworks used by humans to collect, store, process, organise and communicate understanding.

Knowledge-based system (KBS). Part of ES and AI systems technology, that comprises the tools, techniques and information sets for use in ES and AI.

Knowledge engineer. A specialist in ES engaged to elicit information and expertise from other professionals to be used in a knowledge base.

L

LAN (local area network). A term applied to computer networks which operate over a small area, such as one site or building of a business organisation.

Laser printer. A high quality printer which uses laser beams to form characters on paper.

Light-pen. An input/output (I/O) device, that uses a photoelectric cell to indicate positions on a screen.

Line printer. A printer that outputs all characters in a line as one unit.

LISP (list processing). A programming language used mainly in the field of AI.

Load. To enter data into storage locations of computer systems.

Logical design. A description of the underlying goal of an information system in terms of its purpose and logical information requirements.

LOGO. A programming language used in education, particularly for robotics.

Loop. A loop is used when a process needs to be done more than once (iterations). It takes the last instruction of a process back to the beginning.

M

Machine cycle. The series of operations required to execute a computer instruction.

Machine language. A language with instructions in binary code that is used directly by a computer.

Macro. A set of instructions in a computer language that is equivalent to a specific sequence of computer instructions.

Magnetic disk. One of the most popular data storage mediums within computing environments.

Mainframe computer. A large centralised physical computer.

Management information systems (MIS). A system providing information for managers to undertake decision making within a business organisation (e.g. used for monitoring and control of business functions).

Megabyte. A measure of computer storage equal to just over one million bytes (1,048,576 bytes).

Megahertz. A measure of computer clock speed equal to one million cycles per second.

Microcomputer. A small desktop or portable computer.

Microprocessor. A CPU implemented by means of a single silicon chip.

Microsecond. A measure of machine cycle time equal to 1/1,000,000th of a second.

Microwave. A high-frequency transmission medium (popular with mobile phone technology).

Millisecond. One thousandth of a second (1/1000th second).

Modem. A device that allows electronic information to be transmitted and received through various communication channels.

Modulation. The process of converting digital signals into analogue.

Monitor. A VDU used with computer systems to display input and output information.

Mouse. An input device which is moved over the table in order to move a cursor on the screen. Icons can be selected by placing the cursor on them and double-clicking a button.

Multi-media. The integration of text, graphics, pictures, video, sound and annimation into one computer medium.

Multiplexer. A technology that allows a single communications channel to transmit from multiple sources simultaneously.

Multi-tasking. The execution of a number of tasks or operations simultaneously.

N

Nanosecond. An order of magnitude of one thousand millionth of a second.

Natural languages. Languages which are used by humans (e.g. English, French, Japanese)

Network. A set of components within a computerised system interconnected by telecommunications channels.

Network gateway. Links points between different computer networks.

Network topology. The configuration of hardware devices within a network (e.g. star, bus, ring topologies).

Neural network. A network that emulates the patterns and responses of the human brain.

O

Object-oriented programming. A programming technique that combines data and the specific instructions acting on that data into a defined object.

Object-oriented technology. Technology that utilises the connection of data and information objects.

On-line. Directly connected to and under the control of a computer.

On-line database. An external database information service that supplies data and information to an organisation.

On-line real-time processing. Instantaneous data processing as and when data is received, rather than storing data for future processing.

Open system interconnection (OSI). A network protocol model that allows different computer-based network technologies to communicate with one another regardless of the operating system.

Operating system (OS). Software that controls the operation of computer programs on a computer system.

Operational systems. Systems found at the lowest functional levels of a business organisation used to process routine deterministic data.

Optical character recognition (OCR). A device that reads characters from a page or product (e.g. bar code).

Optical disk. A storage medium in which data is recorded by laser beam rather than magnetic means.

Organisational structure. The shape, nature and configuration of information flows and lines of authority within a structured organisation.

OS/2. An operating system that allows multi-tasking that is usually used with 32-bit microcomputers.

Output. The results of data processing.

Outsourcing. The use of external computer vendors and sources to develop, maintain or operate a business organisation's information systems and information technology.

P

Parallel processing. Processing activity in which more than one instruction is processed at any one time.

PASCAL (program appliqué à la selection et la compilation automatique de la literature). A high-level structured programming language.

Password. A word that needs to be typed into a computer system to gain access to data and information.

Physical design. The physical technology (hardware and software) that manifests itself as a result of the logical design of information systems.

Picosecond. A measure of computer machine cycle time equal to one trillionth of a second.

PIN (personal identification number). A secret number used to gain access to a cash dispenser known generically as ATMs.

Primary key. A unique identifying field key of a database record.

Primary storage. The part of a CPU that temporarily stores program instructions and related data.

Processing. The conversion of raw data into meaningful information.

Program. A set of instructions written in a computer language that a computer can recognise and understand.

Programming language. A series of statements used for writing computer programs and instructing computer systems.

Project management. The art and technique of managing and coordinating information systems projects and teams.

Protocol. The set of rules governing telecommunications transmission between two or more computer networks.

Prototyping. The building of an experimental model that can be tested and evaluated.

Pseudocode. The technique of using natural language statements to describe processing and programming logic.

Q

Quality control. The monitoring and identification of variances from established standards that affect the manufacturing and production systems of a business organisation.

Queue. An ordered waiting line of tasks or jobs to be processed through a computer system.

Query language. A usually high-level programming language for accessing data in a database.

QWERTY. Refers to a keyboard used in the UK and USA, so named because the first row of alphabetic characters is QWERTYUIOP.

R

RAM (random access memory). Memory where any location can be read from, or written to, in a random access manner. That is memory where there is no need to go through other records to find the one that is required.

Real time. The response of the computer is at the same rate as the data input (e.g. the automatic pilot system in aircraft).

Record. A unit of related information, or set of data, forming the basic element of a file.

Relational database. An organisation of data within a database in which a data item in one table can be related to a data item in another table.

Remote access. Access gained to a computer system, through data communications, from a remote terminal not located at the site of the computer system.

RISC (reduced instruction set computing). Improving microprocessor speed and characteristics by including only the most frequently used instructions on a microchip.

Robotics. Physical systems that replicate and replace the manual work undertaken by humans.

ROM (read only memory). Memory that can be accessed, but not altered.

Routine. A sequence of operations for a computer system to perform.

S

Scanner. A data input device that electronically reads text or graphics into a computer system.

Scramble. The mixing up of data/information before it is communicated electronically to avoid the data being interfered with and used.

Scroll. The movement of text up and down, or across, a screen or monitor.

Sector. A portion of a magnetic computer disk.

Semiconductor chip. A silicon chip containing hundreds of thousands of etched circuits.

Sensors. Technology that electronically collects data from the environment to be input into a computer system.

Sequential file. A file where records are kept in order or sequence.

Socio-technical approach. An approach to information systems development that recognises the impact and involvement of people, organisation and technology.

Software. A computer program or suites of programs which are used to direct the operations of a computer.

Sort. Arranging data/information into an ordered or structured format, such as alphabetical or numeric sequence.

Spreadsheet. A software package which consists of a grid of cells that can hold alphanumeric data or formulae.

Strategic information systems. Systems for decision making at the highest strategic level of a business organisation (e.g. the executive level).

Structured query language (SQL). A program language for database management systems.

Supercomputer. A very powerful computer that can perform complex and fast computations (e.g. Cray Computers®).

T

Telecommunications. The transmission and reception of data in the form of electronic signals using radio, satellite or transmission lines.

Telecommuting. Using information technology to work or operate from home but still be employed and attached to a business organisation.

Teleconferencing. The use of IT and communications technology to allow individuals to engage in a conference or meeting from remote locations.

Teletext. An information service system available through television transmission channels.

Terminal. A device that is capable of sending and/or receiving data.

Test data. Data which is prepared in order to test the functioning of a specified program or computer system.

Touch screen. A sensitive computer screen that allows a user to command the system by touching specific areas of a screen.

Transaction processing system (TPS). Operational systems that process functional transactions at the lowest hierarchical level of a business organisation.

U

UNIX. An operating system for mainframes and microcomputers which supports multi-tasking and networking.

Upgrade. To improve the specification of a computer system in terms of hardware and software.

Upper case. The capital letters of the alphabet (e.g. 'D' instead of 'd').

User-friendly. A system which users find easy to understand without much formal and lengthy training.

User interface. The device or technology that allows a user to interact with a computer-based system.

V

Value-added network (VAN). A computer network managed by an external organisation which charges a fee for usage, thus allowing a business organisation access to network technology without outright purchase.

VDU (visual display unit). A screen used to display the output from a computer.

Verify. To determine whether a data recording operation has been achieved accurately.

Videoconferencing. A form of teleconferencing where participants see, as well as hear, other participants at remote locations.

Virus. A software program that can destroy or damage a computer system.

Voice mail. The digitisation of the spoken word which is then transmitted over a telecommunications network and stored until the receiver is ready to listen to the message in audio format.

W

Wafer. A thin slice of silicon which forms the basis of a chip.

Wide area network (WAN). A telecommunications computer-based network covering a large geographical location.

Windows. A sub-domain of a screen. A screen can be split into a number of different areas of variable size known as windows, each area being used for a separate function.

Windows NT. A powerful operating system that supports multi-tasking and can be used in networked environments.

Wordprocessor. A computer package or application that can store, handle and manipulate written information.

Wordwrap. A facility in wordprocessing applications whereby text can be typed continuously and the processor wraps words on to the next line as the line length is exceeded.

World Wide Web (WWW). Hypertext technology that allows the linking of documents and information sources over the Internet.

Write. To transfer data to a storage device such as the main memory of a computer disk or floppy disk.

WYSIWIG. An acronym for 'What You See Is What You Get', indicating that the text/data seen on the screen will also appear as seen on the printed page (no hidden data/information).

Z

Zero. Indicating nothing or nought. Also a state of representation within binary code.

Index

Note: A page reference in **bold** indicates a definition.